The Rise & Fall of

THOMAS
CROMWELL

The Rise & Fall of
THOMAS CROMWELL

HENRY VIII's MOST FAITHFUL SERVANT

JOHN SCHOFIELD

For Ann

Cover illustrations: Thomas Cromwell (courtesy of Ipswich School archive); view of Westminster across the Thames from Lambeth, by Wenceslaus Hollar (THP archive).

First published 2008
This edition published 2011

The History Press Ltd
The Mill, Brimscombe Port
Stroud, Gloucestershire, GL5 2QG
www.thehistorypress.co.uk

British Library Cataloguing in Publication Data.
A catalogue record for this book is available from the British Library.

ISBN 978 0 7524 5866 3

Typesetting and origination by The History Press Ltd.
Printed in Great Britain
Manufacturing managed by Jellyfish Print Solutions Ltd.

Contents

Part IV: How Have the Mighty Fallen

Preface

This book sets out to tell the story of the man who, apart from King Henry himself, was the dominant personality in one of the most eventful eras in English history: Thomas Cromwell, the king's chief minister and principal reformer of the church.

In preparing the work I have freely used the definitive studies of the late Professor Elton and other recognized scholars. Most of the evidence, however, is derived from primary sources.

The amount of such material available on Cromwell is huge, including nearly twenty substantial volumes of *Letters and Papers* in which Cromwell's name appears on almost every page. For seven or eight years, there was hardly an issue of any significance in which he was not involved. To keep this book down to manageable size, a number of subjects will be covered as concisely as possible. These include Henry's first divorce negotiations, the theological issues of the Reformation and the constitutional legislation of the 1530s, all of which are elements of Tudor economic and social history. Notes will make reference to works in which these important subjects have been treated more than adequately by other writers.

Unlike many of his contemporaries, Thomas Cromwell left no personal works or memoirs, and the official papers, despite their bulk, do not necessarily reveal much of the inner man.

Occasionally in this book, therefore, I allow myself the luxury of drawing a few inferences. This is done guardedly and with suitable caveats, but I believe that it is justified in the circumstances.

As usual in works on the Tudor period, a note is needed on terminology. To avoid repetition, the words 'evangelical', 'reformer' and 'Protestant' are used interchangeably, 'evangelical' being used in its sixteenth-century sense, meaning Gospel. 'Lutheran' serves well enough for most of the leading English evangelicals during the 1530s, like Cromwell and Cranmer. The 'new learning' and 'the Gospel' are terms synonymous with Protestant faith. 'Catholic' is not always as easy to define as it sounds. Lutherans frequently claimed that their confessions followed the Scriptural 'Holy Catholic and Apostolic Church' rather than the medieval religion which they contested. Unless otherwise indicated, however, I use 'Catholic' to cover all those who opposed Luther and held to the religion in which they grew up. Nothing derogatory is implied by 'medieval', 'Papist' or 'Papalist'; the latter two are most useful in distinguishing those like Thomas More from others, who, though they supported King Henry's Royal Supremacy, remained broadly Catholic on so much else.

Generally the word 'councillor', or occasionally 'servant', is preferred to 'statesman' when discussing the policies of Cromwell and other leading men surrounding the king. By 'statesman' we usually mean one who has some freedom to formulate and execute policy, but of Cromwell's master the Milanese ambassador once said that 'His Majesty chooses to know and superintend everything himself'. I hope readers will not mind seeing these words more than once during the narrative, for often they help to understand what is happening.

Quotations are generally given in modernized spelling, but in order to try and capture a sixteenth-century feel, the Tudor phraseology is usually retained. Foreign names are anglicized unless there is a pressing reason not to do so.

PART I

Rise to Power

I

In My Lord the Cardinal's Service

Well might many a famous individual from the past, were he able to read history's verdict on him, echo the cry of Shakespeare's Cassio: 'Reputation, reputation, reputation! I have lost my reputation'.[1]

In our times – despite the sterling labours of the late Professor G.R. Elton – the very mention of Thomas Cromwell's name is likely to conjure up a baleful spectre in the minds of many. He was, we are repeatedly informed, the chief destroyer of a vibrant, idyllic English medieval church, the man who plundered the monasteries and consigned to oblivion centuries of pious, devotional tradition, imposing in its place an alien creed of justification by faith alone; the prime instigator and enforcer of harsh Tudor treason laws; a ruthless, sinister, unsmiling Machiavellian who cynically cut down Anne Boleyn and all others who dared oppose him, before finally receiving his much deserved deserts when he overreached himself and lured King Henry into an disastrously unsuitable marriage with Anne of Cleves.

I do not remember for sure what made me first begin to wonder whether all of this might be largely fanciful, and whether the real Thomas Cromwell, if only we could meet him and become better acquainted, might take on a less fearsome and altogether more agreeable aspect. It was not a craving to be novel just for the sake of it, but what began as no more than a hunch quickly developed into a conviction. Readers will be able to decide for themselves if they care to go down the same route.

Like many substantial and controversial men in history, only patchy details about Cromwell's early life are known. The main sources are Eustace Chapuys, imperial ambassador to England during much of the 1530s; Reginald, later Cardinal Pole; Matteo Bandello, the Italian writer who became bishop of Agen in France; and John Foxe, the Elizabethan historian and martryologist. Of these four Chapuys knew Cromwell best, but even he is frustratingly brief. Cromwell, says Chapuys, was the 'son of a poor blacksmith who lived and is buried at a small village' near London. His uncle was cook to Archbishop Warham. In his youth Cromwell was somewhat 'ill conditioned and wild' (*mal conditionné*), and he spent some time in prison before travelling in Flanders, Rome and throughout Italy. The reason for the imprisonment is not stated.[2]

Reginald Pole also knew Cromwell personally, though not as well as Chapuys did. Pole confirms Cromwell's birth near London, but calls his father a cloth shearer. Cromwell, Pole continues, then became a private soldier in Italy before pursuing a more secure, if less adventurous, way of life as an accountant in the service of a Venetian merchant.[3]

The Italian connection is taken up by Bandello, with his engaging story of the wealthy Florentine merchant, Francesco Frescobaldi, chancing one day to meet 'a poor youth' (*un povero giovane*) in the streets begging alms 'for the love of God'. Seeing him 'in a bad condition though gentle in appearance' (*mal in arnese e che in viso mostrava aver del gentile*), Frescobaldi was moved to pity, especially when he learned that the youth hailed from England, a country he knew and loved. He asked him his name. 'My name is Thomas Cromwell', he replied, 'the son of a poor cloth shearer' (*d'un povero cimatore di panni*). He had escaped from the battle of Garigliano in Italy where he served as a page or servant to an infantryman, carrying his pike. Frescobaldi invited Master Cromwell into his house as his guest and offered him shelter, food and clothing. After a short stay he gave him money and a new horse. Thus refreshed and replenished, the grateful youth set out to return to England.[4]

These accounts complement rather than contradict each other, though with one interesting exception. Cromwell's father was a 'smith' (Chapuys) but a 'cloth shearer' (Pole, Bandello). Foxe clarifies the matter with the information that Cromwell 'was born in Putney or thereabouts, being a smith's son, whose mother married afterwards to a shearman'. So the smith was Cromwell's natural father and the shearman (or shearer) the step-father. Foxe gives no reason why his mother married again, but the only obvious one, unless the second marriage was illegal, is that his father, the smith, died shortly after Thomas was born. So it is not certain whether Cromwell was the name of the father or step-father.

Foxe also disagrees with Chapuys and Bandello on Cromwell's youth. Bandello has Cromwell arriving in Italy after 'fleeing from my father' (*che fuggendo da mio padre*), which Foxe, in a curiously slanted translation, renders as 'straying from my country'. Elsewhere Foxe, still on the subject of the young Cromwell, tells us that 'a great delight came into his mind to stray into foreign countries, to see the world abroad and to learn experience' – quite a different reason for leaving England than the one given by either Chapuys or Bandello. At first it seems that Foxe might have wanted to cover up the youthful waywardness of one of his greatest heroes. However, this explanation will not do, because later it is Foxe who tells us that Cromwell, as Wolsey's agent, long before he became a Lutheran, was very active in procuring bulls and pardons from Rome. Foxe also quotes Cromwell telling Cranmer that he had been a bit of a 'ruffian' in his younger days, though Foxe includes this in his discussion of Cromwell's pre-Protestant years, not his actual youth.[5]

Fortunately these small variations are not very important. They can easily be explained by the fact that none of these witnesses knew all the details of Cromwell's birth and youth at first hand. Besides, no comprehensive records of births, marriages and deaths were kept until an act of parliament prepared by the adult Cromwell in 1538 required them.

According to Merriman, a certain Walter Cromwell was Thomas's father. As Merriman notes, however, this name appears in records of antiquity from 1475 right up to 1514, so he could not have been the natural father, who, unless Foxe is greatly mistaken, must have died sometime before 1500. It is just as unlikely that Walter was the step-father, because he is described in the *Close Rolls* as a brewer of beer ('berebruer'), not a shearer. He was also a man of some means. As well as his beer business he kept sheep and cattle, he became Constable of Putney in 1495, and he owned lands and property in Wimbledon. This information fits neither the description of Thomas's father as a poor smith, nor his stepfather as a poor shearer. Walter and Thomas Cromwell may have been related, but it is difficult to see how they could have been father and son.[6]

Cromwell's mother came from Derbyshire or Staffordshire. Her maiden name may have been 'Meverell'. According to Cromwell himself, in a conversation with Chapuys, she was fifty-two years old when he was born. The mother's age suggests that Thomas was the youngest child and perhaps an unexpected one. If, therefore, the father died soon after the birth, and the mother married again to a shearer, as Foxe says, it is quite plausible that tensions soon arose between the poor shearer and his energetic and perhaps unruly stepson. A troubled and unhappy childhood, therefore, provided the impulse for the young Thomas to seek his fortune abroad.[7]

A sort of reverse reasoning dates Cromwell's birth to around 1485. Time is needed for him to become old enough to do a spell in prison, as Chapuys says, before venturing out on his own. The battle of Garigliano was fought in late December 1503, so it would have been sometime the following year, maybe spring, before he could have reached Florence and met Frescobaldi. That would put him in his eighteenth year, still young enough to be called a 'youth'.

The matter is, however, somewhat complicated by Stephen Vaughan, a close friend of the adult Cromwell, who knew him better than any of the witnesses named so far. In the middle of a long letter on various points, Vaughan urged Cromwell not to wear himself out through overwork, warning enigmatically that 'half your years be spent'. This letter is dated December 1534. It is not clear how long Vaughan expected Cromwell to live. If he meant the biblical 'three score years and ten ... or four score years' for those who have the strength (Psalm 90:10), then Cromwell would have been thirty-five or forty at the time. This gives two alternative dates for his birth – 1499 and 1494. The first is far too early for Garigliano in 1503, and even the second would make Cromwell only eight or nine when he fled from England and joined the French army. Vaughan may have meant Cromwell's years of discretion, normally regarded as beginning at around the age of twelve, which would take us back to approximately 1485. However, it may well be that Vaughan was simply using a figure of speech, never imagining that anyone would try and calculate the time of Cromwell's birth from it. As Vaughan merely blurs an already indistinct picture, the traditional date of 1485 should suffice until or unless some more positive evidence turns up.[8]

Nothing is known about Cromwell for some years after his meeting with Frescobaldi. However, despite the lack of a formal education, the adult Cromwell was a proficient linguist – he was fluent in French, Italian, Spanish, Latin and Greek – so it is likely that he travelled extensively across southern Europe. His adventures there remain a mystery.

Around 1510 it so happened that the town of Boston in England needed to renew two papal pardons, and one Geoffrey Chambers and a companion were sent as messengers to Rome with provisions and money. Chambers met Cromwell in Antwerp, and because Cromwell could speak Italian, he was persuaded to accompany the two Englishmen to the eternal city. At that time Cromwell had 'no sound taste or judgement of religion', sighed Foxe, the source for this story. Cromwell showed an inventive streak, however, in his plan to persuade

Pope Julius to grant Boston's requests speedily. Cromwell prepared 'some fine dishes of jelly ... made after our country manner here in England'; he then waited patiently until Julius returned from a hunting expedition before approaching him with presents and a 'three man's song', again in the 'English fashion'. The dainty jelly dishes so delighted the Vicar of Christ that he authorised the pardons with little more ado.[9]

By 1512 Thomas Cromwell, with mind broadened and horizons widened by his foreign travels, had settled in England. In November that year, in his new career as a lawyer, he endorsed a legal document entitling one Thomas Empson to lands. He had not given up his interest in commerce, however, and two years later he again paid a visit to the great trading city of Antwerp. Around this time he married Elizabeth Wykys, the daughter of a shearman, and apparently a fairly well-to-do shearman for she descended from an ancient family, one of whom had served as gentleman-usher to King Henry VII. Practically nothing is known about Cromwell's marriage except that at least two daughters and one son survived infancy. Merriman's idea that Cromwell married mainly for money is no more than an uncharitable guess, and there is no reason to doubt that Thomas and Elizabeth Cromwell were a happy couple.[10]

Possibly in 1514, definitely by 1516, Cromwell became part of Cardinal Wolsey's household. He went to Rome a second time in 1517–18, again for reasons connected with the Boston pardons. Cromwell, notes Foxe disapprovingly, was a 'great doer' with Chambers 'in publishing and setting forth the pardons of Boston everywhere'. But Foxe also tells us that Cromwell, seeking to advance simultaneously in learning and piety, learned by heart the recently published Latin New Testament of the great Dutch humanist scholar, Desiderius Erasmus, and the evidence suggests that he did so while on this journey. If this is true, then it is a delicious historical irony that the first faint seeds of Cromwell's future Protestant faith would have been sown during a visit to the Roman See, about the same time that Martin Luther was protesting against the abuse of indulgences in his native Wittenberg.[11]

It was sometime in or just before 1519 that Wolsey – Cardinal, Lord Chancellor and chief minister to King Henry VIII – appointed Cromwell to his council. This did not interrupt Cromwell's legal work, and the following year he was involved in a suit concerning tithes between a vicar and a prioress. It did, however, inevitably raise his standing in society, and a year later comes a hint that Cromwell might have been known to the king: sometime in 1521 he corrected drafts of petitions from a certain Charles Knyvett to Henry, alleging that the duke of Buckingham had defrauded him of money and other entitlements. In January 1522, William Popley asked Cromwell to serve as attorney in a matter he had taken to the king's council. Cromwell's clients in his prospering legal business now included the marchioness of Dorset and Richard Chawfer, alderman of Calais and a wealthy merchant. Cromwell represented Chawfer in a legal suit to be heard in chancery, where Chawfer vowed he would sue his rival to 'the most extreme'.[12]

In August 1522, William Popley reappears in the records asking Cromwell to find out where one Glaskerton was on the night of Lady Eve and on Lady Day. Whether this was a legal matter, or whether Cromwell's freelance activities now included services as a private detective, is not clear. Towards the end of the same year Cromwell was named in another suit, this time a merchant affair, with authority granted to him and others to collect outstanding debts. He also kept up his business interests in the cloth trade. Then in 1523 a new door was opened to him, and he became a Member of Parliament.[13]

Like most late medieval parliaments, this one was summoned to raise money for war. Like many of his ancestors, King Henry dreamed of conquering France, and it seemed that his moment of glory might have come when he made an alliance with Charles V, the newly crowned Holy Roman Emperor, against the dashingly adventurous King Francis I of France. This parliament, however, was not quite as obliging with funds as Henry and Wolsey hoped it would be, and one of its newest members – Thomas Cromwell – went as far as preparing a decidedly anti-war speech. Some doubt has been raised whether this speech was actually delivered; but it is still worth studying in some detail, because it is the first serious guide we have to the political philosophy and rhetorical style of Henry's future chief minister.[14]

Cromwell began loyally. He proclaimed Henry's 'good and just title' to the throne of France – a most worthy cause, and 'who would not gladly give not only all his goods but also his life for it'. Cromwell appreciated the revenues that would stream into England if France were recovered, 'to the great enriching and prospering' of all the king's subjects. He powerfully extolled the king's goodness and virtue. Then the speech takes an unexpected turn. Cromwell looked ahead with dismay to the impending dreadful conflict among the rulers of Christendom, 'so great a number princes, noble men and other subjects', with 'swords in their hands, to try where the pleasure of God shall be to strike … of which slaughter must needs ensue the most lamentable cries and sorrowful wringing of hands that hath happened in Christendom many years'. The heart and outlook of the speaker were surely forged by his personal experience, as a youth, of the horrors of war for ordinary soldiers and people.

Realizing the belligerent mood of many in the country, however, Cromwell accepted that now might not be the most appropriate time to talk of peace. So 'insatiable' was the appetite of the French to extend their boundaries 'to the great molesting and troubling of all the nations about them', that no remedy sufficed except they be 'scourged else they will surely be a scourge to others'. How righteous indeed, Cromwell admitted, was the anger of our dread sovereign and his ally, the emperor; how laudable were Charles's successes in Italy and elsewhere, and Henry's victories over France's ally, Scotland. Many loyal Englishmen would surely contend that the time was now ripe to press home the advantage, to attack France and 'vanquish him utterly and subdue him'.

At this point Cromwell digressed slightly. He had heard something that 'putteth me in no small agony' – our most gracious sovereign intended to take the field in person. 'Which thing I pray God for my part I never live to see.' Cromwell begged his audience's pardon, but he 'cannot consent to obey' for fear of the calamity that would befall the realm should any harm come to the king. For his subjects' sake, his kingdom's sake, and especially for the sake of his 'dear and only daughter' – for upon her, next only to the king, 'dependeth all our wealth' – Cromwell appealed to Henry to restrain his undoubted courage and zeal for a just cause, and remain within his own realm.

Then Cromwell examined the harsh practicalities of war. As many as 30,000 footmen and 10,000 horsemen would be needed. The cost of supplying such a vast army abroad, with the unpredictable Channel in between, could be ruinous for England – it might 'consume all the coin and bullion in this realm'. If the king were taken captive on the battlefield, 'how then should we be able to redeem him back again?' Then to military tactics: the French might not take the field directly, but withdraw to Paris, lie in wait, seek to cut off supplies and leave our main army at the enemy's mercy. Cromwell invoked the memory of Henry VII, who concentrated on Bolougne rather than venturing further inland; and also Charles V, who, in more recent campaigns, had not stretched his forces too far for fear of being surrounded. Further, even if victory in battle was achieved, how 'should we be able to possess the large country of France' without reliable allies there? In times past English invaders of France enjoyed the support of 'assured confederates and allies … and assured friends', while French towns possessed nothing like the fortifications and 'marvellous strength' that they did now.

So, Cromwell concluded, rather than waging war on France, let Henry concentrate on Scotland, to 'join the same realm unto his', and thereby 'win the highest honour', higher than any of his predecessors. This would be a far greater victory for England and a far greater defeat for France, for Scotland was France's traditional ally against England. As the saying went, 'who that intendeth France to win, with Scotland let him begin'. So the maiden speech ends.

It is not the speech of a sycophant, or an unscrupulously ambitious politician seeking only to ingratiate himself with his masters. Cromwell's suggestion that Henry should remain at home was not designed to flatter, because leading armies into battle in person was just the sort of showy but unnecessarily dangerous gesture that would have appealed to Henry. This he would do in the post-Cromwellian 1540s, when the strategic value of his presence on the field was dubious. Cromwell's words demonstrate good sense – a king with no adult heir should not take needless risks, especially with the instability of the previous century and the Roses Wars still alarmingly fresh in the minds of the English people.

Besides Cromwell's concern for costs, trade and the suffering of a nation at war, the speech showed remarkable foresight, because only two years later King Francis was taken prisoner by the emperor's troops at Pavia, and not released until the French were compelled to pay a huge ransom. Cromwell was also right about Scotland, because any English attack on France would expose England to the risk of war on two fronts – on the continent with France, and at home with France's traditional northern ally. Scarcely less interesting is Cromwell's reference to Princess Mary – upon whom 'dependeth all our wealth'. Assuming that Cromwell was reflecting a general view rather than giving his own purely personal opinion, his words suggest that the absence of a *male* heir was not seen as a great threat to the stability of the Tudor dynasty.

Also interesting is the style of speech, and the technique used to try and persuade the king to change his mind. Employing the right kind of flattery at all the right places, Cromwell emphasized at some length the justness of the cause and the zeal of the king. Only after these points were eloquently made did he urge Henry not to go abroad for the sake of the realm. It was the sort of argument that even Henry could hardly reject outright. Then Cromwell focussed on the immense practical difficulties that a guerrilla campaign in France would pose, invoking unpleasant memories of prolonged conflict and hardship in the past – all skilfully calculated to dampen enthusiasm for war.

No evidence survives of any reaction to the speech, if indeed it was given, but a great deal else was discussed in that parliamentary session. Cromwell gave a wry account of affairs in a letter to his friend, John Creke:

> I among others have endured a parliament which continued by the space of seventeen whole weeks, where we commoned of war, peace, strife, contention, debate, murmur, grudge, riches, poverty, perjury, truth, falsehood, justice, equity, deceit, oppression, magnanimity, activity, force, attemprance, treason, murder, felony, conciliation, and also how a commonwealth might be edified and also continued within our realm. Howbeit, in conclusion we have done as our predecessors have been wont to do, that is to say as well as we might, and left where we began.[15]

The letter reveals a little of the personality of the writer, because it continues in similar tongue-in-cheek tone: 'All your friends to my knowledge be in good health and especially they that ye wott of: ye know what I mean. I think it best to write in parables because I am in doubt'. As Elton has already said, it would be foolish to read a cynical contempt for parliament into these words. Elton has quoted several extracts of famous parliamentarians expressing exasperation with the institution, the workload, the disappointments and the frequent difficulty in converting constructive ideas into effective legislation.[16]

However, what Cromwell's letter may reveal is not frustration exactly, but rather a dry, worldly-wise sense of humour, and a judgement of mankind and human affairs that is mature and realistic but neither contemptuous nor cynical. Certainly he was no naïve idealist. In style and content his letter is somewhat reminiscent of the Old Testament preacher:

> One generation passeth away, and another generation cometh ... The sun also ariseth and the sun goeth down, and hasteth to his place where he arose ... The thing that hath been, it is that which shall be; and that which is done

is that which shall be done: and there is no new thing under the sun. (Ecclesiastes 1:4–9.)

When parliament was dissolved, Cromwell resumed his legal and business interests. At an inquest in December, he and others made various claims against church officials and their properties; these included such diverse matters as defective pavements, noisy geese on church lands, brawling neighbours, doors that needed fixing and cantankerous women. The following year (1524) Cromwell was admitted to Gray's Inn, one of the English legal societies that formed the Inns of Court. Land deeds continued to take up much of his time, but he also investigated a dispute among the family of the earl of Oxford regarding inheritance, and he drafted a licence for William Collyns to carry on his trade as a blacksmith in any city or town. Cromwell drafted a petition of Robert Leighton, gentleman porter of the Tower, to Wolsey alleging assault during a church service. He also received a petition from Edward Smything, addressed to him as 'councillor to the lord legate', requesting recovery of cloths depicting Christ on Maundy Thursday, Christ praying in the Garden and bearing the Cross.[17]

Around the turn of the year (1525), Cromwell was forced to put the lands of one John Fleming in Yorkshire into execution for breach of covenant. In May he revised a draft for a lease of church lands in York; the draft was originally composed by Thomas Wriothesley, a man also in Wolsey's service, who would become a lifelong associate of Cromwell's. In June a Mr Cowper sought Cromwell's help to obtain a benefice for a relative, while in November another business dispute concerning alleged non-payment of goods required attention.[18]

In February 1526 he was involved in the allocation of benefices, though the papers do not state whether he had authority to recommend appointments, or whether he was just administering the matter – probably the latter. A more interesting assignment was a draft of a petition to Henry on behalf of the merchants of Hanse for safe conduct and a licence to trade. The licence itself, also in Cromwell's hand, was granted by Wolsey, acting for the king. In June Cromwell was invited to inspect and audit accounts. In July one Lawrence Starkey asked him if he could use his influence to obtain a benefice. Starkey also complained about alleged wrongs done to him by the bishop of London and the abbess of Syon, and asked Cromwell's help. Land and testate affairs remained the most common legal tasks, and they could be pleasingly profitable when clients like George Monoux, an alderman, promised Cromwell twenty marks for a favourable outcome.[19]

Not all his life was taken up with business and law. By now he had acquired a reputation for generosity with money as well as a flair for making it. Lawrence Giles sent greetings to Cromwell and his wife, thanking him for kindnesses he could not repay, observing how God provides for those who help the poor, 'as I understand ... your mastership is provided'. Cromwell was also able to afford an education for his son Gregory. Cromwell's sister had married a farmer with the wonderfully English rustic name of Wellyfed, and in the early 1520s Gregory and young Wellyfed began their schooling together in Cambridge. Letters survive from Gregory to his father promising to do his best and work hard – 'we apply our books diligently', he assured him. School was not 'all work and no play', however, and the boys were thrilled when a local lord took them out for a day's hunting and 'let us see such game and pleasure as I never saw in my life'.[20]

With Wolsey's domestic political policy, Cromwell seems to have had little to do. It was fortunate for his reputation and later career that he was not one of the commissioners appointed by Wolsey in spring 1525 to raise yet more money from the clergy and laity to finance the military aspirations of the king and his cardinal. This so-called 'Amicable Grant' provoked unexpectedly stiff opposition in the country, and had to be withdrawn in the face of threats of a rising in south east England. Nor is there any evidence that Cromwell was a part of Wolsey's foreign policy team in the cardinal's complex diplomatic manoeuvrings with France, Rome and the emperor.

Cromwell was, however, closely involved in the administration of Wolsey's colleges. In January 1525 Wolsey appointed Sir William Gascoigne, William Burbank and Cromwell to survey six monasteries to be converted for the use of Cardinal's College at Oxford, for which Cromwell drafted the letters patent. Cromwell and one John Smith were also attorneys for four other religious houses. At the dissolution of monasteries at Begham and Blackmore, Cromwell was present as a witness, though not the chief officer. It is from Begham that we have the only surviving letter of Cromwell to his wife, though it does not reveal very much about their married life – he sent her a nice fatted doe and asked for news of home.[21]

During the next four or five years until Wolsey's fall, twenty-nine small monastic communities were closed. These dissolutions were not a proto-Protestant measure; they were decided on by Wolsey with the approval of both the king and Rome, with a view to funding and beautifying Wolsey's grand colleges in Oxford and Ipswich. Cromwell's involvement continued in various ways, as surveyor, administrator, and attorney. He was not acting alone, and in February 1525 Wolsey was urging Henry not to listen to bad reports of the behaviour of some of his officers during the suppressions. No names were mentioned, so it is not known for certain whether Cromwell was one of those who had carried out his tasks with heavy-handed efficiency. Two years later, however, Wolsey was told that the 'king and noble men speak things incredible of the acts of Mr Alayn and Cromwell'. If this was meant as a complaint it did Cromwell no harm either with Henry or Wolsey, for in September 152 Cromwell was described on an official document as 'receiver-general' of Cardinal College at Oxford.[22]

So far as can be discerned, Cromwell played no part in Wolsey's anti-Lutheran measures. Following the birth of the Reformation in Germany, a variety of unorthodox religious ideas had been filtering into England. Men like Thomas Bilney and Robert Barnes were preaching justification by faith and attacking the worship of the saints, though they had not yet denied papal authority or the sacraments of the church. A

Protestant underground movement had begun in England, and it was smuggling literature into the country, successfully evading the authorities' book-hunting and book-burning drives. The most famous English evangelical of these years was William Tyndale, now forced to flee and live in exile on the continent where he worked on his translation of the Bible; but in the mid to late 1520s, there is nothing to directly connect Cromwell with either Tyndale or Lutheranism. Cromwell was, however, a friend of Miles Coverdale, a man soon to become part of English Protestant history as a reformer and Bible translator. In a letter to Cromwell dated May 1527, Coverdale thanked him for his goodness, and recalled a conversation 'in Master Moore's house on Easter Eve'. It is not certain whether this was Thomas More. Knowing Cromwell's 'fervent zeal' for 'virtue and godly study', Coverdale sought his help, for he had begun 'to taste of Holy Scriptures ... holy letters ... and the ancient doctors'. He appealed for more books, promised to dedicate himself to learning, and offered his services to Cromwell. The letter reads as though Coverdale was not particularly piously inclined until he came under Cromwell's influence. Soon Coverdale would meet and befriend Robert Barnes, and both would move quickly in a Protestant direction.[23]

Coverdale's letter, though brief, is a useful pointer to Cromwell's spiritual mindset in the late 1520s. It compliments Foxe's story that Cromwell had learned by heart Erasmus's Latin New Testament during one of his visits to Rome. It shows that Cromwell was far from the irreligious secularist depicted by Merriman and others. He was no Lutheran yet, but Coverdale has told us what kind of Catholic Cromwell almost certainly was. He belonged, it would seem, to the ranks of Christian humanists, who, though still 'Catholic' in the broadest sense of the word, had become disillusioned with the medieval scholastic theologians, and preferred to read the Scriptures and the works of the church fathers (the 'ancient doctors'). The seeming relish with which Cromwell went about suppressing monasteries suggests that he had little love for monastic traditions or conventional piety. The term 'Erasmian' – if it means a church still loosely Catholic though stripped of some of the outward piety that Erasmus and other humanists disdained – may be safely used to describe Cromwell in these years.

Meanwhile, he continued his legal business, though there is little sign in 1527 that either his clients or his cases were significantly more prestigious than a few years earlier. He was again involved with several claims between merchants. When his close friend, Stephen Vaughan, suffered losses after having his goods seized on the high seas, and was being pursued by unsympathetic creditors, Cromwell drafted a petition to Wolsey on Vaughan's behalf. A certain Henry Lacy asked Cromwell for help in a testate matter, and also in a property dispute between him and the wife of a cousin who had left her husband. One of the first signs of any contacts between Cromwell and a powerful new political faction – the Boleyns – occurred in December 1527, when Cromwell wrote to Thomas Boleyn, Anne's father, now Viscount Rochford; Cromwell was acting as counsel for the wife of Sir Robert Clare, Rochford's sister.[24]

According to Foxe, Cromwell also found himself 'in the wars of the duke of Bourbon at the siege of Rome'. On this story Foxe is frustratingly brief, but Bourbon's imperialist troops sacked and wrecked carnage in Rome in May 1527. It is possible, though not especially easy, to fit such a visit in with Cromwell's legal business that year – most of the cases noted above, apart from the Clare matter, took place in March or April. This, however, is not enough to reject Foxe's story completely. A hurried, secret visit could have been undertaken on Wolsey's instructions, because Henry and Wolsey were supporting Bourbon against King Francis. Beyond that, unfortunately, nothing is known about it.[25]

An inventory of Cromwell's goods dated June 1527 confirms the impression that, though not excessively rich, he was now a man of some means, who had done rather well for himself since fleeing the country from his step-father as a youth. As well as furniture and clothing, items listed include images of Christ and Mary and the Magi, an ornament of Venetian gold, a picture of Lucretia Romana, and a gold broach with an engraving of Mary Magdalene. Other miscellaneous letters and papers also suggest that Cromwell was a collector of ornaments and furniture. Sub-sections of the inventory include 'Mr Prior's chamber' and 'Mistress Prior's chamber' – these were his in-laws, presumably living with him and his wife. Mistress Prior was quite a lady. Her possessions included a range of clothing and household goods, a silver brooch, purses, a silk Spanish girdle, seven pearls, plus pieces of velvet and satin. Stephen Vaughan, when asking Cromwell to commend him to her, once described her as 'after you my most singular friend'.[26]

Here, then, is a historical snapshot of Thomas Cromwell in 1527. It shows a self-made man, a thriving freelance lawyer with profitable commercial interests, employed in the service of the king's most powerful minister, happily married with a growing family and enjoying a satisfying social life. No sign can be detected of a deep religious conversion or burning political ambition. Independent of, and happily unthreatened by, the intrigues of factions and power struggles at court and in the ruling council, his was an altogether agreeable manner of living. But it was not his destiny to remain in it, and like many of his friends and colleagues, he would soon be caught up and carried along by the momentous events about to unfold in King Henry's reign.

2

To Make or Mar

After the tragic and untimely death in 1501 of Prince Arthur, eldest son and heir of King Henry VII, the king was anxious to preserve the alliance he had made with Spain. Consequently he had arranged for the marriage of his second son, then Prince Henry, to Catherine of Aragon, Arthur's widow. Because a marriage to the wife of a dead brother could be problematic in ecclesiastical law and practice, the English and Spanish authorities decided to ask for a papal dispensation. This they duly obtained from Pope Julius II. Henry VIII then married Catherine when he became king in 1509.[1]

The marriage began happily enough, but it had failed to produce a male heir. Catherine had been pregnant many times, but royal babies, including males, were either still-born or died soon after birth. The queen had also suffered several miscarriages. Princess Mary was the only surviving child, and though Henry did have an illegitimate son in Henry Fitzroy, no royal bastard had ever succeeded his father to the English throne.[2]

At some point difficult to determine, Henry VIII, a prince with a keen interest in theology, and a high opinion of his own abilities in the subject, fastened on to texts in the book of Leviticus which appeared to forbid sexual relations or marriage to a brother's wife, and which warned that anyone who disobeyed this command would be punished with childlessness (Leviticus 18:6, 20:21). However, another text from Deuteronomy *did* allow a man to marry his dead brother's wife, if that marriage had produced no children (Deuteronomy 25:5). Some theologians saw no contradiction between the two, on the grounds that Leviticus simply forbad marrying the wife of a brother who was still alive; in other words, it prohibited bigamy. Others disagreed, and Henry's divines set to work on what would become known as the King's Great Matter. For his own part, Henry became convinced that his marriage to Catherine was unlawful, and that the papal dispensation issued by Pope Julius clashed with the divine law of Leviticus, and was therefore invalid.[3]

It would be easy – perhaps too temptingly easy – to suspect that all this disputing about Leviticus and dispensations amounted to nothing more than a giant constitutional red herring, because Henry's affections for Catherine had now faded, and he was in love with the younger, spirited Mistress Anne Boleyn. It is an undeniable historical fact that in each of Henry's three divorces (or annulments, as he preferred to call them), the appearance of another woman in his life just happened to coincide with the discovery of complications over the validity of his present marriage. However, whether passion for Anne prompted or emerged from Henry's qualms of conscience over Leviticus is something that must be left to others. What matters here is that, according to the Tudor historian Edward Hall, it was in 1527 that Henry's confessor and other clerics told him that his marriage to Catherine was not lawful, and that he was free to consider marrying again.[4]

Anne Boleyn had once been a maid of Queen Catherine's. Then Henry Percy, earl of Northumberland, fell in love with her, though with miserable ill luck he did so at about the same time that she caught Henry's roving eye. Displeased to hear that Percy and Anne were courting and might be wishing to marry, Henry ordered Wolsey to thwart the young couple's plans. Wolsey summoned Percy to appear before him and rebuked him, heir as he was to one of the greatest earldoms in the country, for wanting to marry a mere gentleman's daughter. Wolsey warned him that Henry would never give the necessary royal consent, disingenuously adding that the king already had someone else in mind for Anne. When Percy gallantly maintained his love for Anne, the earl's father, unwilling to incur the disfavour of Wolsey and the king, threatened to disinherit his obstinate son. Eventually the combined pressure of the cardinal and the father, backed by the king, forced young Percy to give way, and instead of Anne he married one of the earl of Shrewsbury's daughters. Anne was furious, though mainly with Wolsey; she did not yet know either the king's involvement or his feelings for her.[5]

It fell now to Cardinal Wolsey, Henry's chief minister and Thomas Cromwell's master, to secure a divorce for the king. International opposition was, predictably, fiercest from the Holy Roman Emperor Charles V, Catherine's nephew. In May 1527 Charles's ambassador in England, De Mendoza, reported that Wolsey 'had been scheming to bring about the queen's divorce', and that Henry was about to assemble a gathering of divines to declare his marriage null. In the diplomatic haggling now under way the French, again according to De Mendoza, promised Wolsey the archbishopric of Rouen. To counter this the ambassador hinted to Wolsey that Charles could make a better offer and facilitate Wolsey's elevation to the papacy – provided his 'actions deserved it'. Meanwhile Catherine and Anne, despite their intense rivalry for the king's affections, at least shared one thing in common – both were equally suspicious of Wolsey's motives. Anne had by now forgotten Henry Percy, but her loathing of Wolsey simmered as intensely as ever, and she suspected him of trying to secretly arrange a French match for Henry. She, her father and the duke of Norfolk, so De Mendoza reported, had now formed a factional league against the cardinal.[6]

It comes as something of a relief for a writer on Thomas Cromwell to be able to say that he seems to have had virtually nothing to do with all of this. This would be, at least partly, because he was neither a bishop nor a divine, and unlikely to be asked to consider the theological aspects of the case. He was, however, fluent in Italian and Latin, and had travelled to Rome two or three times, maybe more, since settling in England; so he could have been employed in some capacity in the long drawn out negotiations that followed between Henry and the papacy. Fortunately for him, he was not called upon.

During 1528 Cromwell was more preoccupied with his son Gregory's schooling than Henry's marital trials. The boys' new tutor, John Chekyng, may have known Cromwell personally, because some of his letters concern subjects of general and presumably mutual interest. Chekyng had been reading Erasmus's edition of Saint Augustine's works, and he praised them highly to Cromwell. However, he was also a bit pressed for cash, and chasing Cromwell for unpaid bills. Gregory's end of term report was somewhat less than glowing – he was a bit slow – but Chekyng blamed his previous tutor for the lack of progress. Once again Gregory's letters to his father were full of promises to work hard and do well.[7]

Still in 1528, while Wolsey grappled with Henry's Great Matter, Cromwell continued his work on the cardinal's colleges at Oxford and Ipswich. He prosaically assured his master that the building 'of your noble college most prosperously and magnificently doth arise' in so imposing a manner that 'the like thereof was never seen nor imagined'. Cromwell was busy sorting out all the documentation, letters patent and administration. He also took up the cause of English merchants whose ships were detained in France, and completed a valuation of Wolsey's lands in York. Suppression of selected smaller monasteries continued, though it is noteworthy that when the priory of Felixstowe was suppressed, Stephen Gardiner, now Archdeacon of Worcester, and Rowland Lee were named as 'judges', with Cromwell present officially only as a 'witness'. Gardiner, Lee and Cromwell then supervised the transfer of all the priory's possessions to Ipswich. Then in October comes the first indication that Cromwell by now knew Thomas Cranmer, when Cranmer went up to London and then to Ipswich with a letter for William Capon, the new dean of Wolsey's college there, which had been written by Cromwell.[8]

Also in October, Cardinal Campeggio arrived in London from Rome as the papal representative to hear the king's case. He and Wolsey then went to see Queen Catherine to officially inform her that proceedings were about to start. She responded regally. 'Is it now', she demanded, 'a question whether I be the king's lawful wife or not, when I have been married to him almost 20 years'? Catherine scathingly reproached Wolsey for his 'high pride and vainglory ... voluptuous life and abominable lechery ... power and tyranny who of malice you have kindled this fire ... especially for the great malice that you bear to my nephew the emperor ... because he would not satisfy your ambition and make you pope by force'. Wolsey pleaded that he was 'neither the beginner nor the mover' of the affair, but had merely been appointed to hear the case.[9]

According to De Mendoza, Henry and Anne were already looking 'on their future marriage as certain, as if that of the queen had been actually dissolved'. Wolsey, however, was trying to delay things. 'It is generally agreed', the ambassador added, that Wolsey and Campeggio 'will secretly agree to keep the matter in suspense'. Wolsey's fear was that he would lose power if Anne, now nagging Henry mercilessly to settle his divorce quickly, became queen. For his part, Henry was 'so blindly in love with that lady that he cannot see his way clearly'. The ambassador suspected that Henry was loading Campeggio with gifts.[10]

George Cavendish, Wolsey's first biographer, agreed that Anne was now keeping 'an estate more like a queen than a simple maid'. Anne was urging Henry to consider 'the danger the cardinal hath brought you', how he had been working to the king's 'slander and dishonour', and that if anyone else had done 'but half so much as he hath done, he were well worthy to lose his head'. At the turn of the year (January and February 1529), De Mendoza reported that Henry was becoming impatient with Wolsey for not fulfilling his promises. Anne was certain that Wolsey was stalling, and her alliance with her father and the dukes of Norfolk and Suffolk to undermine the cardinal was now in full swing.[11]

One of the clearest insights into Wolsey's strategy is revealed in his own letter to Stephen Gardiner dated 7 February 1529. Wolsey urged Gardiner, now one of the king's emissaries to Rome on the divorce case, to do all he could to help Wolsey become pope, a plan that Wolsey claimed enjoyed the king's support. Gardiner will be 'informed of the king's mind and mine concerning my advancement unto the dignity papal', Wolsey wrote, trusting that Gardiner would 'omit nothing ... to serve and conduce to that purpose'. He addressed Gardiner as the man 'whom I most entirely do trust', a view which would soon change. He referred to the king's 'secret matter, which, if it should be brought to pass by any other means than by the authority of the church, then I count this prince and this realm utterly undone'. Wolsey, already fearing the ghastly prospect of a breach with Rome, was convinced that he was the only cardinal 'that can and will set remedy' in the great affair. However, he denied seeking power or glory for himself.[12]

It was around this time that personal tragedy struck the Cromwell family. The last surviving reference to his wife occurs in a letter from Richard Cave to the Cromwells in June 1528. It may have been the deadly sweating sickness plaguing the country that stole her and his two daughters away sometime shortly afterwards. Whatever it was, he decided he must make his will in July 1529, which opened in impeccably medieval fashion:

> I bequeath my soul to the great God of heaven, my Maker, Creator and Redeemer, beseeching the most glorious Virgin, our Blessed Lady Saint Mary the Virgin and Mother, with all the holy company of heaven, to be mediators and intercessors for me to the Holy Trinity, so that I may be able ... to inherit the kingdom of heaven.

The will names Gregory as his heir. Poignantly it refers to his 'late wife', and provisions made for his daughter Anne and his 'little daughter Grace' are crossed out. It provides for his sister, Elizabeth Wellyfed, his nephews and niece, and his mother-

in-law, Mercy Prior, all still living. Smaller gifts are assigned to
Ralph Sadler and Stephen Vaughan along with other friends
and servants. He required his executors to 'conduct and hire a
priest being an honest person of continent and good living, to
sing for my soul by the space of seven years after my death'. A
list of donations to causes he supported included 'the making
of highways in this realm … every of the five orders of friars
within the City of London to pray for my soul', plus gifts to
the poor, not forgetting the 'poor prisoners of Newgate'. He
asked for a funeral 'without any earthly pomp', and named
Sadler, Vaughan, and his brother-in-law, John Williamson, as
executors.[13]

Meanwhile, he had to carry on with his normal duties. He
was occupied with Wolsey's colleges and his own legal business, which included a request to procure a papal bull, though
nothing to do with the king's affair. He also arranged for the
education of one of his nieces. He then stung John Chekyng
with a criticism that Gregory and young Wellyfed had not progressed well enough under his tutorship. Indignantly Chekyng
protested that he had brought up many fine scholars, including six MAs and fellows of colleges. He continued to press
Cromwell for outstanding bills, including the cost of a feather
bed, burned when master Wellyfed fell asleep reading a book
by candlelight and the candle dropped onto the bed starting
a fire. However, the dispute was soon resolved, the bills were
paid, and for the time being Gregory continued as a pupil of
Mr Chekyng.[14]

But far more important affairs of state were now reaching
their climax. In July 1529, Campeggio effectively stymied any
further progress on Catherine's 'trial' by insisting that the court
should follow Roman legal custom and adjourn till October.
It never reconvened. Henry either discovered or suspected
that the pope had yielded to the demand of Charles V to hear
the case in Rome, exactly the thing Henry had hoped Wolsey
could somehow prevent. On 9 August writs were issued for a
new parliament. Eustace Chapuys, Charles's new ambassador
in England, predicted that if Anne had her way, Wolsey would

soon be gone. Henry and Wolsey met for the last time at Grafton on 20 September. Three days later Cromwell received a letter from a friend telling him that the Dukes of Norfolk and Suffolk, along with Thomas Boleyn (Anne's father), were all showing deference to Wolsey, but 'what they bear in their hearts I know not'. Wolsey himself now suspected the loyalty of some in his own circle. The trust he had shown in Stephen Gardiner earlier in the year vanished and was replaced by suspicion and bitterness.[15]

The French envoy, du Bellay, was also convinced that Wolsey would not survive the coming parliament. Both diplomats had read the situation well. On 9 October Wolsey was indicted for praemunire; on 18 he surrendered the great seal, and a week later Thomas More was made Lord Chancellor in his place. Du Bellay confirmed the news to the French – Wolsey was undone, Norfolk was chief of the council, behind him was Suffolk, but 'above them all' stood Anne. The ambassadors had no doubt that the vengeful, ambitious royal mistress was Wolsey's chief enemy and the prime cause of his fall. Already Wolsey, now in great distress, was appealing to du Bellay for help from King Francis.[16]

Shortly after the blow fell, Cavendish entered the Great Chamber of Wolsey's Asher home one morning to behold what he regarded a 'strange sight'. Cromwell was 'leaning in the great window with a primer in his hand, saying Our Lady Mattens', with tears in his eyes. 'Why, Mr. Cromwell', asked Cavendish. 'What meaneth all this your sorrow? Is my lord in any danger for whom ye lament thus, or is it for any loss that ye have sustained?' 'Nay', replied Cromwell with brutal frankness. 'It is my unhappy adventure, who am like to lose all that I have travailed for, all the days of my life'. Cromwell felt 'in disdain with most men for my master's sake, and surely without just cause; however, an ill name once gotten will not lightly be put away'. Within twelve months Cromwell had lost a wife, two daughters and a master. He now faced political and financial ruin. Fortunately, he was also a man of mettle, not one to be cowed by misfortune. He told Cavendish that he would ride to London and court that afternoon, 'when I will either make or mar, ere I come again'.[17]

Fortified by this resolve, Cromwell attended a farewell dinner given by Wolsey. Sometime during dinner the conventional piety of Lady Mattens faded, and the independent, anti-clerical spirit of the late medieval humanist revived within him. Cromwell urged Wolsey to show his gratitude to his servants, and offer them some encouragement in the crisis that had overwhelmed them. 'Alas Thomas', cried Wolsey, 'you know that I have nothing to give them'. Cromwell persisted. He reminded Wolsey of all his gifts to his chaplains and clergy while his lay servants have nothing, despite having 'taken much more pains for you in one day than all your idle chaplains hath done in a year'. At this, Wolsey relented. He summoned his entourage, thanked them for their services, told them that they may 'take your pleasures for a month' and then return to him, by which time he hoped rather forlornly that the king would be reconciled to him. Cromwell pointed out that his servants did not have enough money for a month's holiday, and suggested that Wolsey's chaplains, 'who hath received at your hands great beneficies and high dignities', might care to show some charity to those less well off. Cromwell threw five pounds in gold on the table, then cast his eye around him. 'Now let us see what your chaplains will do', he challenged. 'Go to, masters'. The browbeaten chaplains meekly coughed up, and a sizable sum was collected. Wolsey then bid his thankful servants farewell, and after a long conversation with his former master, Cromwell and his clerk, Ralph Sadler, rode off to London to 'make or mar'.[18]

It is intriguing that Cromwell, instead of retiring to his legal practice and private life, decided to set out for court. It was a gamble for a man from Wolsey's council who had not joined – and was not going to join – the triumphant pro-Boleyn, anti-Wolsey faction around the king. Cromwell's career hung in the balance, leaving his friends anxious. Stephen Vaughan, now in Flanders, was 'greatly in doubt how you are treated in this sad overthrow of my lord your master'. Vaughan offered all the encouragement and help he could. He had heard malicious things about Cromwell, 'yet do I not doubt but your truth and wisdom shall deliver you from danger. You are more hated for your master's sake than for anything which I think you have wrongfully done against any man'. Vaughan prayed God to 'lend you a constant and patient mind' and help you.[19]

The story of how Cromwell recovered his fortunes by becoming a member of parliament once again is complicated and a little uncertain. According to Cavendish, Cromwell 'chanced to meet with one Sir Thomas Rush, knight, a special friend', and 'by that means' Cromwell managed to 'put his foot into the parliament house'. Here Cavendish was giving a summary only. It was not quite as simple as this, and a key letter to understanding what happened is Sadler's to Cromwell dated 1 November. Sadler had seen a Mr Gage, who spoke to Norfolk, who spoke to the king about the possibility of Cromwell entering parliament. Henry agreed, and Cromwell was ordered to wait for further instructions from Norfolk. Sadler had also talked to Rush, and was intending to see him again to learn 'whether ye [Cromwell] shall be burgess of Orforde [in Suffolk] or not'. Sadler continued: 'And if ye be not elect there I will then according to your further commandment repair unto Mr Paulet, and require him to name you to one of the burgesses of one of my lord's towns of his bishopric of Winchester'. Sadler suggested that Cromwell should come to court to meet Norfolk, 'by whom ye shall know the king his pleasure how ye shall order yourself in the parliament'.[20]

So Cromwell had taken the prudent precaution of obtaining the king's approval, via the good offices of Gage and Norfolk. However, the reference to 'Orforde *or not*' proves that Cromwell was not allocated a plumb seat automatically. He had to wait his turn, and wheel and deal a bit. In the event Orforde chose Erasmus Paston and Richard Hunt, while Cromwell took his seat representing Taunton.[21]

Parliament opened on 3 November with a speech from the new Lord Chancellor, Thomas More. Then the Commons elected Thomas Audley, soon to become a close evangelical ally of Cromwell's, as Speaker. Archdeacon Cranmer, meanwhile, was now in the lower house of Convocation, the assembly of the clergy. An anti-clerical mood prevailed in this parliament, and a raft of complaints was quickly lodged against the clergy for assorted abuses ranging from excessive charges levied on the family of a deceased person, to more general gripes about worldly living and pastoral neglect. Audley appointed a committee to investigate, and it is almost certain that Cromwell sat on it.[22]

Somewhat less certain is how prominent a role he played, or the degree of his opposition to the clergy. In Elton's view it was quite decisive, though other scholars of Tudor constitutional history like Lehmberg are not so sure. Lehmberg gives examples of Cromwell's notes actually softening some of the harsher criticisms of the clergy. A virtually irresolvable question is whether drafts in Cromwell's handwriting should be taken as his own personal ideas, or the proposals or conclusions of the committee reached after a thorough discussion. Because there was nothing fundamentally Protestant about the critiques levelled at the clergy, we can pass over this moot point and concentrate on Cromwell's relations with Wolsey during this difficult time in his career.

Norfolk, Suffolk and Thomas Boleyn were now drawing up articles against Wolsey. According to Cavendish, Cromwell supported Wolsey so valiantly in the Commons that 'there was no matter alleged against my lord [Wolsey] but that he [Cromwell] was ever ready furnished with a sufficient answer'. Cromwell demolished the attacks on Wolsey with 'such witty persuasions and deep reasons that the same bill could take there no effect'. Cromwell was now full of confidence, and wearing a 'much pleasanter countenance' than at the recent dinner at Asher. He seemed unfazed by a warning from Sadler that Wolsey's 'enemies' – he mentioned no names – had been talking to Henry, and that Sadler had now lost trust in Stephen Gardiner.[23]

Bitter following his misfortunes, and still suspicious of Gardiner, Wolsey now looked on Cromwell as my 'only aider in this mine intolerable anxiety and distress'. He urged him to 'forsake me not in this my extreme need'. He pleaded with Cromwell to speak with Henry Norris, one of the king's household and a supporter of the Boleyns, to see if the 'displeasure of my lady Anne' might be assuaged; likewise 'my lords Norfolk and Suffolk … must be effectually laboured'. With Wolsey's agreement, Cromwell drafted a grant for George Boleyn, Anne's brother, awarding him an annuity of £200 for lands in Winchester, and another £200 for abbey lands in St Albans. Apparently on Cromwell's advice, more financial sweeteners were arranged for Norris and Sir John Russell, an envoy of the king and another affiliate of Anne's increasingly dominant faction. Pandering to the Boleyns had become a disagreeable necessity because Anne's hostility was widely believed to be the main reason for Wolsey's demise: 'everyone', according to Chapuys, was saying that Henry bore Wolsey no ill will, but the king was forced to get rid of him solely to 'gratify her'.[24]

Cavendish's portrayal of Cromwell's loyalty towards Wolsey has rankled with critics like Merriman, who can only see Cromwell buying off opposition with money to help himself gain popularity and power in parliament and at court. However, whilst it is true that Cromwell had to rebuild his own career, the real point is that Wolsey had begged Cromwell to do all he could to assuage Anne's 'displeasure'; and Wolsey, still dreaming of making a grand comeback, would hardly have agreed to Cromwell's ideas if he suspected that Cromwell had only his own welfare in mind.[25]

During or shortly after January 1530, Cromwell more or less formally entered the king's service. Effectively this meant being part of Henry's administrative staff. He was a long, long way from being the king's chief minister, but the point may be worth stressing that he was in the *king's* service and no one else's. After Wolsey's fall he did not join the Boleyn faction, or the Norfolk faction, or any other vested interest at court. He transferred from the cardinal's employment directly to the king's. This independence from any party loyalty – allied to his natural abilities in law, languages and commerce – would soon ensure advancement and success. Stephen Vaughan, previously worried about Cromwell's fortunes, was now relieved to hear 'all things to have succeeded even as I desired; you now sail in a sure haven'.[26]

Meanwhile, Anne's 'displeasure' with Wolsey had at best only partially abated. She was overheard snapping at Norfolk and even at Henry for not being severe enough with the disgraced cardinal. Despite this, Wolsey's fortunes revived somewhat when, in February 1530, he received a pardon; at this point even Merriman is forced to admit, though reluctantly and through ferociously gritted teeth, that Cromwell's efforts might have had something to do with this. Wolsey certainly showed a deep gratitude towards Cromwell, begging 'our Lord to reward you … for such great pains as you have taken in all my causes'. These 'pains' also included procuring medical help.[27]

But to Wolsey's intense chagrin, Henry was now abundantly helping himself to the cardinal's colleges, lands and fine buildings. This was another affair that Cromwell was called on to manage. Once again he received fulsome praise from Cavendish for the way in which he executed his office, 'so justly and exactly', with such 'faithful and diligent service'. Soon Cromwell found himself swamped with applications for annuities from enquirers who were 'worthily to reward him' for his efforts on their behalf. As a result, Cromwell had more and more direct contact with Henry, and by his competence and 'witty demeanour he grew continually in the king's favour'. Henry was impressed with Cromwell's 'honesty and wisdom', finding him a 'meet instrument to serve his grace'. Again Merriman sees Cromwell chiefly occupied in making money and buying influence for himself, but again Merriman's jaundiced eye overlooks a rather obvious fact. Cromwell was now in the king's service carrying out the king's business, accountable directly to Henry for the administration of lands taken over by the king. Maybe Cromwell did, from time to time, consider his own interests as well as the king's; maybe he gladly accepted the bonuses that came his way – who would not? Nevertheless, he was not free to fleece all and sundry and enrich himself in the process with impunity. Any unscrupulous, dishonest, selfish dealing could easily have been noticed and reported back to Henry.[28]

When Wolsey hankered after a move from Asher to Richmond, he asked Cromwell to obtain the king's permission. This gave Cromwell another opportunity to see Henry personally. Again Cromwell bypassed the council and dealt directly with the king. Permission was duly granted, but when the council heard about it they managed to persuade Henry that Wolsey should live out his days in York. Wolsey demurred and would have preferred Winchester, but under pressure from his council, and maybe from Anne as well, Henry was now adamant that Wolsey must go north. All the while Cromwell was the one shuttling backwards and forwards between Henry and Wolsey with requests and answers.[29]

A sign of Henry's increasing trust in Cromwell is that he confided to him, sometime in May, that Wolsey had been trying to sow discord between the king and Norfolk. Cromwell may also have been gratified to hear from John Russell that Henry 'had very good communication of you' following a recent meeting; the details of this meeting are not disclosed. Meanwhile a Mr Page had delivered certain letters from Wolsey to Anne, though Cromwell had to tell Wolsey that she 'gave kind words, but will not promise to speak to the king for you'. Cromwell continued to look after Wolsey's interests as best he could. Sometime in June he drafted a letter from Wolsey to Henry about a matter of maritime law that Wolsey had dealt with when he was Lord Chancellor, and which had, for reasons not stated, surfaced again.[30]

But in summer 1530, dangerous thoughts were stirring in Wolsey's mind. From his new home in York he renewed his contacts with Rome and, via Eustace Chapuys, Charles V. Wolsey used his physician, a Venetian called Dr Augustine, as intermediary to suggest to Chapuys that now was the time to act for Catherine of Aragon. Cromwell knew Augustine well;

he had helped him obtain his English citizenship, for which Augustine was immensely grateful. There is, however, no evidence that Cromwell was involved in Wolsey's intrigues.[31]

As if oblivious to them, he carried on dealing assiduously with Wolsey's incessant pleas and requests. Somewhat abruptly he told the testy and ever demanding cardinal that he was now 'worse than when your troubles began'. Trying to soothe Wolsey's anger over the loss of his colleges, Cromwell appealed to him to be content 'and let your prince execute his pleasure', and submit to the king in all things. He assured Wolsey of Henry's goodwill, and the goodwill of many in court and country; but Cromwell also felt constrained to point out to Wolsey that his ways and manner of living were 'not by your enemies interpreted after the best fashion'. Reports had reached London that Wolsey was living sumptuously in York, and Cromwell begged him 'for the love of God … as I often times have done, I most heartily beseech your grace to have respect … and to refrain yourself for a season from all manner buildings more than mere necessity requireth'. Such restraint will 'cease and put to silence' those who were speaking ill of Wolsey to the king. Cromwell urged Wolsey to use his liberty to 'serve God', and to learn to 'experiment how ye shall banish and exile the vain desires of this unstable world'. Cromwell's letters to Wolsey in York are not all pastoral, however, and he regularly sent Wolsey news about events abroad and at court. He also promised his continued support.[32]

Unfortunately, neither Wosley's ambition nor his love of fine living had deserted him, and again in August Cromwell warned him that Henry was minded to take over more of the cardinal's lands in York. 'This will be very displeasing to you', Cromwell admitted, 'but it is best to suffer it'. Once more Cromwell appealed to his former master to have patience: for 'some allege that your grace do keep too great a house and family, and that you are continually building – for love of God, therefore, have a respect and refrain'. According to Hall, Wolsey was planning a spectacular enthronement ceremony for himself at York, but Cromwell's letters do not mention this.[33]

Cromwell's last surviving letters to Wolsey were written in October, after he heard a rumour that Wolsey suspected him of 'dissembling'. The letter does not say what prompted these suspicions but Cromwell felt understandably aggrieved – 'I beseech you to speak without faining if you have such conceit, that I may clear myself', he appealed. Cromwell promised he would continue to act for Wolsey in all sorts of ways, but 'truly your grace in some things over-shooteth yourself'. Still calling him 'your grace', however, Cromwell asked Wolsey to provide 'some little office' for one Dr Carbot, and he also commended other servants and scholars in Cambridge. He kept Wolsey up to date with parliamentary business – 'The prelates shall not appear in the *praemunire*; there is another way devised ... as your grace shall further know.' There is no obvious hint or clue in these letters that Cromwell knew of, or even suspected, that something dramatic was about to happen. The clear impression is that he expected to be writing regularly to York during the coming weeks and months.[34]

On 4 November, however, after incriminating letters were found in Dr Augustine's possession, Wolsey was arrested on suspicion of treason. Chapuys blamed Norfolk, Anne and her father for their plotting against Wolsey, with Anne even threatening to leave Henry unless he took decisive action. Augustine, meanwhile, was taken to Norfolk's house, where he was 'entertained like a prince ... singing to the right tune'. Chapuys heard details of Augustine's statement from the Venetian ambassador: Wolsey had asked the pope to excommunicate Henry and put England under a papal interdict unless Henry dismissed Anne from court; and by this means Wolsey hoped to provoke a rising in England, and return to power as the restorer of good order. This may not have been technically treasonable according to the law of England as it then stood, but it was certainly more than enough to enrage Henry and ensure Wolsey's final doom.[35]

It may be harsh to call Augustine Wolsey's betrayer. He may have done nothing worse than answer Norfolk's questions honestly. As for Wolsey, the Venetian ambassador writing retrospectively confirmed the reports of his imperialist colleagues: Wolsey had initially supported the divorce, but had changed his mind after Campeggio's visit to England, when he began to fear that if Rome approved Henry's marriage to Anne, then he (Wolsey) would lose power at home, and might even be ousted by the alliance of Anne, her father and Norfolk.[36]

Wolsey then received a summons to London, but his death on 29 November at Leicester spared him the humiliation of a trial and possibly the scaffold. Cromwell's reaction to the news is not known, but there is no valid reason not to accept Cavendish's testimony that he remained loyal to a fallen master, despite occasional moments of exasperation when it became embarrassingly plain that Wolsey was not prepared to retire quietly and gracefully. Cavendish is supported by Chapuys, a seasoned diplomat, who had been following the events of 1529 closely. Chapuys had been in regular contact with Wolsey throughout the summer, and he would later testify that Cromwell 'behaved very well' towards the cardinal during his unhappy last days.[37]

By January 1531, Cromwell was a member of Henry's council. He was not a senior councillor yet, and his position might be likened to that of a British government minister who does not have a seat in the cabinet. And this might be the suitable place to consider the well-known story that Cromwell rose rapidly to power after one dramatic interview with Henry, in which Cromwell urged the king to break with Rome and declare himself head of the Church, before going on to outline a bold plan that would make Henry the richest king in the world. With only minor variations, this story appears in the writings of Reginald Pole and John Foxe. Chapuys has half of it – that Cromwell promised to make Henry rich – but not that he encouraged the king to break with Rome.[38]

This story does not, however, feature in the works of Hall and Cavendish, two contemporary witnesses who knew Cromwell better than did Pole, Foxe or even Chapuys. Cavendish, as noted already, speaks of a gradual rise to power, and how Cromwell 'grew continually in the king's favour'.

This is, beyond all doubt, right. There was no speedy, sudden promotion for Cromwell. He may have had personal meetings with the king during 1530, and they may have discussed royal revenues and financial affairs; but Cromwell would have to wait three more years before being appointed Henry's Principal Secretary. His eventual pre-eminence on the council would be due to the old-fashioned, unglamorous virtues of hard work and ability, not to one single melodramatic encounter with Henry. Besides, in 1530 there was nothing startlingly novel in the idea that Henry should make himself Head of the Church (see Chapter 4).[39]

According to Cavendish, Anne's father was the 'chiefest of the king's Privy Council' after Wolsey's demise. Chapuys assigned that distinction to Norfolk, and the Venetian ambassador thought likewise. His colleague from Milan wrote that Boleyn senior, Norfolk and Stephen Gardiner now enjoyed most influence with the king. Whilst minor differences of opinion existed between the ambassadors, they all agreed that Cromwell was not yet one of the king's foremost councillors. In fact his name does not appear in Chapuys's surviving letters until March 1533, even though Chapuys in particular took an avid interest in English affairs, and sent regular reports to Charles.[40]

Although Cromwell's star was rising steadily rather than spectacularly, he could nevertheless look back on a long and successful, if at times painful, life's journey. In every sense he had made, not marred. The humble blacksmith's son, the fugitive, the one-time 'bit of a ruffian' was now called by his prince to be a councillor of the realm. Further advance and honour would lie ahead. Before that, however, he would hear a calling of quite a different kind. A new path was now opening up in front of him, as precarious as any he had trodden hitherto. Thomas Cromwell was about to set out on a spiritual journey that would make him, in the coolly dispassionate judgement of the later French ambassador Charles de Marillac, the 'principal author' of the Protestant Reformation in England.[41]

3

The Lutheran

On 16 February 1531 the Schmalkaldic League, the newly formed alliance of Lutheran states, wrote to the kings of France, Denmark and England. The League defended the Lutheran *Augsburg Confession* as being fully in accordance with Holy Scripture and the ancient Christian creeds, and strongly denied accusations that Lutherans were heretics or subversives. Henry sent a courteous reply on 3 May. He was relieved to hear of their commitment to Christian orthodoxy, and he commended them for seeking to make necessary, wholesome reforms to the church. Doubtless with Luther in mind, however, he added that he preferred physicians who 'heal the wound or cure the disease without exasperating the parts'.[1]

It so happened that a mild, gentle physician was now dispensing the Lutheran medicine. Philip Melanchthon was of the same faith as Martin Luther, but of quite a different temperament. 'I am a rough warrior', Luther confessed, 'born to fight with mobs and the devil. I clear away the logs and stones, tear up the briars and thorns. Then along comes Master Philip, softly and gently, sowing and watering with joy'.[2]

King Henry had already experienced a bruising encounter with the spiritual warrior from Wittenberg. Nearly ten years earlier, eager to prove his orthodoxy following the challenge of Luther, Henry had written his *Assertion of the Seven Sacraments against Martin Luther*, only to be stunned by a furious reply. Among other things Luther had called Henry a 'liar', a 'buffoon', a 'big sissy' and a 'stupid king'. Luther's fiery zeal for the Gospel was known and feared by his opponents. It has also elicited a great deal of dreary sanctimonious moralising, as well as largely inept psychoanalysing, from historians down the years (with honourable exceptions like Martin Brecht).[3]

But times were changing, and it was Melanchthon who drafted the League's letter to the kings of Europe. He, too, had composed the *Augsburg Confession*, presented to the Emperor Charles V at the diet in summer 1530. When the Catholic delegation countered with their *Confutation*, Melanchthon made the first sketches of his *Apology of the Augsburg Confession*, which soon developed into the most significant Lutheran work yet written. It expanded on the *Augsburg Confession*, and answered in minute detail the points raised in the *Confutation*. Begun in the autumn of 1530, the *Apology* was not finished until spring or summer the following year. But only a few months after the first editions were running off the printing presses of Witttenberg, Thomas Cromwell received, by special delivery, his own personal copy. How this came to be is the subject of this chapter.

Until now Cromwell's views on Luther were not much different from Henry's or Wolsey's. In a letter to Wolsey during summer 1530, Cromwell reported a rumour that Luther had died, and added curtly that he wished he had never been born. For a man seeking to rebuild his political career in Henry's England, this was a prudent attitude. Two royal proclamations of March 1529 and June 1530 thundered against 'erroneous books and heresies ... printed in other regions, and sent into this realm ... to pervert and withdraw the people from the Catholic and true faith'. The first proclamation, though not the second, condemned Luther by name. Both condemned the books of his English 'disciples', with William Tyndale, Simon Fish and John Frith being the chief targets. All teaching 'contrary and against the faith Catholic' was forbidden.[4]

Tyndale, the foremost English evangelical scholar and Bible translator, was now living in exile on the continent. His decision to remain abroad proved a wise one in view of the fate suffered by Thomas Hitton in February 1530. Hitton, a priest who had returned to England after travelling in Europe, was burned at the stake for smuggling a New Testament and other evangelical literature into the country. Hitton may count as England's first real Protestant, rather than Lollard, martyr. The Lord Chancellor, Thomas More, had cast aside his cultivated humanism to spearhead an anti-heresy onslaught, and like a victorious angel of wrath he condemned Hitton as 'the devil's stinking martyr', who had caught his 'false faith' from Tyndale's 'holy books, and now the spirit of error and lying hath taken his wretched soul with him straight from the short fire to the fire everlasting'.[5]

Hitton was not the only object of More's fury. Suspected Lutherans were being rounded up and questioned. Many recanted under the threat of the stake. One Philip Smith was found in possession of works by Luther, Melanchthon and the Basle reformer, Johannes Oecolampadius; but only, so he claimed, in order to form his own opinions about them. Apparently adept at getting out of tight corners, Smith told his examiners that he accepted Luther only as far as the church did. With More as Chancellor, this would not be very far. Another suspect taken in for questioning had allegedly bought works by Luther and Melanchthon at an Antwerp book fair before bringing them to England. Another early evangelical convert, Hugh Latimer, maintained that he had borrowed nothing from Luther and Melanchthon for his sermons. This may be so, but it does suggest that by now Latimer had been reading the German Reformers.[6]

Yet it was while this campaign was reaching its height we have the first indication that Cromwell's religious views were undergoing a change. In November 1530, four men were required to do penance for reading and distributing Tyndale's works. At least one, Thomas Somer, was known to Cromwell. He had helped Somer when he fell on hard times. How much

Cromwell knew of, and agreed with, Somer's beliefs is far from certain; but his evangelical interest, though rather tenuous at this stage, may well have begun while Wolsey was still alive.[7]

During 1531, someone or something induced Henry to take a more lenient line towards Lutheranism. It may have been the timeliness of the League's letter, because it arrived just when Henry was asserting his authority over his clergy. He demanded from them a massive £100, 000, ostensibly to recover expenses incurred on his divorce case, such as sending emissaries to Rome, soliciting opinions from universities, and so on. After some murmurs of protest the clergy yielded, only to be assailed with a further demand that they acknowledge the king as 'sole protector and supreme head of the Anglican church and clergy'. Following token resistance, the clergy accepted this too, with only a minor qualifier 'as far as the law of Christ allows'.[8]

With his opposition to the papacy now growing, Henry may have felt that he had something in common with the German Lutherans, though at this stage not very much. He agreed to send Stephen Vaughan, Cromwell's friend, to the continent to see if there was any chance of reconciling Tyndale to Henry. Like Luther, Tyndale had opposed Henry's plans to divorce Catherine of Aragon and marry Anne Boleyn. Tyndale did, however, support the principle of kingly rather than papal authority. Henry, influenced perhaps by Cromwell, must have decided that an approach to Tyndale and the Lutherans would be worthwhile. The choice of Vaughan as an emissary is a little curious because during a recent visit to Antwerp, questions had been raised about his Catholic orthodoxy. No formal charges were made against him, but he was not entirely free from suspicion. As we will see, More was watching him closely.[9]

Vaughan's first report to Henry from the continent is dated 26 January 1531. Vaughan had written to Tyndale as instructed by the king, offering Tyndale a safe conduct to England. Tyndale, however, suspected a trap. Fearing that England would be unsafe, he politely declined. Vaughan sent a copy of his report to Cromwell, though with a few interesting extra points. Vaughan doubted whether Tyndale would ever agree to come to England because of the anti-Lutheran drive orchestrated by More. Vaughan thought Tyndale would answer More's attack on him, then write no more. Tyndale, Vaughan added, was 'of a greater knowledge than the king's highness doth take him for; which well appeareth by his works. Would God he were in England!' Obviously Vaughan knew that commending Tyndale, which would have risked arrest had More heard of it, was a safe thing to say to Cromwell.[10]

Vaughan's next letter to Cromwell is dated 25 March. Now he boldly commended Tyndale's book, written in reply to a critique of him by More. Vaughan wondered whether it would be wise to let Henry see it, and he asked Cromwell's advice. His caution was well founded because these were still uncertain and dangerous times for Lutheran men. In the spring Convocation questioned a clutch of evangelicals including Edward Crome, Thomas Bilney, Hugh Latimer and John Lambert, though following a partial climb-down by the accused, no serious action was taken against them. Convocation also summoned Richard Tracy, whose dead father's will had confessed justification by faith alone. He was also spared prosecution, but next year his father's body was exhumed, and, on the directions of the chancellor of the bishop of Worcester, burned at stake. Tracy's supporters and helpers, by now including Cromwell, took legal action against the chancellor, who was forced to pay a £300 fine by way of compensation.[11]

Returning to Vaughan and Tyndale on the continent, on 18 April 1531 Vaughan wrote to Henry again, enclosing a part of Tyndale's *Answer* to More. Vaughan had now met Tyndale, who protested his loyalty to Henry, but was still nervous about returning to England in view of the opposition to him. Vaughan then ventured his own judgement on Tyndale, this time directly to the king, not to Cromwell. 'I have not communed with a man ...' he begins – but here, mysteriously, the surviving manuscript ends. David Daniell, Tyndale's recent biographer, rejects as fanciful the suggestion that Henry tore up the letter in anger. Nevertheless, something unusual must have occurred, because Cromwell's reply in early May is full of harsh words about Tyndale, plus crossings out, underlining and various other alterations before ending on an incongruously calm note with instructions on shipping matters. Then in a supplementary postscript, Cromwell urged Vaughan to carry on as before! Exactly what happened here is a mystery. It may well be that something had displeased Henry, and that Cromwell had succeeded in mollifying the king's initial anger. Whatever the true facts of the case, there was no royal rebuke for Cromwell and no recall for Vaughan, who replied to the king on 20 May, breezily confident as ever. He assured Henry that Tyndale deeply desired to be reconciled to him, and longed for the king to 'grant only a bare text of the Scriptures to be put forth among his people'.[12]

Vaughan's next letter to Cromwell, on 19 June, shows him forging ahead on a mission somewhat more evangelical in purpose than Henry was likely to have authorised. Vaughan had been trying to obtain a book of Luther's (no title is given) but only one was available, and that was taken. He had Melanchthon's *Augsburg Confession* and wished he could send it to Henry, but feared Henry would hand it over to others for an opinion rather than read it himself. Something had happened to make Vaughan anxious to meet Cromwell – I was 'never more desirous to speak with you than now'. Vaughan had no regrets about sending Tyndale's *Answer* to Henry, and he triumphantly announced that Isaiah and Jonah were now translated into English, and it 'passeth any man's power to stop them from coming forth'. Tyndale had just completed his translation of Jonah, while Isaiah was the work of George Joye, another evangelical in exile. Both works were printed by Martin de Keyseer of Antwerp.[13]

At home, meanwhile, Cromwell's steady rise to political power continued. He was now receiving 'instructions given by the king's highness unto his trusty councillor Thomas Cromwell'. These instructions included overseeing legal affairs and formulating drafts for parliament. In Elton's view, Cromwell had advanced to 'an executive minister of the second rank'. He was also involved in managing parliamentary affairs, and a further sign of his growing influence is seen in letters from members of parliament to Cromwell excusing themselves or others from attendance. Sir William Stourton of the Commons asked leave for his aging, sick father as well as for himself, a request temptingly accompanied by a gift of a tub of wine. John Tuchet also obtained leave after an approach to Cromwell, while Sir John Fitzjames, chief justice of the King's Bench, asked to be excused because he had a bad leg. In November that year a report from the Venetian ambassador to his senate on affairs in England included a list of Henry's councillors, with Cromwell number seven on the list. It was a notable advance compared with the previous year.[14]

But Cromwell's political progression ran somewhat uneasily alongside his interest in Luther and Tyndale, because this was not the most opportune time for a career-minded lawyer and politician to be concerning himself with Lutheran heresies. More and John Stokesley, the new bishop of London, were both breathing out threatening and slaughter against Lutherans in England, and More's anti-heresy measures intensified during the second half of 1531. Thomas Bilney went to the stake in August, Richard Bayfield in November. More was now examining the evangelical George Constantine, demanding to know who in England was helping Tyndale, Joye and others abroad.[15]

It is hardly surprising, therefore, that a note of uncharacteristic concern from the normally unflappable Vaughan is detected in two letters of his to Cromwell dated 14 November. These letters are almost identical. Vaughan was puzzled that Cromwell had not heard from him, for Vaughan had written four times. He had also made contact with Robert Barnes, the former Augustinian Friar who had fled England two years ago and made his way to Wittenberg, where he studied for his doctorate in theology at the university under the tutelage of Luther and Melanchthon. Vaughan had sent a book by Barnes – the *Supplication unto King Henry VIII* – and another unnamed German work to Cromwell, and was surprised to hear that they had not arrived. How he knew of their non-arrival his letter does not say, but he wondered whether the bearer had been afraid to deliver them. Undaunted, however, Vaughan sent another copy of Barnes's work – 'such a piece of work as I yet have not seen one like unto it; I think he shall seal it with his blood'. Vaughan urged Cromwell to commend it and its author to Henry. After some news about the emperor's movements, Vaughan asked what Constantine had been saying about him to More. Vaughan must have known about recent developments in England, very likely from letters of Cromwell now lost. Vaughan's jolly confidence was now returning, and he was sure that Constantine could do him no harm, because Henry knew all about, and had even authorised, all his contacts with Tyndale. Fearless as ever, Vaughan promised Cromwell more evangelical books, including Tyndale's commentary on the first epistle of John. However, he did take the precaution of asking Cromwell to write and confirm that his letters had been safely received.[16]

Vaughan does not explain why he sent two letters on the same day covering much the same points. He might have been concerned about letters going missing or even being intercepted, which is not surprising. Both Vaughan and Cromwell were living dangerously, because a further proclamation against heretical books, naming Tyndale though not Luther or Melanchthon this time, was issued on 3 December. In letters dated 6 December, Cromwell urged Vaughan to be extra careful and watchful. Vaughan replied quickly. He knew More was on his trail, and that Constantine might wilt under interrogation and implicate Vaughan as a Lutheran. Vaughan now showed a touch of guile with some pious disapproval of heresies, and a protest that he was 'neither Lutheran nor yet Tyndalin'. In view of what has gone before, and especially what is still to come, these denials are not particularly convincing. It is likely that Vaughan, maybe at Cromwell's suggestion, had decided to cover his tracks by sending something that could be shown to Henry if necessary, to satisfy him that Vaughan was a loyal servant of the king and acceptably orthodox on religion.[17]

With Cromwell's full knowledge and support, Vaughan kept up the search for Lutheran books. At home Cromwell managed to secure a safe pardon for Robert Barnes to return to England. Barnes's *Supplication* defended justification by faith and argued for a Bible in English; it answered some of the most common critiques of Lutheranism, and contained a strong declaration of personal loyalty to Henry. Like Tyndale, Barnes soon came under renewed attack from More. Henry, however, was now willing to give Barnes an audience, no doubt hoping that the Lutherans might endorse his cause in his divorce case, as other European universities had done.[18]

But to the surprise of Henry and many others, Luther turned out to be one of Catherine of Aragon's most unflinching supporters. In his judgement on Henry's Great Matter, Luther held that the text from Leviticus – the foundation of Henry's case for putting Catherine away – merely forbad a man marrying the wife of a brother still alive, so it could not be used against Catherine. Unlike most theologians, Luther was not greatly bothered about the validity of papal dispensations or endless disputes over Leviticus. Far more important in his view were the words of Christ on the subject of marriage – 'What God has joined, let not man put asunder'. Only if one party had been unfaithful could divorce be permitted. (Matthew 19:6, 9). However, Luther was not unmindful of Henry's desire for a male heir for the sake of the stability of his realm, so by invoking the precedent set by godly Old Testament kings, he suggested that Henry might take two wives, Anne as well as Catherine. It was not Luther's intention to re-introduce polygamy into the Church, but he justified it in this special case as the only available solution which would preserve the royal dignity of Catherine and Mary, while also allowing Henry to marry again in the hope of begetting a son to succeed him. It was not an entirely novel idea, because the pope had also mooted it during the lengthy negotiations with Henry's envoys.[19]

Henry's immediate reaction to the advice from Germany is not known. Obviously he did not like it, but it is noteworthy that the king did not summarily abandon his cautious interest in the Lutherans. Neither did he take any action against Barnes, Cromwell or Vaughan. This can be no more than a guess, but Cromwell may have persuaded Henry to keep this idea in his mind, and instead of rejecting it outright as the king might have been inclined to do, treat it as one option available to him. It could at least prove useful during complex negotiations. It would also have greatly flattered Henry to be compared with Old Testament luminaries like David and Solomon.

Nevertheless, other Catholic European universities were much more supportive than Wittenberg, and Luther's refusal to back Henry's case was a setback for English evangelicals. During 1531–2, therefore, no scheming politician on the make, concerned only about his own career and well being, would bother to show much interest in Luther. Henry was no evangelical himself, and his Lord Chancellor More, a man substantially senior to Cromwell on Henry's council, was rampaging violently against Luther's English admirers. Vaughan, still on the continent, told Cromwell that people with Lutheran views had gone into hiding for fear of being apprehended. In England in January 1532, Thomas Dusgate perished in the flames of Smithfield for his Protestant beliefs. Next month Convocation issued a new list of heretical books, and this time proscribed writers included Luther and Melanchthon as well as Tyndale. In spring James Bainham, John Bent and Thomas Harding were burned to ashes like Hitton and Dusgate before them. Yet it was during these hazardous times for evangelicals that Cromwell received his personal copy of the greatest evangelical work produced thus far, Philip Melanchthon's *Apology of the Augsburg Confession*. The sender was not Vaughan or Barnes but Dr Augustine, formerly a physician to Wolsey before turning the king's evidence against him (see pp. 42–3).[20]

A letter from Augustine to Cromwell, dated April 1532 from Regensburg, is unfortunately damaged in parts, but it does reveal the crucial information that 'I gave you the Lutheran *Confession* with Melanchthon's *Apology*'. There then follows a reference to Brussels and John Cochlaeus (*dedit tibi monstran-*

dam confessionem Lutheranorum una cum Apologia Melanchthonis de qua jam pridem cum essem Bruxellis tibi scripsi … momenti … libellus (?) a J. Coclaeo in illius confutationem). It is not absolutely clear whether the *Apology* was sent with this letter or with an earlier one now lost, when Augustine was in Brussels – probably the latter.[21]

But why should Augustine of all people be sending Cromwell the *Apology*, and with it a work of Cochlaeus, one of Luther's most vociferous continental opponents? No explanation is given, so the following section offers a suggested reconstruction of events.

Henry had sent Vaughan to Europe to make limited contact with William Tyndale. Vaughan, however, with Cromwell's connivance, had gone some way beyond his official remit when he started searching for Lutheran books, including the *Augsburg Confession*. Subsequent news from England caused Vaughan to worry whether his letters to Cromwell might have been intercepted. Augustine, meanwhile, following Wolsey's fall, was on the continent in the king's service. He had spent some time in Brussels, where Vaughan had ample opportunity to meet him. We also recall that it was Cromwell who secured Augustine's English citizenship, and a grateful Augustine promised he would be obliged to Cromwell for ever (see p. 42). In other words, he owed Cromwell a favour. We know, too, that Augustine continued in the service of Cromwell and the king, sending Cromwell regular reports of diplomatic affairs as well as requests for money. He went to Italy with Cardinal Campeggio in August 1532 and from there to Rome, where he promised Cromwell that 'I think I may do your cause no small good' (*ubi puto me non parum posse prodesse causae vestrae*).[22]

Putting all these fragmentary strands of evidence together, Augustine would have provided the perfect cover whereby the *Apology* could be smuggled into England at this testing time. There was no risk that a despatch from one of the king's official agents, who was not even suspected of being part of the evangelical movement, would be intercepted. Cochlaeus's book could have been thrown in for the sake of balance, and to defuse any suspicions that Augustine might have had: here was an impeccably orthodox work to answer all this 'new learning' from Melanchthon.

There remains, admittedly, some conjecture in this reconstruction. Nor is it the only point arising from Vaughan's trip to the continent that cannot be answered definitively. It is not clear whether Vaughan, or Cromwell or even someone else first thought of sending the *Apology* to England. After five hundred years, however, absolute certainty is impossible on a subject that had to be carried out in great secrecy, and it is only due to a stroke of good fortune that any evidence has survived at all. Happily these gaps in the account do not really matter very much. What is important – and this can be said with full confidence – is that by 1531, or, at the very latest early in 1532, the most significant conversion during this period of the English Reformation had taken place. Thomas Cromwell was now a Lutheran. In the anti-Lutheran climate of these times, possession of a work like the *Apology* is virtually irrefutable evidence. If Cromwell had no spiritual interest in it, what could he have been doing with it, especially when he had acquired it in such a secretive way? A bishop or cleric might be authorised to read heretical material in order to refute it, but Cromwell was not part of the clergy. He was still a civil councillor; he was not Vicegerent yet, and had no official responsibility for church affairs.

Subsequent events confirm this. In January 1532, at Cromwell's request, Vaughan produced a paper on the English cloth trade and the problems faced by English merchants. It has been suggested that Cromwell was now trying to direct his friend away from forbidden religion and back to safer matters like commerce, but as David Daniell has shown, there could be a connection between evangelical activity and the cloth trade. Since the fifteenth century, trade in books from Europe to England had flourished, and an act of Parliament in 1483 even encouraged the import of books. Antwerp had gradually developed as a printing and commercial centre with agents in England. From the 1520s illegal evangelical works by Luther, Tyndale and others were smuggled into England in bales of cloth, sacks of flour and cargoes of various kinds, and in ever-increasing numbers. A typical print run on the continent would be between 1,000 and 1,500 books, though for Tyndale's New Testament the number might have been twice this. (Tyndale and his printers must have known that demand in England was high.) So sympathetic contacts in the cloth, wool and other trades – men like Stephen Vaughan for example – were becoming ever more useful in ensuring safe deliveries to England. The authorities were partly aware of what was happening, and under Wolsey, Tunstall and More England witnessed sporadic outbreaks of book burning and Bible burning. Nevertheless, the underground trade thrived. Even before Tyndale's death in 1536, as many as 16,000 copies of his New Testament had reached England, whose population at the time was approximately two and a half million.[23]

So Vaughan's renewed involvement in the cloth trade was not necessarily intended to divert him from the quest for Lutheran works. Nor is it surprising to find Vaughan, a year later, once again writing to Cromwell from the continent about German books that Cromwell had asked for. By this time Christopher Mont, another of Cromwell's evangelical allies, had begun translating German works in Cromwell's house. German by birth, Mont had obtained English citizenship, and was now more or less formally in Cromwell's service. It is rather likely that the books Mont was working on had found their way to England via Antwerp, maybe while Vaughan was stationed there, officially reporting on commercial affairs, but unofficially using his contacts and influence to smooth the safe passage of evangelical material to England.[24]

Further evidence of Cromwell's Lutheran activity in the early 1530s comes from John Oliver, a chaplain to the king who subsequently became a friend of Robert Barnes. Oliver recalled how, around this time, he used to be among the guests at Cromwell's house, where theology was often discussed. After listening to Cromwell, Oliver went away to consult his Bible and 'found always the conclusions which you maintained at your board to be consonant with the Holy Word of God'.

These evenings in Cromwell's company prompted Oliver to learn Greek so that he could read his New Testament in the original tongue.[25]

Another witness is Richard 'Hylls', probably Richard Hillis, the merchant, who introduced himself to Cromwell around 1532 as another recent evangelical convert. Hillis also sent Cromwell a short treatise he had written on the epistle of James, and particularly the section describing how Abraham was justified by works (James: 2:20–4). The treatise is now lost, but it must have been written from an evangelical standpoint, because Hillis soon found himself in trouble over it with his employer and the bishop of London, John Stokesley, who had somehow managed to get hold of it. Now out of work, Hillis and his mother both sought Cromwell's help.[26]

It is worth lingering for a moment over Hillis and his work on James. Certain passages in this epistle, like 'faith without works is dead', appear to deny Luther's message of justification by faith alone, as Luther's opponents were not slow to point out (see especially James 2:14–25). Luther's response was characteristically blunt. He dismissed James as 'a right strawy epistle' (*ein rechte stroern Epistel*), hardly worthy to be compared with the gold and silver works of Paul, John and the other apostles (the analogy is taken from 1 Corinthians 3:12.) Luther agreed with those in the ancient church who questioned whether James rightly belonged in the New Testament canon, as it contained nothing about Christ's atoning death and resurrection – a point, incidentally, which has never been answered entirely convincingly. Melanchthon, however, saw the epistle in a much more favourable light, and his *Apology* contains a mini-commentary on it. James, Philip argued, does not contradict the writings of St Paul, on which Luther's message was chiefly based. In Melanchthon's view, James would make a good Lutheran because he writes about good works as *fruits* or *products* of Christian faith. So when Abraham obeyed God, and when Rahab showed hospitality to the spies of the people of God, they acted as believers *already* justified by faith; they were not doing good works in order to *become* justified, as certain medieval interpreters claimed. It would be quite plausible, therefore, if evangelically minded people in England were mulling over these passages in James, and that Melanchthon's evangelical treatment of the epistle in the *Apology* helped sway those hitherto not quite ready to embrace justification by faith alone. Certainly Hillis and his anxious mother both knew that, having incurred the wrath of Stokesley, Cromwell was the man to turn to for refuge and help.[27]

Soon Cromwell began to discreetly introduce some of the less controversial aspects of Lutheranism to the king. He also suggested that the Lutheran princes might make useful allies in European diplomacy. In March 1533, Chapuys reported the arrival in London of an emissary from the duke of Saxony and the Landgrave of Hesse. The man was a German born at Basle, aged about thirty, who spoke French, Italian and Spanish, and had reportedly served in the Italian wars. Chapuys does not mention the visitor's name, but he was well received by Henry. Because Cromwell was 'appointed to treat with him', Chapuys suspected that 'he has been sent here by Melanchthon'. Cromwell's Protestant views were no closely guarded secret any more if Chapuys knew of them. Melanchthon may or may not have been behind this visit, but it is quite likely that Cromwell was.[28]

Later, in July, Henry began to consider establishing ambassadors in Germany, not only in Catholic Bavaria but also in Lutheran Saxony. The king sent Christopher Mont and Stephen Vaughan to Germany for exploratory talks. This may have been Cromwell's idea as well, because he was the one who gave instructions to Mont to 'explore and search and know the state of the whole country of Germany, and of their minds intents and inclinations' towards Henry, England and the emperor. Then sometime during the winter of 1533–4, Henry told Chapuys that he was now ready to renounce Rome, and that he disowned passages in the *Assertion* that upheld papal authority, claiming that he had been misled by Wolsey and other bishops whom he does not specify. Lutheranism was being introduced into England, sighed Chapuys, and even some in the royal court were sympathetic to it.[29]

Next year, Cromwell's remembrances around April 1534 include a note to discover the king's pleasure concerning 'Philipus'. Almost certainly this is a reference to Melanchthon, who received two invitations to come to England that year. Then a report of the diet of the Schmalkaldic League held in May reveals covert evangelical designs at the highest level in England. It describes how envoys from England, 'unknown to the king', had confided that their mission was the policy of certain of England's 'distinguished councillors and people', who hoped to establish formal relations with the Lutherans. These 'distinguished councillors' were men 'who favour the Gospel', who hoped that diplomatic relations with the League would be the means by which the Gospel 'might be brought into England' and commended to the king. We are indebted to Rory McEntegart's research in Germany for this information, and he is surely right to say that one of these councillors was Cromwell.[30]

So there need be no doubt about Cromwell's Lutheran faith. Exactly when it was first kindled in his heart is not certain. It could have been late in 1530 or, more likely perhaps, sometime the following year. As noted already, this was a risky time to be nourishing evangelical beliefs. To safeguard his political survival and progress, Cromwell should have left Luther well alone and remained content with Henry's so-called 'middle way'. This was the safe option, but Cromwell did not take it. He did not wait to discover the religious direction that Henry, after his controversy with Rome, would elect to follow. Cromwell embraced the new learning first, and set about trying to commend it to Henry afterwards.

At the start of 1531, two paths lay ahead of Cromwell – the evangelical and the political – and they seemed to run counter to one other. However, Cromwell trod the twin paths together. The outcome was successful, but in view of the assault on Protestantism by More and Stokesley, that success was neither guaranteed nor even likely when Cromwell began his journey of faith. So the idea that he was the type of man to subject what little religious feeling he had to political expediency is utterly overthrown. There was little political mileage in being a Lutheran in 1531. One false or hasty move and his career could have been ruined, even his life in danger.

It is also worth noting that Cromwell's conversion occurred independently of the man soon to become his closest ally on Henry's council, Thomas Cranmer. In the exchange of letters between Vaughan and Cromwell discussed above, the name Cranmer is conspicuously missing. During 1531 Cranmer was making tentative evangelical contacts of his own, but not with Luther or Melanchthon. He met Simon Grynaeus from Basle on a visit to England during the spring and summer of that year. Grynaeus, like the leading Zürich reformer Huldrych Zwingli, supported the king's divorce, and he may have met Henry as well as Cranmer. Grynaeus was a friend of the Strasbourg reformer Martin Bucer, who was also sending cordial letters to Cranmer around this time. There is little evidence, however, that Cranmer was especially friendly with Barnes or Tyndale, or that he was anxious to read the Lutheran confessional works. Because Luther opposed Henry on the divorce, maybe Cranmer found the Swiss a more agreeable introduction to the European Reformation. Cranmer's biographer, Diarmaid MacCulloch, describes him in 1531 as being interested in evangelical developments on the continent, but not yet definitely part of the evangelical movement. Cranmer then spent much of 1532 abroad as Henry's ambassador to Charles V, and the most striking evidence for his newly found Protestant beliefs seems to have been his marriage that summer to the niece of Andreas Osiander, the chief Lutheran divine in Nüremburg. It would appear, therefore, that not only did Cromwell convert without Cranmer's counsel or guidance, but that he almost certainly converted before him.[31]

So while Cranmer was in Europe breaking his vows of celibacy, Cromwell was reading, assimilating and arranging the printing of Melanchthon's *Apology*. And for Cromwell, soon to become the driving force of the Protestant Reformation in England, the value of this work was inestimable. Though Lutheran books had found their way into England before, the *Apology* was by far the most comprehensive and eloquent outline of the Lutheran faith, covering virtually all subjects from the Creation to justification, the sacraments and church customs. In Luther's admittedly biased view, it surpassed in quality anything written by the church fathers. It dealt, often in exhaustive detail, with some of the most common arguments that Luther's opponents were wont to use against him, answering them point by point and line by line, with an abundance of supporting Scripture texts. As a foundation on which to build and spread the Gospel, it had no equal. Its safe arrival in England ensured that Cromwell did not need to study the new learning from second-hand sources, or spend valuable time gathering assorted Lutheran writings together. In his possession he had the complete product, the finished article. So although the campaign to evangelise England did not begin with Cromwell, under his leadership it would be more organized, effective and incisive than anything hitherto.

It may now be timely to briefly review Thomas Cromwell's spiritual journey. In Wolsey's service he was involved, apparently enthusiastically, with the Boston pardons. He also set himself the demanding task of learning Erasmus's Latin New Testament by heart. He made a very Catholic will. Nevertheless, it is unlikely that he had ever been one of the Roman church's most dutiful sons. Misfortune and the threat of ruin after Wolsey's fall had prompted an outpouring of medieval piety when Cavendish came upon him suddenly saying 'Our Lady Mattens'; but, as Cavendish wryly noted, this was a rare sight and the emotion soon passed. Cromwell had always possessed a strong streak of anti-clericalism and anti-monasticism. He revered the church of the ancient fathers more than the medieval church of his times. It seems that he was genuinely attracted to the Bible, and knew it well. (On these points, see Chapters 1 and 2.) Sooner or later a man with such a religious outlook was bound to think seriously about Luther and his message of salvation as God's gracious, unmerited gift to all who believe in Christ for the remission of sins. But no evidence survives to explain why Cromwell, after wishing that

Luther had never been born in summer 1530, should decide barely a year later to risk his political career by smuggling the *Augsburg Confession* and the *Apology* into England. Something had happened to work this change in his heart, but the mystery of conversion defies historical research. It may be that, as a result of renewed reading of the New Testament, Cromwell became convinced that Luther really had rediscovered the true meaning of the Gospel of Christ, which the medieval church had largely lost. His inmost spiritual thoughts, however, remain secrets that he kept to himself and his closest friends.

Meanwhile, the man who sent Cromwell the *Apology*, Dr Augustine, may have had little idea how vital a role he had played in the English Reformation. So far as is possible to tell, he did not join the ranks of evangelicals, though he did remain in the service of Cromwell and the king. He continued badgering Cromwell for favours, including funding and a benefice. He returned to England in the spring of 1533, and then Henry sent him to Rome again as part of his divorce team to present one more time the case for Henry's new marriage. For his services he received a reward of £100. His fortunes sank the following year when he was imprisoned in England. The reason for his confinement is not known for certain, though it has been suspected that his sympathies for Catherine and Mary had offended Anne Boleyn. After an appeal to Cromwell, however, he was soon released, and he carried on his career comparatively untroubled as a physician in his adopted country.[32]

4

The King's Councillor

This chapter will examine Cromwell's role in Henry's marriage to Anne and the breach with Rome, the religious and constitutional upheaval commonly known as the schism.

While Cromwell was absorbed in Lutheran theology and justification by faith, King Henry's dispute with Rome over his divorce had reached an impasse. For nearly four years he had been striving unsuccessfully to convince the pope that his marriage to Catherine was contrary to divine and natural law. From now on he would act more decisively, and it is understandably tempting to ascribe this increased momentum towards schism to the rise of Cromwell. The unparalleled break with Rome, ending centuries of tradition, strongly suggests a new man at the heart of government, who was a Protestant, with religious as well as political motives to do whatever he could to end papal influence in England.

However, a word of caution may be advisable before the dramatic events of 1532–3 can be ascribed entirely or even substantially to Cromwell. First, the concept of English Royal Supremacy and independence from Rome was not a Cromwellian one. In 1485, the year of Cromwell's birth, the Lord Chief Justice of England declared that the king was accountable directly to God. The superiority of common law and parliamentary statute over canon law was recognised in the reign of the first Tudor king. The second had embraced this philosophy ardently. As early as 1515, stung by French taunts of England's submission to the pope in the days of King John, Henry laid his claim both to the throne of France and to full sovereignty in his own realm. 'We are King of England', he proclaimed majestically, 'and kings of England in time past have never had any superior but God only'. Henry was resolved to 'maintain the right of our crown and of our temporal jurisdiction as well in this point as in all others'. This declaration came after the so-called Standish affair – a fairly minor case resulting from an act of 1512 which sought to restrict certain clerical privileges. When the abbot of Winchcombe unwisely spoke against the act, Henry convened a debate between the abbot and Henry Standish, who argued that the king and parliament enjoyed a measure of independence from the clergy and even from papal decrees. Henry took Standish's side.[1]

The English people's affection for Rome was fading long before Cromwell joined Henry's council. Edward Hall tells how, in 1527, after the sack of Rome by the duke of Bourbon's troops and the pope's imprisonment, Wolsey directed the clergy in all parishes to 'move the people to fast' three days a week. But, adds Hall expressively, 'few men fasted'. Wolsey's appeal drew forth plenty of excuses, but little piety or charity. Priests claimed that the order applied to the laity but not to themselves. Layfolk said the priests should set an example and fast first. Hall tells us that 'none of both almost fasted'.[2]

Nor was it Cromwell who suggested to Henry that he should divorce Catherine. By 1527 Henry was already minded to put away his Spanish wife. He was also, before Cromwell even entered the king's service, becoming aggressive towards the pope. In April 1529 Stephen Gardiner, Henry's emissary to Rome, delivered a veiled warning of the 'solicitations of the princes of Almain'. No details are given, and this may have been nothing more than a bargaining tactic; but it is astonishing that Henry could even think of playing the Lutheran card so soon, and when harsh anti-Lutheran heresy measures were in force in England. Then in June that year Henry bizarrely threatened to appeal over the pope's head to 'the true Vicar of Christ', though he left the identity of this august personage undisclosed. In November – still 1529, when Cromwell was trying to rebuild his career after Wolsey's fall – Henry told Chapuys of his dissatisfaction with the pope and his cardinals, and that if Luther had only attacked the vices and abuses of the church rather than the sacraments, then Henry would have supported him rather than condemned him. Luther's books did contain heresies, admitted Henry, but some truth as well. Henry was now determined on a reform the English church. Next month the ambassador told the emperor about his fears that Henry would soon marry Anne, who was acting as if she were queen already. The English 'will not care much for Rome', Chapuys predicted. 'Neither the leaders nor the rest of the party can now refrain from slandering the pope'. Chapuys and the French ambassador were expecting the measure to be brought before parliament any time.[3]

The English mood grew progressively more belligerent. In September 1530, when Cromwell was only a junior councillor, the Catholic duke of Suffolk and Anne's father, now earl of Wiltshire, brazenly told the shocked papal nuncio that England cared nothing for popes 'even if St Peter should come to life again'. The king, they claimed, was 'emperor and pope within his realm'. In January 1531 the duke of Norfolk, another leading Catholic magnate, gave Chapuys a lecture in church history. By tradition, avowed Norfolk, English kings had no superior in their own country. Relations with the papacy were now going downhill fast, and by March 1531 denying that the pope was Head of the Church no longer counted as heresy in Henry's judgement.[4]

It is true that nothing decisive had been actually done yet. Neither had anything significant been put before parliament. Henry may have been waiting to hear the verdicts of European universities on his Great Matter. However, the point remains that the nationalist, independent anti-papal climate pre-dated Cromwell's rise to power and his Lutheran conversion. According to the available evidence, he was not even involved in the weighty *Collectanea*, written in 1530 and published from the king's printer the following year. Its chief authors were Thomas Cranmer and Edward Foxe, and it justified the crown's spiritual authority over the church in England from various historical sources. It called the king God's vicar in England, and upheld the right of the English church to settle disputes here rather than petition Rome. It drew on supporting evidence of ecclesiastical independence from the church Councils of Nicea (AD 325), and King Wambar summoning bishops to Toledo (589). It highlighted a statement in the Council of Carthage that not even the bishop of Rome should be termed the 'universal bishop'. Henry pored over the findings of the *Collectanea* with unalloyed delight.[5]

So when Cromwell became one of Henry's councillors, he joined rather than originated the movement for English independence from Rome. He was able to bring with him his considerable experience as a lawyer and a member of the Commons, which he would soon put to good use in the king's cause. Two major developments of the parliamentary session beginning in January 1532 were the Annates bill and the Supplication against the Ordinaries. Both were designed to weaken papal control over the English clergy. Annates were payments that new clerical incumbents paid to Rome, and it was almost certainly Cromwell who drew up the bill to have them abolished. The bill's preamble claimed that the papacy had fleeced England of £160,000 worth of annates since the Tudor dynasty began nearly thirty years ago. The bill emphasized the financial burden to the realm. It declared defiantly that should Rome react with an excommunication or interdiction, then the king and country may 'without any scruple of conscience ... lawfully to the honour of Almighty God ... continue to enjoy the sacraments, ceremonies and services of the holy church'. Cromwell was unsure how successful this bill would be, especially when it ran into strong opposition, chiefly from the bishops. Perhaps as a bargaining ploy to put pressure on Rome, Henry offered to delay the effect of the act, but this concession failed to mollify either clerical resistance at home or in the papacy. At length, with support from the lords temporal, the bill was passed by the House of Lords on 19 March, only to run into further opposition in the Commons. After much heated debate Henry intervened in person. He ordered the bill's supporters and opponents – implicitly *his* supporters and opponents – to gather on opposite sides of the house. Thus by royal intervention, the necessary majority was secured.[6]

Henry was now openly contemptuous of Rome. He rejected the right and competence of the pope to be judge of kings. He cared nothing, he boomed, for the pope's authority any more, not even excommunication. Not surprisingly, a second anti-papal measure quickly got under way. The 'Supplication against Ordinaries' was essentially a petition full of complaints against ecclesiastical courts and the conduct of heresy trials, amounting to a general expression of dissatisfaction with clergy. Thomas Audley, an ally of Cromwell, presented the Supplication to Henry on 18 March 1532, three days after Archbishop Warham had made a speech in the Lords, which, according to the Venetian ambassador, provoked the king to cursing. However, Henry stifled his wrath and took no immediate action. Sometime early in April he passed the Supplication on to Warham, and asked for a quick reply. Convocation's answer to it, based on a draft from Stephen Gardiner, rejected the complaints against the clergy. Henry then passed Convocation's answer to the Commons. Gardiner, previously a good servant of the king and loyal member of his divorce team, was unwisely prominent in the resistance, a stance which seriously set back his career.[7]

On 8 May, Convocation appealed to Henry to preserve the liberties of the church. Rather rashly it tried to block Henry's demands that the church should no longer make canons without royal approval. Three days later Henry summoned Audley, and gave him a stark message to relay to the Commons:

> We thought that the clergy of our realm had been our subjects wholly, but now we have well perceived that they be

but half our subjects, yea, and scarce our subjects: for all the prelates at their consecration make an oath to the pope, clean contrary to the oath they make to us, so that they seem to be his subjects, not ours.

Convocation then tried to offer a compromise. Not satisfied with this, Henry demanded the clergy's formal submission. On 15 May the reluctant but browbeaten clergy complied, in a document known as the 'Submission of the Clergy'. Henry was now effectively Head of the Church in England. The chief casualty of these events was Thomas More, who felt he could no longer continue in Henry's service. More surrendered the Great Seal on 16 May 1532.[8]

The precise part Cromwell played in this drama is still difficult to prove beyond reasonable doubt. He was certainly involved in the drafting of the Supplication. There is also a draft bill, written by a clerk with corrections in Cromwell's hand, expressing the general tenor of the Supplication: the realm of England is composed of clergy, commons and nobility, each distinct but all three 'under royal authority and jurisdiction', and that the 'imperial crown of this realm ... is not under the obedience ... of any worldly or foreign prince'. This draft was probably produced sometime between 11 and 14 May, but may not have been actually presented to parliament following Henry's demand that the clergy submit to him. Cromwell did, however, save up some of the papers for later, because similar arguments were to reappear in acts of 1533–4.[9]

Without wishing to minimize Cromwell's part in these developments unduly, it may be safer to see him using his legal and parliamentary skills in a supporting role, but not as the man driving the process forward or leading from the front. He does not seem to have taken as prominent a part as Audley, who was quickly rewarded for his loyal services. On 5 June the evangelically minded Audley was knighted and made Lord Keeper. Six months later he was confirmed as Lord Chancellor. Cromwell, by contrast, was made Master of the King's Jewels in April and Clerk of the Hanaper of Chancery in July. Respectable though these offices were, they fell some way short of the impressive advances achieved by Audley. Cranmer also enjoyed greater royal patronage than Cromwell when Henry appointed him Archbishop of Canterbury following Warham's death in August. On the continent since the beginning of the year, Cranmer left Mantua for England on 19 November to arrive home the following January. By this time, an event had occurred that made the English schism virtually certain – Henry was married again.[10]

As with the king's headship of the church, Henry's marriage to Anne Boleyn was a subject openly talked about when Cromwell was still Wolsey's secretary, yet to enter the king's service and unable to influence the king's policy. Back in September 1528 the Imperial ambassador, De Mendoza, reported that Henry had resolved to marry her. In March the following year Henry threatened that 'if the pope will not annul' his marriage to Catherine, 'I will annul it myself'. In December that year, according to Chapuys, Mendoza's successor, Henry tried to humiliate Catherine at dinner by telling her publicly that she was not his lawful wife, and that he would present his case to Rome; but if the pope did not declare the marriage null and void, then Henry would 'denounce the pope as a heretic and marry whom he pleased'. The 'principal cause' for the divorce was non-existent, countered the queen. A long and heated argument followed, with Catherine getting the better of it. Anne was unimpressed by Henry's performance, and she later reproached him saying, 'Did I not tell you that whenever you had disputed with the queen, she was sure to have the upper hand?' Having been worsted by Catherine, Henry now had to endure the sharp tongue of Anne. 'I have been waiting long', she scolded, and cuttingly reminded him that she could have married well and borne children by now.[11]

By January 1530, the Emperor Charles V heard that Henry as good as looked on Anne as his wife, that he was 'threatening to marry her', and no longer cared anything for the pope. After a meeting with Henry in April, Chapuys was asked directly by Norfolk whether Charles would declare war on England if Henry, with the support of the English clergy, made Anne his queen.[12]

From the evidence of ambassadors' despatches, marriage talk subsided a little before resurfacing the following summer, when Chapuys told Charles that the duke and duchess of Suffolk would, 'if they dared, oppose this second marriage'. To Anne's fury Suffolk and William Fitzwilliam, the king's Treasurer, had been tying to dissuade Henry. Anne warned Sir Henry Guilford, Controller of the Household, that when she became queen she'd have him sacked. Guilford, a plucky fellow by the sound of it, replied that he'd resign anyway. In July Anne was confident that 'her marriage to the king will take place in three or four months at the latest'. Chapuys, Catherine and Charles took this prediction seriously, though Rome seemed less disturbed, at least to begin with. Charles heard a report that Henry's 'infatuation' with Anne simply made the pope laugh.[13]

A year on (July 1532) – having now secured the clergy's formal submission – Henry declared confidently that the pope had 'no power over him'. He was 'determined to accomplish this new marriage with the greatest possible solemnity and pomp'. However, powerful voices had been urging Henry not to take this fateful step. Norfolk later told Chapuys that he was neither the 'originator nor the promoter' of the marriage to Anne, but he 'had always opposed it, and tried to dissuade the king therefrom'. But for him and Anne's father, Norfolk claimed, the marriage would have taken place a year earlier than it did, and as a result, Anne was 'exceedingly indignant' with both of them.[14]

This slightly lengthy background to the events of 1532 suggests that Henry, despite his bluster and bravado, remained indecisive and in need of a push. According to Chapuys's letters, even Anne's persistence, her reproaches, charms and entreaties had all singularly failed to tear the king from Catherine and bind him to her. Something more, or someone else, would be required. Again the obvious candidate is Henry's first Lutheran councillor, Thomas Cromwell.

But as with Henry's headship of the church, there are serious difficulties in assuming that it was Cromwell alone who provided the thrust that Henry seemed to lack. Though Cromwell's influence was growing, he was not yet as high-ranking as Norfolk, Suffolk and Wiltshire, and it would have been reckless to have pressed hard for the Boleyn marriage in the face of opposition or disquiet from more senior councillors. If something went wrong, he would have made himself a very convenient scapegoat, and Cromwell was far too astute a man to stumble into such an obvious trap. What Henry really needed was encouragement from a higher source, such as a fellow prince, and this leads to the subject of Henry's visit to France in autumn 1532.

Henry was eagerly looking forward to meeting King Francis again. He was also hoping to persuade the French to support him in his Great Matter. Anne, meanwhile, was letting it be known that she would be married soon, possibly in September. Chapuys and Catherine were worried by rumours spreading around the court and beyond that the marriage might take place in France. Anne, however, was determined that she would never agree to this even if Henry wished it. She was insisting on being wed in England, where queens were customarily married and crowned. Increasingly concerned, Chapuys told Charles that Henry was taking with him to Calais 'a legion of doctors and priests who hold for the divorce', and that Henry was trying to arrange a conference at Calais with cardinals and councillors of France who might be supportive. The Venetian ambassador noted the widespread expectations of a Calais marriage, news which Charles received with shocked disbelief. Elizabeth Barton, the mystical 'Holy Maid of Kent', claimed she had a vision of a Calais marriage, 'and of the great shame that the queen should have' as a result.[15]

It was in this expectant atmosphere that Henry and his entourage – including Norfolk and Cromwell as well as Anne – arrived in Calais on 10 October, 1532. There are some signs, albeit rather slim ones, that Cromwell's influence with the king and the future queen was steadily increasing. Audley wrote from England to Cromwell concerning various administrative affairs, before asking if Cromwell might care to speak to Anne in the hope that she may make Audley keeper of one of her parks. Cromwell was acquiring international recognition as well, with King Francis reportedly speaking well of him. This apart, records of the Anglo-French summit say nothing significant about him. It was Norfolk, still senior to Cromwell, who was selected to meet the Grand Master of France outside Calais on 16 October. Then on 21 the two kings greeted each other. With Francis was the King of Navarre, the Cardinal of Lorraine and a generous assortment of the French nobility. Henry and Francis returned to Calais on 25 October. Four days of ceremony, festivities and talks followed, though no details were made public. The official communiqué confined itself to fine words about the unity of Christendom and the defence of the faith against the infidel Turk. On the following day (Sunday), after mass in the morning and bear and bull baiting in the afternoon, a sumptuous banquet was held in the evening. The meal over, Anne and her ladies entered, and Anne danced with the French king. She was living like a queen; 'it is said that the marriage of Madame Anne will be solemnised next Sunday', reported the Venetian ambassador on 31 October.[16]

In fact there was no Calais marriage, though the ambassador had caught the mood aright. The day after Henry's return from Calais, on Saint Erkenwald's day, 14 November 1532, Henry and Anne were married in England as Anne had wished, though the ceremony was kept a close secret. So the Tudor historian Edward Hall recorded, and after all the excited build up it would have been a hugely strange anti-climax if nothing at all had happened. However, apart from notable exceptions like Diarmaid MacCulloch, few modern writers want to believe Hall. They prefer instead the witness of Cranmer and Chapuys, both of whom date the marriage to 25 January 1533, by which time Anne was pregnant.[17]

Chapuys and Cranmer would normally make dependable witnesses, but there is good reason to doubt them this time, quite apart from Hall's account. Cranmer, even though he arrived back in England on or about 10 January, admitted that he was not present at the 'marriage' fifteen days later. He did not even know about it until 'a fortnight after it was done'. Now it is scarcely believable that Henry would wed Anne and not invite Cranmer. He was the man the king would appoint to oversee his divorce; he was also the prelate most beloved of both Henry and Anne, and the natural choice to officiate and pronounce the blessing.[18]

Chapuys's testimony also raises uncertainties, and here I must ask the reader to bear with a short but necessary examination of dates to make the point. On 15 February, Chapuys informed Charles that 'eight days ago' Anne said that she was sure she would marry 'very soon'. Her father, Chapuys continued, said the 'day before yesterday' (that would be 13 February) that Henry was determined to marry his daughter 'at once'. These dates do not fit either the November or January marriages. It seems that the Boleyns were sending false signals to Chapuys to mislead him, in the hope of keeping the news from him and Charles for as long as they could, which is what makes his evidence questionable. Not until 23 February, nearly one month after the January 'marriage', did Chapuys report it to the emperor. There is no other letter from Chapuys to Charles between 15 and 23 February.[19]

This subject will be left for a moment, and we will return to it after considering Cromwell's role in all of this. He would later tell Chapuys that he was the one who 'promoted' the king's marriage, and seeing Henry 'much bent' upon it, had 'paved the way towards it'. These words were spoken in April 1536, by which time Anne had fallen from the king's favour and Jane Seymour had stolen his heart. So it was not intended as a boast, and all the evidence suggests it is a thoroughly reliable description of the part Cromwell played.[20]

The words could mean that Cromwell persuaded Henry to marry in November or January. But this is unlikely, because whenever the marriage took place, there is no evidence that Cromwell had arranged it or that he was even present. It is far more plausible that he was referring to the whole sequence of events beginning in late 1532 and extending into the following year – the marriage to Anne, the formal divorce from Catherine, Anne's coronation and the new succession laws. He 'paved the way' to all of this with the Act of Restraint of Appeals, which he began to draw up about the same time as the November marriage, perhaps before, and almost certainly before Anne's pregnancy. This act prohibited appeals in all marital cases to Rome. Employing all the historical and other arguments that Cranmer, Foxe and others had collated in the *Collectanea*, it gave Henry a solid constitutional basis on which to settle his Great Matter in England. Cromwell had now effectively brought all the jurisdiction of the church under the king's control by means of parliamentary statute. The act was presented to the Commons on 14 March 1533, and after some limited resistance, it passed both houses by 7 April.[21]

While parliament was debating the Appeals, Convocation began its discussions on the Aragon marriage on 26 March. After bishops Standish and Stokesley produced the verdicts of European universities favourable to Henry, the Lords dutifully declared for the king on 29 March, with only Bishop John Fisher opposing. On 2 April Cranmer, newly consecrated as Archbishop of Canterbury, called on the Commons to give its view. It, too, declared for Henry. On the delicate point of whether Arthur's marriage to Catherine had been consummated, the consensus was that it had.[22]

According to Hall, the news that Anne was with child was made known at Easter; but it is not clear whether he meant Palm Sunday (6 April) or Easter Sunday seven days later, or whether Easter was just an expression covering the first week or two in April – just as we say 'Christmas time' meaning the period around Christmas and not specifically 25 December. The Venetian ambassador reported the news on 12 April. Two days earlier Chapuys had deduced that Anne was 'in the family way' (after Henry had asked him three times, 'Am I not a man like others'?). Chapuys added that on Saturday (12 April) Anne went to mass 'in truly royal state', acting as if she wore the crown already. Some preachers had even begun calling her the queen.[23]

Meanwhile, Henry had sent George Boleyn, Anne's brother, now Lord Rochford, on an embassy to King Francis. Henry's instructions to Rochford are worth reciting in some detail because they are the nearest thing we have to an official minute of the Anglo-French summit in Calais the previous November. They begin with a reference to 'our previous meeting and the fraternal and familiar communication that we had concerning our affairs' (*Premier, a nostre derniere entreveue sur la fraternelle et familiaire communication que Nous eusmes ensembles de noz affaires venant aux nostres*). A section follows on how the pope and the emperor have combined to thwart Henry's most just cause, and then we get to the heart of the matter:

It is to have a male heir and succession, by which we will (God willing) establish the quiet repose and tranquillity of our realm and dominions (*Cest davoir masculine succession et posterite, en la quelle Nous establirons (Dieu Voulant) le quiet repoz et tranquillite de nostre Royaulme et Dominions*). Francis's brotherly and clear advice, the best that there could be, had been to counsel us to delay or protract no longer, but with all haste to proceed effectively to the accomplishment and consummation of our marriage (*Son fraternel plain et entier advis (et, a bref dire, le meilleur qui pourroit estre) fut tel, et Nous conseil.la de ne dilayer ne protracter le temps plus longuement, mais en toute celerite proceder effectuellement a lacompliment et consummation de nostre marriage*). On this advice and counsel which he gave us (*Sur lequel son advis et conseil, que ainsi Nous donna*) … We, for the firm confidence, hope and trust that we have in his truth and promise, confirming the perfect and infallible amity and perpetual alliance between us, have effectually proceeded to the accomplishment and consummation of the said marriage (*Nous, pour la ferme confidence espoir et fiance, que Nous avons en sa verite et promesse, corrobore de la parfaite et infallible amytie et allyance perpetuelle dentre Nous, avons effectuellement procede a laccomplissement et consummation dudict marriage*).

Henry was now looking forward to his heir, 'which, please God will follow, and which to all appearance is in a state of advancement already' (*qui, au plaisir de Dieu, succedera, et comme bien cuidons est desja en bonne apparence de advancement*). Henry was willing to take Francis into his confidence, and listen to his advice on the delicate matter of how best to publicly announce the marriage (*il Luy plaise en toute diligence Nous donner et mander son bon conseil et advis fraternel, en quelle maniere et quant seroit le mieulx de le publier*).[24]

This is, admittedly, the English version of what the two kings had discussed. However, it should be reliable enough. There would be no point in sending Rochford to France with directions like these if what had actually been agreed in Calais was something quite different.

Further instructions for Norfolk and Rochford followed later, this time in English:

> And … after consulting with our good brother … how and in what sort to disclose to our people our marriage, which we had by his advice and council contracted and consummate, he sent us word that we should first unite and knit in one accord all the nobles of our realm, and so thereupon divulge the same.

This Henry confirmed he had done, Francis 'being councillor, author and chief advisor'. Henry did nothing, he avowed, 'than whereof our good brother was author unto us, though not of form and manner, yet of the substance and matter'. Henry then asked for Francis's continued support against the pope.[25]

Francis's backing for Henry in his Great Matter, and his attempts to persuade the pope to decide in Henry's favour, were no secret in diplomatic circles. Naturally Francis could not openly urge the Boleyn marriage, so the French information service was set to work to deflect any suspicion. According to the Venetian ambassador to France, Henry had brought Anne to Calais with the intention of marrying, but Francis dissuaded him. For how long, he did not say. A similar story went back to

Catherine in England. The Imperial diplomat, Dr Oritz, heard that Francis had reproved Henry for his conduct, but Oritz could not help wondering whether Anne might have 'made the King of France come round to her opinion'.[26]

Francis himself, in a later meeting with the pope, maintained that he had pressed Henry not to go ahead with the marriage, or at least to delay it. Henry, said Francis, was adamant that Catherine was not his lawful wife, but he did promise that Mary would not be struck out of the line of succession. However, Imperial observers pointed out that whatever claims Francis made, French cardinals were now willing to support Henry not only in putting Catherine away, but also in declaring Mary illegitimate.[27]

Despite French denials, the evidence that Francis gave Henry advice, and, at very least, tacit encouragement to marry Anne during the Calais summit is overwhelming. Apart from Henry and Anne, no one stood to gain more from this marriage than Francis. He and Charles V, Catherine's aunt, were the two most powerful monarchs in Western Christendom, co-existing in a state of near permanent rivalry. Making Anne Queen of England in Catherine's place would create an irreparable rift between Henry and Charles, at least as long as Catherine lived. It would be devastatingly effective in destroying any chance of an Anglo-Imperial alliance against France. The imperialists knew the wily French king well, and had long suspected that he might make mischief for them in Henry's Great Matter. Even during Wolsey's lifetime, Charles feared that Francis might lend his support to Henry in the hope of setting Henry and the emperor against each other. This is exactly what happened. On 16 April (1533) an angry Chapuys told Charles how Francis had written to Anne 'addressing her as Queen', even though no coronation had yet taken place, and that Francis was looking on the wreckage of Anglo-Imperial relations with unabashed delight.[28]

This may be a suitable point at which to pause, summarise and reconstruct the events of late 1532 and early 1533. When Henry and Francis met at Calais, Henry secured his brother king's support for his forthcoming marriage. The backing of a fellow monarch was just the boost that Henry needed to embolden him to take the decisive step, especially when senior councillors like Norfolk, Suffolk and even Wiltshire were full of misgivings. To deflect attention away from Francis's involvement, the marriage did not take place in Calais as was widely expected, but was deferred until the English arrived home. It was also kept a closely guarded secret, just as Hall said. To keep the pretence up, something happened in January, probably some kind of confirmation ceremony, which, with government connivance, was understood to be the marriage proper. Anne's pregnancy was then made known while the parliament and Convocation were debating the crucial constitutional and ecclesiastical legislation. It was all rather ingenious, and much of it, apparently, the brainchild of the French.

Francis, it needs to be stressed, was not trying to entice England away from the Catholic faith, or even into schism. His aim was to create an enduring antagonism between Henry and Charles. Francis would then seek to mediate between Henry and the pope, and try to persuade Rome to look more favourably on Henry's marriage to Anne. Francis even wished, if rather vainly, that Henry would accompany him on his forthcoming visit to Rome, where he could meet the pope face to face and conclude an amicable settlement. Had Francis succeeded in his overall aim, he would have completed the isolation of Charles by driving a wedge between him and the pope as well as between him and Henry.[29]

Francis, however, may have underestimated the forceful mood of nationalism now current in England. Neither Henry nor Anne cared much for reconciliation with Rome any more. Though the schism was not yet a *fait accompli*, events were now moving inexorably towards it. Chapuys could only watch and fume helplessly. He reported to Charles the widespread English unhappiness with the new marriage, and how many people – angry with Anne and still loyal to Catherine – wished that Charles 'would send an army' to punish the schismatic king. Chapuys respectfully suggested that Charles could 'hardly avoid making war' on England in view of the great wrong done to Catherine. An undertaking would be easy, for England was ill-equipped in arms, and the affection of most of the people was with Charles.[30]

But Henry pressed on regardless, bolder and more bombastic towards Rome than ever. He warned the pope that St Peter was a 'fisher, who, when he draweth his net too fast and too hard, then he braketh it'; so let St Peter's successor take care to treat princes carefully, for they 'be great fishes' and will not abide any wrong done to them. On 23 May 1533 at Dunstable, Henry's marriage to Catherine was formally declared to be contrary to divine law and invalid. Cromwell was not present at this 'trial', and he heard the news from two of his servants who were. On 1 June Anne was crowned Queen of England, and in what can only have been a calculated insult to Catherine and Chapuys, the Boleyn party commandeered Catherine's royal barge to convey the new queen along the river from Greenwich to the Tower.[31]

Cromwell helped organise the coronation, but a much more starring role was played by Cranmer, who placed the crown on Anne's head, anointed her and sat at the queen's table. While Chapuys stayed away in disgust, the French ambassador conspicuously attended, and Francis continued his discreet but firm support for Henry. He 'has always shown partiality' to Henry, Chapuys reported gloomily. Francis was also 'on good terms with the lady, to whom within the last week he has sent by esquire St Julien a handsome and richly decorated sedan chair, and three mules with harness and accoutrements in very good order'. The Venetian ambassador mentioned the same gift in his letters, which suggests that Francis was not even trying to keep it a secret.[32]

All that remained was for the long awaited son and heir to be born. The end of Anne's controversial pregnancy was fast approaching, and already the expectant father had decided that the infant prince would be named Edward or Henry. And in view of all the indignities and insults suffered by the imperialists, surely Chapuys can be forgiven just a touch of *schadenfreude* when, on 7 September, Anne gave birth to a healthy baby girl. Henry managed to hide his disappointment well, and a royal christening for Princess Elizabeth was held three days later. Again Cranmer was allocated a leading role. Although the baptism itself was performed by Bishop Stokesley, Cranmer confirmed the princess and became one of her godparents. Like most councillors and dignitaries, Cromwell attended the service, though as with the coronation, the position he took was a comparatively minor one.[33]

The English euphoria of the first half of the year now subsided somewhat. Henry consoled himself with the knowledge that Anne was still young and more children would follow; but nothing could disguise the fact that he had desperately wanted and expected a son. The main purpose of the marriage had failed, and the longer Henry had to live without his heir, the likelier it was that sooner or later people would start to wonder whether this was a marriage blessed or cursed in heaven. Catherine remained much loved, while Anne never won the hearts and minds of the English people. To make matters worse, Henry's relations with Francis were deteriorating as Anglo-French recriminations over the previous Calais summit began to set in.

Whereas Francis had hoped to mediate between Henry and Rome, Henry had now begun to damage relations between *Francis* and Rome. Henry was unhappy about discussions underway concerning a marriage between Francis's second son and Catherine de Medici, the pontiff's niece. According to Henry, Francis had promised that this marriage would not go ahead unless the pope decided in Henry's favour in *his* case, so Henry was intensely annoyed when he heard that the Franco-Medici marriage plans were proceeding apace. Henry now feared that Francis, despite his previous assurances, might yet take the pope's side against him.[34]

In October, however, Francis was still hoping to rub salt into Charles's wounds by offering to reconcile Henry with Rome, but he was would do nothing prejudicial to the papacy. The pope now saw little prospect of any agreement. Back in

England, Chapuys quoted Cromwell wishing that Henry had not 'placed all his confidence in the King of France'. Whether this was a slip of the tongue or a deliberate leak, Chapuys had found out a bit more about the role Francis had played in the Boleyn marriage. Around the same time a courier arrived from Marseilles with a personal letter to Henry. Chapuys was not sure of its message, but whatever it was Henry flew into a rage when he read it. He exclaimed bitterly 'that he had been betrayed, and that the King of France had not behaved in as friendly a spirit' as Henry had expected.[35]

For his part, Francis claimed to be distressed by some of the aggressively anti-papal policy enacted in England, like the Appeals Act, since he met Henry at Calais. When the pope urged Francis to stop supporting Henry, according to one imperialist source, Francis replied: 'Were I not at present in want of his friendship, that others may not forestall me, I would play him such a trick that he should for ever remember'. Francis wondered how Henry, 'who presumes to be a wise man, can be such a fool as this to work for the queen's cause'. Nor had Francis expected the sentence against Catherine at Dunstable. He was especially irked to hear of this, because it threatened to undermine his efforts to persuade the pope to decide in Henry's favour. Another of the French king's complaints was Henry's appeal to a General Council of the Church. Francis feared this would only bring the pope and the emperor closer together, when he had spent most of the year doing his best to drive them apart. By now Francis was heartily wishing that he had never involved himself in Henry's affairs at all.[36]

It may now be timely to review the role of Thomas Cromwell in these sensational events. When I began researching this part of Cromwell's life, I was expecting to be quickly buried under piles of evidence showing him in league with Anne and her party, steering, tugging, manipulating and generally urging Henry to throw off the papal yoke, put Catherine unceremoniously away and marry Anne. The real story has turned out differently. The English schism was the outcome of Henry's love affair, his goal of supreme power at home, and of contemporary European power politics. It was not primarily due to Cromwellian ambitions or machinations. There is no evidence that Cromwell was the one who suggested to Henry that he seek the support of King Francis in marrying Anne. If he had been the author of this innovative idea, so successful initially until Anglo-French relations began to sour, there would surely have been some reward for him, either a rapid promotion or even ennoblement; but he would have to wait another year and a half before becoming Henry's Principal Secretary. Nor was Cromwell ever particularly keen on alliances with the French. His sympathies in foreign policy consistently lay with Charles V and the Imperialists.

So whose idea was it to enlist the help of the French? It could have been Henry's, or possibly Anne's. She had spent some time at the French court before she became Henry's lover, and had developed a pro-French outlook. She also, as Chapuys gruffly noted, seemed on uncommonly good terms with the French king. However, in Henry's own words already quoted, he did nothing 'than whereof our good brother [Francis] was author unto us, though not of form and manner, yet of the substance and matter'. This suggests that the initiative might have come from King Francis. Unfortunately, the evidence may not be fully conclusive.

To say all this is not to diminish Cromwell's part entirely. Neither is it to forget the all-important Appeals legislation that he drafted and ushered onto the statute books. Here, however, he was acting as Henry's loyal and competent servant, 'paving the way' for his master, but only because Henry was already 'much bent upon it', especially after he had won the support of Francis. Cromwell did not determine the way, and neither did he push, entice or drag Henry against his will along the way. As the Milanese ambassador once said of Henry: 'His majesty chooses to know and superintend everything himself'. The Appeals was a constitutional framework, erected by Cromwell, to enable Henry to do what he wanted to do and had already resolved to do. Cromwell, therefore, played an important supportive role. But to claim that he masterminded the schism and then railroaded the breach with Rome through parliament is to exaggerate both his influence with the king and his prominence on the council at this stage in his career. Noteworthy, too, is Cromwell's comparatively modest profile at Anne's coronation and Elizabeth's baptism. It would be a mistake to read too much into this: his rise to power was not yet complete, and besides, these were sacred services which he as a layman would not be expected to lead. Nevertheless, there remains a striking absence of any clear evidence that he was ever especially close to the Boleyns. It is quite possible that Anne did not particularly like Cromwell. She may not have forgotten that he was once Wolsey's servant, and a loyal one even after the cardinal's fall. However, the relationship between Anne and Cromwell is a subject that will receive more attention in Part 2. Suffice to say for now that Thomas Cranmer, not Thomas Cromwell, was the new queen's favourite.[37]

In the year of Anne's triumph, Cromwell had not risen as high as his main evangelical colleagues, Lord Chancellor Audley and Archbishop Cranmer. He would soon overtake both in pre-eminence on Henry's council, but not yet. Conversely, it does not seem as though either of these two had travelled as far down the evangelical road as Cromwell had done. Cromwell had by now read and digested Melanchthon's *Apology*, and Christopher Mont was translating Lutheran works in Cromwell's house (see Chapter 3); but whether Cranmer or Audely were yet an integral part of this largely underground Protestant movement is far from certain. And it was still an underground movement, even though men in high places had joined it. From the vantage point of history, the rupture between England and Rome appears as a central element of the Protestant Reformation in England, but hopefully it is not being pedantic to point out that *at the time* things were perceived differently. Even if Lutheran ideas had helped fuel the mood of English nationalism – and even this is debateable – the king who led his country into schism was no Protestant when he married Anne, and he never became one after that. For all his defiance of the pope, Henry would continue to enforce medieval papal doctrines of transubstantiation, the sacrifice of the mass and clerical celibacy; and despite all the subsequent efforts of Cromwell, Cranmer and others to persuade him, he never accepted justification by faith alone. For want of a better and generally recognized term, Henry might be called a rebel Catholic, or maybe a schismatic. Cromwell's evangelical activities, therefore, still had to be conducted in some secrecy and with discretion.

One of Cromwell's last official engagements of the year was to attend, along with many others, Cranmer's enthronement on 3 December, 1532. It was a lavish affair. Thomas Goldwell, the prior of Christ Church at Canterbury, had wanted to send Cromwell 'some pleasure in wildfowl' for Christmas; but after the ecclesiastical festivities he had to regretfully advise that 'all our swans and partridges, with such other things, be consumed and spent'. So Goldwell offered 'fruits of the earth' instead, among which were '*Pome riall*', apples, 'good to drink wine withal'. Thus an eventful year drew to its close.[38]

5

Principal Secretary

Sometime during these historic events, Cromwell renewed an old friendship. Francesco Frescobaldi, the merchant who many years ago had shown a Christian charity to the young Thomas Cromwell when he was a fugitive and wanderer in Italy, had now fallen on hard times. He had debtors in England, so he set out to claim the money owed him and to revive his fortunes. Quite by chance Cromwell saw him one day, recognised him, greeted him fulsomely and invited him to dinner, introducing him to his guests as the man 'by whose means I have achieved the degree of this my present calling'. Dinner over, Cromwell learned the reason his former benefactor had come to England. By now a rich man himself, Cromwell loaded Frescobaldi with gifts, and after taking the names of Frescobaldi's debtors, ordered one of his servants to investigate the case and obtain the money owed. Within days, all debts were recovered. The Italian then stayed for a short while as Cromwell's guest before returning to his homeland. The story has a slightly sad ending; now an old man, Frescobaldi died within a year of arriving back in Venice.[1]

Bandello's appealing tale can be dated to around 1532–3, when the name of Francis Frescobaldi appears in the *Letters and Papers*. Dr Augustine was also in touch with him around this time. There are two separate letters from a Francis Frescobaldi to Cromwell from Marseilles in October 1533 offering his services, though the brevity of these letters suggests that this might have been a different Frescobaldi, maybe a son. Frescobaldi's name appears for the last time in Cromwell's remembrances in 1534. The reunion provided an agreeable interlude for a councillor who now had some grim business to deal with.[2]

When the New Year (1534) dawned, one item demanding Cromwell's attention was the case of Elizabeth Barton, variously described as the Holy Maid of Kent, the Nun of Canterbury, or simply the Nun. Following an illness in 1525, this humble Kentish servant girl had transformed herself into a charismatic, mystic visionary, prone to trances and startling prophecies. With the support of a monk of Canterbury, Dr Edward Bocking, her influence quickly grew. Even the high and mighty of the realm were fascinated by her. She was granted an audience with Archbishop Warham and John Fisher, and also, sometime in 1529, Henry himself. According to one story she had met Anne Boleyn, who offered her a position in her circle at court. By contrast Catherine of Aragon and Thomas More avoided the Maid, Catherine pointedly turning down opportunities to meet her.[3]

Though the Maid had become one of the most vocal opponents of Henry's new marriage, it was not until the summer of 1533 that the king ordered Cromwell and Cranmer to begin dealings with her and followers. At first she was questioned by Cranmer – she hailed from Kent so she was his responsibility – but soon Cromwell was put in charge of investigations. On 11 August Richard Gwent sent a report to Cromwell, describing how 'when my lord of Canterbury had examined the Nun of Canterbury upon your interrogatories ... she then confessed many follies'. No record of these interrogatories has survived, but they were crucial in breaking the Maid's spirit because Gwent added that 'if your interrogatories had not been, she would have confessed nothing'. Soon after this incident the Maid, Bocking and other allies of hers were sent to Cromwell personally. Then, to quote Cranmer, 'she confessed all … that she never had a vision in all her life, but all that ever she said was feigned'.[4]

At one point during the Maid's examination she was asked to reveal past events that she could not have known about. According to Cromwell's protégée, Richard Morison, it was this sudden thrust that shattered her confidence, and confessions quickly followed. Morison is the only source for this story, but it does ring true. It may be suspected that behind this tactic lay the penetrating mind of Cromwell. For if someone can divine the future, why not the past as well? What better way to test the genuineness of this self-proclaimed prophetess? The hapless girl could now do no better than fall back on a platitude. Those who put such questions, she pleaded, would need to be in a 'state of grace' before any answer could be given. Alas for the unfortunate Maid, such pious excuses would never pass muster with an accomplished examiner like Cromwell. True prophets of the Lord in the Bible, like Joseph to Pharaoh or Daniel to Nebuchadnezzar and Belshazzar, never insisted on the prerequisite of 'state of grace' (Genesis 41; Daniel 2, 5). As Cromwell knew, the main point of prophecy in its scriptural sense is to convict the *un*converted, not to preach to those who have the light already. Admittedly this interpretation of the Maid's case is both a little conjectural and based entirely on Morison. Few details of her examination were made public, and Cromwell doubtless preferred to keep his interrogation techniques a secret.[5]

Cromwell's remembrances in January 1534 include reminders to ask Henry what action the king wished to take regarding the Maid and her accomplices. Henry was determined to exact exemplary justice, but a legal technicality stood in his way, because opposing Henry's marriage to Anne was not treasonable under the existing law. Moreover, because the Maid had prophesied in the presence of the king, expert legal opinion took the quite realistic view that she could hardly be guilty of treason against his life. So Henry decided to proceed against the offenders by an act of parliamentary attainder, under which a person could be condemned by Act of Parliament without a formal trial in a court before a jury, and without the opportunity to give a defence. This arbitrary law-enforcement method had existed since 1459; it was not a Cromwellian invention, as is sometimes supposed. Cromwell, however, was the one directed by the king to prepare the indictment.[6]

There is a hint in Cromwell's notes that he held out some hope of clemency for the Maid and her party. The reference is to those who 'shall be attainted of high treason and suffer death *except the king's majesty do pardon them*'. The king's majesty, however, was not minded to be merciful, and in April the offenders faced the full horror of the traitors' death at Tyburn.[7]

The affair of the Maid highlighted the need to prepare parliamentary legislation to alter the succession and treason laws, subjects that Cromwell had been concerned about for some time. After the bill to reduce Catherine of Aragon's status to that of 'Princess Dowager' was passed by both houses by 7 March, the more complex succession bill, drafted by Cromwell and the council, underwent a number of revisions before being debated in parliament. Its main provisions confirmed Henry's marriage to Anne and ensured the succession to their lawful male heirs. Failing male heirs, the succession would pass to Elizabeth and her children. Rather surprisingly, Mary was not mentioned. She was not included in the succession, but neither was she made illegitimate, though this would be the logical outcome of the alleged invalidity of the Aragon marriage. By the end of March, the bill had completed its course through parliament, and members were required to swear an oath to the new act. Almost immediately after this demonstration of loyalty, news reached England of the papal sentence declaring that Henry's marriage to Catherine was valid. Henry was furious, and orders were sent to his clergy to attack papal authority with more vigour than ever in their Easter sermons. Parliament was then prorogued until November.[8]

Sometime early in April 1534, Henry made Cromwell his Principal Secretary in place of Stephen Gardiner, bishop of Winchester. In an uncharacteristically clumsy manner, the normally astute bishop had offended Henry. He had opposed the Submission of the Clergy, and had showed an unwise lack of enthusiasm for the king's Supremacy, though he did eventually comply on both points. Cromwell's appointment was completed with the minimum of fanfare and ceremony, a strange irony considering that he would soon raise the prestige of this office to new, unprecedented heights. Even the date of the appointment is not certain. However, as Gardiner signed his last warrant as secretary on 3 February, and Cromwell his first on 15 April, it most likely occurred during the early part of that month. Cromwell's steady rise to power was now virtually complete, and he had become Henry's foremost minister of state. For his indiscretions, Gardiner was a little fortunate not to forfeit his bishopric. Cromwell did not crow, and he even wrote a friendly letter to 'my very loving lord, my lord of Winchester'; but Gardiner's pride was wounded by this setback, and he harboured a simmering resentment against Cromwell from this moment on.[9]

During summer 1534 Cromwell was closely monitoring affairs in Ireland, but these, like his Irish policy generally, will be discussed in Chapter 11. The situation in England was fairly quiet, as if the king, council and parliament were resting and recharging the batteries before a further bout of anti-Rome legislation later in the year. In September Pope Clement died, to be succeeded by Alexander Farnese as Paul III. The English agent in Italy, Gregory Casale, reported that the old pontiff passed away largely unmourned, and that the new one was welcomed with much rejoicing on the streets of Rome. According to Chapuys – he may have been a bit optimistic here – Norfolk and the marquis of Dorset tentatively suggested to Henry that now would be an opportune moment to seek some kind of reconciliation with Rome. Henry scotched the idea immediately. 'Whoever is elected pope', averred the king, 'I shall take no more account of him than of any priest in this my kingdom'.[10]

The parliamentary session of November and December proved that Henry meant what he said. The Act of Supremacy confirmed Henry as Head of the Church in England, and omitted the clause 'so far as the law of God allows' that had been included in earlier drafts. It also gave Henry the authority to set wrongs to right in the church, and to authorise visitations whenever necessary – a hint of impending action to be taken against the monasteries.[11]

Then the Act of First Fruits and Tenths dashed any hopes the clergy might have had of enjoying their savings now that they no longer had to pay annates to Rome. Cromwell and Audley were its prime movers. The act was full of praise for the king's mercy, wisdom and justice, and it rhapsodised on how blessed a land England was under his most benign rule. As a result it was sure that all clerics would be delighted to pay the equivalent of a year's income, plus a further tenth of their yearly revenue, to the crown. The lack of any significant opposition – the act was passed by the end of November with barely a squeak from the clergy – serves as a powerful indicator both of the anti-clerical mood of the time, and also of the daunting efficiency of the new men around the king like Cromwell and Audley. The average yield in Henry's reign has been estimated at £40,000 per annum, and thus the church paid nearly ten times as much to Henry as it used to pay the pope in Rome.[12]

It is frequently claimed that Cromwell plundered the wealth of the church. Maybe so; but what a lot of wealth there was to plunder, far more than was needful to minister to the spiritual wants of the nation. Not many of the clergy in England had sold all and given to the poor before taking up their calling.

Then a subsidy bill in November secured another £80,000 for Henry, even though the country was not at war. The justification was similar to that in the First Fruits – Henry's wonderful character and beneficent rule. Cromwell had got this ploy off to a fine art, and we will find him using it again. He was proving a far more able manager of parliament than Wolsey had been, particularly in the delicate task of persuading the Houses to fill up the royal treasury. Whenever Henry wanted more money, Cromwell did not lecture parliament on the king's right or entitlement; he appealed instead to the loyalty of the Commons and the Lords to their prince. Half admiringly and half enviously, Chapuys reported parliamentary affairs to Charles, ascribing most of Henry's accumulating wealth to Cromwell, 'who boasts that he will soon make of his master the richest prince in Christendom'.[13]

The most controversial legislation of the new regime concerned the capital crime of treason. Under the existing laws, mainly defined by the 1352 act in the reign of Edward III, opposition to the king's Supremacy was not technically treason. Nor, embarrassingly for the government, was calling Queen Anne a 'whore', which is what a disconcerting number of people up and down the country were doing. As seen already, the activities of the Maid of Kent were not strictly treason either, and Henry had been forced to deal with her by attainder. Consequently a new treason bill, which had been some time under discussion, was debated in parliament in November, and made effective from 1 February the following year. As well as actual acts against the king or the state, treason was now defined as any desire maliciously expressed in 'words or in writing' to kill or harm the king, queen and heir, or to deprive them of their titles. It would also be treason to call the king a heretic, schismatic, tyrant, infidel or usurper.[14]

Elton saw the unmistakable stamp of Thomas Cromwell on the new law. This may well be, but it might also be useful to recall that general comment on English affairs made by the Milanese ambassador that 'His majesty chooses to know and superintend everything himself'. No decisive proof exists that Cromwell was the one who first suggested that words as well as actual deeds should henceforth count as treason, and an image of Cromwell steamrollering draconian legislation through parliament, flattening all opposition that stood in his way, would be exaggerated. The real author of the king's supremacy in church and state was the king himself. This comment is, however, no more than a minor qualifier, because there is no doubt that Cromwell fully supported the act and that he presented it to parliament on the king's behalf. Nevertheless, he was unhappy with a proposal to offer rewards to informers, perhaps because it could invite false charges, and this clause was soon dropped.[15]

The new law has gained a reputation for gratuitous severity among historians, but whether this is entirely justified is debateable. Under Edward's act it was treason to 'compass or *imagine*' the death of the king' (*fait compasser ou ymaginer*). The practical effect of this would depend on what 'imagine' meant. Did it mean to conspire and set the plot in motion, but fail to bring it to completion? Or was it enough to harbour hostile thoughts or intents, whether or not they were spoken or put into action? If it meant the latter, then in *principle* the new act was no more severe than the old one. Leaving aside the obvious difficulty of divining the secret motives of the heart, Edward's act could technically condemn someone for a malicious thought or intention which might or might not result in any treasonable action. So why the Tudor law, which insisted on a malicious word, should be regarded as excessively harsher than Edward's is hard to see, especially as Elton has given various examples of people being condemned for treason for little more than aggressive or ill-judged words before 1534. Having made this point, however, there is no denying that the new law was designed to give the government sweeping powers to repress any opposition to the new regime.[16]

These are the main acts of the parliamentary session of 1533–4. As Henry's Principal Secretary, Cromwell now played the leading part in all government legislation, from the drafting of bills to debates in parliament. He also directed the clergy to preach the Royal Supremacy from the pulpits. He even told them what Scripture texts they should use. The favourite passages were Romans 13 and 1 Peter 2:13–17, as well as the examples of godly kings in Old Testament times, and the obedience due to them. Slightly more difficult to determine is his exact role in the pamphlets, booklets and various other forms of literature now being used to persuade and cajole the people to support the constitutional changes.[17]

The first set of such writings had appeared around summer 1531 dealing with the validity of a marriage to a brother's widow. These were generally dry, uninspiring works composed by academic theologians and canon lawyers who supported the king's divorce. Then the veteran lawyer and writer, Christopher St German, composed his '*New Additions*', arguing that the king in parliament was 'the high sovereign' over the people with responsibility for their souls as well as their material wellbeing. This piece was completed two years before the Act of Appeals and three years before the Act of Supremacy. There is no real evidence that Cromwell had anything to do with these early works.[18]

The *Glass of Truth*, written in 1532, was a spirited little book. Henry may have had some part in its preparation, because it contains quite intimate family details about Catherine's first marriage to Arthur. The work discusses the Leviticus and Deuteronomy texts once more, and slightly ingeniously it argues that Leviticus should be taken literally but Deuteronomy spiritually. To back up this novel line in exegesis, the *Glass* brings in St Augustine on Deuteronomy: 'Every preacher of the Word of God is bound so to labour in the Gospel that he stir up seed to his brother, that is to Christ, which died for us; and the seed so suscitate [sic] must have the name of him departed, that is of Christ: whereupon we be called Christians'. A good try, perhaps, but it hardly carries much conviction in the matter of Henry's marriage. A discussion follows on the pope's power of dispensation, before we read that Arthur's marriage to Catherine was consummated despite Catherine's denials. They allegedly 'bedded together at sundry times'; they lived together as married; and 'some men of the great house' avowed on oath that Arthur 'did report himself unto them that he had carnally known her', and not just for 'youthful boasting'. The *Glass* does not deny that the pope was head of church, only that his dispensation to allow Henry and Catherine to marry was wrong because of Leviticus, and the pope cannot overrule Holy Writ. A hint of what is to come is contained in this thinly veiled threat: 'methinketh the king's highness and his parliament should earnestly press the metropolitans of this realm … to set an end shortly'.[19]

As Elton has noted, there is evidence, though it is not conclusive, that Cromwell might have had something to do with
the production of the *Glass*. However, I would suggest that
he had nothing much to do with its contents. Cromwell's
theological writings are few and far between, restricted in the
main to a few select letters, the Ten Articles and accompanying
Injunctions, and his last words and prayer. These will be discussed when we come to them chronologically; but the point
can be made now that whenever Cromwell had something to
say on theology, it was invariably quite arresting and incisive.
He comes over as a man blessed with above average theological intelligence and insight, features that are conspicuously
missing from the *Glass*. Though bright and breezy in parts, it
contains nothing substantial or stimulating. The advantageous
allegorising of Deuteronomy reads more like a hopeful novice
trying his best to impress the king than a fine theological mind.
There is certainly nothing Protestant about it.[20]

Two little known treatises by Jasper Fyloll had been published around 1532–3. Both tracts include familiar arguments
for the Supremacy. Both read as though they were prepared
with the aim of brow beating the clergy into submitting to
the king. Fyloll had now entered Cromwell's service, so maybe
Cromwell approved these works. As with the *Glass*, however,
there is no direct evidence for this. Cromwell habitually gets
the credit (or the blame) for much of the stuff that appeared
in print around this time, but he did not have the time to read
everything his clients wrote. The only printing and publication activities known for certain to have been organized by
Cromwell during these early years were Melanchthon's *Apology*
and those other unnamed Lutheran works that Christopher
Mont was translating in his house (see Chapter 3).[21]

Sometime in late 1533 – when the new Act of Succession
and Act of Supremacy of 1534 were already being planned –
the *Articles devised by the whole consent of the king's most honourable
Council* were published. They take the Supremacy argument
a stage further than the *Glass of Truth* with an attack on the
institution of the papacy. They argue that in Scripture 'there

is no authority nor jurisdiction granted more to the bishop of Rome than to any other *extra provinciam'* ... and that the pope is 'neither in life nor learning Christ's disciple ... he is both baste and came to his dignity by Symony'. Christian people should, therefore, reject papal authority and follow 'Christ's law, in which is all sweetness and truth, adjoining with it the laws of this realm, utterly relinquishing the other, in which is nothing else but pomp, pride, ambition' and assorted other ills. The following year Edward Foxe and Richard Sampson – one evangelical and one Catholic – both wrote learned works supporting the Supremacy, mainly targeted at the clergy. Also in 1534, and for a larger audience, a tract appeared wittily titled *A Little Treatise against the muttering of some Papists in corners*. In this work there is, at last, definite evidence of Cromwell's direct involvement. A letter in the hand of one of Cromwell's clerks suggests that he had inspired it. The letter also reminds the clergy that they are not to live luxuriously, but should forsake pomp and pride and give what they possess 'superfluously' to the people.[22]

The *Little Treatise* is designed to show that whilst papal power is something that has grown up in Christendom over centuries, it is contrary to Scripture. This claim is reinforced by a plentiful supply of quotes from the New Testament and the church fathers. The message, therefore, is that the king's Supremacy was based on an ancient truth recently discovered, to which mistaken medieval custom must give way. The author of the *Treatise* withholds his name, but gives occasional glimpses of Protestant thought. For example: 'for Christ's laws he (the pope) bringeth forth laws and traditions of his own devising'; now princes 'begin to be lighted with the knowledge of Christ's doctrine', and can see the bad ways of the popes; the bishop of Rome is but a member of the church, not her head or leader on earth. On Christ giving the keys to Peter (Matthew 16:19), St Augustine is quoted as saying that 'those keys He gave to His church', not to the pope alone. The *Treatise* then censures popes for their luxurious living, contrary to the example of Jesus and apostles.

In substance and in style, the *Little Treatise* is far superior to
the *Glass of Truth*. Instead of the routine and rather tiresome
rant against the pope, it actually gets to grips with the crux
of the matter of papal authority by discussing the Scripture
text on which that authority is supposedly based (Matthew
16). It does not, however, liken the papacy to the antichrist or
the monstrous seven-headed beast of the Revelation, as some
Protestants were doing. And this may be a timely moment
to note that the Reformers' sharp attacks on the popes were
aimed primarily at the Renaissance papacy of their times: men
like, for example, Innocent VIII and Alexander VI, who brazenly used bribery and extortion to advance their personal
careers before and during their papal reigns; and who, despite
enforcing all clergy to make solemn vows of clerical celibacy,
fathered a large brood of illegitimate children by various mistresses. It is unlikely that popes of more recent memory would
have aroused the same hostility.[23]

As the decade advanced, talented Tudor writers supporting the Supremacy were increasingly offering their services to
Cromwell. In 1534 William Marshall produced an edition of
Lorenzo Valla's *Donation of Constantine*, and the following year
he produced his translation of Marsiglio of Padua's *Defence of
the Peace* (*Defensor Pacis*). The Valla project was Marshall's own
initiative, but Cromwell approved the Marsiglio work and provided the money to publish it.[24]

The *Donation* had been one of the scoops of the fifteenth
century, if not the entire late medieval age. This document,
in which the Emperor Constantine had allegedly committed the government of his western empire to Pope Sylvester
I, was dramatically exposed as a forgery in 1440 by Lorenzo
Valla, a leading humanist. Valla was supported by two other
scholars working independently of him – Nicholas of Cusa,
who later became a German Cardinal, and an Englishman,
Bishop Pecock.[25]

Marsiglio was a fourteenth-century thinker and writer.
He was attracted to the concept of nation-state sovereignty
in which the clergy were as accountable as any other group

of men to courts and laws, and therefore subject to the civil power. Papal claims to power, he argued, were disruptive of civil peace, and the main cause of strife among nations. Essential functions of the priesthood consisted in teaching the Gospel and ministering the sacraments. Continuing in this proto-Protestant vein, Marsiglio challenged the papal claim to spiritual supremacy as St Peter's successor. Marsiglio contended that Peter had no official superiority over the other apostles, and there was no proof from Scripture that Peter was ever a bishop of Rome.[26]

Either Marshall or Cromwell decided that Marsiglio would need to be adapted before he could be suitable for the Tudor state. Marshall's translation left out about one fifth of the original work, and was not always scrupulously faithful to what it retained. Marsiglio supported an elective monarchy, whereas Marshall, wisely in Henry's reign, defended the hereditary version. Marshall also omitted the passage where Marsiglio defended a quasi-democratic control over the ruler by the community. Then when Marsiglio wrote of the laws being made by the people, Marshall's commentary explained that the author meant parliament and not the 'rascal multitude'. This tactfully doctored English translation of Marsiglio was another imaginative initiative designed to convince people of the justness of the king's cause, though unfortunately for him, Marshall had to admit to Cromwell that it had not sold particularly well.[27]

So how successful was this combination of legislation and literature in persuading the people to give their hearts as well as their outward obedience to the Royal Supremacy? On this question, the debate is likely to continue without ever being answered definitively. Historians may consult Tudor documents, but they cannot meet Tudor people and discover their private thoughts. The government at least was not troubled by serious organized resistance until the so-called Pilgrimage of Grace in 1537, a major uprising in the northern counties that had a variety of causes, though opposition to Cromwell's reformist measures was undeniably a significant factor. A puzzling point, however, is that almost all the propaganda was aimed at convincing the people of the king's rightful Supremacy; but apart from the succession legislation, surprisingly little seems to have been done, either by Cromwell personally or the government as a whole, to endear Queen Anne to a nation that still retained a great affection for Catherine.

But there were some who would not submit, not even outwardly. Though Thomas More and Bishop John Fisher indicated that they would be prepared to swear to the main body of the Act of Succession, they objected to its provocative preamble that specifically condemned papal authority and the Aragon marriage. Cranmer, anxious to spare More and Fisher from Henry's wrath, suggested to Cromwell that this compromise should be accepted. Cromwell agreed, and he took the idea to Henry. However, Henry was adamant that they must swear to the entire act, preamble and all, otherwise they would be an inspiration for others also to resist.[28]

More's own words remain the best guide to his personal relations with Cromwell, who seemed to share Cranmer's willingness to save More from death if he could. Cromwell was glad that More's name was not included on the attainder of the Maid of Kent and her allies, and he made a point of asking More's son-in-law, William Roper, to tell More the good news. In his memoirs recorded during his interrogations, More variously described Cromwell as 'he that tenderly favoureth me', 'my good master', and even – when Cromwell reminded him that the king's goodwill would not discharge him from complying with an act of parliament – 'my special tender friend'. When More used his fine legal mind to avoid implicating himself, Cromwell advised him, apparently in a kindly rather than a threatening manner, that his answer 'should not satisfy nor content the king's highness', and that Henry would want something more definite. Cromwell then assured More that Henry was still willing to be gracious towards him. More's wife, Alice, wrote to Cromwell while her husband was still alive. She was, she assured him, 'most deeply bound ... for your manifold goodnesses and loving favour, both before this time and yet daily, now also showed towards my poor husband and me'. She appealed for Cromwell's continued goodwill, 'for thereupon hangeth the greatest part of my poor husband's comfort and mine'. Now in financial straits, she was 'compelled of very necessity to sell part of mine apparel'.[29]

Despite the clearest possible evidence from the Mores themselves, and without bothering to give a source reference, Merriman writes confidently that Cromwell was spitefully hunting around for 'some mesh' to trap More. Where Merriman gets this from, I have absolutely no idea. The only sign of tension between the two men appears in More's account of one of his last interrogations before his trial. More writes that Cromwell gave a very 'fair' summary of the situation thus far, before telling More that Henry was not pleased with his answer. The king had demanded to know whether More would accept the Supremacy and the Acts of Succession, and confess Henry as Head of the Church. Again More would not commit himself, so Audley and Cromwell warned him that Henry might compel an answer. Cromwell reminded More that he had once compelled heretics to answer his questions, so surely the king could do likewise. More replied that the cases were not identical: when More was Lord Chancellor the pope's authority was recognised throughout Christendom, including in England, but now – and here More spoke with a shrewd vagueness so as not to incriminate himself – it 'seemeth not like a thing agreed in this realm and the contrary taken for truth in other realms'. In that case, countered Cromwell, 'it were as well to be burned for the denying of that as be beheaded for denying of this, and therefore as good reason to compel them to make precise answer to the one as to the other'. More suggested that the law of all Christendom bound the conscience in a way that the law of one dissenting land could not do. Unfortunately, Cromwell's answer is not recorded. The conversation continued at some length but More's account gives no further details except that, at the end, Cromwell 'liked me this day much worse than he did the last time'. This suggests disappointment rather than sheer malice on Cromwell's part. One other interesting point to emerge from More's recollections is that even during the exchanges on theological matters it was Secretary Cromwell, not Archbishop Cranmer, who did most of the talking for the government side.[30]

Unlike More, Bishop John Fisher was not averse to looking for help from abroad to overturn the Henrician settlement, though not to destroy Henry personally. According to Chapuys, Fisher had urged Charles to 'interfere in this affair and undertake a work which must be as pleasing in the eyes of God as war upon the Turk'. Chapuys reckoned that many English people would support the 'strong measures' for which Fisher appealed.[31]

Fisher had also shown more interest in the Maid of Kent than was prudent for a man already viewed by his king with some suspicion, and this led to an interesting exchange between the bishop and Cromwell. Fisher had written to Cromwell on 18 January 1534 about the affair. His letter is unfortunately missing, but some idea of its contents can be gauged from Cromwell's reply in February, which is worth looking at closely because it reveals much about Cromwell's theological mind.

Cromwell was unconvinced by the 'craft and cunning' that he claimed Fisher had used 'to set a good countenance upon an ill matter'. The Scripture texts quoted by Fisher, 'though well weighed according to the places whereof they be taken, make not so much for your purpose as ye allege them for'. Fisher claimed he had believed the Maid because of her pious religious bearing, and reports of her holiness. Cromwell called this a lack of discernment. 'For if credence should be given to every such lewd person as would affirm himself to have revelations from God, what readier way were there to subvert all commonwealths and good orders in the world?' Rather than listen to 'vain voices of the people making bruits of her trances and disfigurations', Fisher should have examined credible witnesses. Fisher had cited Amos 3:7 – 'The Lord God will do nothing, but He revealeth His secret unto His servants the prophets' – as one reason why he trusted the Maid.

Again, Cromwell was unimpressed. He bluntly told Fisher that he was misapplying the text. Is it not self-evident, demanded Cromwell, that 'since the consummation and the end of the Old Testament, and since the Passion of Christ, God hath done many great and notable things in the world, whereof He showed no thing to His prophets, that hath come to the knowledge of men'. Cromwell appealed to Fisher's conscience. What if the Maid's 'revelations' had been of a different sort? What if she had spoken for the king's marriage rather than against it? Would Fisher have believed her then? Maybe not, Cromwell suggested; maybe Fisher might reply that the Boleyn marriage was against the Law of God. But surely the bishop should know 'by the histories of the Bible that God may by His revelation dispense with His own law, as with the Israelites spoiling the Egyptians, and with Jacob to have four wives, and such other' (Exodus 3:21–2, 35–6; Genesis 29–30). So the bishop was without excuse. Now Cromwell closed in for the kill. Fisher's real interest in the Maid was to 'know more of her revelations than to try out the truth or falsehood of the same'. In this the bishop stood in 'great default, believing and concealing such things as tended to the destruction of the prince'. Cromwell rebuked Fisher for not reporting what he knew of the Maid to Henry. It was no excuse for Fisher to say he had kept silent because the Maid herself had spoken to Henry. Fisher had only her word for that, and even if it were true, he was still duty bound to tell his prince. At the end Cromwell delivered a warning to the bishop. 'Surely my lord, if this matter comes to trial, your own confession in these [Fisher's] letters, besides the witnesses which are against you, will be sufficient to condemn you'. Cromwell then urged Fisher, 'laying apart all excuses', to appeal to the king's mercy, 'and I dare undertake that his highness shall benignly accept you into his gracious favour'.[32]

It could never be imagined from this letter that Cromwell was wholly self-taught in theology. Despite this, he entered boldly into a theological bout with John Fisher, a man internationally recognized as one of England's foremost scholars and theologians. He coolly tells Fisher that he has been naïve in his dealings with the Maid, and that the learned bishop has bungled his Bible texts. Then, with an assurance and incisiveness that few theologians can command, he sets forth into sensitive theological territory, such as God overruling his written Word with revelations, and the role of prophecy in the New Testament era as distinct from the Old. Finally he calls on this senior bishop to repent. If anyone has any doubts about why Henry advanced this layman so high in spiritual as well as secular affairs, this letter will amply answer them. Thomas Cromwell was more than a match for the best of bishops in their own specialist field.

It is not clear how or even if Fisher responded. There is a request from him to Cromwell to stop sending angry letters and leave him in peace, but this is undated, so whether it was a reply to Cromwell's letter above we cannot say. But Cromwell's letter is not angry; he just makes his point with his customary vigour and eloquence. However, it was just before Christmas (1534) that Fisher – now in evident discomfort in the Tower and dependent on his brother's charity – appealed to Cromwell for relief from the cold and the poor diet. A certain Anthony Bonvisi, a man Cromwell knew, was wont to send meat and wine two or three times a week to More, and wine and jelly daily to Fisher, but these supplies may have stopped when the prisoners were brought to trial for fear of provoking Henry. Not much else, unfortunately, can be said about this point, except that when he was preparing for his death, More made a point of thanking Bonvisi for his friendship and kindness.[33]

The closing words of Cromwell's letter to Fisher prove that Cromwell was not hounding the bishop to his doom, and it is not absolutely clear what Henry intended to do with him or with More at this stage. Throughout 1534, their fate hung in the balance. Anne Boleyn is sometimes blamed for inciting the king against them, but the decisive factor was the pope's decision to make Fisher a cardinal. Infuriated at this provocation, as he saw it, Henry piled the pressure onto these two most prominent dissidents before bringing them to trial and the inevitable condemnation. Cromwell then had the unenviable task of having to explain, and to try and justify, the executions to foreign courts.[34]

The other leading dissidents of this period were the Carthusian monks of the Charterhouse. Cromwell's agent, Thomas Bedyll, equipped with 'diverse books and annotations', was busy in spring 1534 trying to persuade these monks to accept the Royal Supremacy. He tried to prove to them the 'equality of the apostles by the law of God', and refute Peter's primacy and papal succession. After a long conversation he left certain books with them, hoping 'that they should see the Holy Scriptures and doctors thereupon concerning the said matters, and reform themselves accordingly'. Bedyll comes over as an unsympathetic character in some of his letters, but he was obviously making some attempt to engage the monks and debate with them. Unfortunately for the government, he was unsuccessful.[35]

Matters came to a head in spring the following year. In April 1535 Cromwell's remembrances include notes to ask what the king wished to do regarding the Charterhouse of London and Richmond. Cromwell then sent John Rastall to try once more to prevail with the monks. John Whalley, another of Cromwell's clients, warned Cromwell that Rastall would fail, and that the 'superstitious' monks would only laugh at him. Whalley then put forward an idea of his own. He suggested that some 'loyal' man should stay at the Charterhouse, and then men like the vicar of Croydon – a well known religious conservative who had submitted to Henry – should be invited to preach to them as well. Should this two-pronged approach fail, Whalley advised sentencing the monks according to the law.[36]

Cranmer also offered to try and reason with the monks. Cranmer expressed surprised at the attitude of one of them named Reynold, 'having such sight in scriptures and doctors', and another named Webster, 'which promised me that he would never meddle for the defence of that opinion' – papal authority. As with More, Cranmer was anxious to see the monks convicted 'by communication of sincere doctrine', and then make a public profession of loyalty rather than suffer as traitors.[37]

Again Cromwell seems to have agreed, and soon after this he went to speak with the monks himself. However, he had no more success than his agents. One monk named Houghton struck up a conversation on the subject of Christ giving the keys to Peter (Matthew 16). Evidently not persuaded by the arguments of Bedyll and Rastall, Houghton claimed that ever since the early church, all the fathers and doctors understood that the keys were given first to Peter, then to the apostles and subsequently to the pope and the bishops. How then, demanded Houghton, could the king, as a layman, be Head of the Church? Cromwell's reply was terse: 'You would make the king a priest, then?' With that he closed the subject, apparently deciding that there was little point in going over the same ground yet again.[38]

As with More and Fisher, so with the Carthusians, Cromwell and Cranmer were not rushing to shed Papist blood. Over a period of a year or more, various attempts were made to secure a peaceful end by a mixture of persuasion and pressure. Yet the monks would not yield, and in a savagely ironic twist their resistance led them to a trial where the duke of Norfolk, the leading Catholic peer of the land, presided as judge and passed sentence. Unlike More and Fisher, both quickly despatched by the axe, the unfortunate monks were hanged, disembowelled and quartered. Chapuys reported the executions, attended by Norfolk, Wiltshire, and his son George Rochford, with 'several other lords and gentlemen', including Henry Norris. Chapuys does not mention Cromwell at the spectacle.[39]

Efforts to bring the remaining Carthusians into submission met with only limited success. Jasper Fyloll told Cromwell that the monks he met still preferred reading the medieval schoolmen to the New Testament. When a copy of Marsiglio's *Defence of Peace* was given to them to study, one defiant monk promptly threw it straight into the fire. A renewed offer of royal mercy was made in October if they would submit to the king, surrender their Papalist books and start reading the Bible instead.

Some did accept, and one Nicholas Rawlyns begged Cromwell to release him from the Charterhouse, fearing his health could stand no more – the Carthusian life was known to be exceptionally rigorous. John Copynger, learned Bridgettine Fellow of Christ's College in 1511, was sent from his Syon community to Bishop Stokesley for resisting the Royal Supremacy. He also had a personal interview with Cromwell which must have changed his religious outlook significantly, because he was soon urging the remaining Charterhouse to submit, and thanking Cromwell for the gift of certain books (titles withheld). Copynger was later appointed as Confessor-General.[40]

It is hard to think of a class of men less likely to elicit sympathy from Thomas Cromwell than strict Carthusian monks. Nevertheless, as one of the leading Catholic historians of recent times has already noted, but for Cromwell the fate of some of these monks might have been worse than it was. After the infamous executions Ralph Sadler, Cromwell's assistant, had a meeting with the king, and found Henry displeased that the 'Charterhouse in London is not ordered as I would have had it'. Henry recalled that he had commanded Cromwell 'long ago to put the monks out of the house'. For reasons not too clear, however, Cromwell had delayed carrying out this order. Sadler did his best to help his master out of difficulty by pointing out that Cromwell had managed to get some of the monks 'reconciled', but this achievement left Henry unimpressed. 'Seeing that they had been so long obstinate', the king declared, 'I will not now admit their obedience'.[41]

Eventually government pressure forced many of the remaining Carthusians, some being kept in wretched conditions, to submit. A few who held out were taken to Newgate and left to die. Bedyll told Cromwell that these 'traitorous' monks 'be almost despatched by the hand of God'. Bedyll was not sorry, but he did ask Cromwell to be favourable to the current prior of Charterhouse, 'as honest a man as ever was in that habit'. Why the monks were left to waste away in jail rather than face trial and death at Tyburn is not known. It is hard to believe that Henry took compassion on them, or that he wanted to spare them the customary fate of traitors. Someone may have persuaded him, in view of what had gone before, that public executions for the sake of conscience might be counter productive. It could have been Cromwell's advice, but it is impossible to say for sure.[42]

During the days of their liberty Thomas More, John Fisher and the Carthusians had evinced little sympathy for religious dissidents. More in particular had shown a singular zeal for eradicating heresy by all available means, including the stake. Nobody he examined ever called him 'my special tender friend'. Fate had now made these men the best known examples of tough new laws grimly enforced against the regime's most outspoken opponents. In each case, however, Cromwell can be found making some attempt to avoid a bloody end. The same goes for Cranmer. There can be no reasonable doubt that the decision to exact the ultimate penalty was the king's, and that Henry was not being spurred on by bloodthirsty reformist ministers. It might also be noted that even though the number of people unwilling to conform was potentially quite high, only a few felt the full, concentrated force of Tudor justice. Even at their most repressive, Henry and his councillors can hardly begin to compare with the Dantons or Robespierres of later times, still less the hideous modern monsters of the twentieth century.

6

Vicegerent

A collection of Cromwell's personal notes, possibly made around March 1534, includes measures to proclaim and enforce the Supremacy and the new Succession Act, and later, a separate item, 'to appoint preachers throughout the realm to preach the Gospel and the true Word of God'. It reads as though Cromwell consciously made a nuanced distinction between these two aims.[1]

The previous chapter concentrated on the establishment of the Royal Supremacy by legislation, backed up by booklets, circulars and other propaganda. Apart from a few high profile cases, resistance was generally muted. The formidable new laws sufficed to ensure enough outward conformity to maintain civil peace and good order. But now a new challenge faced Cromwell, namely this: how to win the hearts and minds of the English people for the Reformation. How could he turn a schismatic kingdom into a Protestant kingdom? It was a much more intricate and even dangerous task. By drafting and steering to completion the Appeals and Supremacy bills, Cromwell was acting as the king's obedient though undeniably willing servant; but by spreading the evangelical message throughout the land he would be acting more on his own initiative and taking a considerable risk, because Henry, his sovereign lord and master, was no Protestant. Modern historians talk freely about Henry's 'middle way', but there was no middle ground with Henry on justification by faith, the mass and clerical celibacy. On these fundamental points he was thoroughly medieval. Cromwell would have to win the king round somehow, or at least soften his well-known antagonism to Luther. He would also have to work within the parameters permitted by Henry. Nor was the cause of Reform much helped by the new queen's reformist sympathies, because she remained a highly unpopular figure in the country, while Catherine of Aragon, a very pious Catholic, was still alive and much loved. The Catholic nobility wielded considerable power and influence, while the people remained attached to the medieval religion, more devoted to their images, masses, saints and ceremonies than to the renaissance popes. Weaning king and country away from the medieval faith, and persuading them to accept Luther, would be a greater challenge than tightening up the treason laws or replacing the pope with King Henry as Head of the Church. This and subsequent chapters aim to show how he set about it.

A good start had been made already with the arrival of Melanchthon's *Apology* in England and Christopher Mont's translations of Lutheran works in Cromwell's house (see Chapter 3). The next major phase concerned the monasteries. In January 1535 Cromwell was appointed the king's Vicegerent in spirituals, specifically for the purpose of a national visitation of all religious houses.[2]

Cromwell, according to John Foxe, was the man who persuaded Henry to suppress first the chantries, the friars' houses and the smaller monasteries, then the abbeys and the large monasteries, leaving the 'synagogue of Antichrist ... utterly overthrown and plucked up by the roots'. For all this, Foxe had nothing but fulsome praise for Cromwell. Foxe thanked God for raising up Cromwell, 'His servant', to uproot these 'sinful houses which rebelled against Christ's religion', and it was due to Cromwell that England no longer had 'swarms of friars and monks possessed in their nests'. It is stirring stuff from Foxe at his most entertainingly biased, and Cromwell's reputation as the grim despoiler of the monasteries may date from him. There are, however, reasons to wonder whether Foxe has slightly exaggerated and maybe even misunderstood Cromwell's policy regarding the religious houses. It is likely that Cromwell's mind worked in ways somewhat more subtle than the heavy bulldozer method implied by Foxe.[3]

Henry had been monitoring the monasteries for some years, ever since Wolsey had obtained royal approval to dissolve some of the smaller houses in which, the cardinal had said, 'neither God is served, nor religion kept'. Nearly six years ago, in autumn 1529, Du Bellay and Chapuys both reported that the nobility of England were directing their covetous eyes towards the wealth of the church, and that if Wolsey fell, the lords of the land would try and seize for themselves the clergy's goods. Even then the powerful duke of Suffolk and his supporters at court were advocating dissolution as the answer to the country's financial problems. In December that year, Henry told Chapuys that he had decided on a reform of the clergy; the main reason, says Chapuys, was the king's anger at the pope for insisting that the divorce case should be heard in Rome. Chapuys expected before long to see money from church property flowing in to the king's coffers, and because 'nearly all the people here hate the priests', Henry hoped it might win public support for the divorce. In Convocation that year John Fisher was worried that Henry was already planning some action against the smaller monasteries. Even then Fisher feared that the larger ones might also be in danger.[4]

A year on in November 1530 Henry told Chapuys that it 'would be doing God's service to take away the temporalities of the clergy'. He did not proceed with this threat immediately, but three years later he was once again 'thinking of uniting to the Crown the lands which the clergy of his dominions held'.[5]

Henry, therefore, had had the lands and property of the church in his sights long before Cromwell's time, and the dissolution of the 1530s needs to be seen in this light. Like the schism, the Royal Supremacy and the Boleyn marriage, it was not specifically a Cromwellian measure, or even a Protestant one. It fell to Cromwell to take charge of a policy whose origin pre-dated his rise to power. This time, however, he had the opportunity to turn that policy to direct evangelical advantage.

Cromwell began more gently and discreetly than Foxe implies. When Chapuys reported on the proposed confiscation of church properties, he noted that Norfolk and Suffolk, both nobles of the old faith, had received a generous helping. But 'I am told', added Chapuys, that though Cromwell once supported the suppression of the religious houses, yet 'perceiving great inconveniences likely to arise from that measure, he has since made attempts to thwart it'. For this, Cromwell had angered the king. Chapuys does not name his source but it was not Cromwell personally. This was not a case of Cromwell putting on a show of moderation for the benefit of Chapuys and Charles V in order to improve Anglo-Imperial relations.[6]

A generation later George Wyatt recorded a similar story, presumably based on things he had heard from his parents and grandparents. According to Wyatt, Cromwell addressed the king and council one day, advising a dissolution 'little by little, not suddenly by parliament'. Because this religion is so 'odious to the wiser sort of people', Cromwell had said, 'they may be easily persuaded to leave their cowls and to render their possessions to your majesty'. However, Wyatt continued, the rest of the council opposed Cromwell and pressed the king to proceed by act of parliament, and after this Chancellor Audley and Richard Rich devised two acts for the suppression of smaller monasteries. Elton was inclined to believe Wyatt on the grounds that the act of 1536 was not an especially impressive piece of work, and unlikely to have been Cromwell's.[7]

A word of caution may be advisable before rushing to conclusions about Wyatt's story. Cromwell was a Lutheran diplomat, and every good diplomat knows the art of getting others to do what *he* wants. Cromwell may have been simply pretending to be less eager to act against the monasteries than he really was, tactfully disguising his own Lutheran feelings, and letting popular dissatisfaction with the monasteries, and the laity's greed for monastic lands, do the job for him. However, a clue to his real thoughts, which corroborates Wyatt, may be found in an item from his own personal notes on the 'the abominations of religious persons throughout the realm, and a *reformation* to be devised therein'. My italics here could highlight something significant. Cromwell had in mind a 'reformation', but not, at least not yet, a dissolution or destruction. Rather than close the monasteries down, he would set about reforming them from within.[8]

The first key aspect of Cromwell's policy was the national visitation. The result of this massive undertaking was the *Valor Ecclesiasticus*, a register of all church lands and revenues completed by the end of 1535. Commissioners included bishops and local gentry, most of them in the king's and Cromwell's service. The *Compendium Compertorum*, the commissioners' reports, gave a generally negative view of monastic life. Many historians have assumed that all this was deliberately biased, but bias alone can hardly explain Richard Layton's report to Cromwell after arriving at Langden with a Mr. Bartlett, a servant of Cromwell's. Layton went alone up the abbot's lodging where, 'even like a cony clapper full of starting holes', he spent a long time knocking on the abbot's door. There was no response except for the dog that 'barked and barked'. Eventually Layton forced his way in and found the abbot with 'his whore', who, in panic, 'bestirred her stumps towards her starting holes'. (I think I have this right: the original is 'bestyrrede hir stumpis towards hir startyng hoilles'.) Bartlett, waiting outside, then caught the 'tender damsel', and Layton sent her to Dover to the mayor to 'set her in some cage or prison for eight days'. After finding 'her apparel in the abbot's coffer', Layton brought the 'holy father abbot' to Canterbury. 'To tell you all this comedy, but for the abbot a tragedy, were too long', Layton remarked, and he promised Cromwell that he would tell a lot more next time he saw him. Layton seems to have had a sense of humour, whereas complaints of arrogance reached Cromwell about another of his visitors, Thomas Legh. Not surprisingly, Legh strenuously denied them.[9]

Meanwhile, the visitors were sending their reports to Cromwell. The overall picture was a decidedly unpleasant one. However, the dossiers were not uniformly hostile, and this is what casts doubt on the rather convenient assumption that all this was nothing more than government propaganda designed to bring the religious houses and orders into public disrepute. Layton's indictment of the prior of Shelbrede (sic) is fairly typical: the prior had seven women, each of his monks had four or five, and the prior had also misused funds. But John Tregonwell had visited a number of houses, and, though critical of some, he also reported one abbot, a prioress and her sisters who lived chastely and above suspicion, and another abbot and a prior with a good knowledge of the Scriptures. George Giffard, after visiting several houses in midlands, asked Cromwell if Woolstrope Abbey could be spared dissolution because of the genuine devoutness and hospitality of its monks. Cromwell and his visitors may well have been biased in the sense that they had long since lost their reverence for monasticism, but they were never ungracious enough to ignore or despise examples of sincere, unfeigned piety when they came across them.[10]

The royal injunctions for the monasteries, which the visitors carried with them, are more interesting than the visitors' reports. The first three articles demanded loyalty to Henry and the Succession, and the 'extirpation and taking away of the usurped and pretended jurisdiction of the bishop of Rome … and all manner of obedience' towards him. The next articles forbad monks from going out of the precincts, and banned women from going in, unless they could produce a licence from the king or an authorised visitor. Directions were also laid down for meals. Before they ate, the monks were required to listen to a reading from the Old or New Testament. Meals should be taken in moderation, not from 'oversumptuous and full of delicate and strange dishes …but common meats', and to 'gently entertain strangers and guests'. Surpluses should be distributed to the poor and the sick. Monks should give alms and live humbly. No brother or monk was allowed to 'have any child or boy lying or privily accompanying with him, or other wise haunting unto him, other than to help him to mass'. The abbot should seek university education for 'one or two of his brethren', so that they may 'instruct and teach their brethren and diligently preach the word of God'. Each day one hour had to be devoted to reading the Scripture. All brethren were to 'observe the rule, statutes and laudable customs of this religion *as far as they do agree with the Holy Scripture and the word of God*' – my italics here highlight the obvious implication that not all of 'this religion' *did* agree with Scripture. Furthermore abbots and priors were to instruct their brethren that 'ceremonies or other observances of religion' must be conformable to 'true Christianity, or to observe an order in the church'. In addition, 'true religion is not contained in apparel, manner of going, shaven heads, and other such marks, nor in silence, fasting, uprising in the night, singing and such other kind of ceremonies, but in cleanness of mind, pureness of living, Christ's faith not feigned, and brotherly charity …' – a pretty sweeping dismissal of many monastic values and customs. No one should be 'allured' into the house or order 'with persuasions and blandishments to take religion upon him'. No relics or 'feigned miracles for increase of filthy lucre' were to be displayed. The religious should 'exhort pilgrims and strangers to give that to the poor that they thought to offer to their images or relics'. No 'fairs or markets' would be allowed in monasteries. Prayers should be made for the king and 'his most noble and lawful wife Queen Anne'. Infringements of these injunctions should be reported to the king, his visitor-general or deputy.[11]

These injunctions, which Cromwell as Vicegerent approved and may well have composed, give another clue to his policy regarding the religious. Consider, for example, the first three articles, upholding the Supremacy and denying papal authority. A monastery that denies the spiritual authority of the pope is no longer a monastery at all, at least not in the sense that the word is normally used and understood. The same applies to a house which is not allowed to have any religious relics. We note also the requirements for Scripture readings, and the statements about 'Christ's faith not feigned', and 'brotherly charity' being superior to the monastic habit. Before the birth of the Reformation this might have been fairly harmless, depending on the disposition of a given abbot; but in the religious context and climate of 1535, with Cromwell as Vicegerent, it was nothing less than an open door to Lutheran ideas. Cromwell's meaning when he penned that note for the 'reformation' of the monasteries rather than their disappearance may now be becoming clearer. If monasteries were well run and obedient to Cromwell's injunctions; if the monks denied papal authority, accepted the Royal Supremacy, read the Bible and trusted in faith and charity more than their own ceremonies – if, effectively, they turned themselves into semi-evangelical theological colleges – then for the time being at least they could stay. On the other hand, there was plenty of scope to close down monasteries not this way minded. Then the king and nobility's greed for church lands would also be satisfied. Either way, Cromwell would get what he wanted. The monasteries as learning centres of the medieval faith would go into terminal decline, while those that remained would become sort of evangelical, as well as providing useful service to community.

An integral aspect of this reformation from within was something that, for the sake of convenience, can be called the infiltration policy. Evidence exists of an initiative of Cromwell's to place supporters of the Royal Supremacy and the new learning in the monasteries and abbeys whenever the opportunity arose.

Even before his appointment as Vicegerent, Cromwell had somehow managed to get involved with ecclesiastical nominations. The abbot of St James in Northampton was appointed thanks to Cromwell sometime in 1533. Later he and his house were commended by the commissioners. Cranmer was playing his part as well, in tandem with Cromwell. In May 1533, Cranmer wrote to the abbot of Westminster putting forward one of his own nominees, Sir John Smythe, for a vacancy. About the same time Cranmer and Cromwell were discussing an appointment at St Gregory's in Canterbury. A slight but amicable disagreement had arisen between them about whether the new prior should be an outsider or someone from within. Cranmer preferred the latter, but outcome is not known.[12]

Under the vicegerency, this infiltration stepped up a gear. John Barstabull thanked Cromwell for his preferment as abbot of Sherborne in Nicholas Shaxton's diocese.[13] When the abbot of West Dereham died, Thomas Legh asked Cromwell 'whether it please you to prefer any friend of yours whom ye shall think most meet or convenient', though this time Cromwell accepted Roger Forman, a candidate put forward by Legh.[14] When Commissioner Thomas Parry accepted the resignation of the prior of St Swithin's in Winchester, he mentioned to Cromwell that he had found, among the better religious sort, a certain William Basing, Doctor of Divinity. Besides being an educated man and 'favouring the truth', Basing had 'never consented to any of the abominable spoils and sacrilege and other enormities here committed, but much lamented the same'. Henry's approval was needed for this request, and Basing offered a generous gift of £500 for Cromwell's 'most benevolent and acceptable favour' to obtain it, plus a renewed patent for Cromwell and his son Gregory for life.[15] Basing quickly became prior. He sent profuse thanks to Cromwell, though with apologies that he was unable to pay the full £500 straight away because his predecessor had left him with too many debts to the king and others. Trusting nevertheless that Cromwell would 'continue your goodwill towards me', Basing besought Cromwell 'for the love of God, to be good master to a poor friar, one Cosyn, wrongfully vexed in these parts … whom, I assure you, I never heard preach other than the true Word of God'.[16] This is code for saying that Cosyn was Lutheran. Cromwell was content to wait for his fee, and within a month he issued a certificate licensing Cosyn to preach.[17]

Cromwell may have authorised his visitors to make recommendations and even provisional appointments on his behalf. Sometime in 1535, John Vaughan appointed Dame Joan Skydmore as prioress of Acunbury, subject to Cromwell's approval. Soon after this Layton and Legh reported to Cromwell on the abbot of Fountains, who had allegedly neglected his house and lands, kept whores, stolen property, and confessed that even by the rules of his own order he ought to be deprived. To replace him they recommended a monk called Marmaduke, one of the better religious sort and quite wealthy too, for he 'will give you six hundred marks to make him abbot here', and pay his first fruits within two years. So, they added, 'if ye have not therefore provided or promised such a room for any other of your friends', Marmaduke would be a 'right apt man'. Brother Marmaduke was duly advanced to abbot.[18]

Cromwell's infiltration policy continued to be supported by Cranmer. When Cranmer heard that the Priory of Worcester might soon be vacant, he commended either Dr Holbeach, a monk of Croyland, or Richard Gorton of Burton-on-Trent, both known to him. He asked Cromwell to be good to these two and find suitable places for them; 'for I know no religious men in England of that habit, that be of better learning, judgement, conversation, and all qualities meet for a head and master of a house'. Holbeach later became bishop of Lincoln. On the whole, however, Cranmer's role regarding the monasteries was a surprisingly minor one, and as his biographer has said, the whole story of the dissolution could almost be told without mentioning his name. Cromwell was the man driving things along, and not just as some distant figure behind a desk in London. He frequently undertook evangelising and catechising himself. 'Wherever the king goes', says Chapuys, 'Cromwell, who accompanies him, goes around visiting the abbeys and convents in the neighbourhood, taking inventories of their lands and revenues, amply instructing the people in this new sect'.[19]

The monastery of Winchcombe provides an example of Cromwell's personal evangelising among the religious. Just before his appointment as Vicegerent he received a letter from Hugh Coper, a Winchcombe monk. Coper, whose letter flits between English and Latin, had been reading Daniel 7, from which he concluded, unconventionally for a monk, that the pope was the antichrist. He condemned Rome's 'abominable decretals', and the 'Papistical and monastical' men who have 'more hope and confidence in their laws and pardons … than in the blood of Christ', which alone can cleanse from sin. Coper now believed in justification by faith through grace. His abbot – Coper called him 'our bald bachelor' – was resisting the new learning, and trying with his allies to stop the mouths of 'the pure preachers of the Word of God, like our parish priest, Master Antony'. Coper begged Cromwell to deliver him from 'this prison' (*de isto carcere*). He was, he claims, enticed into the monastic order when not quite fourteen years old by 'fair promises'. Coper's letter then gives a grim, if a little biased, account of monastic life: 'less charity and more malice and envy, less purity and cleanliness of living and more impurity, less quietness and more unquietness, more dissension and strife' than among any other group of men. Some monks in the same house were not even speaking to each other, yet still they 'boast of their goodness'.[20]

Cromwell went to Winchcombe during the summer of 1535.[21] There he had appointed Antony Saunders, presumably Coper's 'Master Antony', as a pastor there to preach to the monks, but Saunders was opposed by the abbot and others of the old faith. Saunders besought Cromwell's help for him and for the schoolmaster in Winchcombe, who 'doth favour the Gospel and doth edify the people', but whose wages had been reduced by the angry abbot. Fortified by Cromwell's visit, Saunders persevered in the evangelical cause against the abbot and an ally of his, a Bachelor of Divinity, 'a great Goliath, a subtle Duns Scotus man'. Saunders was preaching justification by faith alone. Another letter of his to Cromwell includes a confession of faith so impeccably Lutheran that it sounds as though Cromwell may have handed Saunders a copy of Melanchthon's *Apology* during his summer visit.[22] It seems that the abbot and his 'Goliath' were slowly losing ground in their tussles with Saunders, because the abbot later indignantly complained that two of his brethren had eaten flesh during the first week of Advent. One interesting aspect of this case is that whilst Cromwell could and did help his evangelical field activists, he apparently did not have the authority to summarily sack the abbot. Despite being the king's Vicegerent, he still had to work within the system. He could not, even if he had wanted to, pluck it up by the roots and overthrow it.[23]

Cromwell's presence had a striking effect on another Winchcombe monk, John Placet. Placet was now seeking Cromwell's 'discreet and gracious counsel how to order myself' on subjects troubling his conscience. These included 'the authority of the bishop of Rome, St Patrick's purgatory, miracles, dreams, fables, ceremonies, traditions innumerable, hurting and confounding simple souls'. Soon Placet was asking Cromwell's permission to 'take up such books as treat of purgatory'. He had found one 'fair written', which was nothing but 'dry dreams, fancies and fables'. Another had 'torn and tormoylyde [sic] Holy Scripture ... it made the pope equal with the Holy Trinity, and to be of one nature with him in his Deity'. Placet recommended 'my brother Overbury', and asked that he might have permission to teach the Supremacy. He was also upset about 'pyuysche papysche munkyschenes' – a translation of this could be 'peevish, popish monkery'. These medieval mysteries, whatever they were, had been 'exalted to be equal with baptism' by those who 'trust too much by popish pardons, which I know hath diminished the faith ... in the blessed blood of our Saviour'. From personal experience in the monastic life, Placet recalled many souls 'almost in despair by much trust in pardons'.[24]

Placet was now a passionate supporter of the king's Supremacy, quoting Romans 13, a chapter he wished 'to God were written on every monk's bed'. He was, he told Cromwell, 'counted as a wretch' for having composed a short treatise against papal authority. He promised to send his work to Cromwell, for 'you were the very cause that I gave myself to such study, for which I thank God and you'. Placet was not alone in his change of heart. Some of his brethren 'are as glad as I am to set forth the king's power'. Placet recalled how, when Cromwell was among them, 'ye full discreetly and Catholically declared the efficacy of our three vows, in which we trust too much, and I have found your saying true'. Placet was grateful that Cromwell, 'considering my weakness and infirmity, hath excused my rising at midnight', though this dispensation had caused some 'murmur and grudging' among the other monks, who were still required to rise from their beds at all hours to say prayers and sing Psalms. Placet could endure no longer 'the burden and straightness of the religion, as their accustomed abstinence, the frayter and other observances'; so he asked if Cromwell could obtain for him a benefice, though 'without changing my habit'.[25]

Placet's 'brother Overbury' does not sound like a particularly orthodox monk, for he is found addressing Cromwell thus:

> Faithful, trusty and dearly beloved minister unto the high power of Almighty God, of the which you have ministration under our sovereign lord the King, here in earth the only high and supreme head of this his Church of England, grace, peace and mercy be evermore with you: laud and thanks be to God the Father Almighty for the true and unfeigned faith that you have in our Saviour Jesu.

Overbury deplored the many 'perverse men who do dilaniate [sic] the flock of Christ'. He assured Cromwell that he was devoting his time and energies to 'study and exercise of the Holy Gospel'.[26]

Placet, meanwhile, was making good progress in his new faith. He begged Cromwell to permit him to 'instruct the poor people there ... to love God and obey their prince ... and as you have commanded to declare the Holy Gospel meekly sincere and truthfully'. Placet sadly reported that he daily met people who, having sinned against 'unlawful ceremonies' and monastic regulations, sought absolution 'by pardons and by the abbot's power, little considering the blessed blood and passion of our Saviour, and true faith therein only'.[27]

Cromwell's personal commitment was felt beyond Winchcombe. Thomas Redinge (sic), Prior of Kingswoode, thanked Cromwell for speaking the 'divine word' to him in his abbey. Because 'the Word of God, the Gospel of Christ, is not only favoured ... but also set forth, maintained and defended by your honour', Redinge dedicated a book on the Supremacy to Cromwell. He also appealed to Cromwell to 'close up the eye of justice, and open the eye of pity, mercy and compassion' to him and his brethren of Kingswoode, to show 'evangelical charity ... and minister unto us, your daily bedmen'.[28]

Cromwell had now acquired a reputation among the religious. When evangelical monks ran into trouble with their more traditional brethren, they knew where to turn for help. Sometime in 1535 Friar Robert Ward found himself in difficulty with his local vicar and church authorities for saying that satisfactions are 'but a superstition, and that only to believe in Christ is sufficient for our salvation'. Ward appealed to Cromwell, and despite being indicted for heresy, no harm came to him.[29]

Cromwell also had willing informers within the monasteries. Robert Marshall reported his vicar for not proclaiming the Royal Supremacy in church. One zealous monk threatened to report his abbot to Cromwell for failing to read the Injunctions immediately he received them, while the abbot of Kyngeswodd told Cromwell about a friar who allegedly preached contrary to the Word of God.[30]

It is not clear whether all these men were formally in Cromwell's service, or whether voluntary zeal inspired them. They seem evangelical enough, though one who sounds a bit suspect is Andrew Boord, formerly of the Charterhouse. Various letters can be found from him to Cromwell, one recalling the 'great thraldom' he was in until Cromwell 'of your gentleness, set me at liberty and clearness of conscience'. Now realising his former 'ignorance and blindness', he was anxious to serve the king. However, there is nothing explicitly Lutheran in his letters. When the prior of Henton wanted him to return to his monastic ways, Boord excused himself on the grounds that he was 'not able to bide the rigours of your religion'. If Boord was now a man of the new faith, he was unwilling to expressly witness to it, though his excuse may have been an honest one given the austere monastic life of the Charterhouse. Another uncertain case occurred when Thomas Legh went to a priory in the diocese of Norwich. Legh found the monks begging to be 'dismissed from their religion, saying they live contrary to God's laws and their conscience'. As with Boord, it is not certain whether this was a genuine spiritual conversion or not, because Legh gave no reason why the monks were so anxious to escape the cloisters.[31]

Nevertheless, these are all examples of religious men who were, with varying degrees of sincerity and conviction, evangelical or evangelically minded. Many could be called Cromwell's men; they were appointed either by him or on his recommendation to the king, and placed in a monastery with the deliberate aim of introducing the new learning there. Even those who may not have known him personally neverthe-less recognised him as the national evangelical leader. For his part, reformation rather than dissolution is likely to have been Cromwell's policy during these years, and so far as I can see, there is no compelling evidence that he envisaged a complete dissolution at this stage (1535–36). There would be little point in Cromwell trying to evangelize the monasteries if he was about to shut them all down.

There were also practical and political reasons for this more moderate approach. Although the wealth of a full national dissolution would fill Henry's coffers, it could all too easily be squandered on the sort of dubious foreign ventures that Cromwell had opposed ever since his maiden speech in parlia-ment (see Chapter 1). Further, the men most eagerly looking forward to acquiring church lands, and the accompanying prestige and influence, were the leading magnates like the dukes of Norfolk and Suffolk; but Cromwell's policy was always to strengthen the crown, not the nobility. Whereas a national sell-off would enrich these avaricious dukes, lords and earls, a reformation would bring all the religious houses, lands and wealth under the control of the king. Henry would then receive not a once in a lifetime windfall that could easily be misspent, but a regular, dependable annual source of income from the First Fruits and Tenths and other taxes. Moreover, Cromwell's responsibilities now included commerce and economics; and it would have been far better for the Tudor economy if the nobility, gentry and merchants could be induced to invest their capital productively in trade and public works, rather than the comfy, virtually risk-free purchase of church lands.

Because Cromwell left no personal memoirs or an autobiography, it is impossible to be certain whether these really were his own thoughts. However, in one of Chapuys's reports he says that whereas Henry had been 'thinking of getting into his hands all ecclesiastical property and proceeds thereof', he had recently had a slight change of heart. For the time being, Henry was content to let the clergy keep their property, provided they insured him an annual income of £30,000 sterling, plus the value of the First Fruits. Chapuys does not say so, but Cromwell may have been behind this.[32]

Cromwell's policy for the monasteries reveals much about the character of the man. Many reformist ministers might have seen the monasteries as a major obstacle to the cause of reform that had to be removed, but Cromwell saw openings and opportunities there. He had quickly absorbed the lessons of recent church history. In Germany a monk had started the Reformation, and in England Robert Barnes, now one of Cromwell's closest allies, had formerly been an Augustinian friar. So Cromwell decided he could turn the religious to his advantage. By reformation and infiltration, underpinned by a vigorous personal involvement, he would make them, or some of them, agents for the Gospel rather than barricades against it. We will see him taking similarly inventive initiatives later in his career.

Meanwhile, though not strictly part of Cromwell's terms as Vicegerent, he was also busy securing significant evangelical advances in the bishoprics as well as in the religious houses.

Elizabethan historians like Foxe are unsure whether to thank Cromwell or Queen Anne for this development. On Latimer's appointment as bishop of Worcester, Foxe credits Anne in one part of his history and Cromwell in another. The editor of the Parker Society opts for Cromwell, and contemporary evidence is overwhelmingly on his side.[33]

The testimony of the men themselves should decide the matter. We can begin with Latimer. In autumn 1535, when certain little problems arose regarding his appointment, Latimer wrote to Cromwell for help. The details are a bit complicated and not really important, but Latimer was concerned that 'for lack of royal assent with *your* signification, my lord of Canterbury cannot proceed' (emphasis mine). On the matter of the First Fruits, Latimer had intended to write to Henry on a certain sticking point; again the exact details are not clear, but Anne had told him he 'should not need to move the king, but that it should be enough to inform your mastership thereof'. Obviously Cromwell was the one to sort out the administration of bishoprics and any problems that arose. Latimer would later thank Cromwell that 'your lordship hath promoted many more honest men, since God promoted you, than hath many men done before your time, though in like authority with you'. His letter ends: 'Blessed be the God of England that worketh all, whose instrument you be.'[34]

Other rising evangelical stars tell the same story. Even though Anne helped him pay his First Fruits, Nicholas Shaxton pointedly thanked Cromwell for many kindnesses received, especially mentioning his bishopric.[35] Rowland Lee (Coventry and Lichfield) and John Salcot (Bangor) were two more of Cromwell's men on the bench. Thomas Goodrich (Ely), consecrated by Cranmer around the same time, may have been another. Lee was catapulted into the bishopric without ever having been in the pulpit.[36] The evangelical Archbishop of Dublin, George Browne, also acknowledged his appointment 'through your good lordship's [Cromwell's] preferment'.[37]

William Barlow makes an interesting case. Barlow admitted that Anne 'avouched me unworthy the priorship of

Haverfordwest', a position 'under her grace's foundation'. Anne may have enjoyed certain privileges in Haverfordwest because it lay in south Pembrokeshire, where she was created marchioness in September 1532. However, when Barlow encountered opposition to his evangelical preaching there, it was to Cromwell that he wrote for help. When Henry Standish, bishop of Asaph in Wales, died in July 1535, Barlow replaced him. Needing a licence to preach for a supporter of his, one Robert Ferrar, again Barlow approached Cromwell, not Anne. Barlow was transferred to the more prestigious see of St David's in April 1536, and by this time Anne was out of favour with Henry, so she would have had nothing to do with this move. Barlow later thanked Cromwell for his 'manifold benefits', and it is likely that one of these benefits was his bishopric.[38]

Even Archbishop Cranmer seemed unable to make clerical appointments without first consulting Cromwell. When Cranmer was trying to obtain a benefice in Northamptonshire for a friend of his called Bennett, he asked for Cromwell's 'good mind and favour in this and in all other my suits unto you hereafter'. Cromwell did not answer immediately, so Cranmer had to send polite reminders. Apparently the option of appealing over Cromwell's head to the queen was not available, and it is not clear whether Cromwell agreed to this request.[39]

Cranmer had also recommended Nicholas Heath to Cromwell for his piety and learning, regretting that he 'hath also no benefice, nor no promotion', even though in the king's matter 'I know no man in England can defend it better than he'. Heath, evangelical in the 1530s, advanced quickly, and became part of Henry's embassy to Lutheran Germany in late 1535 which Cromwell organized, as we will see. Cranmer also asked Cromwell if John Hilsey, 'or some other worshipful man', may be made prior of the black friars in Cambridge. Whether he got this post is not certain, but Hilsey was another who rose rapidly and soon obtained a better reward – he was made bishop of Rochester after the death of John Fisher.[40]

Queen Anne once wrote to the bishop of Norwich asking him to admit her chaplain, Matthew Parker, to the deanery of the collegiate church at Stoke, now vacant due to the death of the previous occupant; but whether she was acting entirely on her own authority is less than certain. To her chagrin perhaps, even she had to refer such matters to Cromwell. She took up the case of Richard Herman, a merchant and citizen of Antwerp expelled from England under Wolsey for helping 'the setting forth of the New Testament in English'. She asked Cromwell if this 'good and honest' man could be returned to his freedom. Herman later became an agent of Cromwell's.[41] Another request of hers concerned one Robert Power. Cromwell had granted a nomination for a friend of Power, and because a vacancy now existed at an abbey in Lincolnshire, Anne wrote to Cromwell. 'We desire and heartily pray you', she says, that the grant may 'be fulfilled to help his said friend to the preferment of the said house ... for which we shall hereafter have you in our remembrance with condign thanks'. Her letter is headed 'Anne the Queen', while the royal 'we' and 'our' ring out with a flourish; but there is no 'we command you', or 'we require you', or 'it is our pleasure' that you do a given thing. Anne the Queen she may have been, but she still had to ask Cromwell, not give him orders.[42]

Though Foxe's account of Anne has been shown to be based on the testimony of those who knew her, it has to be wondered whether, during the reign of her most illustrious daughter, Anne's influence was being slightly overstated. Evangelicals living in the 1530s, though naturally delighted to have a queen who appeared to favour their cause at least to some degree, had no doubt who the real powerhouse of the English Protestant movement was. Cromwell had framed much of Supremacy legislation, he was the king's Vicegerent in spirituals to reform the monasteries, and he was the architect of the Lutheran policy to be discussed later. More power now belonged to him than to anyone in the realm save only the king. It is sometimes suggested that Anne did not always approve of Cromwell's church policy or his clerical appointments: but if so, her disapproval had little noticeable effect, which only underscores the point that he was the one driving the Reformation forward more than anyone else, including the queen and the archbishop.[43]

Apart from the monasteries and the evangelical promotions, the main religious development of 1535 was the growing warmth in Anglo-Lutheran relations. It was another Cromwellian-inspired initiative, though, as with the bishoprics, technically it had nothing to do with his appointment as Vicegerent.[44]

Henry had no natural love for the Lutherans. But for Cromwell he may never have showed much interest in them. Not only had Luther ridiculed Henry's *Assertion of the Seven Sacraments* and called its author a fool and an idiot, he then added insult to injury by supporting Catherine in the King's Great Matter. Nevertheless, rapprochement with the Saxons offered England diplomatic as well as spiritual advantages. The new pope, Paul III, had shown some interest in the idea of a General Council to settle Europe's religious controversies. Henry and the German Lutherans were suspicious of the pope's intentions, each expecting that any such council would condemn them unilaterally for schism and heresy. This mutual fear provided some common ground between them. Henry also, in Cromwell's presence, had suggested to the French ambassador that Francis in France should do as Henry had done in England and declare himself Head of the Church. Francis declined, but Charles was now aware of, and becoming concerned by, the possibility of an alliance developing between Francis, England and the Lutheran Schmalkaldic League. Despite scruples within the ranks of his own clergy, King Francis, after listening to his evangelically minded sister, Marguerite de Navarre, had invited Philip Melanchthon to France with a promise of safe conduct. Melanchthon was willing to go and Luther supported the idea; but Elector John Frederick, suspecting that the wily French king was more interested in sowing discord between the Lutheran princes and Charles V, refused permission. Melanchthon was deeply disappointed. Diplomatically he wrote to Francis saying that he had wanted to go but circumstances did not allow it.[45]

Henry and Cromwell then sought to capitalize on Francis's failure. In July 1535 the king authorised Robert Barnes and Christopher Mont to go to Germany to renew efforts to bring Melanchthon to England. Barnes reached Wittenberg in September, and next month he was joined by Nicholas Heath and Bishop Edward Foxe of Hereford. The three of them now comprised a formal delegation, sent with Henry's full approval, to discuss the possibility of a political and religious treaty with the Lutherans. This German embassy, organized by Cromwell, is an interesting illustration of the English government's response under diplomatic and moral fire from Rome and elsewhere. The papal censure and condemnations from abroad following the executions of More, Fisher and the Carthusians were still ringing in Henry's ears. At home Chapuys reported that Henry and Cromwell were concerned about the risk of unrest in England, especially after the poor harvest that summer. Chapuys was 'daily assailed on every side' by people – he names no-one – 'soliciting the execution of the apostolic censures'. Many were convinced that 'such a resolution of Your Majesty's [Charles's] part would be a sufficient remedy, considering the great discontent prevailing among all classes of society at this king's disorderly life and government'. But nothing much was done to placate such hostility and fend off the danger. The breaks were not applied to the monastic reforms at home, and no hints were offered that some of the Supremacy legislation might be softened to appease the imperialists and the Papists. Apparently deciding that attack was the best means of defence, Henry and Cromwell pressed ahead with the Lutheran policy. It was a move both bold and astute. It would remove England even further from the Roman church, but at the same time improve England's security through membership of the Schmalkaldic League.[46]

An example of Cromwell's growing confidence was the increasing amount of Lutheran literature now appearing in England with his sanction and support. Even though Luther's works were still officially banned, a primer of Cromwell's protégée, William Marshall, was published in 1535. It drew amply on Luther's writings, particularly in attacking the cult of the saints and purgatory. Another treatise of Marshall's that appeared around the same time, this one based on a work of Martin Bucer, contained a sharp critique of prominent religious images. Bolder still was Marshall's evangelical treatment of the mass, which opposed the medieval moral doctrine – still in practice in schismatic England – of the propitiatory sacrifice availing for the living and the departed. This was too much even for reformist men like Audley, who advised Cromwell to find something less controversial for Marshall to do. Cromwell did not listen, however, and a second edition appeared the following year. Marshall also translated, with only minor amendments, Luther's work of 1522 against the papacy and bishops. Luther's anti-clerical writings might have been safe enough in Henry's England, but the same work also attacked clerical celibacy and vows while defending justification by faith alone, ideas that were still risky in England in the mid-1530s.[47]

However, events were working in Cromwell's favour. In Germany Melanchthon was unsure whether he would be allowed to come to England, but having heard from Barnes and others about the evangelical progress here, he decided to dedicate his new *Loci Communes* to Henry. The work was sent to Cromwell, who presented it personally to the king. Henry was delighted, and sent Melanchthon a gift of 200 crowns and a personal letter signed 'Your friend, King Henry VIII'. Henry did not agree with everything in the *Loci*, but it made a most favourable impression overall, especially as Melanchthon had been nuancing two aspects of early Lutheranism that Henry had profoundly disliked.[48]

The first of these concerned salvation, or 'justification' as theologians frequently called it. During his spiritual crisis that led to the birth of the Reformation in 1518–19, Luther was an almost embarrassingly pious monk. With his fasts, prayers, masses, vigils and confessions, he far surpassed most of his brethren in zeal. Nevertheless, a close study of Scripture, and especially St Paul, convinced him that all this monastic piety was useless for the soul's salvation. Slowly and painfully he became persuaded that by virtue of Christ's atoning death on the Cross for the sins of the world, justification was a free and entirely gracious gift of God, which could never be earned by any human act or effort. Man's salvation, therefore, depended on receiving this gift by faith rather than earning it by works or sacrifices. Thus Luther raised the Reformation banner of justification by faith alone (*sola fides*). Luther did not mean to disparage genuine good works such as loving thy neighbour, gifts to the poor, prayers and so on; but these were *fruits* of a true faith, and they played no part whatever in justification. Some of his opponents, however, accused him of making good works and charity redundant, thereby threatening a complete breakdown in civil order and peace. Henry had enthusiastically joined these accusers; and in his *Assertion of the Seven Sacraments*, written more than ten years beforehand, he charged Luther with making faith a 'cloak for a life of sin'. Luther was furious, hence his vitriolic reply, but such accusations spread like a fire impossible to put out.[49]

Melanchthon joined Luther in trying to combat the charges and clarify the Lutheran teaching. His new *Loci* defended *sola fides*, but it also contained the statement that good works were 'necessary for salvation'. He meant a necessary consequence, not a necessary cause. Resting his case on St Paul (Romans 8:12; I Corinthians 9:16; Ephesians 2:10), Melanchthon stressed that baptised believers were called to live according to the will of God, and were indebted to do so. He was not, as some within his own church strangely suspected, slipping back into medieval ways. He fully supported Luther on justification as a divine gift impossible to earn or to merit, and he defended it at some length in the *Loci*. Melanchthon was also anxious to counter the so-called 'antinomian' tendency that had sprouted up in parts of Germany, which dismissed charity and good works as all rather meaningless if justification is awarded solely through faith. Henry's reaction to the *Loci* proves that the king was pleasantly surprised at what he read there, and much of his former antipathy towards Lutheranism dissolved away. Unfortunately, he did not quite grasp the fine distinction between a necessary consequence and a necessary cause. This point, and the repercussions of it, will become clearer in subsequent chapters.

Another aspect of Lutheranism that had shocked Henry in the 1520s concerned the subject of freewill. The early Luther had broadly followed the predestinarian teaching of St Augustine – the doctrine of the salvation of the 'elect', divinely foreknown before the world began. This implied, without expressly saying so, that salvation was a gift predetermined only for a section of the human race, not freely offered to all of it. It also left little or no room for freewill in Lutheran theology, at least so far as salvation was concerned. Luther's opponents, including Henry, seized gleefully on this, accusing Luther of denying all human responsibility and thereby making God accountable for everything that happened, the evil as well as the good. Naturally they never levelled this charge at Augustine, but this inconsistency soon became a bit academic when Melanchthon, patiently but firmly, sought to entice Luther and the Lutheran church away from predestination. In his writings from the 1520s, and especially in his new *Loci*, he contended eloquently for its antithesis, known technically as the doctrine of universal grace – the belief that God desires the salvation of all mankind, and that there is no secret decree arbitrarily nominating some to blessing while consigning others to perdition. Melanchthon gave this, and the related subject of freewill, a great deal of space in his *Loci*: God's grace is for all, and God's Spirit seeks to draw the hearts of all men to Christ; empowered by this divine influence, the human will is able to believe the Gospel and be converted; man may reject Christ and carry out all kinds of evil, but if so the responsibility is his, not God's.

The timeliness and significance of the *Loci* in the English Reformation can hardly be over-stressed. Though Melanchthon wrote it for the widest possible European audience, in these two important theological subjects it could almost have been calculated to assuage the hostility to Luther that Henry had shown in his *Assertion*. It was not enough to induce Henry to unconditionally accept the *Augsburg Confession*, but it did make a huge improvement in Anglo-Lutheran relations. Having broken England's ties with Rome, Henry needed religious as well as political allies, and suddenly he was able to see the Lutherans in a far more favourable light. The king who had once called Luther a 'serpent' and a 'hellish wolf' – and had been called worse still in return – was now minded to parley with the Germans, even to consider a formal alliance with them. We must, however, emphasise the word 'consider'. Henry was not yet ready to commit himself. Nor was he a man to be rushed or stampeded into alliances against his will. Cromwell and his allies still had much work to do to persuade Henry to become a Lutheran.

Nevertheless, Cromwell lost no time in exploiting the much improved situation. As well as the monasteries, he was now reforming the major universities on evangelical lines. He sent Richard Layton to Oxford, from where Layton reported that daily lectures in divinity, philosophy and Latin were now 'well kept and diligently frequented'. But Cromwell in England, like Luther and Melanchthon in Germany, was determined that the language of the New Testament should be more widely taught and known, so Layton directed all Oxford's colleges to establish lectures in Greek as well as Latin. Layton triumphantly added that the medieval scholastic theologians had been given the boot – 'we have set Dunce (Duns Scotus) in Bocardo, and have utterly banished him from Oxford for ever, with all his blind glosses'.[50]

A similar reformation was underway in Cambridge, quickly becoming an evangelical seat of learning. Cromwell was now the Chancellor of Cambridge University, and he issued a set of injunctions to be followed. These included daily public lectures in Latin and Greek, and in the Old and the New Testament; additionally, students were to read the Bible in private. From now on there would be no lectures on, and no degree course in, canon law. As at Oxford, the medieval theologians were sent packing. As at Wittenberg University, this evangelical curriculum would be complimented by the finest of the humanities, with courses in logic, rhetoric, arithmetic, geography and music. Compulsory reading included the works of Aristotle, Rudolph Agricola and also Melanchthon. Officially the injunctions specified only Melanchthon's humanist writings, though the likelihood must be that his *Apology* and *Loci* were discreetly admitted as well. The university was delighted to receive Cromwell's injunctions, or so they told his visitor, Thomas Legh.[51]

Soon after this Legh issued a subsequent set of injunctions confirming those of Cromwell, though with a few interesting additions. One added Hebrew to the curriculum, while another forbad masters and fellows from selling fellowships or accepting bribes to receive scholars. A third instructed all heads of houses, scholars and students to attend a mass each month 'for the souls of the founders of the university ... and for the happy state of the king and the lady Anne, his lawful wife and Queen'. Cromwell would have approved the first two and he may have ordered them, but whether he gave the directive for the mass is less certain. Maybe Legh was acting on his own initiative and authority as Cromwell's authorised visitor.[52]

Cromwell's university reforms were well received, at least in official replies. The fellows of Magdalene College at Oxford sent him thanks for royal directives, for the reformation of learning, and in particular the requirement for tuition in Greek. Cambridge students thanked him for having done more good for the advancement of learning than any previous chancellor. However, Legh counselled Cromwell to keep a watchful eye on Cambridge and make sure that his injunctions were obeyed, because a number of tutors there still favoured the scholastics.[53]

The year 1535 had been a most gratifying one for Cromwell. It saw reforms to the monasteries and the universities, and a marked improvement in Anglo-Lutheran relations. Hopes were high that Melanchthon might come to England. Foxe, Heath and Barnes were in Germany as guests of Luther and Melanchthon, and in December Foxe addressed a conference of the Schmalkaldic League. Melanchthon was being read not only at Oxford and Cambridge, but also in the monasteries where religious evangelicals, backed by Cromwell, had gained an entrance. The Protestant Reformation of England was now underway in earnest, directed and energised by the most powerful man in the country apart from the king.

PART II

Cromwell and the Royal Ladies

7

Her Special Friend

Catherine of Aragon, Henry's wife for nearly twenty-five years, was now officially and humiliatingly downgraded to the status of princess dowager. Anne Boleyn reigned as queen in her place, although when Chapuys habitually called Anne the 'concubine' or 'mistress', he was echoing the secret sentiments of more than a few English hearts. The feelings of the two royal ladies for each other can be left to the imagination and need no discussion here. This chapter will examine the strong but contrasting views each of them entertained about Thomas Cromwell. One called him 'my special friend', while the other wished she could see his head struck off. The sweet words fell from Catherine's lips, the shrill ones from Anne's (and this is not a misprint).

Divided though Catherine and Cromwell were spiritually and politically, Cromwell struggled to disguise a strong personal admiration for the Spanish queen during her sorrowful last years. With Anne it was all so different; his relations with the Boleyns were never noticeably close. A number of reasons would easily account for this. He came from the service of Wolsey, a man Anne had cordially detested. Worse, he had remained loyal to Wolsey after Anne and her party had finally managed to get rid of him. Cromwell was also Lutheran, while her religious outlook was shaped by reading the French Christian humanists. This difference in religion might not have mattered too much, as they could both have formed part of a broad evangelical front; but Cromwell's Lutheranism was a provocation to Anne because the Germans were still supporting Catherine in the divorce controversy. Cromwell's policy of engagement with the Lutherans had to be conducted in spite of Anne, not because of her. The Elector of Saxony, the most powerful of the Lutheran princes, was at first unwilling to consider establishing diplomatic relations with Henry for fear of needlessly antagonizing Charles V. With some difficulty Cromwell had to persuade the politically cautious Elector that England might be fertile ground for the Gospel. Anne was further incensed by Cromwell's increasingly good working relationship with Ambassador Chapuys. Anne hated Chapuys, and the feeling was mutual.[1]

Between Cromwell and Anne, any real evidence of the warmth that undoubtedly existed between Anne and Archbishop Cranmer is elusive. Capello, the Venetian ambassador, called Cranmer Anne's 'tutor'. Cranmer was grief-stricken when Anne perished on the scaffold, but Cromwell carried on as if nothing much had happened, and he quickly took the Reformation to new levels. An undated letter from Anne to Cromwell on a minor matter is signed 'Your loving mistress, Anne the Queen'; but this may be no more than a customary Tudor civility.[2]

Contrary to many popular accounts of the Tudors, Anne was never Cromwell's patroness. Cromwell was Henry's appointment, not Anne's. It was not Anne's recommendation, but Cromwell's abilities, his capacity for hard work, his successful implementation of parliamentary legislation, and not least his ability to induce parliament to part with money and fill up the royal coffers that impressed Henry to advance him. Neither in his political rise, nor in his evangelical conversion, was Cromwell one tiny iota beholden to the queen. From the day he set out to court to 'make or mar', Thomas Cromwell was the *king's* servant, indebted to Henry and to nobody else. Should Henry's love for Anne ever fade, Cromwell was duty bound to serve and support the king.

The next chapters will trace Cromwell's surprising relationships with the two queens. The story begins around the time of Catherine's 'trial' at Dunstable in spring 1533. Cromwell seems to have deliberately avoided taking any overtly hostile stance against her. The luckless duke of Suffolk was the man sent by Henry to Catherine to demand that she should renounce her queenly title and move from Buckden to Somersham. Both demands met with a swift rejection. On one of these visits, Catherine locked herself in her room and dared the visitors to break the door down. Chapuys absolved Suffolk for this hounding of Catherine – he was only obeying orders, and doing so reluctantly. Chapuys put all the blame on the 'iniquity and detestable wickedness' of Anne, now plotting the ruin of Catherine and also Princess Mary who was now also officially downgraded, being known merely as 'Lady Mary'.[3]

Chapuys was also discussing Anglo-Imperial relations with Cromwell. Again and again he stressed the harm this second marriage was doing. Cromwell listened patiently; he replied that Henry was acting out of his 'love and affection for Lady Anne', and that 'if his conscience was at rest, nobody had a right to interfere'. Without wanting to read more than is warranted into these words, there does seem to be a curious absence of any deep, religious conviction in Cromwell's attitude to the Great Matter. Cromwell did not take the normal line that Henry was under some kind of moral duty to put Catherine away because their marriage contradicted the Levitical law. His position was more pragmatic than dogmatic. Henry was in love with Anne, Henry was the king and his conscience was at peace; he was acting on the advice of numerous theologians and divines in England and abroad. Besides all this, Cromwell was Henry's servant not his master, with no right to gainsay the king.[4]

Cromwell was also moved by Catherine's performance at her trial. 'I am told', Chapuys wrote to the emperor, that Cromwell had said that 'no human creature' could have given 'a more wise or courageous answer' than the one Catherine gave to her examiners. Cromwell added that 'God and nature had done great injury to the said Queen in not making her a man, for she might have surpassed in glory and fame almost all the princes whose heroic deeds are recorded in history'. Cromwell followed this up with 'many other things in praise of the queen'. An unnamed confidant at court had supplied this information to Chapuys.[5]

The case went against Catherine, but Anne's joy at seizing her crown did not last long. As early as 3 September, four days before the birth of Elizabeth, Chapuys reported signs of tension between Henry and Anne. When something she said had riled Henry, he told her roughly she should 'shut her eyes and endure, as those better than herself had done, and she ought to know that he could at any time lower her as he had raised her'. Chapuys hoped that this was more than just a lover's tiff, because 'those who know the king's nature and temper' see this as a 'good omen and a sign that the king will soon begin to think of recalling the queen'. At this advanced stage of Anne's pregnancy Henry was an anxious man, trusting in the predictions of 'his physicians and astrologers' that Anne would indeed bear him a son. Seven days later, and with scarcely concealed pleasure, Chapuys reported the birth of a girl, 'to the great disappointment and sorrow of the king, the lady herself and others of her party, and to the great shame and confusion of physicians, astrologers, wizards and witches (*sorciers et sorcieres*), all of whom affirmed it would be a boy'; but the people rejoiced at their discomfort.[6]

Henry's employment of astrologers is not as strange as it may sound. Many Renaissance humanists were interested in astrology, and many courts had a resident astrologer. It was seen not as black magic but as a real science, a study of the heavens and their influence, if any, on events on earth. However, the reference to 'wizards and witches' – apparently intended as a separate group from the more respectable 'physicians and astrologers' – is puzzling. Unfortunately Chapuys does not elaborate; but his words can only mean that Henry, desperate for a son, had been seeking advice and help from all kinds of sources, disturbingly reminiscent of King Saul and the woman of Endor (1 Samuel 28).

Chapuys tried to capitalize on the king's disappointment. He tried a bit of flattery on Cromwell, hoping he might use his influence with Henry to persuade the king to restore Catherine. Again Cromwell avoided the subject of the validity or otherwise of the Aragon marriage; he simply replied that Chapuys was asking for the impossible, because Henry's 'love is far too passionate and strong'. Chapuys sounded out Norfolk as well, only to receive the same answer. Nevertheless, the miscellaneous memoirs of the French diplomat, du Bellay, include a story that Henry did have a plan should relations with King Francis worsen significantly: Henry could, if only as a last resort, make peace with Charles by taking Catherine back and keeping Anne as the royal mistress, and that Anne lived in a near-constant fear that some settlement might yet be made to her loss.[7]

However, Henry's attitude later that year supports the view of Cromwell and Norfolk that the king was still in love with Anne. Now very angry with Mary for refusing to formally accept his divorce, he decided to take away her servants and staff, and make her live as '*demoiselle d'honneur*' to Elizabeth. Catherine and Mary, naturally aggrieved, asked Chapuys to speak to Cromwell 'and see what can be done to arrest the blow'. Chapuys did so. He warned Cromwell that Charles may be forced to act if such flagrant injustices were not stopped immediately. Cromwell tried to diffuse the situation. He assured Chapuys that he was working hard to restore good relations between Henry and Charles; and that he was doing, and would continue to do, all he could for Catherine and Mary.[8]

The immediate outcome of this encounter is not known, but subsequent letters from Chapuys suggest that he was encouraged. Cromwell was now showing 'great affection' for the emperor's subjects in England and trading with England, and he promised to do 'all he could in the queen's favour, so that no injury should be done to her'. Cromwell recalled that during his examination of the Maid of Kent he had thoroughly satisfied himself that Catherine had no dealings with her; and for this Cromwell praised Catherine highly, saying that 'God had directed the sense and wit of the queen' for refusing to meet and pay any heed to the Maid.[9]

To some degree, Cromwell succeeded in calming troubled waters. Chapuys kept a watchful eye on Catherine and Mary. He also monitored Cromwell's movements to make sure that Cromwell was as good as his word. Occasionally he suspected that Cromwell might have been fobbing him off, but for the most part he seemed satisfied with Cromwell's good intentions. However, there was little Cromwell could have done in the face of Henry's wrath against his ex-wife and daughter. What is really striking from these letters is that when Catherine and Mary felt desperately in need of help, they both saw Cromwell as the only one on the council able and willing to provide it.[10]

Catherine's humiliation during this distressing time was cruelly aggravated by only lukewarm support from Rome. The French were convinced that the pope, but for fear of the emperor, would by now have recognized Henry's new marriage. In near despair Catherine wondered whose fault was the greater, Henry's or the papacy's, which 'applies no remedy to the evil the devil is doing' in England. At home men of the old faith, who might have been expected to show some sympathy, were acting as heartlessly as Anne's party. Chapuys was particularly disappointed with Norfolk over his aggressive behaviour towards Mary; he had taken away her ornaments, saying that she was no princess, and that her pride had to be humbled.[11]

Cromwell, meanwhile, kept up expressions of goodwill. During the spring of 1534 he was concerned to hear rumours that Charles might be preparing for war against England, so he probed Chapuys for news. Again Cromwell assured the ambassador of his personal desire to see relations between Henry and Charles improved. This time Chapuys gave little away. He was too worried about the safety of Mary. On Henry's orders she was now confined, allegedly to appease Anne. Chapuys feared that Mary's execution might be imminent; he had heard Henry speak threateningly of it. Chapuys was convinced that 'some treachery' would befall Mary unless Charles took 'some preventative measure very soon'. He urged the emperor, the time was ripe for 'an undertaking', and the people deeply resented the cruel treatment of Catherine and Mary. Chapuys suggested trade sanctions against England. Maybe 'some commotion might be created' in Ireland if the pope sent an emissary there and publicly censured Henry, because 'all Irish ... are subjects of the Holy Apostolic See'.[12]

In May Henry sent yet another delegation to Catherine to compel her to submit. Harsh and threatening words were used, including thinly veiled threats of the axe. Chapuys protested again, this time directly to the king. 'Nobody doubts here', he told Charles, 'that one of these days some treacherous act will befall the Queen', for Anne 'will never rest until he [Henry] has put her out of the way'. Chapuys had long since suspected that dangerous mischief was afoot. He recalled Northumberland, Anne's former fiancée, saying that he knew 'for certain' that Anne was thinking of poisoning Mary. Chapuys was convinced of the truth of this because of Northumberland's 'intimacy and credit' with Anne. Chapuys was also trying his best to persuade the Scots not to make any treaty with Henry until Mary's succession was secured.[13]

Despite the danger to her and her daughter, Catherine refused to submit. To the consternation of Henry and the council, she insisted on oath that her marriage to Prince Arthur was never consummated, thus emphatically contradicting the government's line. Yet it is against this unlikely background that one of the strangest letters of the English Reformation is to be found. It is from Catherine, dated probably 1 September, to an unnamed recipient, but calendared in the *Letters and Papers* as having been sent to Cromwell. My 'special friend' (*especial amigo*), it began. 'You have greatly bound me with the pains you have taken' in speaking to the king, 'on my behalf', regarding Mary. 'The reward you shall trust to have of God. For as you know, in me there is no power to gratify what you have done, but only with my good will'. What had happened is clear from the contents of the letter. Cromwell had interceded with Henry, who had made a partial concession by agreeing to let Mary be nearer Catherine, though not actually by her side. Catherine was grateful for small mercies, but she longed to see her daughter again. She appealed to Cromwell, for the sake of a mother's love, to 'do what you may, that this may be yet done'. Having heard that Henry was suspicious of her motives, she assured Cromwell that 'I am determined to die (without doubt) in this realm'. She begged Cromwell to continue to help her as a 'trusty friend, to whom I pray God give health'.[14]

Despite the anonymity, there are sound reasons to see why the editor of the *Letters and Papers* believed that Cromwell was the receiver. It fits the evidence seen already, and more of the same is still to come, that he had become her unexpected helper. The missing addressee's name has a fairly obvious explanation in the circumstances: she wanted to express her thanks and ask for more, but not get him into trouble in case the letter fell into the wrong hands. Moreover, the letter is written in her native Spanish, a language Cromwell knew. How many others in Henry's government knew Spanish is impossible to say; probably not many. Chapuys, a possible alternative recipient, normally wrote and spoke in French or Latin, and Catherine could have written to him in either of these. But in that case, there would be no need for the secrecy. There is also evidence from Dr Butts, Henry's physician, that Cromwell had approached Henry about Mary; Cromwell first persuaded Henry to let Butts attend on Mary, then Butts and Cromwell between them managed to arrange for Catherine's own physician to see Mary.[15]

Cromwell had timed his intercession well, for it was also in September that Henry's roving eye had alighted on an attractive young woman. Chapuys, who reported this development, does not name the lady, but the name of Jane Seymour does not appear in letters and documents just yet. When Anne furiously tried to drive this rival from the court, Henry gruffly reminded her that she should be grateful for what he had done for her, adding ominously that 'were he to commence again, he would certainly not do as much'. Chapuys was trying hard to suppress his hopes that Anne's hour had come. He knew both Henry's changeable nature and Anne's cleverness – for she 'knows well how to handle him' (*que le sçat (or sait) bien manier*). French diplomats also noted that Henry's ardour for Anne had cooled, and that he now had 'other loves' (*des nouvelles amours*). But again, no names were mentioned in despatches. Ambassador D'Interville, however, gave a grim report of a country now gripped by fear of war and a trade embargo, with the nation's hostility to Anne as universal as its love for Catherine and Mary. Abroad a dangerous alliance threatened. Charles was now thinking of making overtures to his great rival, King Francis of France, and forging a Franco-Imperial front against England. One of Charles's ideas was to seek French support for a marriage between Mary and the Dauphine. This did not come to anything, and neither is it clear how seriously Henry was taken to his 'other loves'. There is no real evidence of a strong attachment to Jane Seymour yet.[16]

In October, Chapuys received fresh intelligence from his contacts at court that Anne was harassing Mary. Again he went to Cromwell to seek help. Cromwell made soothing noises, confiding that Henry secretly dearly loved Mary '100 times more than his last born'. Cromwell assured Chapuys that 'in time everything would be set to rights'. Chapuys took this as a hint 'that there was some appearance of the king changing his love'. Chapuys was unsure whether Cromwell was serious, or just saying this to humour him, but before he could ask any more Cromwell cleverly changed the subject. Cromwell had intelligence from France, Spain, Scotland and Ireland that Charles had sent agents to these countries to 'foster rebellion and troubles' against Henry, particularly in Ireland. Cromwell was sure that such reports could not be true – the French must be stirring up trouble between England and Charles again – and Cromwell was certain that Chapuys would be able to categorically deny it all. Now it was Chapuys's turn to go on the defensive. Rather lamely he suggested another meeting to discuss these matters. He then managed dexterously to turn the conversation back to Catherine once more. Why, he demanded, had Henry taken away Catherine's jewels and given them to Anne? Cromwell (says Chapuys) was compelled to agree that the ambassador was in the right. However, Chapuys was satisfied with Cromwell's assurances of goodwill towards Catherine and Mary. He acknowledged that Henry had recently given an order, following Cromwell's intercession, that Mary should be well treated.[17]

In spring the following year (1535), Cromwell introduced a new and disquieting theme in his meetings with Chapuys. He reminded the ambassador that Catherine was 'old and would not live long, while the princess was in bad health, and her early death very probable'. Cromwell then explained how eager Henry was for unity among the princes of Christendom, notably himself, Charles and Francis. If a General Council could achieve concord, there would be a common defence against the Turk. Maybe a renewed offensive in the Holy Land could be considered, resulting in more dominions and wealth for Europe's princes. Cromwell warned Chapuys to abandon ideas that Henry would name Mary as his successor. He also suggested that the affairs of Catherine and Mary should be kept 'in the background', and not be allowed to sour Anglo-Imperial relations. Both women were mortal, added Cromwell, so 'what harm or danger could there be in the princess dying just now? Would the emperor have reason to regret her death?' Taken aback, Chapuys worried about the consequences if Mary died 'suddenly, in these times, and in a manner open to suspicion'. Neither was he happy about putting the issue of Catherine and Mary in the background. Cromwell did not press the point, but Chapuys was sufficiently concerned to suggest to the emperor a plan for helping Mary to escape. Charles agreed, though everything would have to be done 'with the utmost secrecy, and great discretion'. Soon after this, Cromwell met Chapuys again. Cromwell said that Mary was 'an obstacle to all negotiations, and that he wished to God ...'. And here Cromwell left the sentence unfinished. Chapuys was alarmed, lest Catherine and Mary 'be despatched secretly, if not in public'. He had no doubt where the blame lay – it was Anne, 'helping with all her power towards that end'. She was now 'fiercer and haughtier than ever'. Catherine, too, had heard frightful rumours hinting at the danger to Mary.[18]

Cromwell's motive in raising the startling prospect of the death of Catherine or Mary is perplexing. It is possible that he had heard something, and that he was preparing Chapuys for bad news. However, Cromwell's words do not read like a hint or a coded message. It may be better to take them at face value without trying to decipher some clever, hidden meaning from them. Cromwell was a tough, hard-boiled character, who lived and moved in the pitilessly unsentimental world of international politics and statecraft, and his words contained a grim logic which Charles could hardly fail to see. An alliance with England would offer significant advantages for Charles in his rivalry with Francis, and also his attempts to repel the Turkish forces in the east. Should, therefore, Catherine's divorce – now a *fait accompli* – and the matter of Mary's succession, really be sufficient to entrench permanent enmity between the two monarchs? Besides, Tudor minds were more likely than modern ones to believe with St Paul that 'to be with Christ is far better' (Philippians 1:23), especially for someone like Catherine, overtaken by incurable misfortune. Was it really cruel to wish that God would take Catherine or Mary out of her misery and into eternal rest? Seen through Tudor eyes with a Tudor mindset, Cromwell was not being uncharitable, just brutally unsentimental.

Chapuys must have taken Cromwell's words in this spirit because, to Anne's intense annoyance, the two men continued to hold regular meetings. During one of them, in mid-May, a remarkable conversation took place. Rather than look for the passing of Catherine as a blessing for all concerned, Chapuys suggested that Cromwell should consider the issue from the reverse angle. Let Henry dismiss Anne and restore Catherine, the ambassador urged. That would be a far more satisfying way of securing a lasting peace between England and Charles.

Chapuys had been doing some homework, soliciting expert medical opinion. He was convinced that there 'is every probability, as physicians and others tell me', that Henry could still beget his male heir from Catherine rather than 'that woman', meaning Anne. Cromwell pointed out that Catherine was now nearly fifty (she was born in 1485). Chapuys had prepared himself well for this meeting, and he produced examples of women in England giving birth at the age of fifty-one. Now Cromwell knew he was beaten. Here he admitted that his own mother was fifty-two when he was born. Cromwell then spoke 'many pleasant things' of Catherine personally, but he criticized those who had arranged her marriage to Henry. Sensing his advantage, Chapuys insisted that the marriage, while it lasted, had contributed much to England's welfare and security. A long conversation followed of which Chapuys gives no details; except that at the end, 'after much contention and dispute, Cromwell owned openly to me that most of the above and other reasons I had alleged were just and indisputable'. Then Cromwell, like a loser graciously conceding defeat, confessed that 'it is not in mine, nor in any man's power to persuade the king, my master; he will hazard all rather than give in on such a point'.[19]

Ambassador Chapuys now held the distinction of being one of the few people to have got the better of Thomas Cromwell in debate. Chapuys had uncovered a family secret, and skilfully forced his opponent onto the defensive. For once, Cromwell had dropped his diplomatic guard and made a very candid, personal admission, one that he would never have made to the king or anyone in the council.

The despatch in which Chapuys described this conversation is dated 23 May 1535. In his next letter, barely a fortnight later (5 June), we read that Anne wanted Cromwell's head off. Chapuys heard this from Cromwell, and he was not sure whether to believe it at first. He had good reason to be a little sceptical. Cromwell was second to none in the art of political gamesmanship, and pretending to be out of favour with the 'concubine' could be a useful ploy designed to win the good opinion of Chapuys and Charles in the hope of smoothing the troubled Anglo-Imperial relations. In view of all that had gone before, however, the likelihood must be that the story was true. The sharp-eyed Anne, jealous of her position as queen, but still terribly vulnerable without an heir, had sensed that Cromwell had a soft spot for Catherine, and that he was also building up a good relationship with Chapuys. For good measure, Chapuys added, Anne was also scheming to bring Norfolk into disgrace with the king, and she had recently had a blazing row with him as well. She 'heaped more injuries on the duke than on a dog', provoking the goaded peer to storm out of the Royal Chamber in a rage calling her a 'great whore' (*grande putain*). Cromwell's reaction to the waspish queen was altogether more relaxed. He breezily assured Chapuys that 'she can do me no harm'.[20]

Some assessment of Cromwell's relations with the two queens may now be called for. No councillor of state can afford to allow his heart to rule his head, so the first explanation for Cromwell's attitude towards Catherine and Mary must be statecraft. On Henry's Great Matter, Chapuys presents Cromwell as being markedly less dogmatic than others. His position was really quite simple. Henry was the king and Cromwell the servant, whose duty it was to do the king's will. So far as Cromwell was concerned, Henry could marry whomsoever he liked – that was his affair. On theological issues like the validity or otherwise of the Aragon marriage according to the Levitical Law, Henry had theologians and bishops to advise him. If Henry was satisfied with that advice, then that, too, was the king's matter, and Cromwell had no right to interfere. However, any wise councillor could see that the Boleyn marriage was a provocation to Charles that exposed England to the risk of trade sanctions and even war. To prevent, or at least minimize this danger, it made good diplomatic sense to treat Catherine and Mary with as much dignity as was possible in the circumstances. With Charles pressed between the need to contain the Turk in the east, and others urging a punitive invasion of England, considerate conduct towards his aunt and her daughter could make the difference between war and peace.

Cromwell's approach showed political astuteness as well. Through parliamentary legislation, especially via the Act of Appeals, he had done more than anyone apart from Henry to secure the Royal Supremacy; but he had also ensured that the real ire of the Aragon party, including Chapuys and Charles, was directed not at him but at the Boleyns. So Cromwell could now use his growing power to encourage evangelical progress in the country, and at the same time keep diplomatic channels open with the imperialists. Catherine could even call him her 'friend', and while Chapuys was not exactly a close friend of Cromwell's, he was willing to speak with him and deal with him. Cromwell was also keeping his options open. The possibility that Henry might restore Catherine, though remote, could not be discounted entirely. In view of all of this, it is hardly surprising that Anne had no great affection for Cromwell.

It would be tempting to leave it there, and to assume that Cromwell was motivated by cold political calculations only. But there is more to it than this. That Cromwell was loyal to the king in all things can hardly be doubted. That he had a high regard for Catherine personally, and was moved by her suffering, and her dignified demeanour in it, can not be doubted either. These two outlooks are not necessarily mutually exclusive. Cromwell found himself in one of life's painful dilemmas, duty pulling him one way and sympathy another. As a councillor of state, duty had to prevail, though it could never extinguish sympathy entirely. Cromwell, therefore, did what he could to make life a little more tolerable for Catherine and Mary. His efforts may not have been astoundingly successful, but they were nevertheless enough to merit a personal letter from the emperor, warmly thanking him for the 'good service which he has rendered' to the former queen and her daughter.[21]

Anne, meanwhile, continued her troubled and sonless reign. As others have noted before, an alluring mistress is not always successfully transformed into an ideal wife, especially when the wife had yet to bear her royal husband the heir to the throne that he desperately wanted. Leading councillors were now openly unafraid of Anne. In the face of her anger, Cromwell was sanguinely unruffled, while Norfolk did not scruple to call her a 'great whore' and get away with it. Her unpredictable husband had now met the Lady Jane Seymour, though it is not known whether any serious attachment had formed yet, or whether she was one of the 'other loves' that the French diplomat had noticed. The volatile nature of the Boleyn marriage, and of the couple themselves, is arrestingly clear from ambassadors' letters. In the same month (June 1535) the Venetian ambassador reported that Henry was 'tired of her', while according to Chapuys the king 'loves his concubine now more than he ever did'. Each account could be true in its own way; this was a disturbed marriage, with Henry blowing hot and cold towards his unhappy wife.[22]

The couple's only child, Princess Elizabeth, had now become the focus of marriage talks with the French, and a match between her and the duke of Angoulême was considered. An English delegation to France to negotiate the matter during spring 1535 was originally to have included Norfolk, Foxe and Cromwell, though for reasons unclear, Cromwell did not go as planned, and Rochford, Anne's brother, took his place. Maybe Anne was behind this rescheduling. Francis was still supporting Henry's second marriage in his talks with the pope, though somewhat less enthusiastically than before. To his councillors, Francis was saying highly uncomplimentary things about Henry, calling him unstable, arrogant and 'the strangest man in the world'. Francis feared that no good would come of Henry, but 'I must put up with him, as it is no time to lose friends'. Francis was grieved to hear of John Fisher's death, and his fondness for Anne had cooled. There were no more personal letters or gifts of luxurious sedan chairs as seen in Chapter 4. Cromwell was kept informed about the negotiations, but no marriage treaty with the French was actually agreed. One difficulty was Henry's insistence that the young duke should be brought up in England. The atmosphere among the English party may not have been particularly cordial; for although Norfolk repeatedly avowed his

loyalty to Henry and Anne, the Boleyns and the French suspected that Norfolk was secretly hoping to marry one of his
own sons to one of Henry's daughters, in the hope of securing
the crown for the Norfolk dynasty. It also appears that Henry
and his council had now accepted that his second marriage
might not, after all, produce an heir. It was even suggested that
Angoulême might be included in the succession to the throne
of England if he married Elizabeth.[23]

The missing heir remained an acute dilemma, a huge disappointment for the king and a constant threat to the queen.
According to one French visitor to England, Anne's dearest
wish was to have a son. (Her second was to see the queen of
Navarre again.) In October, however, her fortunes revived; she
was pregnant once more, and king and queen were reportedly
merry on a trip to Hampshire. Next month Chapuys was hor-
rified to hear a rumour, which he feared could be true, that
Henry had decided to 'rid himself' of Catherine and Mary at
the next parliament. Again he blamed Anne, who now 'rules
over and governs the nation; the king dare not contradict her'.
But once more appearances were deceptive, and within a few
short weeks Henry would be heard muttering darkly about
being seduced into his marriage by witchcraft, and vowing to
take a new wife.[24]

On 7 January 1536, Catherine's miserable last years came to
a merciful end. Chapuys, still convinced that Anne had been
plotting to poison her, was shocked at the tasteless celebra-
tions that followed. 'No words can describe the joy and delight
which this king and the promoters of his concubine have felt
at the demise of the good queen, especially the earl of Wiltshire
and his son'. Cromwell is not mentioned in this part of the
letter. Elsewhere, however, Cromwell remarked to Chapuys
that Catherine's passing would be 'advantageous' for the
Anglo-Imperial friendship that they both wanted. Again, this is
likely to be more unsentimental than unsympathetic. Chapuys
gives no indication that he took offence, and relations between
these two men, already quite good in the circumstances, would
soon get even better.[25]

The joy of the Boleyns did not last. According to Hall, Anne miscarried in February. Chaupys dated this fateful event to 29 January, with cutting irony the day of Catherine's funeral. Wriothesley records it 'three days before Candlemas'. Candlemas was 2 February, so if he calculated three full intervening days, his account would tally with Chapuys. As the evidence is in favour of 29 January, the following discussion will assume that this is correct.[26]

The usual version of events in accounts of Henry and Anne is that the miscarriage aroused Henry's suspicions of divine disfavour on his second marriage, after which the various factions at court set to work to contrive Anne's downfall. The evidence, however, tells a different, a stranger story.

On this point Chapuys is very specific with his dates. It was on the *morning* of 29 January that he heard, from 'sufficiently authentic' sources, that Henry had recently made an astonishing admission to one of his 'principal courtiers'. Chapuys immediately dashed off a letter to Charles telling him that:

> This king had said to one of his courtiers in great secrecy, and as if in confession, that he had been seduced and forced into this second marriage by means of sortileges [sic] and charms, and that, owing to that, he held it as null. God, he said, had well shown his displeasure at it by denying him male children. He, therefore, considered that he could take a third wife, which he said he wished much to do.

This letter says nothing about the miscarriage. Chapuys had not heard of that yet. It had not even happened when a messenger brought this news to him.[27]

Henry's confessions, therefore, and his anxiety about divine disapproval, and his belief that his marriage to Anne was null, and even his intention to marry again, were not a set of knee jerk reactions to the tragic news of the miscarriage, as is commonly supposed. These were the thoughts flooding through his restless mind *before* the morning of 29 January and *before* Anne miscarried. The miscarriage is thought to have occurred in the afternoon or early evening of the 29th, probably when Henry was out hunting. Faction theories employed to explain Anne's fall are now rendered redundant. The worst that Anne's enemies at court could do was to try and hasten the inevitable. Henry personally, not some faction or other, had decided that he no longer wanted Anne as his queen. The miscarriage would have forcefully confirmed his fears and his plans; but it was not the prime cause of them.

Chapuys had also heard, though on this point he admitted that his sources were not quite as reliable, that even though Anne had rejoiced at Catherine's death, she had also 'cried and lamented ... fearing lest she herself might be brought to the same end'. Chapuys was amazed to hear all this, and promised he would do his best to find out more.

So even during Anne's latest pregnancy, even before she miscarried, neither king nor queen could look ahead to a blessed outcome. Fear and apprehension, not expectancy or hope, filled the hearts of both, while Henry was already minded to marry another woman. How much this shared despondency owed to these strange 'sortileges and charms', only Henry and Anne will ever really know; but we have already seen Henry consulting 'witches and wizards' as well as 'physicians and astrologers' before the birth of Elizabeth (see p. 142). It now looks as though this troubled, turbulent king had been taking similar mysterious soundings before marrying Anne, which were weighing on his mind and vexing his conscience.

Fascinating though it would be to learn more, and tempting though it is to indulge in speculation, this is as far as the evidence allows us to go. The veil covering the inmost thoughts and the dark secrets of Henry and Anne is only partly lifted. Readers who would like a more inventive (and controversial) interpretation of these words will find one in Retha Warnicke's account of Anne Boleyn, wherein are contained, to quote Elton's apt understatement, 'highly original variations' on the usual version.[28]

Meanwhile, news of the miscarriage filtered out, and rumour spread quickly around the capital. The Tudor chattering classes were saying that Anne would never conceive, and the still birth was an ill omen. Anne blamed her miscarriage on Norfolk for his ill-timed announcement that Henry had suffered a riding accident. Chapuys was not convinced. He put it down to her fear of rejection – for Henry had recently made 'very valuable presents' to Jane Seymour.[29]

This was nothing less worrying for Anne than the loss of her child. For it is a curious feature of Henry's moral make-up that in spite of the occasional fling, he seems not to have approved of an official royal mistress. He would put away his wives for another woman, bastardize his innocent daughters, lead his realm into religious schism and constitutional crisis, cut off the heads of his best ministers for no good reason; but his conscience would not suffer him to have a mistress, at least not for long. Once he got attached to another woman, he had to make her his queen. By January or February 1536, therefore, the reign of Anne Boleyn was effectively over.

However, the view that Anne's fall can be explained by her husband's love for Jane is far too straightforward for some tastes. The modern age loves a conspiracy theory, especially one with a really nasty villain at the centre of it, and a novel account of Anne's demise has assigned this role to Cromwell. Provoked by Anne's disapproval of him, so the story goes, Cromwell devised a fiendish plot based on lies and fake charges to ruin her. To bring it to execution he bullied and threatened innocent people into making false confessions which convinced Henry of his wife's unfaithfulness. Thus Thomas Cromwell's hands are stained with the blood of a guiltless queen. None too subtle variations on this theory have Henry more or less conniving at Cromwell's bloody deeds.[30]

With the end of Anne's reign now as imminent as it was certain, the first reaction to such a story must be to wonder how anyone could be so foolish as to waste his time and go to all the unnecessary trouble. Nevertheless, the conspiracy theory has attracted a large following, for it can be found in one form or another in most accounts of Henry and his wives. The next chapter will be devoted to answering it on Cromwell's behalf.

8

In the Line of Duty

Like most conspiracy theories, this one draws on various sources. The first has been noted in the previous chapter – Anne told Cromwell to his face that she would like to see his head off. Hence Cromwell and Anne are supposed to have been at each other's throats.

These pleasantries, however, have nothing to do with Anne's fall or the events leading up to it. They were uttered in June 1535, nearly a year before her arrest, and during the intervening period the main cause of Anne's anger had disappeared with Catherine's death. Besides, Cromwell was not particularly worried about Anne, and he had shrugged the incident off. It would have to be proved that she still wanted his head off a year later, and also that something pretty devastating had occurred to turn Cromwell's unconcern into deadly hatred.

The second piece of evidence comes from an account of Anne's life written twenty-three years after her death by Alexander Alesius, a Scots Protestant divine, for Queen Elizabeth I in 1559. From this it is alleged that Anne had provoked Cromwell by opposing his policy on the monasteries.[1]

It is a strange claim for a Protestant writer like Alesius to make, especially as he admitted that he was out of the country for much of the time when the early dissolution was underway. More importantly, as seen in Chapter 6, Cromwell's policy regarding the monasteries was to place supporters of the Royal Supremacy and the new learning into positions of influence wherever and whenever he could. Nowhere does Alesius explain why Anne should have objected to this. Anne's admirers like Alesius now contradict themselves. She is decked out as the evangelical darling, and then made an adversary of Cromwell. She cannot be both. If she really did oppose Cromwell's evangelical reforms, then she had an evangelical outer shell but not much more. Jeremy Collier's verdict on Anne may have been a perceptive one: he described her as a 'favourer of the Reformation, but not to the length of Foxe's opinion'. It is difficult to avoid the suspicion that Anne was a bit like Henry on religion, neither wholly medieval nor wholly Lutheran; a free-spirited lady, who, though she certainly absorbed evangelical ideas, may have preferred to seek her own independent way. It is also possible that Cromwell, more perceptive than some of Anne's over zealous supporters like Alesius, sensed this better than they did; hence the coolness between the queen and the Vicegerent.[2]

Be that as it may, it is also claimed that Anne sharply disagreed with Cromwell on the most beneficial way of spending the revenue from the sale of the monasteries. She wanted to see much more being done for poor relief, and she was filled with righteous indignation against Cromwell for abundantly feathering his own nest with bribes. We will return to this point in a moment, but meanwhile more needs to be said about our friend Alesius.

He seems to have been captivated by Anne Boleyn. He claims he knew evangelical bishops whom Anne had 'appointed' – but in fact whatever recommendations Anne or Cromwell may have made, bishops were only officially 'appointed' by the king (and in any case, Cromwell was the one behind these appointments – see Chapter 6). Alesius also likes to call Anne 'your most holy mother', a unusual way to describe a woman who had schemed her way to the throne, contrived Wolsey's ruin en route, rowed with most of the council, and, unless Chapuys was dreaming, had harboured ideas about poisoning Catherine and Mary. But even Alesius is overdoing it when he says that 'true [evangelical] religion in England had its commencement and its end' with Anne. Alesius has apparently forgotten about Tyndale, Cranmer, Latimer, Ridley and nearly 300 Protestant martyrs under Mary.

Sentimentalising over Anne is matched by whinging about Cromwell. Alesius claims that he sought to leave England after Anne's death, but Cromwell dissuaded him and 'retained me for about three years with empty hopes' until the Act of Six Articles was passed. Yet it was this same Alesius who wrote a detailed account of Cromwell's first Vicegerential synod in 1537, in which he speaks well of Cromwell as the evangelical leader (to be discussed in more detail in Chapter 10). Moreover, an examination of Cromwell's accounts shows that he supported Alesius financially while he was in England: payments or gifts include £5 in January, March, May and October 1537; 10 marks in February 1538, and a further £5 in October. Then, after the anti-Lutheran Act of Six Articles in 1539, Alesius left England for Wittenberg from where he wrote a seemingly cordial letter to Cromwell. He thanked him for his kindness when he was in England, wrote that he appreciated that Cromwell was not responsible for the act, and that he hoped that Cromwell might be able to soften its effects.[3]

Alesius also has difficulty sifting fact from fiction. He claims that Anne was the one who persuaded Henry to send an embassy to the German Lutherans. But there is no evidence that Anne had any love for the Lutherans, especially as they continued to take Catherine's side in Henry's Great Matter. All contemporary evidence – as the most detailed analysis of Anglo-Lutheran relations (Rory McEntegart's) has shown – points to Cromwell as the man organising and driving Henry's Lutheran policy forward (see Chapter 6).

Alesius further claims that Henry was angry with Anne because the German princes would not make an alliance with him. Here, too, he is much mistaken. In Anne's last year the German princes *were* prepared to offer Henry a religious and political alliance, including membership of the Schmalkaldic League, if agreement could be reached on theology. At the time of Anne's fall, the Germans were waiting for Henry's answer to their proposals and the Wittenberg Articles – a set of articles based on Melanchthon's *Loci* which had been agreed between the Lutherans and the English delegation to Germany. In fact, Henry's anger with Anne had nothing whatever to do with the Lutherans. It had everything to do with their sonless marriage, with Jane Seymour, and stories about Anne's infidelities that emerged from within her own circle.[4]

Richer still is Alesius's tale that Cromwell, when in prison four years later, repented that he 'had caused many innocent persons to be put to death, not sparing your most holy mother, nor had he obeyed her directions in promoting the doctrine of the Gospel'. It is all syrupy, sentimental nonsense. Not only was Alesius in Germany when Cromwell was arrested, but the letters Cromwell wrote from prison are preserved in the British Library and elsewhere, and no such stuff is found in them.

Alesius's account of Anne's life and death is, to borrow a phrase from his own countrymen, pure blethers. Just for the sake of argument, however, let us assume that Anne did disagree with Cromwell over how the monastic revenue should be spent. Even if this were true, it would not amount to very much. Such a difference of opinion at this early stage of the dissolution, when only the smaller monasteries were being suppressed, might prompt an exchange of words or letters, but it is nothing like enough to incite a murderous power struggle between the Vicegerent and the queen. Among evangelicals and humanists, various ideas for the monasteries were being floated. Robert Barnes and Thomas Starkey hoped to see the extra income diverted to the poor or for education, and Cromwell did not try to destroy them because of it. On the contrary, he was willing to consider these and other suggestions as well.[5]

In June 1535, Cromwell told Chapuys that Henry was now so rich thanks to his increased ecclesiastical revenues and other taxes that he could easily afford to join a crusade against the Turk if an Anglo-Imperial alliance was made. Cromwell also commented on how 'fond of hoarding' Henry was; he reckoned that sooner or later 'all the gold and silver of England will ultimately fall into his hands', giving him a treasury certain to arouse covetous interest from other nations like Flanders and France. 'I and other Privy Councillors', Cromwell added, 'are now looking for the means of checking this king's avarice and making him spend his money for the benefit of the nation'.[6]

Among Cromwell's policies was a new act for poor relief, more radical than anything envisaged before. A draft bill prepared that autumn, based on ideas and proposals from various sources including men in Cromwell's service, listed many causes of poverty: idleness, sickness, invalidity, over-indulgence, maltreatment by cruel employers, even poor upbringing. An ambitious plan of public works for the unemployed was then laid out. It included new buildings, repairs to harbours, highways and fortresses, 'scouring and cleansing of watercourses', all under the direction of officers reporting to a central council. This council would be authorised to issue legally binding proclamations and summonses to the able-bodied unemployed to work, for which they would be paid 'reasonable wages'. Those who refused to report for work risked prosecution, and, if found guilty by the testimony of three witnesses, they would be branded. There would be free medical treatment for poor persons unable to work through sickness, and provisions were made for those too old or terminally ill. Officials would be appointed to make sure no one was abusing the system; their task would be to seek out and report idlers to the authorities, but also to identify the old and the incapacitated, and care for them. They would record the details of men who had become impoverished through no fault of their own and were unable to live on their wages, either because they had too many children to feed, or because they were victims of robbery or some natural disaster. In such cases, local justices would provide assistance from public funds if necessary. But giving money to beggars who were fit to work was forbidden. Healthy child beggars would have to serve as apprentices to craftsmen and other masters in order to learn a trade.[7]

Cromwell intended that this plan, unprecedented in England, would be funded from three main sources. The first was the resources of the crown, subject only to the king's discretion. Second, direct taxes would be levied on the better off classes, including the clergy. Third, collections in local parishes for poor relief would be organized. The first of these would almost certainly include money received from the monasteries. Unfortunately, Cromwell did not succeed in winning the support the bill needed from parliament and the king, and the actual Poor Law act of 1536 was much more modest than the drafts. No real national program of public works was possible, and many other proposals were left to the responsibility of local authorities. The act was an improvement on the situation hitherto, but nothing on the scale that Cromwell and his allies had hoped for.

Nevertheless, these proposals and the draft bill should suffice to answer the cheap accusation that Cromwell was callously unmindful of the poor, concerned only to fill up the king's coffers and his own pockets with the wealth of the church. He did indeed want to make Henry rich; but he also hoped to persuade Henry to spend money on worthwhile projects for the common good, not hoard it in his palaces like a miser. Cromwell seems to have decided that he could begin the spiritual reform of England by evangelising in the monasteries, and that he could best help the poor and the economy generally through his Poor Law legislation, backed up by a productive public works program. Anne may or may not have approved; the evidence is not conclusive. But almost all contemporary economists and politicians would agree with Cromwell that government sponsored work-creation measures are far more useful to the poor and unemployed than, say, unconditional cash handouts.

Enough has now been said about Alesius and the monasteries. It is significant that his call for a formal, posthumous vindication of Anne Boleyn went ignored even in her daughter's reign. Elizabeth's government did review Anne's case, but wiser heads decided to leave this unhappy affair in the past. Readers will draw their own conclusions.[8]

Another piece of evidence that needs to be considered is an anonymous work on Henry's reign written by a Spanish visitor, commonly known as the *Spanish Chronicle*. Though Eric Ives wisely treats this work with scepticism, other accounts of Anne draw freely upon it to support the utterly baseless claim that, on the orders of this arch villain Cromwell, witnesses were compelled by torture or the threat of torture to testify falsely against the queen.[9]

According to the *Chronicle*, a young court musician named Mark Smeaton has been reported to Cromwell for his behaviour. Suspicions were raised because Smeaton, penniless only a few months ago, is now living like a lord in the queen's service. He has also, 'on many occasions', been seen going into the queen's chamber. Smeaton is taken to Cromwell for questioning, and Cromwell warns him that he must tell the truth, or Cromwell will get it out of him by force. Smeaton is tongue-tied, so Cromwell warns him again. Still Smeaton gives only an evasive answer. Now Cromwell summons six of his heavies, and a knotted rope is tied round Smeaton's head and tightened. After a dose or two of this medicine Smeaton is singing like a canary, and he confesses he is the queen's lover. Cromwell is 'terror-stricken', and asks if any other men are involved. Smeaton provides a list of names, Cromwell sends a message to Henry, and Smeaton is despatched to the Tower.[10]

It is a spicy, entertaining story, but as with Alesius the devil is in the detail. A knotted rope was a novel form of torture in England, while torture of any kind was used far more sparingly in Tudor England than on the continent, and seldom if ever on the whim of a councillor so early in an interrogation. Then for the story to reach the chronicler, someone from Cromwell's household would have to tell it, and it is not clear why a servant of Cromwell's would report this to a visiting Spanish writer, and a known supporter of Catherine of Aragon.

The *Chronicle* also claims that when Anne was taken to the Tower on 2 May, Henry sent Cranmer, Audley, Norfolk and Cromwell to examine her, and that Cranmer took the lead in the questioning. Actually on 2 May Cranmer was summoned to Lambeth from Knole, where he had been for some days. The following day, still unable to see Henry face to face, he wrote an anguished letter to the king about what he had heard 'reported' of the queen. So he had *not* seen her on the 2nd.[11]

Furthermore, the *Chronicle* calls Anne's brother a duke – actually he was Viscount Rochford. It describes the executions of Anne's lovers as if the writer had inside information, but nowhere does it mention the name of one of them, Francis Weston. It also informs us that Anne's father 'died of grief' a few days after her death. Actually her father lived on nearly three more years.[12]

Then leafing through later pages of the *Chronicle* the reader is puzzled to find Cromwell, who died in 1540, investigating adultery allegations against Catherine Howard, which were not uncovered until the following year. The solution – and it takes a moment or two for this particular penny to drop – is that the chronicler has been engaging in some rather radical historical revisionism. He makes Catherine Howard Henry's fourth wife, followed by Anne of Cleves. Which brings us to Cromwell's own fall (and presumably we are now in 1542 or thereabouts). After discussing Henry's unhappiness with Anne, the *Chronicle* describes how certain lords devise a plot against Cromwell. One of these lords is the marquis of Exeter (who died in December 1538). Then at a dinner given in the honour of the emperor's ambassador, Cromwell announces to all the guests that he intends himself king. Not too surprisingly, he is promptly reported to Henry and arrested.[13]

Reverting to the section on Anne Boleyn, the *Chronicle* has got the main point right – it was Smeaton's confession that led to the arrest of the queen and her other lovers. On this, all evidence agrees. This apart, the *Chronicle* is far too cavalier with facts, dates and details to be a credible witness. At best the knotted rope story must be highly dubious, and very likely an invention.

However, as with Alesius, let us suppose for the sake of argument that the story in the *Chronicle* is true. It still does not support a conspiracy theory. Cromwell does not make up

the charges about Anne, then torture Smeaton into confess-
ing them. What happens is that suspicious behaviour, which
might implicate the queen, is reported to Cromwell and it is
Cromwell's job to get the facts. He allegedly uses strong-arm
tactics not to get Smeaton to sign a *prepared* confession, but
simply to get Smeaton to open his mouth and say *something*.
Cromwell, says the *Chronicle*, is 'terror-stricken' when he hears
that Smeaton is the queen's lover, not glad to have discovered
what he has been looking for at last. So even in this colourful
version of events, not a trace can be found of a Cromwellian
conspiracy against Anne.

Finally to Ambassador Chapuys, the trump card for the
coup theory, according to whom Cromwell was supposed to
have 'planned and brought about the whole affair'. Readers
may care to see these words in their proper context. The relevant passage is as follows, taken from a letter of Chapuys to
Charles V, dated 6 June, nearly three weeks after Anne died.[14]

First, the original:

> *Et que a luy avoit este lauctorite de descouvrir et parachever les*
> *affaires diçelle concubine, en quoy il avoit eu une marveilleuse pene,*
> *et que sur le desplesir et courroux quil avoit eu sur la reponce que le*
> *roy son maistre mavoit donnee le tiers iour de pasques il se mist a*
> *fantasier et conspirer le dict affaire, et que une des choses que lavoit*
> *mis en soupeçon at anime pour senquerre du cas …*

The translator of the *Calendar of State* papers (*CSP*) has, not
unreasonably, broken up this long, sprawly and still unfinished
sentence into something more manageable, as follows:

> He [Cromwell], himself, had been authorised and com-
> missioned by the king to prosecute and bring to an end
> the mistress's trial, to do which he had taken considerable
> trouble. It was he who, in consequence of the disappoint-
> ment and anger he had felt on hearing the king's answer
> to me on the third day of Easter, had planned and brought
> about the whole affair.

Regarding the first sentence, the *CSP* assumes that the authorisation came from the king. Literally it reads that Cromwell 'had the authority', or 'to him had been given the authority'. However, the *CSP*'s rendering is a fair one, because only the king could authorise such action against the queen, and, as Cromwell was the most powerful minister in the land, no one but the king could commission him to do something as grave as this.

Chapuys's very first words, therefore, scotch any notion of a clandestine Cromwellian coup against Anne. Whatever Cromwell did, he did lawfully and properly, acting under orders from Henry. Allegations about Anne have presumably reached Henry, as the *Chronicle* also says, and Henry has appointed Cromwell to take charge of the case, which resulted in her prosecution and conviction.

There is no suggestion that Cromwell has done anything illegal, unauthorised, or perfidious; still less that he has framed the queen on false charges and then convinced Henry of her guilt. Henry, not Cromwell, is directing events. The only oddity of the passage is that after telling us that Henry authorised Cromwell to act, it goes on to say that Cromwell carried out his commission not as an obedient servant of the king exactly, but 'in consequence of' his disappointment with Henry's answer on the third day of Easter (that would be 18 April). This would appear to introduce a new idea, hinting that Cromwell had motives of his own. So is Cromwell acting under orders or not? The text is now ambiguous. It is also nonsense, because if Henry gives Cromwell a royal command, then Cromwell has to carry it out whether he is angry or happy; he does not, as this phrasing implies, obey Henry's orders when it suits his mood to do so. This text, either in transcription or translation, has become garbled.

Here I must ask the reader to bear with a point of grammar. The *CSP* has curiously translated the French '*sur*' as 'in consequence of' (*sur le desplesir et courroux,* 'in consequence of his disappointment and anger'). However, the French for 'in consequence of' is *par* or *en conséquent*. The word *sur* usually means 'on', and although it may have other meanings besides, 'in consequence of' is not listed in the authoritative Collins or Robert dictionary as one of them.[15]

The nearest Collins gives to a causal meaning is this: *sur invitation/commande*, 'by invitation/order'; and *sur un signe du patron, elle sortit*, 'at a signal from the boss, she left'. 'In consequence of' would be misleading here because it would introduce a motive that is not intended. She left, not because *she* wanted to leave, or was motivated for her own reasons to leave, but simply when and because the boss told her. Further, *sur* can also indicate a point of time or proximity: *Il est arrivé sur les 2 heures*, 'he arrived about two o'clock'; *la pièce s'achève sur une reconciliation*, 'the play ends on/with a reconciliation'.[16]

An example of the absurdity and inconsistency of rendering 'in consequence of' for *sur* is clear from the rest of Chapuys's report, which continues:

One of the things which had mostly raised his [Cromwell's] suspicions, and induced him to inquire into her case, was certain prognostications made in Flanders of a conspiracy against the King's life, by people, it was said, nearest to his Royal person. After which avowal (*sur ce*) Cromwell went on to extol beyond measure the sense, wit and courage of the royal mistress, as well as her brother' (*Et sur ce loua grandement le sens, esperit, et cueur de la dicte concubine et de son frere*).

This time the *CSP* has translated *sur* as 'after which' – just like the examples from Collins. Translating it as 'in consequence of' would give 'Cromwell suspects a plot against the king, in consequence of which he praises Anne's sense, spirit and courage'!

So applying the rules of grammar according to Collins to Chapuys's letter, the third day of Easter marks the day when Cromwell began, on Henry's order, to investigate the case against Anne; but it does not mean that Cromwell's disappointment over what happened that day motivated him to launch an action of his own against Anne. The absurdity of this, if it is not obvious already, will become so soon enough.

Chapuys is simply reminding Charles of what happened that day, a very dramatic day about which he had already sent a long report. A detailed discussion of these events will have to wait until the next chapter; but for now readers may rest assured that Cromwell's anger and disappointment with Henry on 18 April had nothing, absolutely nothing whatever, to do with Anne Boleyn.

An alternative, free translation may now be suggested, as follows:

> On (or just after) the third day of Easter, the day when Cromwell was so disappointed and angry on hearing the king's answer to me, Henry authorised and commissioned him to prosecute and bring to an end the mistress's trial. Since then he was the one who planned and brought about the whole affair, which had taken him considerable trouble.

Besides being grammatically acceptable, this would also remove the ambiguity in the *CSP* translation.

An alternative rendering might be that because Cromwell was so upset, Henry authorised him to follow up these prognostications from Flanders and examine evidence against the queen, as a sort of consolation. But even if this were grammatically passable, it is scarcely sensical. Any intelligence that the king's life was in danger would have to be investigated regardless of what happened on 18 April, regardless of whether Cromwell was angry or not.

By now the reader has probably had enough of points of grammar. Chapuys is no longer with us to clarify his meaning, so the issue will have to be settled from the context. Of two things at least we can be certain. First, 'in consequence of' for *sur* is a mistake, or at best unreliable. Second, the opening words – that Cromwell was 'authorised and commissioned' by the king – cannot be arbitrarily struck out or overlooked. Because they come at the head of the sentence in the original document, it is reasonable to assume that they govern what follows. It can hardly be acceptable to turn it all around and say that Cromwell made up the charges against Anne and then persuaded Henry to authorise an investigation. Chapuys's letter, therefore, is wholly inadequate as a foundation for a conspiracy theory.

The reader now has all the evidence commonly cited for Cromwell's alleged perfidy against Anne Boleyn. It comprises fly-by-night stories from Alesius and the *Spanish Chronicle*, words of Chapuys taken out of context and an untrustworthy translation in the *Calendar of State Papers*. As a result, a wholly imaginary power struggle between Anne and Cromwell, unnoticed by Chapuys and all other contemporary witnesses, now dominates many modern accounts of Anne's last weeks. This, unfortunately, is the chief problem with faction theories and conspiracy theories – they succeed only in diverting attention away from the central point. The threat to Anne in spring 1536 came not from Cromwell but from her intimidating husband, now in love with another woman, and from the Seymour party, eager to exploit the king's affections and hasten Jane to the throne. According to everything seen so far, Cromwell became involved in the royal marital drama only when Henry ordered him onto the case.

What needs investigating now is the extent of his involvement, because this letter of Chapuys is by no means a comprehensive account of the affair, and it actually raises more questions than answers. Besides the points discussed already, it is hard to believe that Cromwell needed to take 'much time and trouble' when most of the evidence was readily provided by Smeaton, certain ladies of the court and Anne herself when in the Tower. Then these Flanders 'prognostications' are neither explained by Chapuys, nor ever referred to again. It could be that Cromwell received reports from his agents abroad – the sort of thing that modern intelligence services call 'chatter' – that aroused his suspicions; but at Anne's trial no witnesses were called from Flanders, and according to the surviving records nothing at all was ever said about Flanders. Also, as Chapuys's letter is dated 6 June, nearly three weeks after Anne's death, there is always the possibility of a little embellishment or spin. Certainly the account he gives here differs noticeably from the reports he was sending back to Charles during the crucial period at the end of April and early May.

Having come thus far, perhaps I may state what I believe happened. On or just after 18 April, Cromwell received an order from Henry – he had been expecting this for some time – to prepare the legal and constitutional case for the king's second divorce and his third marriage. When allegations of Anne's adultery followed some days later, Henry ordered Cromwell to investigate these as well. Chapuys has combined the two together; but also, and in order to foster good Anglo-Imperial relations now that the 'concubine' had been disposed of, he has exaggerated Cromwell's role just a little in order to impress Charles V. Readers will be able to judge for themselves after the next chapter.

9

Around the Throne the Thunder Rolls[1]

On the European diplomatic stage throughout 1535, King Francis of France was performing a dexterous, threefold balancing act. While earnestly assuring the pope of his loyalty to the Holy See and the Catholic faith, at the same time he kept up friendly overtures to the Lutheran Schmalkaldic League. Additionally, in his recurrent rivalry with Charles V, Francis needed the support of the schismatic Henry VIII. Francis coveted the duchy of Milan, one of Charles's most prized possessions, and Henry dangled the offer of substantial financial help – up to one third of the expenses of an army to invade Italy and recover Milan, and also Genoa, from Charles. In return, Francis would take Henry's side if either the pope or Charles attacked England.[2]

In December Anglo-French talks had reached a delicate stage. Henry remained willing to support Francis against Charles, but he did not want to be seen urging Francis into war against the emperor. To increase the diplomatic pressure on England, the French seized English ships at Bordeaux. Cromwell then sent letters to France to try and get them and their crews released. Cromwell also urged ambassadors Wallop and Gardiner in Paris to do all they could to discover Francis's real intentions, and persuade the French to pay outstanding sums of money owed to Henry under previous treaties.[3]

On 8 January 1536, Cromwell wrote to Gardiner to officially inform him and the French of the death of Catherine of Aragon, 'whose soul God pardon'. He had just finished this short despatch when a message arrived from Henry, and Cromwell hastily added a postscript. Because Catherine's death had removed the main cause of enmity between Henry and Charles, Henry now instructed Gardiner to be 'more aloof ... in relenting to their [French] overtures or requests'. The French should be left in no doubt 'what fruit' Henry may expect to receive from the emperor, who may offer him 'great pleasures and benefits', besides 'dominions or possession'.[4]

This postscript is crucial to understanding the diplomatic negotiations that followed. Henry had seen opening up before him the prospect of a new relationship with Charles following Catherine's death, and he was determined to take full advantage of it. So when Cromwell approached Chapuys in February with proposals for Anglo-Imperial amity, he was not following his own personal agenda, but acting entirely in accordance with Henry's wishes. Chapuys, however, had divined the English tactics well, and he took a tough, though courteous, opening negotiating stance. He would be delighted to see relations with England restored to their former friendship, but he specified four conditions. First, Henry should be reconciled with the Holy See. Second, Mary must be declared legitimate. Third – and subject to agreement on the first two – an Anglo-Imperial alliance would be formed against the Turk. Fourth, a general, comprehensive treaty could then be made.[5]

To points three and four Cromwell responded warmly. He also promised that he would continue to do all he could for Mary and reach a 'settlement of her affairs' in a manner acceptable to Charles. The first point, the most difficult, Cromwell saved till last. Eventually, obviously stalling he suggested that the matter should be considered by deputies appointed by Henry and Charles and Cromwell continued thus for several weeks. Meanwhile he struck a positive note, urging Chapuys to 'hope for the amicable settlement of all pending matters'. But Chapuys continued with his probing, and somehow he managed to turn the conversation to the Lutherans and the English delegation to Germany comprising Foxe, Heath and Barnes (see p. 129). Their mission, replied Cromwell reticently, was to 'get the opinion of several men in that country respecting their own affairs, and hear how the people govern themselves'. (For 'own affairs' read detailed theological discussions on the *Ausgburg Confession*, possible membership of the Schmalkaldic League and a major Lutheran delegation to England headed by Melanchthon.) Chapuys was not convinced. He suspected that something more than a routine fact-finding mission was underway in Germany. He had heard of the invitations to Melanchthon to visit England, he knew that Foxe's embassy had authority to 'negotiate and conclude' with the Lutherans; he knew, too, that Melanchthon had dedicated his *Loci* to Henry, and that Henry had sent Philip a personal gift in response. Nor was he blind to the fact that Cromwell was on the Lutheran side. For the time being, however, he let the matter drop.[6]

So Chapuys had reacted to Cromwell's overture with commendable skill. Chapuys knew that if his first condition – Henry's reconciliation with Rome – was met, then not only would Charles and Catherine of Aragon be fully vindicated, but also that no Anglo-Lutheran treaty would be practicable. For his part, Cromwell was prepared to do all he could for Mary, but if he wanted to continue with his pro-imperialist policy, he would have to induce Chapuys to soften his first demand somehow. A complex diplomatic poker game had now begun between two of the most intelligent and practised operators in Europe, each eager to restore relations between their respective princes, but each determined to do so on the most advantageous terms achievable. The task would be an intricate one; nevertheless, a useful start had been made.

After his discussion with Chapuys, Cromwell consulted with Henry. Realizing and making full use of his greater diplomatic manoeuvrability following Catherine's death, Henry was now taking a tougher line towards the French. He upbraided them for their unfriendliness to him, and he noisily called the emperor his friend in front of French diplomats; he also haughtily rejected a request from Francis for financial support in any Anglo-French action against Charles. In an interesting move of royal personnel management, Henry now assigned Cromwell to deal with Chapuys and Norfolk with the French. Norfolk, traditionally more pro-French than Cromwell, intimated to the bishop of Tarbes that if Charles attacked France, Henry would support Francis. However, Tarbes treated Henry no less warily than Chapuys. Probably rightly, Tarbes suspected that Henry's main aim was to keep the rivalry between Francis and Charles simmering so that Henry could help himself to whatever spoils came his way.[7]

Chapuys, meanwhile, noted approvingly that many on Henry's Council were supporting Cromwell's pro-imperialist line. He had the additional satisfaction of hearing from his own sources (not Cromwell) that Henry was 'much disappointed and discontented' with Anne following her miscarriage. During the last days of March Cromwell and Anne were reportedly on bad terms, and those in the know were talking of a new marriage. Chapuys then picked up something much more interesting from his French sources – Henry had asked Francis for his daughter. The prospect of an Anglo-French marital alliance made Chapuys uneasy, so he approached Cromwell to find out the facts.

He began by advising Cromwell to be wary of likely attacks from Anne, and to remember Wolsey's fate. Chapuys then delicately brought up the subject of a new royal marriage. Cromwell listened patiently and thanked Chapuys for his concern. After musing on the hazards of high office Cromwell began, in Chapuys's words, to 'excuse himself for having promoted' Henry's marriage to Anne; it was only because he had seen the king 'much bent upon it' that he had 'paved the way towards it' as we saw in Chapter 4. Then, with his hand over his mouth trying hard to keep a straight face, Cromwell said that he expected Henry to 'lead a more moral life' from now on.

This was diplomatic gamesmanship from Cromwell – he was playing with Chapuys, keeping him waiting for the information he really wanted. At last Cromwell proceeded to satisfy the ambassador's curiosity. He assured Chapuys that if Henry married again, 'it is certainly not among the French that he will look' for a wife.

Chapuys was relieved to hear this, though not altogether surprised. He had heard from the marchioness of Dorset, one of his most trusted sources, that Henry's love for Jane had 'marvellously increased' of late. Henry had recently sent Jane a gift which she had returned, sweetly avowing that nothing meant more to her than her honour, and beseeching Henry to 'reserve it for such a time as God would be pleased to send her some advantageous marriage'. Jane, Chapuys continued, had been 'well tutored' by Anne's opponents 'not in any wise to give into the king's fancy unless he makes her his queen'. So the Seymour party was naughtily copycatting the wiles that the Boleyns had used in the 1520s. In fact, Jane's faction had found a way to outsmart Anne's. In a wickedly clever ploy, one that the Boleyns could never have made about Henry's marriage to Catherine, Jane was instructed to tell Henry 'how much his subjects abominate the marriage' with Anne. Delighted to hear all this, Chapuys was now confident enough to say, in an official despatch on 1 April, that he hoped to see Henry's marriage to Jane go ahead soon.[8]

The formal, matter-of-fact documents preserved in the *Calendar of State Papers* offer only the faintest glimpse into the passions the crisis aroused. Once Anne Boleyn had captivated a king; now she was a scorned woman, and scorned in favour of Jane Seymour, an amiable though by all accounts a rather plain, uninspiring young lady. Determined not to surrender her crown, Anne fired back through a sermon given by her chaplain, John Skip. In a loyal if hardly convincing attempt to envelop Anne with a mantle of Christ-like guiltlessness, Skip took his text from John 8:46 – 'Which of you convicts me of sin?' Skip then rummaged around the Old Testament for material that could be topical. He started off with Solomon's moral decline after taking many wives, then Rehoboam for not listening to wise councillors, and ended up with Haman, the Persian king's wicked minister who sought the destruction of the godly queen Esther and her people. Even Parliament did not accept the preacher's wrath, which was actually that of Anne.[9]

The account of Solomon's spiritual apostasy, recorded in 1 Kings 11, is a devastating indictment of the man who was once the Lord's anointed king over His people Israel. He took foreign wives, he turned from the true religion to idolatry, he built an altar for 'Chemesh, the detestable god of Moab, and for Molech, the detestable god of the Ammonites', and offered sacrifices to them. Divine anger was kindled against him 'because his heart had turned away from the Lord', who warned him that the kingdom of Israel will henceforth be divided in two. The direct connection between the foreign wives and idolatry was a cutting thrust from a queen now furious at all the mischief her enemies were making. It was clever, too, because condemning gossip about a likely new marriage was not technically treasonable.

A digression is now necessary because our conspiracy theorists give this sermon quite a different emphasis. They waste few words on Solomon, and home in instead on Haman as if he was Skip's (or Anne's) main theme. This, they claim positively, was a direct attack on Cromwell because of his policy regarding the monasteries, and it riled him so intensely that he began putting together his evil designs to murder the queen.[10]

If, however, Anne had ever borne any ill will towards Cromwell over the small monasteries, she now had far more than that to vex her. Henry's heart had turned against her and his affection for Jane was an open secret; while Anne, queen though she was, had to watch and endure the shenanigans of the Seymour party and all the rumours of a new marriage. Cromwell was not the one stirring all this up; he was simply waiting to see what Henry would do, and meanwhile carrying on negotiations with Chapuys and dealing with other government business. And where is the evidence for Cromwell's deadly retaliation? Only in those words clumsily mistranslated and taken out of context from Chapuys's letter of 6 June seen in the previous chapter. The facts tell a wholly different story, and even Eric Ives is compelled to admit that Cromwell isn't doing a thing about Anne at this stage.

When Skip quoted the wicked deeds of Haman, he was complaining about councillors (the plural), not one in particular, and Anne had more dangerous enemies on the council than Cromwell – Norfolk for example, and Jane's factional supporters. Because none of Henry's ministers except Cranmer was showing much sympathy for Anne, this could have been a swipe at all of them. It is, however, true that Cromwell had been called Haman before, and he would be labelled Haman again in the Pilgrimage of Grace of 1537; but this was the invective of aggrieved Papalists of the old religion, never of reformers. Our conspiracy theorists have now got themselves into a pickle. If Anne is an evangelical queen, as they say, why is she likening Cromwell to Haman, when Cromwell has been smuggling Melanchthon's *Apology* into England, reforming the monasteries along evangelical lines and encouraging Henry to treat with the Lutherans? Those who seek to set Anne at enmity with Cromwell succeed only in delivering a devastating indictment of her evangelical credentials.[11]

For the sake of argument, however, let us suppose that Cromwell was, as is alleged, the prime or even the sole target of Anne's anger. How did he react? He did nothing at all. The taunts of the doomed queen and the excitable Skip, if they really were aimed at him, passed him by like the idle wind. As Ives himself well notes, when Skip was taken to task for his sermon, he was interrogated on all aspects of it *except* the Esther-Haman point. Skip later re-appears in the records with Anne when she was in prison in the Tower. Again Cromwell does nothing. Obviously no one, least of all Cromwell, was getting excited over this rather worn and silly Haman jibe. Now in the thick of complex negotiations with Chapuys, he had far weightier things on his mind. Besides, likening a minister to Haman was pretty tame stuff when set alongside the comparison of Henry, Defender of the Faith and Head of the Church, to the apostate Solomon.[12]

Astute, adult men of state are not like petulant six-year-olds, who must get their own back whenever someone calls them names. Nor do they waste valuable time on petty, personal vendettas, especially when there is nothing worth getting worked up about. And should the time ever come for a sharp, surgical strike against an opponent, they make sure that someone else's fingerprints are on the knife. So even if Cromwell had wanted to be rid of Anne, he needed only to wait patiently for Henry and the Seymours to do the deed for him. Cromwell was never afraid of this queen's sharp tongue. 'She can do me no harm', he assured Chapuys a year ago. It was true then and it was even truer at this stage. Comparisons with Anne's putsch against Wolsey in 1529–30 are not valid here. In Wolsey's last years, Anne was Henry's true love, the woman who would bear him his heir. In April 1536 she was neither. Her place in the king's heart had been stolen by Jane. It did not matter any more whether Anne wanted Cromwell's head off. She may have wanted Jane's head off too, but there was nothing she could do about it. Henry, not Anne, decided whose heads should roll. The crumbling Boleyn faction had become toothless, and it held no terrors for Cromwell.

To revert from the intrigues of court to those of diplomacy, sometime in the first week of April Chapuys received the emperor's reply to his letter in which he had described the approaches made to him by Cromwell previously discussed. After commending his ambassador's conduct, Charles agreed that Chapuys should do all he could to induce Henry to be reconciled to Rome. Charles issued a veiled warning that if the pope proceeded to the 'depravation' of England, and asked for the help of the princes of Christendom, 'we and the rest of them could not well refuse'. Charles offered to mediate on Henry's behalf if that would help. However, if Chapuys perceived that it was 'impossible to withdraw Henry from the error in which he is', then Charles was prepared, though reluctantly, to 'set this point aside for a while' rather than abandon negotiations with Henry and Cromwell altogether. Chapuys should do whatever he could to secure Mary's legitimacy; but here again, if Henry refused, Chapuys may 'allow the matter to drop and things remain as they are for the present'. Chapuys should continue to act in Mary's best interests, with Cromwell's assistance if he was willing to give it – and Charles called Cromwell the 'most fit' of Henry's ministers. The emperor welcomed the prospect of English help against the Turk and a more formal alliance with Henry, but he cautioned Chapuys to be wary lest the anti-French feeling in England among the king and his councillors 'be only feigned'. With Charles prepared to be flexible, therefore, the prospect of an Anglo-Imperial accord edged a little closer.[13]

Some assessment of Cromwell's own aims may now be called for. An imperial alliance would undoubtedly benefit English trade, but Cromwell was interested in more than commerce. Besides talking to Chapuys, Cromwell was also eagerly awaiting the outcome of the embassy to Germany, and corresponding cordially with Martin Luther and Justus Jonas in Wittenberg. Luther's letter to Cromwell, dated 9 April, commended Cromwell's goodwill 'in the cause of Christ', which he had heard about from Robert Barnes. Luther prayed that the Lord would 'complete the good work begun in him', meaning Cromwell. Jonas assured Cromwell that if agreement could be reached in religion, a political treaty with England would follow.[14]

Certainty is difficult without any personal memoirs of his own to draw on. However, it seems as though Cromwell saw within his grasp the hugely advantageous prospect of a twin alliance, one with the Schmalkaldic League and another with Charles. If handled skilfully, the two could compliment rather than clash with each other. The Lutheran princes were Charles's subjects, anxious to live in peace with him so far as was possible, and willing to support him against the Turk if called upon. Additional support from England would be greatly welcomed. In that case, therefore, Charles could hardly object too strongly to a separate Anglo-Lutheran treaty, which might be a price worth paying, certainly until the Turkish threat could be dealt with. And if Henry and the Lutheran princes were rallying under the emperor's banner to the defence of Western Christendom, even Rome's hostility would be neutered. Cries of 'heretic' and 'schismatic' would be silenced, briefly at least, leaving England free from the danger of attack by Europe's Catholic powers. Events at home could also work to Cromwell's personal gain. Apart from earning Henry international prestige, an English army abroad would need commanders to lead it, and Henry's most prominent general was Norfolk, one of Cromwell's main rivals on the council. With Norfolk and Gardiner both conveniently out of the country, Cromwell could consolidate his grip on power at home, and advance the evangelical cause more thoroughly. Henry would take all the credit for English military success, and Norfolk all the blame for any failure. It was, therefore, a bold and imaginative plan, and it would have been a stunning diplomatic coup if he could have brought it to pass. However, Chapuys's condition that England should tacitly accept papal authority again was unacceptable for Cromwell. Nor would Henry ever humble himself before the pope. This obstacle remained, and Cromwell would have to overcome it somehow.

An opportunity presented itself near Easter, when Chapuys and Cromwell held a further meeting. It began with a discussion of the emperor's letter. Sensing a little flexibility in the Imperial negotiating position, Cromwell decided to exploit it. He pointed out the difficulties regarding any reconciliation with Rome – the pope had offended Henry personally, while acts of parliament had been passed and could not quickly be altered. Still, Cromwell was determined to do all he could to help. He enigmatically hinted that Charles 'might in time have greater authority and credit to persuade his master to reconciliation with the Apostolic See'. Cromwell then referred to a letter he had recently received from Rome, sent on the instructions of the pope's son, Peter Louis Farnese. This letter promised that should 'the king my master feel inclined to treat, he would find the pope disposed to gratify and please him as much as he possibly could'; but if Henry refused, then 'His Holiness would be obliged to give up altogether the friendship of France'. Cromwell then sent for the secretary who had the letter, to show it to Chapuys. The secretary, however, was not in his office. While Cromwell was 'much displeased' at this, Chapuys was wondering what the words about 'giving up the friendship of France' might mean. Cromwell gave 'an evasive answer'. Chapuys persisted. Why, he asked, should the pope, having lost England, 'be so careless of French friendship' as to risk losing France as well? Chapuys now suspected something else. Was Henry secretly tempting Francis to ally with England on religion against the papacy? To this 'Cromwell made no reply, save to say that he really could not understand what was meant by the words'. Another possibility then occurred to Chapuys. Maybe this mysterious letter could explain Rome's recent chilliness towards Charles, and warmth to Francis. Maybe Francis had been hinting that *he*, not Charles, might be the one to reconcile Henry and Rome.[15]

Behind this intricate diplomatic dealing lay a simple message. Cromwell had sent Chapuys a veiled warning. If Charles remained too demanding in his conditions for an Anglo-Imperial alliance, then Henry might be tempted to make an alliance with Francis instead. It was a subtle reminder to Chapuys of Henry's advantageous bargaining position; he could swing either to France or to the emperor, whichever option looked the most attractive. Chapuys, however, accomplished diplomat that he was, gave nothing away. He piously reflected that any offer made for the sake of the unity of Christendom should be welcome. Cromwell agreed, and 'added that he sincerely hoped all would be set right in time'.

If a cricketing metaphor may be employed to sum up the latest exchange between the two, Cromwell had varied his line of flight only to be met by an impeccably straight bat from Chapuys. Nevertheless, the point had been made, and soon it would get back to the emperor, just as Cromwell wanted. A further concession might be forthcoming. To encourage this, Cromwell then assured Chapuys that he was doing all he could to make Henry look favourably on Mary. The council, he added, were mostly supportive of friendship with Charles. This support would increase yet more if reports that Francis had made an agreement with the Turk were confirmed.

Cromwell then sent one of his clerks to inform Henry about this discussion. Henry seemed well pleased; he invited Chapuys to meet him the following Tuesday, promising him that he would 'be welcome, and get such an answer as would greatly please me'. Chapuys duly arrived at court on the appointed day. It was Tuesday 18 April, a day of high diplomatic drama, and a fateful one for Queen Anne.

In the morning all went agreeably well. The ambassador was met first by Cromwell, before being received by other councillors as an honoured guest. Cromwell raised a delicate matter of protocol – would Chapuys be prepared to meet Anne and kiss her hand? Very politely Chapuys excused himself – that would be going too far too soon. This was accepted with good grace, and Henry appeared at his most affable when Chapuys was presented to him. On the way to mass, Chapuys and Anne met face to face, and exchanged the faintest of bows. After mass and dinner, Henry saw Chapuys again, and took him into a private room. Cromwell and Audley followed them. Chapuys gently raised the subject of Anglo-Imperial relations with Henry. Then the ambassador noticed the first signs that things were not going as expected. Henry's mood altered; he abruptly introduced the subject of the duchy of Milan, and stung Chapuys by saying that Francis had as good a title to Milan as Charles. Soon Chapuys suspected that 'the affection this king professes' for Charles was 'neither sincere nor disinterested', and he withdrew to speak with Jane Seymour's brother. From a discreet vantage point he could see Henry with Cromwell and Audley, though he could not hear what was said. Between the first two, 'much altercation and angry words' soon arose. Suddenly Cromwell turned his back on Henry and stormed out of the room into the foyer where Chapuys and Seymour were standing together. Seething with anger, Cromwell sat down on a chest and demanded a drink. After a short while

Henry followed him out. The king turned to Chapuys and brusquely demanded that Chapuys put his requests in writing. Chapuys protested respectfully – this was an attack on his integrity. Then Henry launched into a tirade – Charles had no right to meddle in Henry's affairs, either regarding his relations with the pope or with Mary; Henry would deal with Mary exactly as he pleased, depending on whether she was obedient or disobedient. 'I am no longer a child', bawled Henry, 'to be whipped ... then caressed and petted, and urged to come back and called all manner of sweet names'. Henry then started to 'play with his fingers on his knees, and do as people who want to appease a crying child'. Complaining bitterly of Charles's ingratitude to him, Henry demanded that Charles write a personal letter apologising for past wrongs and asking Henry's forgiveness. While this performance was being played out, Cromwell and Audley sat with heads in their hands, downcast and dejected.

Briefly but courteously, Chapuys took his leave. Later that day he saw Cromwell again, who was 'so affected that he could hardly say one word ... never in his life had he been so much taken aback'. Chapuys commiserated; he suggested dropping or delaying the matter, and concentrating on less contentious points like improving diplomatic relations generally, and helping Mary. At these consoling words Cromwell 'suddenly recovered his wits, and said that the game was not entirely lost, and that he still had hopes of success'. The following day (Wednesday), led by Cromwell, Henry's Council begged the king to relent and seek Charles's friendship; but Henry would not yield. Cromwell assured Chapuys that during their talks together he had always acted with Henry's authority. He could not imagine why Henry changed his mind so abruptly. 'Whoever trusts in the words of princes, who one day say one thing and on the next retract it, relies on them, or expects the fulfilment of their promises, is not a wise man, as I myself experienced last Tuesday'. So Cromwell confessed to Chapuys.

This astonishing sequence of events now calls for a moment of reflection. Merriman predictably blames Cromwell for pursuing his hopes of an Anglo-Imperial alliance too far, when Henry simply wanted to stay neutral. But this does not convince for a moment. Henry was not consistently neutral between Francis and Charles. Before Cromwell's rise to power, and again after his fall, Henry fought on one side or the other. Besides, Henry himself had looked forward to better relations with Charles following Catherine's death, and Cromwell had kept Henry fully informed about his discussions with Chapuys. If Henry disapproved of what Cromwell was doing, he could at any time have ordered him to stop seeing Chapuys; and he would not have invited Chapuys to court on the Tuesday morning, first holding out the hope of an agreement and then dashing it in a manner embarrassing to his ministers and humiliating to Chapuys. Henry's royal tantrum – whining about Charles's past unkindness, playing on his knee – suggests that he could not resist this opportunity to take sweet revenge for all the wrongs he imagined he had suffered from Charles. Cromwell, by contrast, wanted to keep negotiations with the imperialists going, hoping that Charles might give further ground on his demand that Henry should submit to Rome.[16]

One clue to Henry's odd behaviour comes from letters of French diplomats. On 19 April, the day after the scene with Chapuys and Cromwell, the bishop of Tarbes saw Henry and also Norfolk, who assured him that relations between France and England would remain unchanged, no matter what the emperor might promise. Henry then showed Tarbes a letter he had received from Charles, allegedly asking Henry to make peace and help him (Charles) against Francis and the Turk. Believing that Charles was preparing to attack French forces in Italy, Henry then offered Francis advice on military tactics. Francis was naturally delighted to be receiving such useful intelligence about the emperor's plans.[17]

Henry, it would seem, was not only playing Francis and Charles off against each other. He was doing the same with his two most powerful ministers at home, Cromwell and Norfolk. He used the one to deal with the imperialists, the other with the French. In his own eccentric way, Henry was trying to keep a balance of power not only in Europe but also in his own council, watching to see which way things would go before making his mind up – and in the end, not really making it up at all. The only certainty is Henry's unpredictability. Anyone who has ever worked for a boss who changes his mind at the last minute without bothering to keep his management team fully informed will know how Cromwell felt on the morning of 18 April.

But maddening though this can be, it is not life threatening. Nowhere does Chapuys, who reported minutely on all these events, even hint that Cromwell's position was now imperilled. He was not isolated, and he had much support in the council for rapprochement with Charles. Nor was he under any threat from Anne and her rapidly crumbling faction. She was *not* actively opposing Cromwell's pro-Imperial policy, though whether she opposed it or supported it no longer mattered very much. Her removal had never been one of Chapuys's pre-conditions for an imperial alliance. In fact, Charles was now prepared to recognize her as queen provided only that there was some sort of posthumous rehabilitation of Catherine and reconciliation with Rome. So unless Cromwell had gone momentarily insane, there is absolutely no reason whatsoever (apart from a dodgy translation in the *Calendar of State Papers*) to believe that he would want to vent his frustration with Henry on Anne. Cromwell's quandary was what to do about Henry's exasperating changeability, not what to do with a queen whose demise was already determined.[18]

However, though Anne was a mere bystander in England's foreign diplomacy, she now returns to the centre stage of domestic policy. From Chapuys's letter of 6 June (see Chapter 8), it was on or just after 18 April that Henry set in motion the sequence of events that would lead to the downfall of Anne and the crowning of Jane. It may have been at the council meeting on 19 April that Henry 'authorized and commissioned' Cromwell to prepare the case for a second divorce and a new marriage. The only reason he had not done this earlier, says Chapuys, was that 'one of his Privy Councillors hinted that he could not divorce himself from Anne without tacitly acknowledging the validity of his first marriage'.[19]

This information is the best clue yet to explaining Henry's volte-face of the previous day (18 April). If Henry sought peace with Charles at the same time as he ended his marriage to Anne – the marriage that had caused the rift between the two monarchs in the first place – that could all too easily be seen as an admission of guilt for putting away Catherine of Aragon, the emperor's aunt. A vindication of Catherine and a victory for Charles: this, surely, was how it would be interpreted by observers on the continent. It was more than this proud Tudor king could endure. So this was Henry's dilemma: how could he divorce Anne without appearing to be the loser? Answer: he would give a grand display of his political virility with a rebuff to Charles and a public humiliation of his ambassador. This done, and when no one could accuse him of weakness or defeat, he would 'authorise and commission' Cromwell to end his marriage to Anne.

Subsequent events confirm the view that the king's mind was made up. On 22 April Cranmer, who had missed the rumpus at court having been at Knole for a few days, dashed off a letter to Cromwell. Cranmer began unremarkably enough by asking Cromwell to remember a master Smyth of the exchequer. Then the archbishop suddenly changed the subject and broke into an impassioned appeal – 'I was ever hitherto cold, but now I am in a heat with the cause of religion, which goeth all contrary to mine expectation, if it be as the fame goeth; wherein I would fain break my mind unto you'. This 'cause of religion' is such a vague expression that it reads almost like a coded message. Could it mean, perhaps, the cause of the Reformation, which Cranmer feared might be threatened if, 'as the fame goeth', Anne was about to be replaced by Catholic Jane? The most likely explanation in the circumstances is that rumours of Anne's impending rejection had reached Cranmer, perhaps the only real ally Anne had left on the council, and he desperately wanted to speak to Cromwell about it. However, no reply is traceable. It may well be that Cranmer was being kept away from court deliberately. It is also plausible that he was the lone voice on the council who had been trying to dissuade Henry from divorcing Anne.[20]

Then on 24 April a commission of *oyer and terminer* was named to investigate unspecified treasons. Issued from the Lord Chancellor's office, it included Cromwell, Norfolk and Thomas Boleyn. This is a curious document, because it did not bring any specific charge against any named individual. So what could these treasons – as yet unnamed and uncommitted – be? No allegations of the queen's infidelity had yet been reported. The most probable answer in the context is that Henry, Cromwell and now Audley were preparing the ground in the more than likely event that Anne would not depart meekly. Under existing legislation her refusal to surrender her crown would not be treason – but it could be *made* treason if the right laws were hurriedly passed and the judicial machinery put in place.[21]

Next day, 25 April, Henry wrote to Richard Pate, his ambassador with Charles, advising him of the recent discussions with Chapuys, and justifying his uncompromising stance. In one part of the letter – on the subject of Mary's legitimacy and her place in the succession – Henry's choice of words suggests that he was anticipating a happy event that had yet to be publicly and formally announced:

> The emperor's second overture and request was that, forasmuch *as there is great likelihood and appearance that God will send unto us heirs male to succeed us* … we would vouchsafe … to legitimise our daughter Mary in such degree, *as in default of issue by our most dear and most entirely beloved wife the queen*, she [Mary] might not be reputed unable to some place in our succession.[22]

How could Henry be so confident of male heirs if he was apparently resigned to a 'default of issue' from his present queen? Henry was getting ahead of himself, his heart now fixed on his new dearly beloved. Pate may have heard unofficially about Jane, so he was unlikely to be misled by this 'most dear and beloved wife the queen', as if Henry was still attached to Anne. This is the language of diplomacy. Henry was being indiscreet, but he was not speaking from the heart. Nor was this the right time to officially announce to his ambassadors abroad that he was about to put Anne, the barren wife, away for another woman. Yet it is scarcely credible that Charles or Chapuys would have put the matter as tactlessly as Henry implied – We know God will give you male heirs, but in case you have no children by Anne, will you admit Mary to the succession! It must be one of the strangest letters Henry ever wrote, but we will have to leave Pate to puzzle it out for himself, because events at home were moving ahead swiftly.

A new queen would require new succession laws, so writs were issued on 27 April for a new parliament to assemble with all haste; the previous parliament had been dissolved on 14 April. Chapuys was also full of news. Nicholas Carew, one of Jane's most lively supporters, had been invested with the Order of the Garter much to the frustration of Anne's brother, who had coveted it for himself. Carew was daily conspiring against Anne, and increasingly confident that she would soon be 'dismissed'. This word 'dismissed' – not 'destroyed' – is worth noting well. There is a world of difference between Anne being dismissed and Anne being destroyed. Henry was 'tired of her', Chapuys continued; he cannot 'bear her any longer'. Henry and Cromwell must have reckoned with the likelihood that Cranmer would be reluctant to consent to Anne's 'dismissal', so Bishop Stokesley of London had been sounded out on whether Henry could 'abandon' her. Stokesley was cagey; he would not give an opinion unless asked to do so by Henry, and even then he would try and 'ascertain what the king's intentions were' before committing himself. The word 'abandon' is as significant as the 'dismissed'. All the talk is of Anne being divorced, as Catherine was, but nothing more. Not yet.[23]

Cromwell, meanwhile, had spent four days in conference with Richard Sampson, dean of the Chapel Royal. This news comes from another letter of Chapuys dated 29 April. So he meant either 25–28, or 26–29 inclusive. No reason was given for this conference, but it should be easy enough to deduce it. Sampson took no part in Anne's subsequent trial for adultery. Nor does his name appear on the *oyer and terminer*, or on her indictment, or on any other document related to her trial. Sampson was, however, an expert in canon law, who had been a key member of Henry's team during his first divorce. So Cromwell and Sampson must have been the men assigned by the king to work on the legal and constitutional aspects of the second divorce. Cromwell, therefore, was not busily framing *criminal* charges against Anne during the last days of April. He would not need the company of a *canon* lawyer for that.[24]

Preparations for Anne's 'dismissal' were proceeding apace. Chapuys, beavering away eagerly as ever for news, heard 'from certain authentic quarters' that there were 'many witnesses ready to testify and to prove that more than nine years ago a marriage had been contracted and consummated' between Anne and Henry Percy, earl of Northumberland. Percy, it will be remembered, was the man Anne might have married had Henry not set his eyes on her; and only the combined pressure of Percy's father, who threatened to disown his son, and of Cardinal Wolsey, ordered by Henry to separate the couple, compelled the young earl to forsake her (see p. 29).[25]

It is fascinating to hear that 'many witnesses' could prove that a marriage had been consummated. Be that as it may, attention now needs to focus on this pre-contract between Anne and Percy, and it is virtually certain that some sort of bond had existed between them. If there was never even a likelihood of a marriage, why would Henry have ordered his then chief minister Wolsey to intervene and bring their relationship to an end? Why would Percy be threatened with disinheritance if the young couple were just friends? Unfortunately it is not possible to say whether it was a formal, legally binding contract because the relevant papers have been lost; but if evidence had now come to light for a consummation as well as a marriage agreement, whether formal or informal, then Henry could have his marriage to Anne declared null and void in law, leaving him free to marry Jane. So Henry's case was cast-iron; or rather, it could be made cast-iron without difficulty. Anne had little support in the government or in the country, and unlike Catherine she had no foreign potentate like Charles V to defend her cause. With witnesses willing to testify, with parliament about to be recalled to confirm the new marriage, with the *oyer and terminer* ready if needed, with no diplomatic complications whatsoever, no obstacle stood in the way to frustrate Henry. No one would bother to ask awkward questions, like why the Boleyn marriage was allowed to take place at all if Anne was pre-contracted to Percy. Within a few weeks everything would be settled and Anne 'dismissed'. It did not matter one whit to Henry that all of Europe would see that the whole thing was a convenient fix. Henry cared nothing for Europe's opinions.

Most writers on Henry and Anne have simply assumed that in order to be rid of Anne and marry Jane, Henry had no alternative but to commit or countenance an act of judicial murder. This is the utterly wrong-headed assumption that spawns the many fanciful conspiracy theories surrounding Anne Boleyn, and the vilest of crimes and motives are liberally imputed to Henry, Cromwell or some other councillor. Henry is a monster, Cromwell a bloody butcher, Cranmer a craven toady, and so on. The evidence that had now apparently come to light, for a pre-contract and a consummation, ensured that Henry did *not* need to destroy Anne before he could wed Jane. He had already nullified his first marriage through parliament and the courts. He could, therefore, follow his own precedent and do the same with Anne if a sufficiently plausible constitutional rationale could be found; hence the secondment of Richard Sampson, already a specialist in royal divorces, to help Cromwell prepare the case. Everything points conclusively to the fact that Henry and Cromwell were determined to resolve the affair in a sort of constitutional manner. There was no crude conspiracy being hatched.

Then, though admittedly this is conjectural, just as Catherine of Aragon had been downgraded from queen to princess dowager, Henry could have done something similar with Anne. She had been made marchioness of Pembrokeshire before her coronation in 1532, and she could have been allowed to keep that title as a consolation prize on the condition that she lived quietly and obediently for the rest of her days. Any resistance would be made treasonable under the new legislation soon to be enacted in parliament, and be dealt with ruthlessly.

In fact, it is not clear what Henry intended to do with Anne at this stage apart from dismiss her, though later reports of uncertain reliability indicate that the plan was to send her off to a nunnery. It had no doubt occurred to him that she might prove troublesome, and that the option lay open to him to compel her submission to the new settlement on pain of the axe. That eventuality, however, was some weeks off. For now, according to ambassadors' reports – and Chapuys was intimately informed by his well-placed sources – there were no rumours of criminal charges or treason trials flying around the court. Right up to the last days of April, all the well-versed diplomatic and court gossip focussed on the king's divorce and Anne's 'dismissal', but nothing more. No arrests had been made, and no one was committed to the Tower for interrogation.

Neither is it clear whether Henry had given Cromwell and Sampson a deadline. The king had not yet cancelled a pre-arranged royal tour to the south coast. Cromwell and Anne were originally part of the entourage, and although Cromwell may have changed his plans, Henry was still intending to go. As late as Saturday 29 April an instruction was sent from London to Lord Lisle in Calais to ship the double cannon over to Dover so that Henry could see it when he arrived there. Not until Sunday was the royal schedule altered. Henry was due to set off for Rochester the following Tuesday, but the trip was abruptly called off. Then the news filtered through that the entire Dover tour was cancelled.[26]

The classic account of what happened to throw Henry's court into turmoil on the eve of the month of May is that given by a French diplomat, Lancelot de Carles, now on an embassy to England as secretary to the bishop of Tarbes. It is a narrative of the life and death of Anne Boleyn, dated 2 June 1536. The following discussion concentrates on the section dealing with her arrest, but first a word is necessary about de Carles's *bona fides*. His work is not a vulgar anti-Boleyn diatribe of the kind that later appeared, for in parts it speaks quite well of Anne. It is an independent account, because a French diplomat would not compose an obituary of Anne on the say so of the English government; and he would certainly not circulate false propaganda to oblige Cromwell, the chief advocate of the pro-Imperial policy. De Carles wrote poetically and gives some facts that are not found elsewhere, but much of what he says is verifiable from other sources, so there is no reason to imagine that this is a romance or a fantasy. Unlike Alexander Alesius and the *Spanish Chronicle*, de Carles contains no obvious howlers. His account, therefore, is a reliable one. One final point: de Carles does not mention Cromwell's name.[27]

One day, says de Carles, a certain lord of the Privy Council had words with his sister for being over affectionate in her ways. She admitted it; but she also said that her behaviour was nothing compared with Anne's, and that if they questioned Mark Smeaton, the young court musician, they would find out a few interesting things. She claimed Anne had a string of lovers, including her own brother. This lord, realizing what a scoop this was certain to be, immediately sought out two fellow councillors. All three then went to tell Henry. The king ordered an immediate investigation, during which Smeaton confessed that he had slept with Anne three times. He also named her other lovers – Henry Norris, Francis Weston and William Brereton as well as her brother George. Henry was quickly convinced of Anne's unfaithfulness, and after a day spent watching the jousting on 1 May, he personally accosted Norris. Within twenty-four hours all suspects, including Anne, were in the Tower.

Chapuys was amazed when he first heard the news on 2 May. Despite all his contacts at court, and despite all his watchfulness, he had no inkling of these dramatic developments. Anne had kept her love nest well hidden. Chapuys had been wondering if somehow the preparations for her divorce and 'dismissal' could be speeded up, but now he hurried off a despatch to Charles telling him that 'things have come to a head much sooner and more satisfactorily than one could have thought'.[28]

Apart from the games on 1 May, de Carles is not quite as precise with his dates as modern scholars aim to be. However, though he does not say so specifically, it reads as though these three lords went to see Henry on 28 or 29 April. Fortunately we should be able to confirm these crucial dates quite accurately, because it is known that the chief witness, Smeaton, was committed to the Tower on 1 May. Working backwards, therefore, we need allow a maximum of forty-eight hours, and more likely twelve or twenty-four, between Henry hearing of Anne's infidelities and Smeaton's committal. It is impossible to account for a delay longer than this. So the delegation must have gone to the king on 28 or more likely 29 April. This conclusion is consistent with de Carles, and it would also fit in with the sudden cancellation of the Dover visit on the 29 or 30 April.[29]

The identity of the informers is not known, and a great deal of speculation has led to nothing conclusive. Perhaps because he was here on diplomatic service, de Carles preferred to withhold names. It is virtually certain, however, that Cromwell was not one of them – he was otherwise engaged with Richard Sampson preparing legal and constitutional documents. It was probably late on 29 April that Cromwell received an urgent message from Henry ordering him to break off this work and examine Smeaton.[30]

Now it is taken for granted by most writers that Smeaton was tortured, threatened with torture, or roughed up somehow. In fact, the only evidence for this is the *Spanish Chronicle*, the book which has Cromwell investigating Catherine Howard and other enjoyable but farcically wide-of-the-mark yarns as we saw in Chapter 8. In his balanced and sensible narrative, de Carles is quite specific – Smeaton confessed *without torture*. George Constantine, writing sometime later, endorsed this. Though Constantine had heard a story that Smeaton had been 'grievously racked', he added that 'I could never know this of a truth'. This qualifier, though left out of some accounts of Anne Boleyn, is important because he was a servant of Henry Norris, one of Anne's alleged lovers, and he wrote to Norris after his condemnation, handing the letter to 'Mr Lieutenant' of the Tower. So if any racking had been going on, Constantine could have found out – but he did not. This is not surprising. A man who had been 'grievously racked' on or about 1 May would be expected to show signs of wounds at his trial and execution barely two weeks later, but none of the surviving accounts, either by Chapuys or anyone else, even hints at it. Besides, racking Smeaton on his own makes no sense at all in the context, because if his confession had been successfully procured through torture, then the obvious thing to do would be to rack the rest of them and get them to confess as well. Then the case for the prosecution would be nicely wrapped up.[31]

Despite the confident assumptions of many modern writers, therefore, no reliable evidence exists for torture. On the contrary, reports soon circulating around London claimed that Smeaton confessed embarrassingly freely because he was jealous of the queen's other lovers. Though the accuracy of this story cannot be proven, it does contain an uncomfortable ring of truth. The last time Smeaton saw Anne he was standing disconsolate by a window, and she reminded him teasingly that he was not a noble man, and she could not speak to him as if he were. 'No, no, Madam', sighed the youth. 'A look sufficed me, and thus fare you well'. Within hours of this little exchange Smeaton was under arrest, and once in the hands of an interrogator as skilled as Cromwell, no racks or knotted ropes would have been needed to get this jealous young lover to open his heart and blurt out a few secrets.[32]

According to the above account of events, while the government was preparing the mind-numbing constitutional legalities for a divorce and re-marriage, the royal sex scandal suddenly exploded like an unforeseen firecracker. Such a view will never satisfy addicts of conspiracy theories, but it is worth noting that scandals in high places during our own times (there is no need to mention names) often come to light purely by chance. After the news breaks the vultures circle overhead, and political opponents rush to seize whatever spoils they can; but the discovery of the story itself is often more accidental than designed. Scandals are frequently exposed when the press stumble on something, like the lord whose sister was a flirt, or when someone close to the central character spills the beans, like Smeaton. There is no reason why the Anne Boleyn affair should be any different.

Some may feel that this is all a bit too accidental. They could be right. The Seymour faction was certainly trying to speed up Anne's dismissal, and it may seem suspicious that those unnamed lords went to Henry just when Cranmer was away at Knole and Cromwell locked in discussions with Sampson over the divorce matters. A delegation bent on mischief could hardly have picked a more opportune moment to fill Henry's suspicious mind with stories about Anne. This, however, is straying into the realms of conspiracy theories once again without any convincing reason. The identity of the informers remains unknown, and there is no evidence that they had any ulterior motive. Besides, there is a hugely compelling argument against any kind of conspiracy, namely this: there was absolutely no need for one. The constitutional apparatus to remove Anne and crown Jane was fast being assembled, and was almost finished.

Meanwhile, Anne and her co-accused were confined in the Tower. William Kingston, Constable of the Tower, sent reports to Cromwell of statements and confessions that Anne made there. The following is a sample of the evidence that arrived on Cromwell's desk and are Kingston's own words:

> I hear say, said she, that I should be accused with three men; and I can say no more but nay, without I should open my body. And therewith she opened her gown.

Anne also admitted her last exchange with Smeaton ('Madam, a look sufficed' – see above). Another one with Norris went as follows: after a tiff between them she turned to Norris and said, 'You look for dead men's shoes ... if ought came to the king but good, you would look to have me'.

She once told Francis Weston that he did not love her kins-woman, Mrs. Skelton, or his wife. Weston replied that he loved another better than both. 'Who?' asked Anne. 'It is yourself', he answered. In one of his last messages before he died, Weston asked forgiveness from his father, his mother and his wife – but especially his wife.[33]

None of this was extracted under torture. Some of it was overhead by others.

So had Anne, desperate for a son to secure her position as queen and retain the king's favour, ceded to the temptation to take lovers in addition to a husband? Gilbert Burnet, one of the greatest of the older historians, who may have had access to evidence no longer available to us, did not believe so. Burnet admitted, however, that 'she had rallied some of the king's servants more than became her', that 'some indiscretions could not be denied', and he added – with most exquisite tact – that 'her carriage seemed too free', all of which led to her sudden, tragic undoing. A recent re-examination of the case by Greg Walker has broadly endorsed Burnet. It is gentlemanly to seek to absolve Anne in this manner, though whether the argument would have impressed hard-nosed Tudor prosecuting lawyers must be rather unlikely. They might have pointed out that a virtuous queen, knowing how precarious her position was, would have been a good deal more prudent with her 'carriage' than this one. We are, however, nearly half a millennium away from the scene of the alleged crimes, and it is impossible to decide for sure between this view and that of George Bernard, who would find Anne guilty of some charges though maybe not all. Suffice to say that for those who cannot believe the evidence, the Burnet-Walker analysis offers a sounder defence than a conspiracy theory. At least it recognises that there is ground for suspicion if not a conviction. For it must be as plain as plain can be that something peculiar had been going on in Anne Boleyn's circle, and it was not normal, harmless 'courtly love' of the kind that Tudor queens and titled ladies were wont to engage in. No evidence exists even from court gossip of Elizabeth of York, Catherine of Aragon, Jane Seymour and Catherine Parr 'opening her body' or flirting with grooms and assorted gentlemen of the king's Privy Chamber; nor were they ever overheard muttering sweet nothings with handsome young musicians by the window at twilight; and none of them ever, either in jest or in earnest, mused aloud on who might bed her if the king were to suddenly die.[34]

On the basis of Kingston's reports, Smeaton's confession, and other confessions now pouring from the lips of various ladies of court, the formal charges against the accused were drawn up. It is sometimes claimed that some of these charges cannot be valid because either Anne or her 'lover' was somewhere else at the time stated. But apart from the obvious problem of proving where people were on exact days 500 years ago, when not all the relevant evidence has survived, this asks us to believe that government lawyers could not get the dates right on the indictment. Also, as Bernard has already noted, the distances involved – usually Greenwich and Richmond or Westminster – are not great, and with a good horse and cart could easily be covered in a day with time to spare. Besides, illicit lovers are seldom so stupid as to leave themselves without an alibi. Anne's 'lovers', incidentally, were not enemies of Cromwell that he needed to get rid of – they were not big enough.[35]

Chapuys, meanwhile, was showing a generous spirit in his letters, sending generally balanced reports of the trials and subsequent events without crowing. Not so Henry – he was now adamant that Anne had had 'upwards of 100 gentlemen' for lovers. Nevertheless, he seemed strangely unconcerned about being cuckolded by his wife on so grand a scale. 'You never saw a prince or husband show or wear his horns more patiently and lightly than this one does', the ambassador noted wryly. As well as adultery charges, Anne and her co-accused had allegedly cast doubts on Henry's prowess in the marriage bed; but despite these aspersions on his manhood – or maybe in answer to them? – Henry has 'more joy and pleasure now' than ever before, and he has 'daily gone out to dine here and there with the ladies, and sometimes had remained with them till after midnight'. There was little public sympathy for Anne, Chapuys continued, but 'still a few find fault and grumble at the manner in which the proceedings against her were conducted'. Apart from Smeaton, the accused 'were sentenced on mere presumption or on very slight grounds, without legal proof or valid confession'. Henry's menacing shadow loomed over the trial; at nine o'clock in the morning he told Jane that Anne would be sentenced by three o'clock that afternoon, and so she was. Chapuys was not greatly impressed with Jane – no great beauty or wit – and already he was wondering how long it would be before Henry found witnesses and excuses to put her away too. Despite his disapproval of Anne and his opposition to the Boleyn marriage, however, Chapuys was magnanimous enough to remark on Anne's courage and readiness to meet death.[36]

There is something chilling about Henry in the aftermath of Anne's arrest. Once he was so infatuated with her that he had rebelled against the Holy See and suffered excommunication for her sake; now her ruin has become his entertainment. His whole performance defies analysis as he showed that curious mixture of mercy and vengeance, so characteristic of him when finishing off prominent victims. He allowed the condemned to die quickly by the axe, but then he insisted on carrying through the original plan to declare his marriage to Anne null; and not only on the basis of her 'pre-contract' with Percy, but also on the grounds of an affinity with Anne's elder sister, Mary, who had once been Henry's mistress. Besides bastardizing a second innocent daughter as cruelly and needlessly as the first, this was Henry at his most baffling in view of Anne's unexpected conviction; because as Burnet noted long ago, if she was never his lawful wife, she could not be an unfaithful wife guilty of adultery. Henry's reasoning must have gone something like this: though the marriage was always null, until it was *known* to be null, Anne owed him wifely fidelity.

It is an unusual line in logic. No evidence survives to tell us what advice Henry was receiving from his councillors, so we have to guess what Cromwell's involvement might have been. He was a lawyer by profession, with years of experience preparing documents for presentation to the courts that would be examined and challenged minutely. As Henry's councillor and Principal Secretary, Cromwell also drafted bills on constitutional, social and economic matters, every clause of which was subjected to parliamentary scrutiny and debate. He was expertly well practiced in preparing a watertight case for the king, parliament and the judiciary. Is it therefore remotely credible that he would have put forward a settlement containing such a glaring legal anomaly? Hardly. Even if Cromwell was the ogre that modern accounts of Anne imagine, at least he would be a competent ogre capable of getting the details and the documentation right. The ruling bears all the hallmarks of Henry superintending everything, as so often in the Boleyn tragedy, determined to doubly avenge himself on the woman he once loved but now loathed – a faithless woman who should never have been his wife at all. It then fell to the unfortunate Archbishop Cranmer to formally pronounce this nullity the day after he heard Anne's last confession. Quite justifiably, though frustratingly for inquisitive historians, no record is available of what was said at this final meeting between Anne and Cranmer.[37]

It is not surprising that doubts about the affair were soon rising in the minds of those at liberty to speak freely. In Flanders Regent Mary was weighing up Jane's chances of survival, while others on her council suspected that Henry might have invented the whole thing simply to be rid of Anne. Understandable though these suspicions were, the fact is that Henry, bizarre though his conduct was, did not invent the reports of the three lords, or the confessions of Smeaton and the other witnesses. What is at issue here is not the *existence* of evidence – there is no doubt of that – but the *interpretation* of it: whether it is enough to prove actual adultery, or whether it can be convincingly explained away, as Burnet sought to do, by Anne's 'indiscretions' and her undeniably 'free carriage'. Thus a tantalizing historical mystery is set to remain.[38]

This mystery, however, will not be solved by blackening the reputation of Henry's finest minister, and as the main purpose of this chapter is to answer the charges laid at Cromwell's door rather than stage the trial of Anne Boleyn one more time, it may now be timely to consider his own version of events given in an official letter dated 14 May to Gardiner in Paris. The points I have highlighted are especially relevant to the discussion that will follow.[39]

'*The king's highness* thought that I should advise you' of the queen's trial, so 'I shall express unto you some part of the *king's* proceeding in the same'. The queen's 'abomination both in incontinent living, and other offences' towards the king was 'so rank and common' that her ladies 'could not contain it within their breasts'. Soon it 'came to the ears of *some of his grace's council*, that with *their* duty to his majesty *they* could not conceal it from him'. Then, 'in most secret sort', certain persons of the privy chamber and Anne's entourage were examined, 'in which examinations the matter appeared so evident, that besides that crime, with the accidents, there broke out a certain conspiracy of the king's death, which extended so far that all *we who had the examination* of it quaked at the danger his grace was in', and gave thanks for the discovery of it. Then Smeaton, Norris, her brother, Weston and Brereton were sent to Tower. 'I write no particulars, the things be too abominable', but this shall be enough for you 'to declare the truth if you have occasion to do so'.

Virtually all of this can be independently verified. Various other reports mention ladies of the court – including Lady Worcester, Lady Wingfield and Nan Cobham – as witnesses who testified against Anne. The point about councillors reporting the matter to the king tallies with de Carles. The impersonal 'some of his grace's council', 'their duty' and 'they' who could not conceal it, strongly implies that Cromwell was not one of them. Again this agrees with Chapuys that Cromwell was working with Sampson at the time.[40]

More interesting is how Cromwell's own version differs notably from Chapuys's now famous letter of 6 June, stating that Cromwell, though acting under Henry's authority, had 'planned and brought about the whole affair' beginning on the 18 April. Cromwell, by contrast, calls the matter the 'king's proceeding'; he never claims that he instigated anything himself, or that he was acting on a tip-off following 'prognostications in Flanders'. Investigations do not begin until after reports of Anne's infidelities have reached the council, and it is *during* those investigations that a conspiracy against the king's life is uncovered. Neither does Cromwell claim to have taken the leading part – note the 'we' who examined the case, not 'those with me' or 'those under my direction'. This, too, agrees with various independent accounts that mention Norfolk, Fitzwilliam the Treasurer and Sir William Paulet of the King's Household all involved in questioning suspects and witnesses.[41]

Incidentally, these 'Flanders prognostications' may, unfortunately, have to remain a mystery, so far as I have been able to trace. As already noted, nothing was said about Flanders at Anne's trial. Cromwell's remembrances, possibly in early February, include a note to send Stephen Vaughan to Flanders, but no reason is given and it is not clear whether he even went. There is another letter from Cromwell to Vaughan about a journey to Germany, which includes a passing reference to your 'last voyage into Flanders', but the date of this letter is uncertain, and again no reason for the visit is given. Cromwell did have agents abroad who reported regularly on diplomatic affairs, but so far as the record goes, nothing was said about a threat on the king's life. There is also the case of William Latymer, a chaplain to Anne, who arrived back in England from Flanders on 7 May to be told that Anne had been taken to the Tower. Latymer had been buying books on the continent, and was whisked off to Henry. But no harm came to him; he was soon released, and he lived on till Elizabeth's reign.[42]

Perhaps the part Cromwell did play in the whole affair can now be quickly reviewed. On 18 April he was commissioned by the king to prepare the constitutional case to remove Anne and make Jane queen. During the last week of April he was carrying out this unenviable task with the assistance of Richard Sampson, one of the king's foremost canon lawyers. Enquiries were focussing on the alleged pre-contract between Anne and Henry Percy. Meanwhile the *oyer and terminer* was issued from the office of Lord Chancellor Audley. When stories of Anne's adultery broke, the king ordered Cromwell, along with Norfolk and others, to examine witnesses. Once the investigations were completed, Cromwell must have handed Kingston's reports over to government lawyers, because his own name does not appear on the indictment against Anne. Stories about Cromwell bribing, bullying and otherwise intimidating juries are no more than fictional tit-bits intended to spice up a conspiracy theory: there is no substantive evidence for them anywhere. Nor is there anything sinister in the fact that Cromwell knew who the jurors were; he was the king's chief administrative councillor, and this was the most high-profile treason trial imaginable, so obviously the jurors would be men of some standing and influence known to the government. Besides, Anne was tried by the peers of the realm, and Cromwell had no control over peerages. At this point Cromwell must have turned his attention to the forthcoming parliament and the drafting of the new succession bills. It was Norfolk, as Lord High Steward of England, who presided at Anne's trial and passed sentence. Norfolk also issued the precepts for the trial: to Judge John Baldwin, to return the indictment against Anne; to Kingston, to bring Anne from the Tower; and to the sergeant-at-arms, to summon the lords of the kingdom. Then Cranmer heard Anne's last confession before formally pronouncing the nullity.[43]

The conclusion must be, therefore, that Chapuys has slightly exaggerated when he implies that Cromwell brought the whole affair to completion. *Henry* was the one in overall control, and, quite understandably in such a momentous case, he ordered his most distinguished councillors – Cromwell, Norfolk, Cranmer and Audley – to deal with various aspects of it.

Chapuys is an indispensable source of information for researchers of the Tudor period. There is no reason to doubt him when he narrates plain facts or conversations, but when he starts to interpret events or give opinions or make judgements, he does have a tendency to exaggerate. He once gave his opinion that Cromwell had 'more influence' with Henry than Wolsey, and that Anne and her father were 'more Lutheran than Luther'. The first comment is very debateable and probably wrong, while the second is obviously wrong. Chapuys is also on record as saying in October 1533 that but for fear of a rebellion like the German Peasants' War, Henry would already have declared himself a Lutheran. In fact, Henry's Lutheran policy did not properly begin at all until the following year, and the reason he never declared himself a Lutheran is that he never *was* a Lutheran – the peasants had nothing to do with it. Chapuys likes to spray the word 'Lutheran' around rather copiously, applying it to just about anyone vaguely unorthodox in religion. Moreover, when the 1536 parliament confirmed the submission of the clergy, Henry was asked to appoint thirty-two men – sixteen clerics and sixteen parliamentarians – to scrutinise the canons and laws of the church to ensure that they contained nothing contrary to the Royal Supremacy. Now Chapuys overdoes it again when he fears that 'the whole of parliament's authority and power has been transferred' to this committee.[44]

A touch of hyperbole, therefore, is the likeliest explanation for Chapuys's letter of 6 June. Nevertheless, the possibility must be reckoned with that sometime after Anne's death Chapuys learned something new, that there was after all some plan, even as early as 18 April, to bring adultery charges against her. It is never easy to prove a negative, but this has to be extremely unlikely. Why would the government leave Smeaton, the key witness, free for nearly two weeks? Why would Cromwell spend four days at the end of April with Sampson, a canon rather than a criminal lawyer, who played no part in Anne's trial? And why was Chapuys as amazed as anyone when he first heard the news of Anne's arrest on 2 May? Alert observer that he was, with many well-placed contacts at court, he never remotely suspected anything treasonable or scandalous. Then there was the Dover visit, planned for some weeks and not called off until 30 April. Was all of this an elaborate government hoax just to deceive Chapuys until he could be told the facts on 6 June? It is getting too far-fetched for words. The only realistic solution is that on 18 April or just after, Henry ordered Cromwell to prepare the divorce case; then about ten days later, after hearing the allegations against Anne, Henry directed Cromwell and others to examine witnesses. Chapuys, three weeks later, when his discussions with Cromwell had resumed, spun the story just a little.

This, surely, is how Chapuys's letter should be understood. Having previously told Charles all about Anne's conviction for adultery, was he now trying to say that murder most foul had been committed? Of course he was not. He was commending Cromwell for the part he had played, and taking the opportunity to talk it up a bit. It might, after the disappointment of 18 April, help restore Anglo-Imperial relations if Charles knew that Cromwell had been the chief prosecutor of the royal mistress, the woman who had stolen the queenly crown from the emperor's aunt.

Over the years hundreds of thousands of words on the story of Henry VIII and his second wife have poured from the printing presses, recounting the long, passionate courtship that turned into a doomed marriage with a violent and bloody end. Many more will no doubt follow. Most take Anne's side, which is understandable though probably credulous. We will never know for sure. This account has necessarily concentrated on Cromwell, because he has been cast as Iago, a pitiless, scheming villain who machinated the destruction of his master's innocent wife. But Anne Boleyn was no Desdemona, and Othello had no Jane Seymour. Once Henry had turned irrevocably against Anne in January 1536, there was nothing that Cromwell could have done for her except perhaps secure for her as painless a divorce settlement as was possible in the circumstances, and even this slim hope vanished when three anonymous lords went to Henry one day with information that the queen was false to him.

Henry and Jane were married on 30 May at Whitehall. Cromwell readily accepted the new queen, even though she and her family belonged to the old faith. Never was he troubled by doubts that he had been a party to a terrible travesty of justice. When Stephen Gardiner tried to flush some more details about Anne's trial out of him, Cromwell had nothing more to say. Henry was married to Jane, Cromwell replied; she was the 'most virtuous lady and truest gentlewoman that liveth, and one who varieth as much from the conditions of the other as the day varieth from the night'.[45]

10

A New Queen of the Old Faith

John Foxe eulogised Thomas Cromwell for 'setting up Christ's church' in Henry's reign, and devoting his entire life 'to advance and further the right knowledge of the Gospel and reform the house of God'. He was the 'mighty wall and defence of the church', who 'first caused the people to be instructed in the Lord's Prayer and Creed in English', before putting an end to the worst pilgrimages to 'rescue the vulgar people from damnable idolatry'. He reduced the number of 'idle holy days', so that ordinary folk were not prevented from trading on such days and earning a decent living, and he used his office to 'procure for them liberty to eat eggs and white meat in Lent'. Foxe was biased, of course, but his is not the only testimony to Cromwell's pre-eminence among reformers. Cromwell has 'done more than all others together' in the cause of the 'reformation of religion and the clergy', agreed Archbishop Cranmer, seemingly content to be Cromwell's deputy in the evangelical movement.[1]

So Nicholas Shaxton was fretting needlessly when he urged Cromwell not to abandon the cause of reform after Anne's fall. Anne's demise and Jane's accession left some evangelicals forlorn and jittery, but for the steely, phlegmatic Cromwell, substantially nothing had changed. His task of spreading the

Gospel in England remained the same as before. His problem – to persuade Henry to accept the *Augsburg Confession* – also remained the same as before, because despite the noticeable thaw in Anglo-Lutheran relations, Henry was not ready to make that commitment to the Protestant faith.[2]

Due to the influx of evangelical ideas, parishioners had been hearing mixed messages from the pulpits, and many were becoming confused. On 7 January 1536 the government had issued a royal circular to bishops regretting the disunity, and condemning the growing number of 'indiscreet persons which, although they be furnished neither with wisdom, learning nor yet good judgement, are nevertheless authorised to preach and permitted to blow abroad their folly'. Bishops were implicitly rebuked for having failed to 'stop the mouths of such as rather sow sedition than with wisdom travail to remove out of men's hearts' the abuses of Rome. The king desired that his people should be 'educated, fed and nourished with wholesome and godly doctrine, and not seduced with the filthy and corrupt abominations of the bishop of Rome or his disciples and adherents, nor yet by the setting forth of novelties and the continual inculcation of things' that lead only to contention and disturbance. Bishops were ordered to examine all preaching licences.[3]

A letter from Cromwell accompanied the circular, which may well have been drafted by him. It contains a carefully constructed Cromwellian vagueness that is a feature of many of his public pronouncements on religious matters. On the one side were the Papists, but those noisy preachers of novelties are not so easy to identify. By now Henry had started his Lutheran policy, and Melanchthon had dedicated his *Loci* to Henry. Henry had also sent a personal letter and a gift to Melanchthon, while Foxe, Heath and Robert Barnes were in Germany with Henry's blessing. So it is difficult to believe that Henry meant to attack Lutheran preachers too strongly, especially when men such as Cranmer, Latimer and Barnes now enjoyed his favour. The government's targets may have been religious radicals like the Anabaptists, known chiefly for their rejection of infant baptism and their opposition to Christians joining the civil government. Alternatively, it may be an example of Cromwellian gamesmanship, giving the public impression of steering a respectable, measured middle way between two opposing factions, all the while pursuing his Lutheran policy circumspectly.

Henry was now willing to consider an alliance with the Germans, depending on the terms. His embassy to Germany enjoyed some success, and the Germans' response in the spring of 1536 was encouraging. The Schmalkaldic League invited Henry to indicate his willingness to accept the *Augsburg Confession*. If he would do so, a formal alliance would be made, and a German embassy sent to England headed by Melanchthon, whom Henry greatly wished to meet. If Henry was not prepared to accept the *Augsburg Confession* yet, then some limited alliance might still be concluded; for example, England and the League might agree that neither would support an attack on the other, and neither would attend a General Council of the Church without first consulting the other.[4]

Henry was listening closely to Cromwell and Cranmer on religion, but men of the old faith were not bypassed entirely. Stephen Gardiner, now English ambassador in France, tried to draw Henry back from a treaty that, he claimed, would leave England 'bound to the churches of Germany'. Gardiner cleverly pointed out that whereas Henry was a king, the electors of Germany were 'only dukes and lower degrees, such also as acknowledge the emperor as their supreme lord'. So German Lutherans were apparently beneath the King of England and Defender of the Faith. It was a skilful ploy, calculated to play on the king's vanity. It may well be one reason why Henry's attitude to the Germans, though interested and friendly, remained cautious as well.[5]

In May and June, however, constitutional affairs were more pressing than matters of religion. The newly assembled parliament was required to pass a new succession law. Cromwell had been promoting parliamentary candidates favourable to the king, and he was now organising parliamentary business. On

8 June the opening speech was given by Chancellor Audley. In what sounds like a deliberate rebuke of Skip's sermon of 1 April – the one that compared Henry to Solomon taking foreign wives – Audley likened Henry to Solomon for his divinely given wisdom and benevolence. The chancellor went on to confirm Anne's treason and Henry's new marriage, and he urged all present to pray to God for the blessing of an heir. Richard Rich, believed to be Henry's preferred choice, was then elected as Speaker.[6]

Another outstanding issue concerned Princess Mary, now officially Lady Mary, who had still not formally accepted her downgraded constitutional status. In a frank letter to Cromwell on 10 June, Mary promised that she would now follow his advice. She urged him, however, 'as one of my chief friends', to intercede for her so that no more may be demanded of her; because 'if I be put to any more (I am plain with you as with my great friend) my said conscience will in no ways suffer me to consent thereunto'. Cromwell's relations with Mary are no less intriguing than those he had had with her mother. The likelihood of further resistance to Henry's rule would be considerably lessened if Mary as well as Jane – both royal ladies of the old faith – were seen to be accepting the Royal Supremacy, and Cromwell was pressing Mary to yield, apparently forcefully. One of his letters severely scolds her for her obstinacy and disobedience, and threatens to give up trying to help her if she refused to obey. So it is surprising to find Mary, on 13 June, thanking Cromwell 'with all my heart for the great pain and suit you have had for me'. Mary made her formal submission two days later. More grateful letters were then penned to Cromwell. She thanked him for having 'travailed' for her, she promised her prayers, and was delighted at the gift of a horse, 'which is a great pleasure ... for I am wont to find great ease in riding'.[7]

Chapuys's report to Charles on 1 July helps understand what has been happening. To obtain Mary's submission, says Chapuys, Henry had sent a formidable deputation to her that included Norfolk, Suffolk and the bishop of Chester, but despite bullying and threats it was unsuccessful. Meanwhile, Mary and Chapuys were communicating in secret. He advised her that if her life was in danger, then she should obey Henry; this would be acceptable to Charles, because on her depended the 'tranquillity of this kingdom and the reform of the many great disorders and abuses by which it is troubled'. Henry knew nothing about these secret contacts, but her tardiness in obeying him had aroused his anger. Henry was also, according to Chapuys, furious with some of his councillors, including Cromwell, for 'having shown sympathy' for Mary. The marquis of Exeter and Fitzwilliam the Treasurer were dismissed from the Council; but after efforts behind the scenes by Cromwell and Jane as well as Chapuys, Mary duly made her submission and Henry's wrath was mollified somewhat. Because Mary's conscience was troubled by what she had felt compelled to do, Chapuys sent soothing messages to her, and Mary asked for secret absolution from the pope. Cromwell told Chapuys that the love of the people for Mary has 'increased of late', but some uncertainty remained about her title and her future as heiress. Mary acknowledged Cromwell's 'good intentions and affection towards her, and that he has been, and is still, working for her welfare and the settlement of her affairs' (Chapuys's words). Chapuys commended Cromwell's conduct towards Mary.[8]

After what has been seen already regarding Cromwell and Catherine of Aragon in Chapter 7, there should be little reason to doubt what Chapuys was saying about Cromwell and Mary. Her letters to him go far beyond normal Tudor niceties. Strange to relate, he had behaved more considerately towards her than Catholic magnates like Norfolk had done. It is likely, therefore, that Cromwell's severe letter to her discussed above was composed more for Henry's eyes than Mary's: Cromwell had to convince the king that he was doing his utmost to press his troublesome daughter to submit. Then either something gentler went to Mary, or else Mary understood Cromwell's tactic and did not take the harsh tone to heart.

Chapuys at least was convinced of Cromwell's good intentions. In subsequent despatches he described Cromwell doing all he could to reconcile Mary to Henry and Henry to Charles. Chapuys had also heard, from 'honourable and good men', that Henry was thinking of marrying Mary to someone in England in order to keep her under his control and deny her any opportunity to revoke her submission. Rumours suggested that Cromwell might be the privileged man, though Chapuys doubted this.[9]

The crisis with Mary over, Cromwell's fortunes continued to rise. On 16 June William Peter, a servant of Cromwell's, argued that because Cromwell represented Henry as Vicegerent, he should have the chief place in Convocation. With barely a murmur the clergy agreed, and on the 21st Cromwell took his place in Convocation to hear Cranmer declare Henry's marriage to Anne void. Then on 1 July Cromwell was made Lord Privy Seal, replacing Thomas Boleyn, Anne's father, though Boleyn did not disappear from public life entirely, and he remained on more or less friendly terms with Cromwell, occasionally dining at his house. Incidentally, this presents another predicament for conspiracy theorists: for why should Boleyn senior socialise and dine with the man who had masterminded the judicial sacrifice of his daughter?[10]

On 4 July the new Succession Act was passed. The previous act of 1534 named Elizabeth as an heir if Henry and Anne had no sons; but because Henry had nullified his marriage to Anne, Elizabeth was now declared illegitimate like Mary. The succession would pass to Henry's sons by Jane, or any lawful future wife and their heirs, and failing any male heir, to his legitimate daughters. Technically this ruled out Mary and Elizabeth. Should Henry have no suitable heir either male or female, the act gave him discretion to name an heir either by letters patent or in his last will. Various other clauses were added to try and forestall the danger of a disputed succession. The act was first presented to the Lords by Audley, and it is not clear exactly what role Cromwell had in preparing it.[11]

Meanwhile, some foreign observers had wondered whether Anne's fall would prompt Henry to seek reconciliation with Rome. Cardinal Campeggio hoped that Norfolk, Suffolk,

Tunstall and Gardiner might be able to lead Henry in the right direction, and he even dreamed of being the mediator nominated to obtain absolution for a penitent Henry. Such fond expectations were dashed by another act of the summer session, the Act to Extinguish the Authority of the bishop of Rome. Drafted by Cromwell and Audley, the act denounced the pope for distorting Holy Scripture, for his worldly pomp and his pretensions to authority over kings and princes. However, it stopped short of calling the pope the Antichrist, which Cranmer *had* done in a lengthy sermon at Paul's Cross earlier in the year. Whether this omission was mainly for diplomacy's sake, or whether Cromwell did not share Cranmer's view, we do not know. Apart from reinforcing the Royal Supremacy, the new act also tightened up on those who, while appearing to accept Henry's headship of the church, at the same time continued to show some sort of loyalty to the pope, for example by failing to blot his name out of service books. From now on, any act of support for the papacy 'by writing, ciphering, printing, preaching or teaching, deed or act' would risk praemunire proceedings, resulting in loss of lands and possessions, though not the death penalty. It was emphasised, however, that act was not 'prejudicial or derogatory' to godly ceremonies and decent order in the church.[12]

On 4 July, Edward Foxe finally arrived back in London from Germany. Seven days later he presented the Ten Articles to Convocation, which were accepted surprisingly quickly in view of the agitated discussions on religion that had taken place there. The articles were substantially the work of Cromwell, whose authority and prestige had never been higher. The king rewarded him with lands, including the manors of Wimbledon and Mortlake in Surrey, and two manors in Norfolk that once belonged to the bishop of Norwich. He was made Baron Cromwell of Oakham on 8 July, though the official ceremony did not take place until the last day of the summer parliamentary session on the 18th. That day also saw Cromwell confirmed as Vicegerent in spiritual and ecclesiastical affairs for the entire church and kingdom, not just for the visitation of the monasteries. Wriothesley records that Henry and all the lords assembled together, and Cromwell, 'otherwise called Lord Cromwell, Lord Privy Seal, and Secretary to the King, was made knight there in the parliament chamber … and high vicar over the spirituality under the king, and sat diverse times in the Convocation house among the bishops as head over them'.[13]

So despite having incurred Henry's anger for being too sympathetic to Mary, when Exeter and Fitzwilliam fell from grace for the same offence, Cromwell had not only continued in office, but had also accumulated titles and honours. In less than three weeks in July he became Lord Privy Seal, Baron Cromwell and full Vicegerent. Frustratingly, the surviving records of this period provide little insight into events taking place behind the scenes, and nothing is available to suggest a power struggle at court. If Chapuys is to be believed, it was Henry, not Cromwell, who bundled Exeter and Fitzwilliam off the council. Skilful opportunism and the king's good will are the best explanations that can be offered for Cromwell's hugely successful summer. Significantly for the evangelical cause, he was now drawing up articles of faith on behalf of Henry.

The Ten Articles were a skilful fusion of Melanchthon's *Loci Communes*, recently dedicated to Henry, and St Augustine, with a few morsels of medieval religion left in them to conciliate the still powerful Catholic party. They were either composed or edited by Cromwell, and subdivided into two main parts. The first five were described as 'principal articles' of the faith, and the remainder, by implication secondary, covered 'laudable ceremonies used in the church'. The 'principal' articles began by upholding the authority of the Bible and the ancient Christian Creeds before going on to deal with baptism, penance, the Eucharist and justification. Justification was attained by 'contrition and faith joined with charity', which sounds like a defeat for Luther's justification by faith alone – until, that is, we read a little further on and find this:

> Not as though our contrition, or faith, or any works proceeding thereof, can worthily merit or deserve to attain the

said justification; for only the mercy and grace of the Father, promised freely unto us for Christ's sake, and the merits of His blood and passion, be the only sufficient and worthy causes thereof.

This extract proves that Henry may have superintended nearly everything himself, to adapt the Milanese ambassador, but not quite everything. He certainly did not superintend this article particularly carefully, because this was far from the king's own belief on the more intricate aspects of the salvation of mankind, as will be clear soon. In substance this statement is pure Lutheran, though couched in language that could easily be defended by reference to patristic writings, especially Augustine. By adroit phraseology, Cromwell had managed to persuade Henry to authorise a document containing a statement that Henry did not agree with. So Henry *could* be manipulated, though not very often. What wiles or charms Cromwell used, we do not know; his papers do not disclose such secrets. He must have caught the king at an agreeable, unguarded moment sometime during his honeymoon with Jane.[14]

The articles on 'laudable ceremonies' dealt with religious images, the saints, church rites and purgatory. Images should be retained in churches, but not abused in any 'superstitious' manner. It was not until Edward's reign that the destruction of images in churches became government policy – no such move was instigated by Henry or Cromwell. Saints may be honoured, and praying to them was not abolished; but in another Lutheran touch it was stressed that Christ was the only Mediator between God and mankind. Ceremonies like candles at Candlemas and ashes on Ash Wednesday were retained, though with the Lutheran sounding reminder that none of these rites had the power to remit sin or make the soul righteous before God. Finally, whilst Rome's pardons and indulgences were forbidden, it was accepted that prayers may be made for souls departed to commend them to the mercy of God.

Despite the Catholicity of some of these points, like the last one, the overall flavour of the Ten Articles is distinctly Lutheran.

Apart from the quote above on justification, the prohibition of 'superstitious' use of images could easily be used to undermine much devotional medieval piety. The role of the saints in the life of the church, especially their mediatorial role, was now being emphatically watered down. Then, even though purgatory had not yet been abolished, like praying to saints it was now semi-officially relegated to a non-essential article of faith. Taken as a whole, therefore, the articles represent a noticeable departure from the medieval religion in the direction of Luther. They might be described as an induction course in the new learning, carefully designed for the re-education of a nation still largely attached to the old ways. It was a stage by stage, step by step Reformation. Cromwell's tactic was to introduce the Gospel progressively, as much at one time as he safely could, while waiting patiently until, as he hoped, Henry would be ready to accept the *Augsburg Confession* in its entirety.

These articles were reinforced by a set of injunctions, issued by Cromwell acting on his authority as Vicegerent. The preamble begins grandly: 'I, Thomas Cromwell, knight, Lord Cromwell, Keeper of the Privy Seal of our said sovereign lord the king, and Vicegerent unto the same, for and concerning all his jurisdiction ecclesiastical within this realm … '. The Injunctions were essentially a set of directives to the clergy, much of it still medieval in faith. But medieval or not, all clergy were now directed to read the Ten Articles in their sermons, as well as uphold the Royal Supremacy. They also had to 'plainly show' the distinction between articles necessary for salvation (the first five) and those primarily useful for good order in church services – this way Cromwell had removed saints, images and purgatory from the vocabulary of salvation. Further, the clergy had to confirm the 'abrogation of certain superfluous holy-days' and drive away 'superstition and hypocrisy'; they should not set forth images, relics or encourage them 'other wise than is permitted in the articles'; in other words, they should hardly set them forth at all. Effectively this directive does away with pilgrimages. The clergy were to impress on their parishioners that loving the Lord thy God and loving thy neighbour, and giving to the poor, was far more blessed in the sight of God than going on a pilgrimage, or doting on a relic or an image. The clergy had to urge parents, governors and others in authority to teach their children and servants at home the Lord's Prayer, the Ten Commandments and 'Articles of Faith' as part of their upbringing; that would include the Ten Articles. Clergy were not to spend leisure hours in taverns, but should devote themselves to reading and studying Scripture; they should also provide for the poor in their parishes from the wealth of the church, and make a contribution to education.[15]

A consummate evangelical strategy was now underway. The temperate Lutheranism of the Ten Articles was to be taught in every church, every parish, every home and every school in England, Wales and subsequently Ireland. Every priest, parent and schoolmaster was now under royal command to teach that salvation was promised through divine grace and mercy alone, even though that was not the king's own view. Charity and good works were not excluded from the new teaching, but their character was subtly changing. No longer could preachers instruct their flock, or parents their children, of the merits of monasticism, pilgrimages and relics. They even had to play down the efficacy of images and the saints. The medieval world's catalogue of good works was dwindling fast. Preachers had to concentrate instead on charity, love to neighbour, virtues like patience, honesty, humility, and not least, obedience to princes. No good priest could object to this so far as it went, but many among them must have realized that if these articles and injunctions were followed thoroughly, several layers of medieval religion would quickly be stripped away, and its hold on the people fundamentally weakened.

This brings us back to the first article, on the authority of the Bible and the ancient Creeds. For why should this point be made at all when it was not disputed among Catholics and Lutherans? Maybe the government wanted to counter religious radicals like the Anabaptists, but even these people did not deny the truth of the Bible; they merely interpreted much of it differently. Article One, I would suggest, is another facet of Cromwell's evangelical strategy. It gave the discreet Lutheranism of the remaining articles the most authoritative seal of Christian orthodoxy. Justification by faith, solely through grace and for Christ's sake; the watering down of the mediatorial role of saints; the effective abolition of pilgrimages – all this was implicitly declared to be entirely consistent with Holy Scripture and the apostolic church. In other words, this new learning was not really new at all; it was a recovery, or rediscovery, of the pure, ancient teaching of Christ and the apostles that the medieval Roman church had distorted and corrupted. This was the message that Cromwell wanted to get out into the parishes of England. It was the same point that Luther and Melanchthon had been making for the last fifteen years.

This was also the message that all the clergy were required by royal directive to read out, whether they liked it or not – and many did not like it one whit. Strategy was at work again, because one of Cromwell's problems was that, unlike Elector John Frederick in Saxony, he did not have, nor could he get, a steady supply of good Lutheran preachers trained at Wittenberg University under the guidance of Luther and Melanchthon. So Cromwell made the Catholic clergy preach the Lutheran Gospel, only slightly diluted. This creative method of evangelising – a well-known and familiar figure proclaiming moderately Lutheran articles issued in the king's name – would have helped to commend the Gospel to its audience. Cromwell doubtless had in mind the hundreds of as yet uncommitted Tudor folk, men and women who might be amenable to the new faith if it was introduced considerately, but who might be repelled by anything too radical. He also had the intelligence to see that the people needed not only to be instructed, but, more importantly if his evangelical aims were ever to succeed, to be persuaded.

As he probably expected, not all priests proclaimed his articles and injunctions with relish. Some might do so through gritted teeth, others might drop hints that these novelties in religion would soon pass away and be forgotten. Such attitudes could be dangerous, however, because Cromwell had also directed sheriffs and local justices to make sure that his injunctions were being followed. A justice sympathetic to the old faith might wish he could ignore this unwelcome duty, but if he was unwise enough to do so, he would run the risk of being reported by one of Cromwell's agents or some watchful evangelical parishioner.[16]

The word 'strategy' has been used, perhaps rather freely, in this narrative, but it is not intended to mean that Cromwell had formulated a master plan sometime in the mid-1530s that he pursued doggedly throughout his vicegerency. His church policy was essentially that of the skilled opportunist; he would do his best for the Gospel wherever he could whenever he got the chance, and in summer of 1536 he grasped a golden opportunity. Elton once described the Act of Appeals of 1533 as Cromwell's 'masterpiece in statute-making'.[17] So it was, in the constitutional arena. However, the Ten Articles and their accompanying injunctions were no less a masterpiece in the spiritual realm. They show Cromwell, hamstrung though he was by a king who did not share his Lutheran faith, was nevertheless at his most imaginative in getting a broadly evangelical message across to the widest possible audience. He probably did not expect immediate success, a point not always allowed for by our 'revisionist historians', who delight in claiming that the Reformation was not received with open arms by the English people. Cromwell and his allies were not mere crowd pleasers jumping on some fashionable ideological bandwagon. These early Reformers were men of principle prepared to stake their own necks, literally in Cromwell's case, for the Gospel. Nor was the king's Vicegerent ever so stupid as to expect that fresh ideas on grace and salvation could, at a single stroke, replace centuries of medieval tradition. With Henry still attached to so much of the old faith, Cromwell had to sow the evangelical seed discreetly, and let it bear fruit in its own time. He would not live to see that day. Edward and Elizabeth would reap the harvest. But the main reason they were able to do so was the resourcefulness of Cromwell in the 1530s, which ensured that enough English people heard enough of the Gospel for it to take root in the spiritual heart of the nation, and make a real if not an instant impact.

However, although Cromwell was able to make spiritual progress on the home front, he could do little for English evangelicals who had fallen into enemy hands abroad. William Tyndale had now endured more than a year in a jail near Brussels after being betrayed by one Henry Phillips with, it was alleged, the connivance of certain English bishops. In May Cromwell had received an anxious letter from Stephen Vaughan beseeching him: 'If you could now send me but your letter to the Privy Council, I could deliver Tyndale from the fire, so it come by time, for else it would be too late'. Freeing Tyndale, unfortunately, was a far more complex task than just getting the paperwork right. Extraditing him to England could have created more problems than it solved, because he might have been in danger of charges of heresy, or even, because of his opposition to Henry's first divorce, treason. Cromwell's reply to Vaughan is lost, but Hall records that Tyndale 'was laboured for by letters written by the Lord Cromwell'. These labours proved unhappily fruitless. After a long drawn out trial, and several wearisome disputations with 'diverse lawyers and doctors in divinity', Tyndale was condemned as a heretic in August. During his imprisonment it was said that 'he converted his keeper, the keeper's daughter, and others of his household'; while many others who came into contact with him 'reported of him that if he were not a good Christian man, they could not tell whom to trust'. Hall noted that even the procurator-general commended Tyndale's piety and learning.[18]

But no eloquent testimony availed to save him now. On 12 August John Hutton wrote to Cromwell to tell him that Tyndale was condemned to die within a week. By the time Cromwell received this dread news, Tyndale should have been beyond hope. Cromwell did not know it, but Tyndale's execution was delayed, probably in order to obtain final confirmation from Charles V. Sentence was not carried out until 6 October. Then, tied to the stake, Tyndale cried, 'Lord, open the king of England's eyes'. As custom in Flanders and the Low

Countries allowed, he was strangled before the fire was lit. Cromwell later heard from Hutton how many witnesses 'speak much of the patient sufferance of Master Tyndale' in the hour of death.[19]

The loss of the great Bible translator, bitter blow though it was, may have renewed the resolve of Cromwell and others to try and persuade Henry to authorise an English Bible for use in churches. It might also have prompted Cromwell to reconsider his traditional preference for Charles in the European power struggle between the emperor and King Francis. Henry had once again officially proclaimed his neutrality in the war between the two monarchs, but in October Chapuys was troubled to hear that Francis had offered Cromwell a pension of 2,000 ducats per annum. Charles was also concerned by reports that Francis was sending Cromwell gifts as well as offering him a pension, and that Cromwell was now inclining to the French. To counterbalance the French initiatives, Charles authorised his ambassadors to send Imperial gifts to Henry's councillors, especially Cromwell, in the hope of retaining their support.[20]

However, plans for the English Bible and foreign policy matters were overshadowed when, at the end of 1536, the English government was confronted by insurrection at home. Large areas of the north erupted into revolt in the Lincolnshire rising and the subsequent, larger northern rising commonly known as the Pilgrimage of Grace. Cromwell might have been expecting trouble in northern parts. The previous year Richard Layton had warned him that he would have to 'beat the King's authority into the heads of the rude people of the north' because they were 'more superstitious than virtuous, long accustomed to frantic fantasies and ceremonies, which they regard more than either God or their prince, right far alienate from true religion'. Even before that (in September 1534) Lord Darcy had told Chapuys that he could endure no longer the lurch into schism and heresy. Darcy was ready to stir the people to resist, and he appealed for Charles's support. Up to 1,600 of the northern nobility agreed with him, he claimed, though his boast was rendered somewhat less threatening by his admission that he had only sounded out one or two of them.[21]

Besides economic grievances, the pilgrim-rebels complained bitterly over the abolishing of holy days, the attacks on the saints and purgatory, the suppression of the monasteries, the advancement of evangelical clergy and ministers 'of low birth' like Cromwell, and various other reformist measures associated with him. Cromwell was the chief target of the rebels' bile. A Buckinghamshire official wished he could kill the Vicegerent with his own hands, while a chaplain in Wakefield taught boys rude ditties about him. A crowd in Dent wished it could 'crum him that he was never as crummed'. A mob seized one of his servants and set a pack of dogs on him. The rebels demanded that Henry 'put down the Lord Cromwell, that heretic, and all his sect, the which made the king put down praying and fasting'. Rebel leader Robert Aske charged Cromwell – along with Audley, Cranmer, Latimer and Barnes – of filling the realm with heresy. Lord Darcy accused Cromwell of being the 'very original and chief causer of all this rebellion and mischief', and like Anne Boleyn before him, Darcy longed to see Cromwell's head struck off. This 'naughty Cromwell', once a mere 'shearman', was compared the villain Haman again.[22]

Cromwell was unfazed and unharmed by the howls, screams and taunts flying at him from the north. Because Henry had sanctioned the reforms that had roused the rebels to fury, the king saw the rising as a challenge to his own royal authority. He sent Norfolk north, first to play for time, and then, as soon as the royal armies had gathered sufficient strength, to crush the rebellion without mercy. When Queen Jane, fearing that the disturbances might betoken divine judgement on a schismatic kingdom, appealed to Henry to restore the abbeys being suppressed, Henry roughly told her not to meddle with matters of state, and reminded her of Anne's fate. This was not the only sign around this time (November 1536) that Henry's love for Jane was fading. Chapuys heard from Mary that Henry no longer expected male children from his new wife, and that he was hoping for a grandson as an heir. Cromwell also confided to Chapuys that 'the king has no hope of male succession'.[23]

Meanwhile, though Cromwell did appeal to Henry to show restraint during the early stages of the rising, he assured Sir Ralph Evers that if the rebels continued to defy the king, they would be 'so subdued as their example shall be fearful to all subjects whiles the world doth endure'. By January 1537, Cromwell was receiving reports from his own men like Ralph Sadler, now darting between York and Newcastle. Soon it became clear that the rebellion had failed. By April the Council was confident that danger had passed. At Cromwell's suggestion, letters were sent to all justices urging action against the 'Papistical faction', and regretting how too many people 'retain their old fond fantasies and superstitions, muttering in dark corners as they dare'. Justices were also ordered to deal with those who spread false rumours about the honour of the king and the laws of the land.[24]

In more ways than one, the northern rebellion actually worked to Cromwell's advantage. From a witness at Aske's execution Cromwell learned, if he did not know it already, Chapuys had had contact with rebel leaders. Aske had admitted hearing from Darcy that Darcy had spoken to Chapuys about his purpose in the rebellion, and had received encouragement. The rising also ensured that Norfolk, a potential rival of Cromwell's, instead of making trouble for Cromwell at court could now be sent north to do the things he was good at doing and enjoyed doing, like fighting, soldiering, besieging towns and hanging rebels. Norfolk went lustily about his task. He ordered his officers to 'spare not frankly to slay plenty of those false rebels', and 'pitch now no courtesy to shed blood of false traitors'. He told Mr Comptroller on the Council to get himself a new bailey because Norfolk was going to hang the present one, 'and I think some of your tenants will keep him company'. Henry approved Norfolk's stern measures, and on the basis of reports from others, he commended the duke for proclaiming the Royal Supremacy vigorously in the north.[25]

Norfolk proved his unqualified loyalty to Henry throughout the course of 1536 and into 1537, even though he might have been expected to feel a little secret sympathy for some of the rebels' attacks on Cromwell. Nevertheless, it was Norfolk who recommended to Cromwell that Henry should befriend Aske, 'and wade him with fair words', and thereby make him 'cough out as much as he knows concerning Lord Darcy and Richard Constable'. As events turned out, therefore, the chief suppressors of this very medieval religious rising were not the hated evangelical trio of Cromwell, Cranmer and Audley. What began largely as a resistance movement against Cromwellian reforms was ruthlessly put down by a king still broadly Catholic at heart, and by his foremost Catholic peer and military commander.[26]

A further sign of the government's confidence in the face of danger was that Cromwell continued to push forward with the Lutheran policy. Contacts between England and the Schmalkaldic League were renewed in early 1537. The League decided to send a messenger to Henry explaining its position regarding a future General Council of the Church, but this friendly intent was almost ruined by clumsy diplomatic mismanagement. Instead of a formal embassy to England, a humble Hamburg sailor arrived with little advance announcement and the minimum of ceremony. He was introduced to Cromwell by John Whalley before giving an unimpressive performance at court. Henry and Cromwell were not amused. Cromwell then despatched a trusty young evangelical agent to Germany to protest, and to urge the League to treat Henry with more respect. The initiative worked. Arrangements quickly began for a major German embassy to England to discuss religion, politics, and a common Anglo-German approach should the pope call a General Council. Henry continued to hope, and ask for, a visit from Melanchthon.[27]

Henry was now putting his mind to religious affairs again. The Ten Articles of the previous year were not intended to be a completely comprehensive statement of faith, and neither had they succeeded in laying all discussions to rest. For example, four sacraments of the medieval church – marriage, ordination, confirmation and unction – went unmentioned in the articles, leaving some observers wondering what the official policy was on these points. Leaving them out of the Ten Articles was another Cromwellian success. It is, as he no doubt calculated, easier to delete something than restore it, and the onus now lay on his opponents to explain why the missing sacraments should be reinstated.[28]

The following is a summary of the narrative of Convocation in 1537 written by Alexander Alesius, now living in England, and, according to his own account, on cordial terms with Cromwell. One day Alesius met Cromwell in the street, and at his invitation, accompanied him into Westminster. At the sight of Cromwell, the bishops rose and 'did obeisance unto him as to their vicar-general'. Cromwell saluted them and sat down 'in the highest place'. Cromwell then opened proceedings; invoking the king's name, he called for a dignified debate on theology, and he urged all present to be guided by Scripture, as the king wished. When the debate began, Bishop Stokesley argued the case for the four missing sacraments. Cranmer replied for the evangelical party. He appealed to Convocation to consider the substance of Christian doctrine, the grand themes of salvation, forgiveness of sins and the true use of sacraments; and to reflect on whether ceremonies of confirmation, ordination and healing really were worthy to be compared with baptism and the Eucharist. Quoting the Sermon on the Mount – 'Blessed are the peace-makers' – he appealed for an end to brawling, and for sober reflection.[29]

Cromwell then intervened and bid Alesius speak, introducing him slightly flatteringly as the 'king's scholar'. Quoting Augustine and other ancient authorities, Alesius argued that Scripture recognised only two sacraments, baptism and the Eucharist. Stokesley was furious at having to suffer a lecture on theology from this upstart, and he rose noisily to press the case for the Seven Sacraments, as many prominent doctors in the history of the church had done. This was a mistake; it allowed Edward Foxe, a Cromwell supporter, to remind the company that even the church fathers occasionally had their disagreements, so Convocation should settle the matter from Scripture

alone. Foxe then commended the Germans for their translation of Bible, so that 'many things may be better understood
without any glosses at all, than by the commentaries of the
doctors'. He followed this up with a broadly Lutheran speech,
defining a sacrament as a divine institution accompanied by
a promise of grace, which cannot be altered by popes or the
church. Again Stokesley leapt to his feet, insisting furiously that
Convocation should consider the merits of church traditions,
not the Bible alone. At this point, Alesius recalled, Cromwell
and the evangelical bishops 'smiled upon one another'.

Bringing Alesius into Convocation was another piece
of Cromwellian gamesmanship designed to wind up the
clumsy Stokesley and derail his case, because the terms of
debate – authorised by Henry and Cromwell – required
speakers to stick to arguments from Scripture, not church traditions. Officially supposed to be above the fray as Vicegerent,
Cromwell was manipulating events to the advantage of the
evangelicals. Though debates and disagreements over the four
missing sacraments continued, they failed to regain equality with baptism, penance and the Eucharist. It was another
Cromwellian, evangelical victory.

Cromwell did not attend Convocation every day, but Foxe,
Cranmer and Latimer kept him informed of developments. In
July Cromwell heard that discussions on religion had almost
finished, and that a book entitled the *Institution of a Christian
Man* – more commonly known as the Bishops' Book – would
soon be ready to submit to Henry for his approval. Shortly after
the synod was prorogued, Cromwell was made Knight of the
Garter. He was also absorbed in another project especially dear
to him after the death of William Tyndale – the English Bible.[30]

Miles Coverdale, a long time friend of Cromwell's, had
finished his translation of the Bible in late 1535. Recognizing
Cromwell's 'preferment of God's Word', he then sought
Cromwell's help to persuade the king to accept it. It was in
circulation the following year, and the first draft of Cromwell's
1536 Injunctions required a Bible in every parish, though
for reasons not entirely clear, this point did not appear in the

final version. Coverdale's biographer suspects that because Anne Boleyn had also supported Coverdale's work, Cromwell withdrew this requirement in case it angered Henry. This may be so, though there is no definite proof. Another possibility is that Coverdale's edition was based largely on the Vulgate, Erasmus and Luther, and that Cromwell was already thinking of an English translation directly from the original Biblical languages. Whatever the reason, Coverdale's Bible narrowly missed being the first authorised Bible in the country.[31]

It was, however, reprinted in 1537 by James Nicholson of Southwark, though by now it had a rival known as the 'Matthew Bible'. Printed in Antwerp, this work bore an arresting title: 'The Bible ... translated by Thomas Matthew', with a call to 'Hearken to ye heavens and thou earth give ear: For the Lord speaketh'. The Matthew was made up as follows: the New Testament was Tyndale's 1534 version; the Pentateuch was also Tyndale's, though with minor revisions; the Psalms and Prophets were from Coverdale; while the origin of the historical books of the Old Testament (Joshua to 2 Chronicles in our English Bibles) is uncertain, though they were probably Tyndale's as well. Thomas Matthew was an alias for John Rogers, another of Cromwell's evangelical protégées, and a friend of Tyndale's.[32]

The Matthew met with almost instant princely sanction. On 4 August Cranmer commended it to Cromwell, and asked him to present it to Henry and obtain royal authority for it to be 'sold and read of every person' in the land. Within days Cromwell had done so. Cranmer was delighted, and thanked his friend for his 'high and acceptable service' for God and the king, 'which shall so much redound to your honour that, besides God's reward, you shall obtain perpetual memory for the same within this realm'. Cranmer's joy at the tidings suggests that Henry's approval was far from a formality. What persuasions Cromwell used on Henry to secure so favourable a result so soon, we do not know. However, as Queen Jane was now in the last weeks of her pregnancy, it may not be too fanciful to wonder whether Cromwell delicately invited the king to consider what imminent divine favour he might look forward to if he approved the publication of the Word of God right now. The safe delivery of the heir Your Grace has desired so long, perhaps? A subtle hint would be enough. Whatever actually happened between the king and his minister, Grafton the publisher then sent Cromwell six Bibles as a gift, and asked for a license 'under your Privy Seal' as a defence against 'all enemies and adversaries'. Grafton also asked for a monopoly to prevent others undercutting him – these were valid fears and he was not being merely mercenary. Cromwell did not comply exactly with Grafton's request; instead he arranged for Nicholson to produce the Coverdale Bible and Grafton the Matthew.[33]

On 12 October, to universal rejoicing throughout the land, Prince Edward was born. The gratifying duty of announcing the birth to foreign ambassadors belonged to Cromwell. The christening three days later seemed to have an agreeably unifying effect, bringing together such diverse parties as Mary, Elizabeth and Thomas Boleyn, as well as all the leading councillors, lords and ladies of the realm. At last Henry could look upon his son and heir. Yet unhappily for Henry, and also for Cromwell as events would ere long turn out, the joy was short-lived. Scarcely had the strains of thanksgiving faded away when fate exacted a cruel price for this long delayed blessing. Within a fortnight Queen Jane was dead, following a severe post-natal illness. She was buried at Windsor on 12 November, in a very Catholic funeral.[34]

Shortly after the tragedy, Henry turned his attention to the Bishops' Book, sent to him for his comments and approval. The notes he wrote down while alone and with no one to guide or influence him are the nearest we have to a personal confession of faith of the adult king. And astonishingly for a man so eager to see Melanchthon in England, and so willing to seek an alliance with German Lutherans, Henry's thoughts on justification by faith are about as different from Luther as any man's in Christendom could be. Henry writes about 'following precepts and laws', about 'living well', and how 'by penance and other good works' we shall be made 'meet and apt'; but nothing can be found from Henry on free grace, saving faith or the righteousness of Christ imputed to the believer. At one point he even contradicted the Ten Articles issued in his own name, when he jotted a note to the effect that justification was 'chiefly' due to divine grace (according to the Ten it should be 'solely'). Cranmer, when his turn came to reply to the king, faithfully and painstakingly explained the classic Lutheran teaching of justification by faith alone, and how good works and right living were fruits of that faith. Cranmer then diplomatically referred 'all mine annotations to his grace's most exact judgement'. No reply from Henry is recorded. He may never have even read Cranmer's comments. If he did, they singularly failed to register, because Henry would continue with his policy of engagement with the Lutherans, even though he neither agreed with them, nor properly understood them, on the most important theological issue of the Reformation. Luther's one thing needful – that man's salvation is entirely God's gift – was lost on Henry.[35]

Cromwell, not Cranmer, was the man who would soon be overwhelmed by the repercussions of this royal gaffe. Both men were living dangerously, and one would pay the price. As the year 1537 drew to its close, Cromwell's position looked secure enough; but appearances were deceptive. If Henry's scribblings in the Bishops' Book faithfully represented his real beliefs – and there is no reason to doubt that this – then in faith and religion the king and his Vicegerent were well nigh an ocean apart.

PART III

The King's Chief Minister

II

The Administrator

Once he had entered the king's service, Thomas Cromwell held various offices of state. He was made master of the king's jewels in April 1532, clerk of the hanaper of chancery in July the same year, and Chancellor of the Exchequer in April 1533. The following year, in April, he became Principal Secretary, and in October, Master of the Rolls. In January 1535 he was the king's Vicegerent for the visitation of the monasteries. By July 1536, as Lord Privy Seal and full Vicegerent, he had risen as high as any of the king's subjects could.

The first three were comparatively junior offices. As master of jewels he was responsible for the safe keeping of national reserves in jewellery and plate; as clerk of hanaper, for financial administration in chancery. As Chancellor of the Exchequer Cromwell was able to gain more control over revenue and auditing, but this position was far from being the chief finance minister of the crown, as is the case in Britain today. These posts were held by patent and for life. In each case Cromwell took the office following the death of previous holder but nothing sinister need be read into this. It is not known whether Cromwell applied for the posts, or whether he was appointed to them by Henry without asking.[1]

The Principal Secretary was the foremost administrative officer of state. This was the office that Cromwell took to new, unprecedented levels, becoming responsible for government administration, revenue, justice, foreign policy, trade, education, defence and even the church.[2]

Master of the Rolls was another office normally held for life. However, when the then holder, Dr John Taylor, resigned in May 1534, Cromwell was preferred to another candidate, Dr John Tregonwell. When Cromwell later succeeded Anne Boleyn's father as Lord Privy Seal, he resigned from the Rolls and Sir Christopher Hales took his place. The Master of the Rolls was one of the government officers authorised to 'write to the seal' – that is to write documents worthy enough to have the great seal attached to them. It also gave Cromwell more control over government administration. Today the Master of Rolls is a judge, but it does not appear that Cromwell ever acted as a judge in chancery. It was a lucrative office with a salary of £300-330 per annum, and one of its attractions was an official residence, the Rolls House in Chancery Lane. Cromwell obviously appreciated his new home, and he made sure he kept it when Hales succeeded him.[3]

The vicegerency has been discussed in previous chapters, while the chief advantages of being Lord Privy Seal were prestige and a handsome salary.[4]

Considering his range of responsibilities, Cromwell can safely be called the king's 'chief minister', provided it is remembered that this was not an official title, and that all appointments to the council were made by the king not Cromwell. His fitness for high office and its multifarious tasks was not disputed by contemporaries, even those who opposed him. Though Cromwell had little formal education, his experiences as a traveller, merchant, lawyer and parliamentarian, and his fluency in languages, combined to make him more qualified than any rival. During his lifetime and since his death he has attracted commendation and carping, praise and hostility, goodwill and antagonism, while opponents have seldom been slow to use his low birth against him; but so far as I have been able to trace, no one ever questioned his ability and proficiency, or his formidable capacity to manage a heavy and arduous workload.

He was also blessed with a gift of eloquence, as Chapuys and other witnesses testify. When Cromwell was made Knight of the Garter in August 1537, it was said that he replied to the honour 'with all the eloquence he was master of, and certainly he was master of the best'. Gabriel Harvey, the Elizabethan critic and scholar, described Cromwell – and also Wolsey, More and Gardiner – as an outstanding orator.[5]

Cromwell's religious faith has been treated already. His political philosophy is territory that needs to be entered into circumspectly, and not for the first time a set of personal memoirs is sorely missed. Some of what follows is therefore conjectural, but there are signs which serve as a guide, and which will hopefully prevent the historian from straying too far from the facts. We can begin with Cromwell's concept of kingship and kingly government.

When Thomas More resigned as lord chancellor, he gave Cromwell a few words of advice on how to deal with Henry. 'Ever tell him what he ought to do, but never what he is able to do. For if a lion knew his own strength, hard were it for any man to rule him'.[6]

Cromwell's response to this counsel is not recorded. However, there is scant evidence that he took it to heart. Cromwell never imagined that he could rule the king, and neither did he particularly want to. So much of what he did was geared towards strengthening rather than restraining kingly power. His famous Act of Appeals, for example, was specifically designed to allow Henry to settle his Great Matter in England, giving Henry a constitutional freedom and authority that he did not otherwise have.

The first Tudor king had brought stability and good government to England, and Cromwell did his utmost to consolidate and entrench that stability through a strong monarchy. Never did he equate kingly power with tyranny. An enfeebled crown could fling wide the door to upheavals, wars and confusion, as the previous century had shown. A crown strong and secure was the guarantor of the liberties of his people and the wellbeing of the nation.

Besides a keen knowledge of recent English history, a Protestant minister was bound to be influenced by the Reformation and specifically the Bible. The New Testament enjoins the faithful to obey rulers, even when the rulers were pagans (Romans 13:1–5; 1 Peter 2:13–17). These soon became standard texts used by Luther and Melanchthon to uphold the divinely required duty of princes to exercise government in the civil sphere, free from clerical interference and claims of papal authority. The Old Testament also offers many examples of godly men in the service of pagan kings, like Joseph with Pharaoh and Daniel with Nebuchadnezzar and Darius (Genesis 41–49; Daniel 2–3, 6). Naaman the Syrian, following his conversion in the Jordan, returned to his own country to serve his natural, lawful but heathen king, and with the prophet Elisha's blessing (2 Kings 5). With these examples at hand, it would not matter to Cromwell that he and Henry were not of the same mind in religion. Cromwell could still serve the king faithfully, and with a clear conscience. He might yet be able to persuade Henry to become a Lutheran too; but even if he did not, the English crown remained an authority ordained of God, and the wearer of that crown was entitled to the unswerving obedience of his subjects and ministers. Only in the very last resort – only if the king commanded something directly contrary to the law of God – could the subject invoke the example of Daniel and the apostles and 'obey God rather than men' (Daniel 6:6–10; Acts 5:29). This apart, Cromwell's loyalty was unquestioning but not unthinking – Reformers had thought this out carefully.[7]

A little anecdote will aptly illustrate this loyalty. For murmuring against the king's early supremacy plans, Sir George Throckmorton was summoned one day to Henry's presence. He warned the king that if he married Anne Boleyn he would compound his sin, 'for that it is thought ye have meddled both with the mother and the sister'. Henry's guilty conscience reduced him to sheepish excuses. 'Never with the mother', he pleaded tamely. 'Never with the sister neither, and therefore put this out of your mind', rapped Cromwell who was also present. Like everyone else, Cromwell knew that Henry had indeed 'meddled' with the sister: Mary Boleyn was once – fortunately for her only briefly – Henry's mistress. But on no account would Cromwell tolerate gossip or anything derogatory to the king's honour, even if it was true. Cromwell was also reported to be furious when stories of Henry's lack of virility leaked out of the courtroom during the trial of Anne Boleyn and her co-accused. Cromwell had wanted this stuff hushed up to protect the king's reputation.[8]

Not that relations between Henry and Cromwell were always harmonious. We have already witnessed, with Chapuys, the two men exchanging sharp words, and Cromwell storming out of the room in anger when Henry abruptly wrecked his minister's hopes and plans for Anglo-Imperial relations (see Chapter 9). Henry was a difficult master to serve, not least because of his fixation with getting involved in details that ought to have been delegated to others. Another reminder of the Milanese ambassador's words – that Henry 'chooses to know and superintend everything himself' – may be timely. Henry once made it very clear to a French envoy that whilst he would seek the opinions of his council on various matters when it pleased him, he and he alone made the decisions.[9]

Henry's servants were under no illusions about their prince. Norfolk told Chapuys one day that Henry did not really need a council at all because he decided all his business himself. Henry, Chapuys wryly observed, has a 'natural propensity to dispute on all matters', and he added that Cromwell was only too well aware of it. On another occasion, when protracted negotiations left Chapuys anxiously waiting for an overdue royal reply, Cromwell, after yet another meeting with Henry, wearily told the ambassador that 'the king, my master, is a great king, but very fond of having things his own way'.[10]

So Henry was undisputed lord and master in his own realm. He was the chairman and chief executive officer, Cromwell the general manager. Whereas, however, many managers would simply do as they were bid and nothing more, this one, fired with boundless energy and brimming with ideas, took all kinds of reformist initiatives in church, state and economic affairs. Recognizing that Henry was in control does not mean that his ministers could never try and influence him, or persuade him to change his mind, or steer him in their own preferred direction. Cromwell tried to do so, though inevitably with mixed results. He contrived to secure Henry's approval for articles of religion on justification by faith that the king did not fully agree with; but no appeals from Cromwell, or even Melanchthon, would induce Henry to relax his uncompromising hostility to the marriage of priests. Cromwell may have used subtle persuasions regarding the English Bible, but he had failed to win Henry's support for his Poor Law proposals or the Anglo-Imperial alliance. Cromwell could introduce Henry to the German Lutheran states, but he could not compel Henry to accept the *Augsburg Confession*. Henry could be prevailed upon, but only up to a point. He could never be ruled by an ambitious, over-mighty subject. Like all Henry's ministers and servants, Cromwell knew his rightful place; he was the man standing beside the throne, not the one sitting on it. He would have it no other way.[11]

Reports exist that Henry would occasionally biff Cromwell's ears and push him out of the Privy Chamber when disagreements arose between them. All was apparently good natured, and Cromwell would laugh it off afterwards. The source is one George Paulet, who may not be the most trustworthy witness. Among his other far-fetched tales are these: Cromwell urged Henry to give away lands of those attainted in Ireland for treason; Cromwell does nothing except for money; Cromwell has recently (spring 1538) been near death; Cromwell uses up all Henry's revenues. Much of this is either nonsense or overblown, and Paulet soon found himself in the Tower, though whether this was for gossiping about Cromwell is not certain. Still, it could well be the case that Henry and Cromwell had rows from time to time. Rather ruefully Cromwell was wont to tell Cranmer how he (Cranmer) was the 'most happy of all men; for you may do and speak what you list: and, say what all men can against you, the king will never believe one word to your detriment or hindrance'. Cromwell, by contrast, for all his efforts, felt 'everyday chidden, and many false tales now and then believed against me'. Cranmer agreed that the king's goodwill rested on him in a unique way, but he doubted whether Cromwell stood much in need of sympathy on this account. 'Your wisdom and policy', the archbishop replied, 'is such that you are able to shift well enough for yourself'.[12]

But working relationships are seldom so affable that nothing is ever said in anger. Moments of exasperation do not undermine the main point that for a Tudor minister, and especially a Protestant one, loyalty to the king was a religious conviction as well as a civil duty or career. It is also worth remembering that even though historians tend to take a dim view of Henry, he possessed qualities of personal magnetism and charm that made him genuinely loved and honoured by those who served him. Under Henry, kingly authority was a divine ordinance that drew forth a willing, not a grudging, obedience.

Cromwell's appointment as Principal Secretary set in motion what Elton memorably described as the 'Tudor revolution in government'. This was never meant to imply that the system was abysmally inept until Cromwell came along and put everything to right, because the first Tudor king had consistently kept meticulous records and accounts. What Cromwell did, or began to do, was to shift the centre of power from the king and his household to the king and his council. Between 1534 and 1536–7 the loose group of councillors around the king became institutionalized as the Privy Council, the king's national executive and policy-making body, roughly the Tudor equivalent of the modern British cabinet. Exactly how this developed remains uncertain, because Cromwell's own correspondence and ambassadors' letters give few clues, and no official document for the formal creation of a Privy Council has survived. Nevertheless, the brain and impetus of Cromwell behind the new developments can still be seen, if dimly. A more efficiently organized council – and Cromwell made sure that all councillors were provided with a clerk and other useful necessities – could implement royal and government policy much more effectively. Membership of the council now became entirely dependant on the king's discretion and less so on ancestry. The nobility were not automatically excluded, but they would have to compete for the king's favour on a more or less level playing field with men like Cromwell and his allies. And although the Privy Council of late 1536 was split roughly equally between evangelicals and those of the old faith, evangelicals of low or humble birth are now found holding key offices of state – Cromwell as Principal Secretary and Vicegerent, along with Cranmer and Audley as Archbishop of Canterbury and Lord Chancellor respectively. Cromwell doubtless hoped that this trend would continue, and that the balance on the council would tilt further in the reformers' favour.[13]

Apart from 'chief minister', another of Cromwell's unofficial titles might be 'manager of parliament' on the king's behalf. Here, too, his own experience as a parliamentarian served him and the king well. Money was the main reason why late medieval and early Tudor kings convened parliament – all seven parliaments between 1510 and 1523 were summoned to raise money – but increasingly under Henry and Cromwell, parliament was required to legislate on major constitutional changes such as the king's Supremacy and divorce. A royal circular issued before the elections in May 1536, for the parliamentary session needed to pass the new succession act following Anne Boleyn's demise, referred to 'our high court of parliament to be assembled for that purpose'. The crown could not arbitrarily repeal an act of parliament, so the king needed parliamentary affairs to be managed with some skill to ensure than nothing contrary to royal policy found its way onto the statute.[14]

Men sought election to the House of Commons generally for prestige, personal advancement and to further their own interests and those of groups with whom they were associated. Consequently, the various vested and conflicting interests of members – including merchants, manufacturers, lawyers and corporate bodies like the city of London – ensured that getting legislation passed was seldom easy or routine. A great deal of detailed planning and discussion went on even before a bill

Lord Privy Seal, Vicar General & Lord Chamberlian.
Created Earl of Essex 17. Ap. 23.H.8. Beheaded 28 July. 1540.

1. Thomas Cromwell.

2. A page of the first edition of the Great Bible, 1539. By permission of the Master and Fellows of St John's College, Cambridge.

3. Thomas Cromwell by Hans Holbein.

4. Henry VIII by Hans Holbein.

THOMAS
WOLSEY
Cardinall.
Archbishope
of Yorke and
Chaunceloure
of England,
Obiit Nou: 29
1530

Non secus vnda mari paulatim accrescit et alta
Neptuni frontem supereminet, at sua tandem
Vis ruit, et pelago labens deuoluitur imo,
Quam tua te WVOLSEDE tumens evexit honoris
Aura, et sublimen super—extulit ardua regis
Culmina, sed tandem conuerso CARDINE rerum
In scopulos, rigidasqz extrusa est gloria syrtes
Terra olim corpus, tumuit, iam corpore tellus

5. Portrait engraving of Cardinal Wolsey.

6. Coin of Henry VII.

7. Portrait miniature of Henry VII.

8. Christening of Prince Arthur.

9. Archbishop Warham by Hans Holbein.

10. George Neville, a Tudor nobleman, by Hans Holbein.

11. Thomas More by Hans Holbein.

12. John Fisher by Hans Holbein.

13. Thomas Cranmer by Gerlach Flicke.

14. The infant Prince Edward by Hans Holbein. Henry's 'godly imp', as Cromwell called him.

15. Catherine of Aragon by Hans Holbein. Author's collection.

16. Anne Boleyn by Lucas Cornelisz. Author's collection.

17. Jane Seymour by Hans Holbein.

18. Anne of Cleves by Hans Holbein.

19. Sir Thomas Eliot by Hans Holbein.

20. Sir Thomas Wyatt by Hans Holbein.

21. Duke of Norfolk by Hans Holbein.

22 & 23. Two Tudor ladies, believed to be by Hans Holbein.

24. Catherine Howard.

was ready for debate. Many times Cromwell faced opposition to his bills, forcing him to make do with a compromise (as with, for example, his Poor Law proposals – see p. 163). Nevertheless, Cromwell did not despair of parliament or seek to circumvent it. The evidence shows that attendance at parliament increased under his management. Whenever something important needed doing he would usually draft a bill; he even produced a bill to give legal sanction to royal proclamations.[15]

Cromwell's commitment to parliament, an institution that frequently frustrated him, may be surprising, for there can be little doubt that he was virtually a royal absolutist. Once he tried to put his rival, Stephen Gardiner, on the spot in the king's presence by demanding: 'Is not that that pleaseth the king a law?' At times Cromwell intervened in elections on behalf of the candidate most acceptable to the king. He rebuked the magistrates of Canterbury for selecting candidates 'chosen at your own wills and minds contrary to the king's pleasure and commandment'; Cromwell insisted that the elections be revoked in favour of names Henry preferred. In a more friendly spirit he advised Sir Edmund Knyvett to accept the king's nominees, not because 'I do think either of them more able for the office than yourself', but because they were 'minded by his highness', and Cromwell wished that all his friends would 'apply themselves to satisfy his grace'. With some satisfaction he reported to Henry, in March 1539, that 'your Majesty had never a more tractable parliament'.[16]

This is probably a lot less sinister than it sounds to modern ears accustomed to parliamentary democracy and free elections. It was really nothing more than a bit of Cromwellian manipulating and management in the king's interest, which was believed to be in the national interest as well. Parliaments were not called to restrain kingly authority, but to underpin and strengthen it. Neither, however, were they required to be excessively pliant. Parliament was expected to debate vigorously, and it could even seek to persuade Henry to change his mind, as Cromwell himself did in 1523 (see pp. 18–21). All this was permitted, and neither Henry nor Cromwell wanted a parliament stuffed with vegetables or clones. The aim, as Lehmberg says, was partnership – king and parliament united and working together. As the Dispensations Act put it: 'In all and every such human laws made in this realm ... Your Royal majesty and your Lords Spiritual and Temporal and Commons, representing the whole state of your realm in this your most high court of parliament, have full power and authority'.[17]

In Cromwell's parliamentary management, a distinction needs to be made between fundamental pieces of legislation like the Royal Supremacy, and day-to-day government bills concerning revenue collection, agricultural policy, land reform and so on. Regarding the second category, Henry's parliaments could be quite independent and at times downright difficult; but on affairs close to Henry's heart, once Cromwell became Principal Secretary, Henry generally got what he wanted fairly soon. Cromwell would even urge evangelicals to support, or at least not to obstruct, the anti-Lutheran Act of Six Articles, even though Cromwell himself strongly disliked the act, as we will discuss in Chapter 16.

So was Cromwell a 'parliamentary statesman'? This question begs another. If Henry was an autocrat who made most of the major decisions himself, can the word 'statesman', suggesting someone who plans and directs affairs of state, really be applied to any of his ministers if their room for manoeuvre was so limited? Henry's ministers existed to advise, serve and obey the king; they were not appointed to dictate policy, or even to formulate policy without the king's approval. 'Councillor' is a less imposing word, but it may be more suitable to describe Cromwell.

But quibbles aside, for Cromwell parliament was an integral institution of royal government. Its purposes apart from raising money were to enhance royal prestige and authority; to provide a national forum to debate subjects of national interest; to make and unmake laws for the common good; and, generally, to enact the will of the king as God's anointed on earth. Cromwell would do nothing of any significance without it. If, however, by 'parliamentary statesman' we mean a John Pym or an *Oliver* Cromwell – one who saw parliament as a check on royal authority, who would advance the authority of parliament at the expense of the crown, making it an equal to the crown rather than a pillar supporting it – if this is what a 'parliamentary statesman' is, then the expression can hardly fit the Tudor Cromwell. Nor is there any sign in this Cromwell's thinking of even the germ of the later constitutional monarchy as it is understood in modern times. Though his increased use of parliament may have helped it acquire progressively more power and prestige, future generations of parliamentarians would use that power in a way that would have appalled Thomas Cromwell. He believed in a just and godly despotism, not in a monarch who reigns but does not rule.

One feature of Cromwell's period in office was a strengthening of the king's writ and rule in all parts of the realm, including outposts like Calais. In his first year as Principal Secretary, Cromwell was investigating the administration of affairs in Calais, and giving a mild rebuke to the deputy, Lord Lisle. In 1535, a royal commission under William Fitzwilliam carried out an official survey. Early the following year an act was passed to reform and improve the town's administration and defences, and establish an executive council under Lisle. As a sign of the government's integrationist policy for remoter parts of the kingdom, the act also provided for Calais to send two burgesses to parliament. Cromwell's personal relations with Lisle were not always especially agreeable, not least because Calais soon became a hotbed for religious troubles. However, a discussion of these can be deferred until later because of their association with Cromwell's fall.[18]

Altogether more satisfying from Cromwell's point of view was his Welsh policy, and his relationship with the man appointed as President of the Council of the Marches, his friend and ally Rowland Lee. Until now such government that existed in Wales had been left largely to local magnates, with little central control. For some time London had been concerned by reports of disorder in Wales, and when Cromwell became Principal Secretary, maybe earlier, he was determined to improve the situation.[19]

The so-called Act of Union of 1536 is a slight misnomer, because unlike the Anglo-Scottish Act of Union in 1707, approved by parliaments in each country, no equivalent Welsh parliament existed. All the legislation was passed in the English parliament, which had no Welsh members. Besides, the act claimed that a *de facto* union already existed, and it invoked the crown's alleged historical rights over the Welsh marcher lords laid down in previous acts of 1275 and 1352. Be that as it may, the map of Wales was effectively redrawn with a border that survives to this day. It was reorganised into counties with representatives in parliament, as in England. The Welsh were allocated twenty-six members in 1536 compared to 349 in England, which meant roughly the same proportion of the total estimated population (278,000 and 3,750,000 in Wales and England respectively). Local government would be exercised by sheriffs, justicies and other officials, again as in England, and English common law was to apply throughout Wales. Though English became the official language, no attempt was made to abolish the ancient Welsh language entirely, and royal proclamations continued to be read out in Welsh. Many of the Welsh gentry, the men now responsible for the practical administration of the country, were already bilingual.[20]

Rowland Lee was an energetic, enthusiastic administrator. His letters to Cromwell, 'my most entirely beloved friend', indicate that his first priority was to restore law and order. He asked for money to repair castles and prisons so he could keep thieves securely locked up while awaiting trial. Soon he was reporting that 'all the thieves in Wales quake for fear'. Sir Thomas Englefield, a justice, agreed – cattle thieving had reduced dramatically, and no one now dared buy cattle suspected of being stolen. Lee was particularly anxious to assure Cromwell that he hanged 'gentlemen thieves' as well as common ones – reports must have reached Cromwell that better off villains had an easier time of it with Lee in charge.[21]

Cromwell and Lee did not hesitate to intervene if they felt that local justice was not functioning adequately. When Cromwell directed Lee to deal with complaints against two knights 'by diverse poor men', Lee promised he would do so. Lee also reported the case of a Welshman, Roger Morgan, charged with rape, but despite overwhelming evidence against him, acquitted 'to the evil example of others'. This, added Lee, was a 'vice that is and hath been commonly used in Wales, and hath most need of reformation'. Lee ordered the jury to be arraigned before Star Chamber and the next assizes, because 'if this be not looked on, farewell all good rule'. Cromwell then introduced legislation under which juries in Wales could be fined or imprisoned if it could be shown that, either out of partisanship or some other reason, they had knowingly let guilty men go free.[22]

Law and order was not Cromwell's only concern for Wales. On Cromwell's instructions, John Vaughan had 'put to execution such enormities and sinful living as we have found here, both to the pleasure of God ... and to the comfort of all good people'. Directed by Cromwell to instil some Protestant moral values in the natives, Vaughan sent back a heartening progress report: young men and women previously cohabiting, and with illegitimate children, were now married, while 'priests with their concubines be now reformed'. Many local people welcomed these developments, said Vaughan; they were 'thanking God highly that ever such power should come among them to call them from their sinful living unto the knowledge of God'. People attending sermons 'wail their errors, and be as appliable [sic] to the truth as any that we know'. Nearly 1,000 attended a recent congregation to hear a Bachelor of Divinity, a learned man, proclaim 'Scripture and the commandments of God'. After this wholesome instruction the people were saying that they had been 'this great while mocked and deceived by the priests of the churches'. But for a certain Elice Ap Robert – who claimed to have a commission for visitation, but spent his days riding about with his whore – Vaughan was sure Wales could be brought into 'as good a trade' as any part of England.[23]

Not everyone was as buoyant as Vaughan on the prospects for the spiritual renewal of Wales. Bishop Barlow of St David's was setting forth the evangelical message and the king's Ten Articles, and lamenting the 'ungodly superstition and abominable idolatry' prevalent in Wales, and the 'horrible blasphemy against God and detestable delusion' of the people. Nevertheless, a few were 'sensibly seeing the long obscured verity' of the Gospel, and Barlow hoped that his efforts might yet yield some fruit. Barlow was also concerned for the education of the people in his diocese, which did not have a single grammar school. This was the main reason why the clergy, in Barlow's judgement, were largely ignorant. So Barlow petitioned Cromwell on the subject of setting up local schools. Cromwell's immediate response is missing, but Barlow did eventually establish a school in Brecon. Cromwell may have been more successful in his campaign for law, order and good administration in Wales than he was in evangelising the country.[24]

To keep watch over the northern counties of England and the border country, Yorkist and Lancastrian kings in former times had employed a sort of northern council, usually controlled by a loyal noble. In 1537, after the northern risings and the Pilgrimage of Grace were successfully put down, Cromwell set up a much more formalized Council of the North to impose the king's will and rule there. This institution enjoyed jurisdiction over all of England north of the Humber except certain parts of Lancashire. It held sessions every quarter in York, Newcastle, Durham and Hull to hear civil and criminal cases. Effectively it became a Privy Council of the north rather than some mere dependency on central government, though it did not have the authority to enact laws independently, and it had to carry out the policy laid down by the king in parliament.[25]

These reforms were not quite the same as devolution, as the word is understood today. Letting the Welsh and the northerners have a greater say in running their own affairs was not Cromwell's chief concern. By appearing to devolve power, his real aim was to increase royal control and authority over the whole kingdom. This policy met its greatest challenge in Ireland, so frequently the political graveyard for English statesmen.

In late medieval times, Ireland was a land of two cultures, English and Gaelic. English areas, known as the Pale, included

Dublin and most of the surrounding districts where the authority of the English king was, in theory at least, formally recognised. Gaelic Ireland comprised largely independent lordships. Before Cromwell's time, Henry was more concerned with fame and glory on the European continent, and he had not given Ireland a great deal of attention. Too many changes of deputy and too much feuding among Irish lords, aggravated by insufficient funding from central government, all combined to weaken English control. Revenues from Ireland were also dwindling, so the situation that Cromwell inherited was not a very satisfactory one.[26]

Though not directly involved with Irish affairs in Wolsey's time, Cromwell was no novice on Ireland. His Irish policy began around the summer of 1533, when he started making his own appointments. Almost immediately Cromwell met with stiff opposition from traditionally dominant lords like Kildare, who was entertaining rebellious ideas as early as that autumn. Cromwell tried to diffuse the situation by diplomacy and persuasion, but he also persevered with his administrative reforms, including the appointment of a deputy, local justices and other officials. These measures, designed to strengthen royal government at the expense of local magnates, were ready by May 1534. They were seen by powerful figures like Kildare as a threat to their authority and influence. They were more than Kildare could stomach, and open revolt soon broke out.

Cromwell then put his reform program on hold until the crisis was successfully dealt with. His Irish policy, as Brendan Bradshaw has emphasised, was not a response to Kildare's rebellion. His reforms began before the rebellion and were interrupted by it. These reforms were also mainly political, not religious. The reformation of the church in Ireland had hardly begun yet, and although some Irish may have hoped for help from abroad, little real, substantial support was forthcoming from Charles, Francis or Rome.[27]

Chapuys was slightly adrift in his judgement on Irish affairs. In July 1534 he suggested to Charles that the Irish, because of their loyalty to Rome, 'ought to be encouraged ... or at least entertained with hope'; and that Ireland 'ought to be secured for our plans, for the Irish only want a chieftain to rise like the others'. Henry and the council, the ambassador continued, were anxious about the risk of an Irish rising with Spanish assistance. Actually the Irish, including Kildare, were neither excessively pious nor especially loyal to the pope, and the rising was defeated much sooner than Chapuys had anticipated. Cromwell knew all along that aid from Charles was unlikely. His agents abroad, including Stephen Vaughan, were keeping him well informed about Irish-imperial contacts. From Cadiz, William Pepwell reported that an Irish emissary to Charles had to return empty handed after the emperor refused to supply arms and men. Here, incidentally, may be one other reason why Cromwell favoured an Anglo-Imperial alliance – it would cut off the possibility of outside help for any Irishmen harbouring rebellious thoughts against Henry, and help bring stability to Ireland.[28]

After the defeat of the Kildare rebellion, Cromwell received conflicting advice on how to manage the country. Some urged a ruthless policy to 'discharge this land of all the sect' of these rebels. Conversely Norfolk, with plenty of experience of Ireland behind him, warned against repressive action that might alienate the Irish. As so often the case, Cromwell preferred moderation, and he concentrated on constitutional rather than punitive measures. He was tasked by the king with devising an act of parliament which would either entitle Henry to all Irish lands, whether spiritual and temporal, or else require all landowners to pay contributions to the king. Lord Leonard Grey was appointed deputy of Ireland, and plans were laid for an Irish parliament to confirm the Supremacy and the Succession laws. Most of this was completed by summer 1536 with surprisingly little opposition, though some lesser bills for the suppression of monasteries and land taxes were rejected. Like the English parliament the Irish one could, and quite frequently did, refuse to do everything that central government wanted.[29]

Cromwell could take some encouragement from reports now arriving from Ireland. John Alen, Master of the Rolls, advised that the king's sessions had been kept in five more shires than usual, and as a sign that law and order was being imposed, eighteen thieves had been hanged in Kildare. Government employees reported good order, peace and quiet where strife and misery were formerly rampant. One of them sent Cromwell a roll of white Irish blankets, a blue Galway mantle, and a barrel of *aqua vitae*. The most serious problem was money, or, more accurately, Henry's continued reluctance to spend much of it on Ireland. Grey was able to report some military successes, but due to lack of cash much of his army had gone unpaid for three months. His soldiers were mutinous and plundering uncontrollably, contrary to articles and orders. Grey was not universally loved by the Irish, some of whom, he admitted ruefully, 'delight to put one of us Englishmen in another's neck'.[30]

Shortly after the Supremacy was accepted by the Dublin parliament, three merchants petitioned Cromwell for a passport into Ireland to permit them to sell malt and beans. Unexciting though this piece of information may be it at least serves to illustrate Cromwell's close involvement with Irish affairs, and it suggests that comings and goings to and from Ireland were supervised carefully. Cromwell also issued detailed instructions to Irish commissioners concerning property rights and land affairs. When the city of Limerick petitioned Cromwell against their mayor, Edmund Sexton, for abusing his office, and when the aggrieved mayor submitted a lengthy defence, all these claims and counter claims had to be studied closely by Cromwell. Henry, meanwhile, remained more interested in increasing his revenues from Ireland than investing in the country. This only added to the government's problems because financial records, especially of royal revenues, were virtually non-existent in Ireland. According to reports of government agents, corruption was rife.[31]

As well as administration and political issues, Cromwell also gave close attention to the Irish church. The late medieval Irish were not an extravagantly religious people. Clerical celibacy, for example, was routinely ignored, and many bishops dabbled in political affairs. However, the legitimacy of English overlordship was not controversial, because it was after an unsuccessful rising against Henry VII in 1487 that the pope had directed the Irish clergy to be subject to the English king. Evidence exists of some religious revival on the eve of the Reformation, but the Irish were no more intrinsically inimical to the new learning than the English or the Europeans.[32]

The new archbishop of Dublin, George Browne, was appointed on Cromwell's recommendation. After arriving in Dublin in July 1536, he wrote to Cromwell with hearty thanks for his 'benevolent and great goodness'. Browne was now at the ready to 'execute and follow all your pleasure and commandment … and good counsel, trusting that it shall be to the pleasure of Almighty God'; he would do all in his power 'to fulfil and accomplish all my promises made unto your good lordship'. Browne was true to his word, and his opening sermon on Irish soil received a glowing report by Martin Pelles in a letter to London. Browne had 'set forth the Word of God in his sermon sincerely', with the result that the 'learned and unlearned both do give him as high praise as I have heard given to any other man'; those that 'favour the Word of God are very glad of him and pray for him so to continue'. Pelles was probably a government agent, and in his reports from Ireland he was bubbling over with ideas about how best to govern the country.[33]

But as in England, the new learning soon encountered opposition, some of it quite inventive. One mischievous monk embarrassed Browne by spreading a story that Browne was failing in his duty to preach the Royal Supremacy and the 'sincere word of God, avoiding all superstition'. This report reached the ears of Henry and Cromwell, and the intensely irritated archbishop had to send strenuous denials to London.[34]

As in England, so in Ireland, the keenest resistance to reform came from the clergy, who preferred their Seven Sacraments, saints and medieval piety to justification by faith alone. Thomas Agard, probably a government employee, reported to Cromwell that 'the blood of Christ is clean blotted out of men's hearts' by the pope and his followers, especially the

Observant Friars. Browne was preaching the Word of God, supported by other leading figures on the council, but resentment quickly surfaced when 'abuses' were criticised. Browne himself complained to Cromwell of opposition from the bishop of Meath, who was trying to undermine him, and how some clergy refused even to proclaim the king's Supremacy. Out of twenty-eight cathedral clergy, Browne found only three with 'any learning', and hardly any favoured the Gospel. This dispute between Browne and Meath rumbled on interminably with accusations, defences and counter-accusations from both men stacking up on Cromwell's desk.[35]

Bickering among Irish ministers was endemic almost from the moment Grey arrived in Ireland. Anthony Colley, son-in-law to Lady Skeffington, widow of the late deputy, complained that letters to Cromwell were being intercepted, and that dissatisfaction with the new deputy was widespread, partly because of his hostility to the previous deputy's staff. Colley asked for an impartial commissioner to be sent over. Lady Skeffington personally joined in the complaints about Grey. Then, on Grey's behalf, one Matthew King assured Cromwell that these complaints were untrue. Others on the council weighed in on Grey's side, pointing to English achievements in Ireland since Kildare's defeat and the surrender of his lands to the king. Cromwell took these reports up with Grey, who naturally put up a vigorous defence of his record as deputy.[36]

But reports of bad feeling on the council persisted. Browne suspected the Treasurer, Brabazon, of misleading Henry regarding the revenues of the bishopric of Dublin, while relations between Browne and Grey were deteriorating alarmingly. Browne complained to Cromwell of opposition not only from the clergy but also from Grey, who tried to imprison him (Browne) and subsequently expel him from his house. Grey was frustrating the Reformation of the church, Browne alleged. The only way Browne could get the pope's name written out of service books was by sending his own servants to do it because the clergy, with Grey's connivance, ignored his directives. Grey was now under attack from other members of the

Irish council, and in 1538 articles were drawn up against him. The main charges were that he had favoured the Geraldines in Ireland and abused his authority and trust. It fell to Cromwell to try and sort all this out, which meant asking for, and having to study, detailed and lengthy statements from all parties.[37]

Frustrating and time wasting though this turned out to be, the news was not all bad. Grey was partly successful in extending English influence in areas beyond the Pale, and he did so to the 'joy of the inhabitants', at least according to reports that reached Cromwell. This raises the subject of the government's attitude to the Gaelic Irish.[38]

The act for the 'English order, habit and language' relating to 'the part of the land that is called the English Pale', was passed in the Dublin parliament of 1536. It condemned the diversity between the people of Ireland 'in tongue, language, order and habit', which deceived them into imagining they were 'of sundry sorts, or rather of sundry countries, when indeed they be wholly together one body whereof his highness is the only head under God'. This preamble suggests that although the English language and English laws were intended to have priority in Ireland, as in Wales, the natives were not to be set apart as a class of untouchables. The emphasis was on unity – all the Irish were the king's subjects.[39]

If this was the government's will for the Pale, then it might suggest that some sort of rapprochement towards the Celts was envisaged, at least by Cromwell. It was Cromwell who persuaded Henry to appoint Dr Richard Nangle, an evangelically minded Irish speaking professor of theology, as Bishop of Clonfert in the west of Ireland. Unfortunately for him, he too ran into opposition from local clergy. Browne got embroiled in the row, and accused Grey of refusing to support Nangle even though he knew that the king and Cromwell had sent him to Ireland. But the very fact that Nangle provoked hostility at all indicates that at least some Gaelic people were listening to him, just as Browne had attracted interest in Dublin. And the deliberate choice of a man competent in the native language suggests willingness by Cromwell to win over

the Gaelic Irish if possible, and entice them into the kingdom rather than treat them as an underclass under some kind
of apartheid system. The natives were not beyond redemption in Cromwell's eyes. Nor was Nangle the only occasion
on which Cromwell made use of Gaelic speakers. He once
produced some of them from within his service to examine
an Irish monk suspected of treason who could not speak (or
pretended he could not speak) English.[40]

Meanwhile, Grey's problems were mounting. Antagonism
towards him on the Irish council increased, and reports reached
not only Cromwell but also Henry. Many Irishmen were now
confidently expecting the deputy's dismissal, though he was not
actually recalled to England until 1540, and partly at his own
request. Browne was not sorry – only 'Papists would miss him'.
Grey was committed to the Tower in June 1540, coincidentally
the same month as Cromwell, though the two men's falls were
not connected. Convicted for various offences connected with
misrule in Ireland, Grey was executed the following year.[41]

This short survey of Ireland is confined to one small period
of Tudor rule, the years that Cromwell was Henry's chief minister. It can hardly be called a resounding success. Cromwell
had three main problems to tackle: years of neglect before
his term began, Henry's exasperating unwillingness to invest,
and fractious backbiting among those appointed to govern.
Cromwell could do nothing about the first; he had to manage
as best he could with the second, and then try to sort out the
undignified squabbling from an inconvenient distance. It is not
surprising that little real progress was made.

However, the picture is not all bleak. One might even ven-
ture to claim that the ingredients for a good Irish policy were
present. A chief minister who understood Ireland, and took
Irish affairs seriously, was an advantage in itself. Attempts to
bring order and better administration to Ireland were overdue,
uncontroversial and generally welcomed. Sooner or later someone would have had to implement reforms like these. Irish
opposition to the king's Supremacy was certainly no worse than
in England, and despite the troubles he faced, Browne found

willing listeners to his evangelical preaching. Then both before and after the Kildare rebellion, Cromwell preferred diplomacy and persuasion to force or the threat of it. Military conquest and harsh repression did not feature in his plans. As Dr Nangle's appointment showed, Cromwell made some attempt to reach the hearts and minds of the Gaelic people. The general policy with Gaelic chiefs seems to have been to live and let live, and try to extend English influence little by little.

Although the story of English rule in Ireland all too often makes depressing reading, this brief Cromwellian period – though too brief to make any real, lasting impact – does read like one of the few brighter, or at least less gloomy, interludes. At worst, no major blunder was committed to burden and bedevil successive generations. Maybe Cromwell regretted not replacing Grey sooner. Ironically, a touch of the ruthlessness that popular accounts of the Tudors ascribe to Cromwell might not have been entirely amiss in dealing with Grey and his wrangling council. Often the key to a successful policy lies in the one appointed to execute it, and Grey turned out to be a huge disappointment for Cromwell. If Cromwell had had a Rowland Lee – a man more after his own heart – as deputy, more good might have come of it.[42]

Wales, Ireland and Calais all came under the category of domestic affairs. An insight into Cromwell's negotiations with foreign ambassadors has been given already in Chapter 9. Similar discussions with Chapuys and the French continued almost weekly, but two or three thick volumes would be required to treat all of them in detail. Suffice to say that Cromwell continued broadly pro-Imperialist, though this was never the equivalent of an article of faith; he would do whatever he felt was in Henry's and England's interests.

Foxe noted approvingly that during Cromwell's period England was never at war, and that his policy was to 'nourish peace' with Charles, Francis, the Scots and even Rome if the pope was willing. Cromwell seems to have believed that whereas close relations with France would inevitably drag England into a continental war against Charles, friendship or an alliance with Charles would be sufficient to deter French adventurism and aggression, perhaps without the need for conflict. Whilst Cromwell was prepared to offer English soldiers and funds to help Charles against the Turk as part of an Anglo-Imperial treaty, he was determined to avoid the inconclusive and often wasteful foreign ventures that had been a feature of Henry's reign in Wolsey's time, and would become so once again after Cromwell's fall. When, in early 1535, the French were suggesting that Henry might join Francis and make war on Charles, Cromwell resisted. He assured Chapuys that 'I will never allow the king my master to carry war across the channel, or try to gain one more foot of land on the continent than he has already'. It was a promise he managed to keep.[43]

Chapuys also noticed that Cromwell was very friendly with the Scots ambassador. At the peace treaty with Scotland in May 1534, Cromwell was part of the English negotiating team, along with Audley and Edward Foxe. The treaty held during Cromwell's lifetime, though not Henry's. From time to time Cromwell hinted diplomatically to King James that he might consider doing in Scotland what Henry had done in England, and establish his Supremacy in his own kingdom.[44]

Though allegations of an elaborate Cromwellian spy network are often exaggerated, Cromwell nevertheless prized a good spy in both his foreign and domestic policy. It seems, however, that he was expected to pay their wages and expenses himself rather than from government funds, because he once complained to Cranmer that his spies 'in foreign realms, at Rome and elsewhere cost me above 1,000 marks a year'. Some of his spies came from unexpected quarters, like the Irish-speaking agents in his service (see p. 253). The movements of two suspicious Observant Friars were once reported to Cromwell by another friar named Lawrence, who, displaying a cunning not normally required for his order, recommended that they should not be arrested just yet, but rather kept under observation to discover what their 'cankered intents' really were. Lawrence suspected that a London merchant was bankrolling them. The outcome is not clear.[45]

Cromwell received regular reports on diplomatic events in Europe, and his agents could be quite resourceful. With the help of a page servant to a Portuguese dignitary, Richard Herman's brother managed to get hold of some of the pope's letters to the king of Portugal, and made copies for Cromwell. Simon Heynes in Paris befriended Jacob Sturm from Germany, and through his good offices Hayes secured duplicates of correspondence between King Francis and the German princes at the time when Francis had invited Melanchthon to France. Another alert agent discovered that Reginald Pole, now in exile on the continent, was staying in the old palace in Liège.[46]

As well as domestic and foreign policy, Cromwell's responsibilities also extended to finance, trade and economics. This, however, is a subject more appropriate for specialist journals than a biography, and even then it is fraught with more difficulties than are usually present in historical research. When assessments of contemporary economic trends and policies can be highly subjective and debateable, similar exercises undertaken on the Tudor age 500 years ago face near insuperable obstacles. The following section is, therefore, a very general survey of Cromwell's policy in this area included mainly for completeness, and to show how varied and wide-ranging his workload was.

As a rule, Cromwell preferred to see government income and expenditure managed by departments of state or courts than by the royal household. The Court of Augmentations was made responsible for revenues received from the monasteries. Another court was set up to administer the First Fruits and Tenths and other income from the church. Altogether six different courts or departments existed in Cromwell's time, each with its own terms of reference and officials. As far as his own office of Principal Secretary was concerned, Cromwell, like Henry VII before him, liked to exercise close personal control over income and expenditure, even to the extent of attending to some fairly routine accounting.[47]

The English coinage had been debased under Wolsey, and it would be debased more frequently and drastically in Henry's last post-Cromwell years. However, in a royal proclamation in summer 1538 it was *re*valued. How much of this can be credited directly to Cromwell's management of the Tudor economy is hard to say, but a welcome degree of financial stability attended his tenure of office. The cloth trade, the source of much profit and wealth, generally did well in the 1530s, though customers were becoming increasingly discerning and selective – European buyers were insisting on white or unfinished cloth, as the Merchant Adventurers kept stressing to the government. Cromwell listened to the merchant classes and supported trade in various ways. He relaxed price controls without abolishing them entirely, but he was unwilling to restrict foreign competition as much as the Tudor business community would have liked. An act of 1531 had virtually banned all export of foreign exchange unless licensed by the Lord Chancellor; but Sir Richard Gresham, a merchant who knew Cromwell, seems to have convinced him that such severe restrictions were harmful to trade. Cromwell then successfully persuaded Henry and the council to allow free exchange. He also supported Gresham's proposals for a London *bourse* (Stock Exchange), and he introduced a bill in the 1539 parliament. It won the support of the Lords, but it turned out to be another of Cromwell's bills that failed to pass the Commons – Elton suggests simply for lack of time. It was left to Gresham's son, Thomas, to make the Royal Exchange of London a reality in Elizabeth's reign.[48]

The following table, taken from the much respected Phelps Brown researches, shows the indexes of price rises for food (1) and industrial products (2) in the period 1501–1600 (1471–5 = 100):[49]

	(1)	(2)		(1)	(2)
1501–10	106	98	1551–60	315	186
1511–20	116	102	1561–70	298	218
1521–30	159	110	1571–80	341	223
1531–40	161	110	1581–90	389	230
1541–50	217	127	1591–1600	530	238

Readers will hardly need reminding that statistics, even when expertly researched and prepared, may need to be interpreted with caution. Nevertheless, these facts speak for themselves eloquently enough. The Cromwellian 1530s resemble a monetary oasis compared with most of the rest of the century, and especially the periods just before and after. Uncommonly low inflation combined with a strong currency and a healthy trading position is, as anyone with a bare smattering of economics can appreciate at a glance, a huge economic success story.[50]

Like most prominent ministers of his time, Cromwell favoured moderate state intervention in economic affairs. He introduced a bill that would have prevented wealthy landowners buying up farms to turn them over almost entirely to pasture in order to profit unfairly from the wool trade, a practice allegedly responsible for rising food prices. From now on, no one would be allowed to keep more than 2,000 sheep; at least one eighth of leasehold land had to be reserved for tillage; and restrictions were placed on the amount of such lands any one person could own. Cromwell had high hopes of this bill, and he boldly promised Henry that if it passed successfully it would be the 'most beneficial' thing done for your people 'since the time of Brutus'. Cromwell managed to steer his bill through the Commons only to see the Lords block it, perhaps because it clashed with vested interests. About the only major provision of the draft that became law was the maximum allowance of 2,000 sheep per person. This disappointment may have somewhat dampened his enthusiasm for trying to regulate the economy more than was really practicable.[51]

Cromwell's career as a lawyer, and all the cases concerning land deals in which he was involved, may have provided the impetus to substantial reforms on law and property. He made plans to bring in a comprehensive system of land registration that would consign to history the endless claims and disputes that arose after bargains and sales had been made without any written agreement. The resulting Statute of Enrolments required all land transactions to be sealed and enrolled within six months in a court or before a justice. However, as with his

Enclosure and his Poor Law bills, the act was somewhat more modest than the drafts; Elton suspects that Cromwell ran into organized opposition from landowners and conveyancers.[52]

Landowners and landlords did not always react positively to Cromwell's ideas. One study of the conditions of towns sent to Henry by a servant of his, John Baker, blamed landlords for raising rents far too high for local tenants, with the result that homelessness was increasing, and many buildings falling into decay. Many local corporations received parliamentary authority to intervene and repair decaying properties if the landlords failed to do so. Cromwell, however, recognized the practical difficulties of central government getting too involved in such affairs. He preferred to work with local contacts and interests, using persuasion and influence rather than statute.[53]

This chapter has outlined Cromwell's main official, public policies. The next two will examine the nature of his rule, his relations with the Tudor populace, and also the persona of the king's chief minister.

12

The Widows' Helper

A note survives from Cromwell's remembrances, as recorded in the *Letters and Papers*, to send the Abbots of Reading and Glastonbury 'to be tried and executed' for offences against the king's Supremacy. This served as a cue for Merriman to deliver a sternly sanctimonious lecture on Tudor, and specifically Cromwellian, injustice – 'no pretence of a fair hearing … it mattered little whether this serious charge was proved or not, his execution was determined beforehand'. However, as Elton and others have since pointed out, the original document in the British Library contains the rider to 'see that the evidence be well sorted, and the indictments well drawn against the said abbots and their accomplicies'.[1]

Now a truer picture emerges. Both abbots had almost certainly offended against the law as it stood. Anticipating the dissolution of his abbey, the abbot of Reading had been selling sheep, corn and other items to reduce the value of his lands. At Glastonbury three government agents – Pollard, Moyle and Layton – found a book opposing Henry's first divorce, as well as 'diverse pardons, copies of bulls, and the counterfeit life of Thomas Becket'. They examined the abbot and sent a detailed report to Cromwell, which, they claimed, made manifest his 'cankered and traitorous heart'. They also found a gold chalice and other items which 'the abbot hath hid secretly from all other commissioners'. More extensive searches of the abbey uncovered money and plate hidden in walls and vaults. Further investigations revealed that other valuables had been 'conveyed to diverse places of the country', and that the abbot and some of his monks had allegedly 'embezzelled and stolen' enough plate and ornaments 'to have begun a new abbey'. Cromwell's agents then paid the servants six months' wages, and the monks not involved in the swindle were given their pension and allowed to leave. 'We find them very glad to depart', Pollard added. Other witnesses, including the French ambassador, linked the abbots with the Exeter conspiracy as we will see in Chapter 14, though this does not seem to have been part of the original set of charges against them. Cromwell later received a report of the execution of the abbot of Glastonbury; he had asked 'God's mercy and the king's for his great offences', before he took his death 'very patiently'.[2]

So Cromwell's note about the abbots was not quite the grim indictment of a despotic ruler arbitrarily singling out one or two hapless monks and sending them to death regardless of facts or the due processes of the law. Under the law of the land the case against them seemed clear and straightforward, but Cromwell insisted that all evidence should be properly prepared. This was the Cromwell that Tudor people knew, as Elton's magisterial study of law enforcement in the Cromwellian regime has shown. It is a far cry from the Cromwell imagined by Victorians and Merriman, and some of our modern writers who copy him.

Treason trials in Cromwell's day were by no means foregone conclusions. The king's supremacy laws were enforced rigorously, but invariably fairly, and in accordance with the due processes of law. The accused had first to be presented or indicted by the grand jury of the shire. Presentation was a charge made by the jury. For an indictment to be brought, the jury considered a charge put before it by the crown. If the grand jury rejected the charges, the accused was free to go, otherwise he was sent for trial. There the crown had to prove the case before a new trial jury, and although the defendant had no legal representation, trials were seldom a pushover for the prosecution. The evidence had to convince. Technically the accused could be convicted on the testimony of one witness, but the government generally preferred two.[3]

Here are some bare facts of Henrician and Cromwellian justice. From 1532–40, nearly 900 people were investigated for treason. Of 74 cases, practically nothing is known of the outcome. Of the remainder, 308 are known to have been executed, while 20 more might have been – the evidence is not certain. This figure of 320 or so deaths includes high profile cases like Anne Boleyn and the Exeters, as well as 178 rebels condemned for their part in the northern risings. It also includes over 40 executions that had nothing to do with Henry's Supremacy laws – these were people who would have died as traitors under the previous reign – and a further 23 who were sentenced by the Council of the North without reference to London during the years 1537–40.

Regarding cases of treason by words only, brought under the revised 1534 Treason act, Elton's estimate is that Cromwell investigated nearly 350 such allegations. Of this number, 40 persons were convicted and put to death. About 20 were pardoned or reprieved. This gives a conviction rate of approximately 16 per cent (60 out of nearly 350), and an execution rate of 11 per cent. These surprisingly low figures cannot be explained by the reluctance of local justices to implement the law, or of juries to convict. In only 16 cases did the government fail to secure an indictment from the grand jury, and in only 14 did the trial jury return a verdict of not guilty. But these 30 acquittals make up less than one tenth of the total allegations. The real reason for the low conviction rate was that more than half of the cases reported to Cromwell never reached the courts at all, because after investigating the matter Cromwell decided that the evidence was not strong enough to proceed. Elton's researches reveal that 89 cases were dropped and 95 were probably dropped, though we cannot be absolutely sure of this second figure. The outcome of 68 more allegations is unknown due to missing evidence, but it is at least plausible that these were dropped as well. Some are believed to have fled or died in prison; again the number is not certain.[4]

Treasonous words or acts were frequently reported by ordinary folk to local authorities, who would then inform Cromwell or the Council. Informers were not rewarded, and Elton suggested that the patron-client structure of Tudor society served as Cromwell's eyes and ears, with much of the information being supplied from those who might have sought his patronage or good opinion. An elaborate police state did not exist in Tudor England. Cromwell never went beyond sketching a few very general ideas for creating any sort of national law and order enforcement unit, though these ideas might have developed into something more substantial had he lived longer. For the most part, Cromwell heard of suspicious words or activity only when someone close to the accused, or a local justice, wrote to him about it.[5]

All treason allegations in England were referred to Cromwell except those in the north of the country, which could be dealt with by the Council of the North. Cromwell studied each case on its merits, and all charges were rigorously investigated. Cromwell was well aware that allegations might be motivated by malice or revenge. Occasionally he wrote to the men accused to summon them to him. This could be an intimidating prospect, as it was for one William Wetheral. Escorted by Bishop Tunstall from Kent to London to be examined by Cromwell, Wetheral contrived his escape after breakfasting with the bishop. He was soon caught, however, and confessed that fear of coming face to face with Cromwell drove him to flight. Of the many men questioned by Cromwell, few left any record of the experience. Two who did were Gabriel Pecock, warden of the Observant Franciscans who resented the new teaching against papal authority, and Richard Master, a cleric and associate of the Maid of Kent. Pecock was allowed to go free and Master received a pardon; both described Cromwell as fair, reasonable, even 'noble' in manner. In fact, the only surviving evidence of Cromwell behaving aggressively towards a defendant is the

Spanish Chronicle's tall story about Mark Smeaton with a knotted rope tied and tightened around his head.[6]

Evangelicals reported to Cromwell on suspicion of heresy could count on a sympathetic hearing, but the case of Dr John London shows that Cromwell did not try to fix charges against men of the old faith on flimsy evidence. London, warden of New College at Oxford, was reported by his nephew Edward, apparently an over enthusiastic young evangelical, for allegedly Papist sympathies. Actually London had supported Henry's marriage to Anne and had taken the oath of succession promptly. London defended himself against Edward's claims, and he wrote to Cromwell personally. He lived on untroubled.[7]

Even on the most controversial aspect of Henry's treason laws – where malicious words alone could send the accused to his death – examples survive of those who escaped justice after living and speaking dangerously. The pulpit was a common platform for criticism of the Supremacy and the Reformation, sometimes diplomatically, other times less so. One priest was alleged to have urged his flock 'not to follow the saying of evil princes or evil rulers, but rather put on your harness and fight against them'; but there is no evidence that he was ever prosecuted. The government could be lenient. A few anti-supremacy preachers escaped with a caution, maybe after a climb down. One William Smyth, servant to Sir Roger Wentworth, allegedly asked a visiting evangelical in an inn: 'Were there not in times past as wise kings reigning over us as this king is now, and yet they all obeyed the pope's power? And I beg thee, who gave the king leave to put him down?' Smyth was reported to Cromwell, but there is no evidence that he was committed for trial. The religious and constitutional changes also produced a number of fanciful prophecies up and down the land – Henry and Cromwell were cursed of God, England would soon be ruled by king of Scotland, Henry would be made to do public penance, and more of the same. Some of these were investigated, but only a few were deemed serious enough to be sent for trial; many were simply dropped. It is likely that, except in the most watertight cases, suspects were given the benefit of the doubt, maybe after an acceptable apology and a profession of loyalty, followed by a warning from Cromwell to behave in future.[8]

In Tudor England, unlike most of Europe, torture was not normally used in criminal investigations. Nevertheless, there could be exceptional cases, mainly when national security was believed to be in danger. Cromwell once committed two 'very sedicious' friars to custody until Henry had time to consider their case. Cromwell suspected that they would 'confess some great matter if they be examined as they ought to be, that is to say by pains'. One of them in particular was a 'subtle fellow and much given to sedition'. In the event, these friars suffered no pains. Maybe the threat was enough to loosen their tongues.[9]

No one would deny that Tudor laws could be severe, but any comparison between the Cromwellian period and the reign of terror of the French Revolution would be ludicrously wide of the mark. Nevertheless, Cromwell's forbidding reputation persists, and he is still from time to time made guilty by association with one of the most malignant of all hobgoblin figures of the past – Niccolò Machiavelli.

It was in 1539 that Lord Morley sent Cromwell a copy of Machiavelli's *History of Florence* in Italian, knowing Cromwell's interest in Italian history, and how conversant among the Italians he was. Morley was amazed at the Italian 'frauds, mischiefs, treasons and conspiracies' he had read of. He also recommended *The Prince*, a book 'surely a very special good thing for your Lordship to look upon for many causes'.[10]

According to Reginald Pole, however, Cromwell had read *The Prince* ten years earlier, and had warmly recommended it to Pole. Merriman believed Pole's account though others, including Pole's recent biographer, are sceptical. *The Prince* was not published until 1532, three years after Pole alleged that Cromwell had applauded it; so if Pole's story is true then Cromwell must have seen an early manuscript copy. Because he was fluent in Italian, this is quite possible, so the following discussion will assume for the sake of argument that Cromwell had indeed read *The Prince* as Pole claimed. He was not the only Englishman to have done so; one of his clients, Richard Morison, had also read it, and he found it a most interesting work.[11]

So was Cromwell a Machiavellian? The term has become a carelessly used catch-all insult for any politician who may occasionally display a touch of guile, so in order to try and answer the question, a summary of *The Prince* might help.[12]

To begin with, *The Prince* contains sections on making war and conquering new territory. As seen already, however, the chief aim of Cromwell's foreign policy was to keep England at peace, and to dissuade Henry from oversees adventures. Then much of *The Prince* concerns a ruler who has acquired power by conquest or other means, not a hereditary monarch like Cromwell's master. Machiavelli also writes admiringly of the Renaissance Pope Alexander VI, who, 'more than any other pontiff who has ever lived, showed how much a pope could achieve with money and armed force'. After him, Pope Julius 'not only continued but also improved' on the feats of Alexander. Thanks to these two, Pope Leo 'found the papacy in an extremely strong position'. Machiavelli hoped that Leo, 'by his goodness and countless other virtues, will make it very great and revered'. Not much here to arouse the admiration of Henry's Lutheran chief minister.[13]

Here, now, are some of Machiavelli's more general points. Generosity is a virtue, but not necessarily a good thing in a prince; it will be misused and resources squandered. Cruelty is acceptable if it keeps his people united and loyal. If a prince is too compassionate, he risks provoking disorder and murder, which harms the whole community; but a few well-timed executions affect only individuals. Nevertheless, his behaviour 'must be tempered with humanity and prudence'. Ideally a prince should be loved and feared; but rarely is this possible, so it is better to be feared than loved if he cannot be both. An act of love is easily despised, but fear compels obedience. The art of statecraft is to be feared, but not hated. The best way a prince will avoid being hated is to leave his subjects' property and their women alone. A war leader needs to be cruel to keep discipline: Hannibal showed 'inhuman cruelty', and was a great commander; Scipio showed leniency, and his armies mutinied.[14]

One of the most controversial passages from *The Prince* reads as follows:

> A ruler must not honour his word when it places him at a disadvantage, and when the reasons for which he made his promise no longer exist. If all men were good, this precept would not be good; but because men are wretched creatures who would not keep their word to you, you need not keep your word to them ... One must know how to colour one's actions and to be a great liar and deceiver.

A good prince, the author continues, should be capable of kindness, honesty and mercy; but he should also know how to be the opposite. Reasons of state demand it. He should 'not deviate from what is good, if that is possible; but he should know how to do evil, if that is necessary'. To appearances a prince should be compassionate, honest, and especially religious; because 'everyone sees what you appear to be, but few experience what you really are'.[15]

Some may find this offensive, though others may feel that Machiavelli was merely stating some uncomfortable truths rather forcefully. There can be few rulers and statesmen, however honourable, who have not behaved with a certain ruthlessness or guile at some time in their careers.

Machiavelli has an interesting passage, which might have caught Cromwell's eye, on the relationship between a prince and his key ministers. The prince should not injure any minister 'close to him in his affairs of state' – a lesson Henry VIII habitually ignored. 'Nothing brings a prince more prestige than great campaigns and striking demonstrations of his personal abilities'. As noted already, Cromwell hated great military campaigns. A prince must try and 'win the reputation of being a great man of outstanding ability', and be a 'true friend or a true enemy'. But he must avoid neutrality. A prince 'should never join in an aggressive alliance with someone more powerful than himself unless it is a matter of necessity', because 'if you are the victors, you emerge as his prisoner'. Cromwell, however, *was* prepared to consider an alliance between Henry and a more powerful monarch, Charles V, against the Turk, as we saw in Chapter 9. A minister should think always of his prince, never of himself. A prince should honour such a minister and share responsibility with him. A good prince must choose wise ministers and allow them, but only them, 'the freedom to speak the truth to him, though only concerning matters on which he asks their opinion'. A 'prince who is not himself wise cannot be well advised, unless he happens to trust himself to the hands of one individual who looks after all his affairs, and is an extremely shrewd man'. The danger with this is that the prince would 'not last long, because the one who governs for him would soon deprive him of his state'. So a prince needs more than one advisor, and he needs also the wisdom to understand and decide on the often conflicting advice he receives. So if Cromwell entertained ideas about becoming an all-powerful minister ruling without rivals, Machiavelli offered no encouragement.[16]

Of fortune or providence in the affairs of nations, Machiavelli has little to say. He does not 'rule out our free will', so he makes fortune 'the arbiter of half the things we do'. Fortune is like a 'great river which may bring floods and destruction; but when such a river is flowing quietly it is sensible to build dykes and embankments, so that when the storm comes it may be less dangerous'. Fortune 'shows her potency when there is no well-regulated power to resist her'. Machiavelli discusses the career of Pope Julius II, an 'impetuous' man; and concludes that 'it is better to be impetuous than circumspect, because fortune is a woman, and if she is to be submissive it is necessary to beat and coerce her'. Machiavelli hoped that Lorenzo de Medici, to whom the work was dedicated, would be the one raised up of God to liberate Italy and lead her 'to her salvation'. It is noteworthy how the theme of salvation appears in a political, though not a religious, context.[17]

However, Machiavelli was not entirely irreligious. In a separate work – his *Discourses* – he commended religion, but chiefly as a force for inspiring and maintaining a well-ordered society, as the ancient Romans applied it. He was critical of the Roman Church of his time; he was also, though indirectly, critical of the Christian piety that lauded humility, weakness and gentleness while belittling grandeur, strength and greatness. About Christian themes like salvation, regeneration and sanctification, he has little to say.[18]

The Prince was written following Machiavelli's own experiences as a diplomat and observer of the tangled Italian conflicts of his age, when he had the chance to watch and assess the campaigns of Cesare Borgia and Pope Julius II.[19] So it is not particularly relevant to England in the 1530s, a unitary state with a hereditary monarchy undergoing a period of unprecedented constitutional change. No advice is to be found in Machiavelli on how to persuade the pope to grant the king his heart's desire, or carry out a religious and political reformation. No hints are given on how best to infuse Lutheran ideas, which the king still only dimly understands, in the hearts and minds of the English people. The admiration for the military and political skills of the renaissance popes sits uneasily with the campaign of Henry and Cromwell to reject papal authority, and to turn the peoples' affections away from the pontiffs by attacking their worldly, unchristian living.

To revert to the original question, therefore, calling Cromwell a Machiavellian is the sort of thing that makes a catchy headline but has little real substance to it. Cromwell may indeed have read *The Prince* around 1529, as Pole claimed. Maybe it made an impression then; maybe he retained, and from time to time practiced, one or two Machiavellian ideas. But Cromwell had moved on since Pole knew him, to a wholly new spiritual and political order. The thoughts and counsels of *The Prince* were of little use to him when he became Henry's chief minister. In fact, as a reformer of the Tudor church and state, Cromwell had no man's writings or works to draw upon.

He was one of those men destined to make history, not to follow where others had gone before.

Another tale about Cromwell is that he was extortionate, rapaciously fond of money and a habitual exactor of bribes. Again the flimsy evidence that exists comes mainly from hostile witnesses. Elton has already demonstrated that two letters in Merriman's collection (numbers 163 and 180), which appear to show Cromwell demanding bribes, are almost certainly forgeries. The fact that these letters have been preserved indicates that the targets of the deception probably reported the tricks to Cromwell.[20]

Beyond doubt, Cromwell profited from his position, and before the hazards of high office dragged him to his downfall, he saw no reason why he should not enjoy some of its benefits. He lived handsomely, though never craved the flamboyant extravagance that Wolsey delighted in. Many of those enquiring about monastic lands for sale offered Cromwell a fee; but this is no more disturbing than a business lunch, a free ticket to the opera, a weekend in the country, or some other inviting perk that is likely to remain a part of daily commercial life. Besides, letters enquiring about church lands came invariably from the nobility and wealthy gentry, and there was no reason why such fortunate people should not be expected to offer something in return for a favour. It is impossible to trace how Cromwell spent all this money, but as many as 400 people depended on him either directly or indirectly for their livelihood. It is also likely that Cromwell used the gentry's cash to fund his evangelical allies and their cause.

A study of Cromwell's relations with the West Country by Dr Mary Robertson has shown how concerned he could be for the wellbeing of a region in which he had little vested interest, and little opportunity to enrich himself. It was comparatively remote from London, generally conservative in religion, and the stronghold of the Exeters, a clan not among Cromwell's natural supporters. Nevertheless, Cromwell made good use of personal contacts with local gentry, merchants and justices that he had forged since first entering parliament in 1523. Some, though not all, were formally in his service. Cromwell's contacts supplied him with regular news on a range of subjects including law and order, poverty in Falmouth, building works, tin works, repairs needed to ports, a fight between French and Spanish sailors off the Devon coast, and a similar scrap near Falmouth. These were not routine reports that Cromwell merely read and discarded. Many had a positive outcome. For instance, bills were brought before parliament to improve ports and harbours. When a complaint reached Cromwell that local officials had covered up a crime allegedly committed by a nephew of one of them, and the sheriff failed to take any action, Cromwell quickly sent one of his own men, Richard Pollard, to resolve the matter to general satisfaction. However, Cromwell made no attempt to pack the Devon and Cornish benches or local authorities with loyal evangelical protégées.[21]

The West Country may not necessarily be representative of all England, but it is nonetheless a useful pointer to Cromwell's style of government, and how it impacted on the lives of people in the regions. What emerges from it is a narrative of good, sound practical government, and the right sort of central intervention when needed. This, and the knowledge that the king's chief minister cared about the welfare of the region, would help foster goodwill among the people, and maybe win acceptance for the sort of religious change which normally would go against the grain of Catholic Devon and Cornwall.

In fact, there was far more to Tudor government than major constitutional change, and the following examples are selected in order to illustrate what a more or less typical day in the life of Thomas Cromwell could have been like. They will also shed light on his reputation among the Tudor populace. All events occurred between 1534 and the period shortly before his death. Some of the more intriguing cases are petitions from ordinary and not excessively rich folk on day-to-day problems. We begin, however, with a few miscellaneous tasks he undertook just after he was made Principal Secretary.

In July 1534 he issued an order to detain suspected murderers from Yorkshire, who, after the crime, had fled to Scotland

and subsequently returned to Durham. He then sought to reconcile a dispute over property between the abbot of St Austin's
and one George Goldwyn, who had been pursuing Cromwell
relentlessly with his 'continual suit'. He sent directions to Lord
Cobham about a 'farm of the parsonage', instructing him to
'cause the corn and other duties to be gathered together', and
promising to 'order your lordship' concerning the rent. He
summoned Sir Roger Reynolds, Robert Wolf and John Kytch
to answer charges against them. An admonitory letter had to
be sent to Lord Lisle in Calais, though Cromwell promised
Lisle and his wife his friendship. He arranged a lease of a farm
for one Mr. Allen. He then wrote to Scottish authorities on
behalf of Thomas Miller, a merchant and an English subject,
whose ship had run aground, and whose goods were detained
'against good equity and conscience' by authorities in the
north of Scotland. After being petitioned regarding a land dispute, Cromwell asked that lands belonging to one Reginald
Williams should to be restored to him. On Henry's behalf, he
rebuked the authorities of Oxford University for their 'abu-
sions, usurpations and ungentle demeanour' towards the king's
subjects in Oxford and its suburbs. Cromwell marvelled that
'ye being men of learning and in who should remain both
wisdom and discretion' should behave in such a way. Their
offence is not explicitly stated, but it reads as though they had
used unreasonable heavy-handedness regarding university
appointments. Later in the year, keeping watch on all kinds of
government projects, Cromwell sent a stern letter to Thomas
Wingfield, controller of the works at Dover, giving him a
rocket for wastefulness and inefficiency.[22]

Cromwell also received many letters from the king's subjects seeking redress, help or simply making a complaint. A
great many of these are disputes regarding lands and property,
or requests for annuities, appointments and applications to
this or that post. These can be passed over for this purpose
– they are repetitive and somewhat dull – in favour of more
interesting cases. The outcome of these requests is seldom
certain from the surviving records, but when there is clear

evidence it will be noted. We begin with letters of a semi-official nature.

John Peryns of Herton complained about a prior, who, with two of his monks – all disguised with coats, swords and bucklers – entered Malvern Chase to hunt and kill the king's deer. When William Maunsell, an employee of the sheriff of Yorkshire, was arrested for felony, he wrote to Cromwell asking for a personal hearing. Sir Walter Stonore appealed to Cromwell on behalf of his brother Edmund, who had killed a servant who attacked him; Stonore gave a meticulous account of the event, insisting that Edmund had acted only in self-defence. Lord Lumley complained to Cromwell that Ralph, earl of Westmoreland, had illegally stopped a water-course; Westmoreland then submitted a lengthy defence (this occurred before the Council of the North was established).[23]

When seven convicts escaped from the bishop of Lincoln's prison, the anxious bishop, now liable for a forfeit, appealed to Cromwell to intercede with Henry and obtain the king's forgiveness. When a labourer on the king's works in Dover was injured and unable to work, one John Wynfeld kindly pro-vided for him. Then, when some official advised Wynfeld that he might be able to make a claim for compensation, he wrote to Cromwell asking if his costs might be refunded. Bailiffs of Kingston-upon-Thames, embroiled in a dispute over rents, asked Cromwell to obtain an allowance from the Exchequer. From the north of England – this time when the Council of the North *was* established – Robert Ferrer, one of Cromwell's agents, reported that gentry on the borders were oppressing and cheating the poor. Ferrer does not say why he did not take the case to the Council of the North. What really matters, however, is that Ferrer knew this was the sort of thing that ought to be reported to Cromwell.[24]

The next three pieces show local officials contacting Cromwell. When Thomas Crofte of Kent, for seditious words, was sentenced to the pillory and to have both his ears cut off, Cromwell somehow heard of the case. He reviewed it, and decided that the pillory alone should be enough. The local justice agreed, and a grateful Master Crofte survived his ordeal with ears intact.[25]

Thomas Long was a local officer in the London area. One day, quite lawfully, he set a fellow called Rygeley in the stocks. Soon after this, and quite by chance, Long and Rygeley came face to face in the street. Determined to get his own back, Rygeley set about Long with his fists. Rygeley was getting the better of the brawl until a passer-by restrained him. Long, now heavily bandaged, lodged a most indignant complaint to Cromwell.[26]

Richard Smyth was a physician of dubious merits living and working in Cheapside, whose patients quickly got worse after being treated by him. One, who took medicine prescribed by Smyth as a certain cure, died four days later. Eventually an official complaint against Smyth landed on Cromwell's desk.[27]

Nor were private citizens slow to petition Cromwell. Prisoners at Ludgate complained to him about the harsh, unlawful treatment they had to endure at the hands of the prison keeper. He was overcharging for little luxuries like blankets and sheets, taking bribes and keeping alms intended for the prisoners. He would not provide cheap beer, and he refused to attend to prisoners who fell sick. If a prisoner's wife visiting her husband was a pretty woman, he would 'labour to fulfil his foul lust'. (From this it sounds as though prison conditions were not all terribly bad in Tudor times.)[28]

A certain merchant once suffered losses at the hands of French pirates. Unable now to support his wife and nine children, he appealed to Cromwell for help. When a Mr Gostwycke was holding back expenses owed to Robert Barnes, Barnes asked Cromwell to intervene. When John Burton's wife was ejected from a farm rented from Merton Abbey, and the abbot ignored her husband's demands for restitution, Burton knew what to do – he wrote to Cromwell for help. However, not all requests came from the needy. William Hawkins of Plymouth was a sea-faring merchant, whose travels may have included Brazil. Needing brass, powder and loans for his ships, the enterprising Hawkins approached Cromwell to ask whether government funding might be available.[29]

Richard Manchester, once chaplain of Sir John Russell, complained to Cromwell alleging false imprisonment due to the malicious accusations of one Mr Moore. A learned, if somewhat conceited man, Manchester's letter recalled Synon and the Trojan horse, before likening himself to Cassandra, who prophesied truly but was not believed. Manchester begged Cromwell's help and understanding. Moore, he alleged, was a deceitful character, and had tricked even Wriothesley, one of Cromwell's staff, into believing his mischievous tales. Soon after this for reasons not stated Moore found himself in trouble with the authorities, and Cromwell received another begging letter, this time from Moore's wife pleading for his freedom. Several other examples could be given of letters to Cromwell from people claiming wrongful imprisonment.[30]

Overseas visitors to England as well as the king's subjects enjoyed Cromwell's patronage and protection. François Regnault was a French bookseller who had lived in England for several years, but he began to fear that English booksellers wanted to stop him printing and distributing here. He wrote to Cromwell, in French, asking for help, and for permission to carry on his trade. Regnault may have been a man of evangelical sympathies, because he later played host to Coverdale and Grafton during their visit to Paris to print the Great Bible (see Chapter 14).[31]

Cromwell's responsibilities also extended to the king's lands and livestock. Sir Edward Croft enjoyed lands as a gift from Henry, and one of his privileges was to have a deer in summer and winter. Then one day Geoffrey Blount, Keeper of the King's forest of Wyre, abruptly and without any explanation, told Croft that he would not be allowed any more deer. Croft was outraged; in his opinion this was a subject worth bringing to Cromwell's notice.[32]

Inevitably matters concerning religion and the church were referred to Cromwell, not least by eager beaver evangelicals seldom slow to offer the Vicegerent some advice. Around August 1534, an anonymous draft called for an end to clerical celibacy, veneration of images and prayers for the dead. A little later, another anonymous writer to an anonymous recipient, though probably to Cromwell, suggested an act of parliament to establish evangelical articles of faith: that Christ was the sole Mediator between God and man; that 'the blood of Christ sufficeth to man's redemption without the blood of martyrs'; that purgatory was a popish myth; that it is more charitable to pray for the living than the dead; that God alone can forgive sin; and that images should not be worshipped. This writer, a man with more zeal than sense, seemed blissfully unaware that Cromwell had to spread the Word discreetly; there was not the remotest chance of securing legislation on these subjects so soon.[33]

Further Lutheranesque proposals were sent to Cromwell from John Rastell, brother-in-law of Thomas More, though whether by invitation is not stated – probably not. Another evangelical, Thomas Mereall, was accused of heresy, and at his trial he noticed servants of the bishop of London on the jury. He knew exactly what to do – he dashed off a letter to Cromwell.[34]

Evangelical strategist though he was, Cromwell might have done better without the likes of Richard Quiaenus, who took it upon himself, apparently without any calling or permission, to preach justification by faith at a church in Stamford. On leaving the church he was set on by a group of Dominicans, strenuously averring that justification could never be attained without good works. Quiaenus asked for Cromwell's help, and provided some local information. A nearby abbot, in the service of the bishop of Lincoln, had attacked those carrying the New Testament. Quiaenus demanded that the Gospel be set forth everywhere, including brothels. He had also been involved in a row with the abbot regarding images and the mediatorial role of Mary and the saints. He was afraid of his bishop, but claimed many witnesses could vouch for his good character.[35]

Details of family disputes and even marriage rows demanded Cromwell's attention. Soon after Maud Knevet was widowed in 1526, she secretly married Master Knevet of the King's Privy Chamber; but for reasons not stated he did not treat her as his lawful wife, so she married a fellow called Smythe. Knevet's jealously was kindled, and he summoned her to appear before Wolsey, who commanded her to divorce Smythe. She obeyed, and 're-married' Knevet. After living together as man and wife for eight years, Master Knevet now denied that Maud was his lawful wife; exact reasons are not given, but there is a hint that money was involved. Whatever the facts, Maud begged Cromwell to compel Knevet to acknowledge her as his wife so she could keep a good living.[36]

Less intricate, but still faintly bizarre, was the case of Thomas Barton who had married a divorcee. The divorce decree had been approved by the Archbishop of York, but he was now reconsidering the matter, prompting an anxious Barton to urge Cromwell to intervene. Then there was Godfrey Somersall, who, apart from having an affair with a married woman, was also maltreating his own wife, Anne, despite a warning from the local justice to behave. A friend of Anne's, William Assherby, fearing that local authorities were remiss in settling the matter, appealed to Cromwell to come to the aid of the cheated wife.[37]

Tudor women were not slow to turn directly to Cromwell for help in time of need. Elizabeth Burgh (Borough) was delivered of a son sometime in late 1537. It was a premature birth, and the relieved mother was convinced that only the power of God had saved the child's life. However, her tyrannical father-in-law Lord Burgh now claimed that his son, her husband, Sir Thomas Burgh was not the true father. Because her husband was scared of *his* father, she begged Cromwell to intercede and help, chiefly for the child's sake in case he was unjustly disinherited. Cromwell dealt with her appeal sympathetically, but as so often in these cases the trail quickly goes cold and the outcome is not known.[38]

Agnes Awstyd's husband was detained falsely for no better reason, so she claimed, than having once done a kindness to a man subsequently condemned to death. She begged Cromwell to secure his release. Ellen Wryne appealed on behalf of her son, John, prevented by the local mayor and sheriffs from doing his job as recorder, even though Cromwell had approved the appointment. They were only angry, she maintained, because her husband once complained to Cromwell about them for robbing a ship. Thomas Martin, a London merchant, had been pursuing a law suit in Poland for fifteen years to recover a large sum owed to him. The affair had dragged through four courts, and had even come to the attention of the King of Poland. Currently it was in the hands of Polish councillors. Impatient with all the delays, Martin's wife took matters into her own hands and wrote to Cromwell asking him if he would expedite the case.[39]

Word must have spread that Cromwell dealt understandingly with women in distress. Elizabeth Constable was a rejected wife with no one to support her. Appealing to Cromwell's kindness, she was, she pleaded, ashamed to beg or play the harlot. Margaret Lyle was deserted by her family for being a loose-living woman; undaunted she turned to Cromwell, urging his intercession to get her an honest living somehow, somewhere. Nor was Alice Parker, a former servant of Cromwell's, afraid to ask her former master's help when two other servants refused to pay money owing to her.[40]

Especially noteworthy are letters from widows. Katherine Torner and her late husband had lived on land belonging to a Mr Barton for fifty-six years; but following her husband's death, Barton allegedly took away their cattle and stopped her servants bringing in the hay. The distressed widow wrote to Cromwell – would he please help her, and tell Barton to stop harassing her. Dame Elizabeth Whettyl and the marchioness of Dorset, both widows suffering from ungrateful sons, wrote to Cromwell for succour and support. In Dame Elizabeth's case – her son refused to honour his late father's will and provide for his mother – it can be said for certain that the outcome was a happy one, because she subsequently sent Cromwell a letter warmly thanking him for his goodness.[41]

Katherine Audelett, another widow, complained to Cromwell about one Harry Huttoft, who was delaying a settlement due to her. Huttoft received a sharp rebuke from

Cromwell, so presumably this one ended agreeably as well. Sometime later the same lady reported a case of assault to Cromwell. Perhaps she received no satisfaction from the local justice – she does not give a reason – but obviously she knew where to go in time of need. So did the widow of Sir Robert Lee, Lettys Lee, when burdened with various legal wrangles and uncertainties following her husband's death. Finding the law confusing, and suspicious of the motives of greedy lawyers, she sought Cromwell's advice. She, too, was successful and well provided for. Another petitioner was Ellen Ewer, whose husband had been executed (the crime is not stated) and was left penniless because the recorder would not provide her with her husband's money to which she was entitled. The recorder claimed that Ewer's imprisonment had cost him 40s, but the widow begged Cromwell's intervention; she assured him that the figure was only 16d, and she could prove it.[42]

Let the last word on this most ruthless and notorious Tudor tyrant go to Mawde Carew, widow of Sir Richard, father of Nicholas. Cromwell had gone to some trouble on her behalf after thieves had robbed or defrauded her of her savings. For this she poured out her gratitude for 'your great pains taken about the redress of my great late losses'. Now a frail old lady and nearly blind, she felt 'most bounden to' him; she begged God to 'prosper and continue your good lordship, for the comfort of all poor widows'.[43]

13

Patron and Persona

An illustration of the renaissance humanist passion for the past is that Tudor men deemed worthy of high praise were wont to be likened to some towering figure of the classical age. Gabriel Harvey, the Elizabethan writer, was greatly impressed by Cromwell's 'natural heroic audacity' and 'pragmatic experience'. Harvey admired self-made statesmen of humble birth 'like Marius, especially Caesar, and in our time, Cromwell'. These, he judged, were far better motivated and equipped than academics, thinkers or intellectuals to turn fine ideas into real, substantial benefits. Others likened Cromwell to Maecenas, chief councillor to Augustus and patron of the Roman arts.[1]

With men from a lowly background, it is often the case that their unprivileged background spurs them on to attain heights beyond the reach of more fortunate people. Thomas Cromwell was one such man.

Encouraged by his foreign travels, he was able to develop his natural aptitude for languages to become the most proficient linguist in Henry's government. Chapuys testified to Cromwell's ability to read and speak French, Latin and Italian fluently. Cromwell retained a particular love of the Italian tongue. Frequently he received letters in Italian from contacts abroad, some of them agents of his. When time permitted he enjoyed reading Italian works like the *Triumphs of Petrarch*, *Il Cortegiano*, a book on Venetian society and diverse Italian verses.[2]

Chapuys does not mention it, but on the evidence of letters sent to him, Cromwell must have been competent in Spanish as well. Catherine of Aragon's letter to him was written in Spanish as we saw on page 146. Don Diego Hurtado de Mendoça, an envoy from Charles V to England and a colleague of Chapuys, wrote to Cromwell in Spanish about diplomatic affairs. So, too, did an Englishman on official government business in Spain, presumably wanting to practice his Spanish with a fellow countryman who also knew the language. These letters are quite detailed and informative, obviously not intended for beginners. Maybe Cromwell's youthful foreign travels included parts of Spain.[3]

It was Cromwell's mortal enemy, Stephen Gardiner, who, perhaps without intending to, left liberal testimony to Cromwell's knowledge of classical languages. In Edward's reign, when Gardiner's fortunes had fallen somewhat, he recalled how Cromwell was habitually 'very stout towards me … for that conceit he had, what so ever he talked with me, he knew ever as much as I, Greek or Latin, and all'.[4]

Cromwell once translated Gardiner's minutes of a meeting with the king from English to Latin. Whatever the reason – it may have been a favour before the rivalry set in – the task was completed to the bishop's satisfaction. However, whilst it was unremarkable for a Tudor minister to be competent in Latin, similar accomplishment in Greek was rare. Gardiner was the last man in the world to put in an undeserved good word for Cromwell, which is what makes this hostile witness so compelling. Gardiner was no mean scholar himself. He described with satisfaction how, in June 1535, he completed his translation of the Gospels of Luke and John. Elsewhere Gardiner's letters contain references to, or Greek quotes taken from, Euripides, Gregory of Nazianen, Plato and Aristotle. After Cromwell's death, Gardiner engaged in lengthy scholarly discussions with Sir John Cheke, Regius Professor of Greek at Cambridge and tutor to Prince Edward, on various aspects of Greek including the right pronunciation.[5]

It is possible that Cromwell had set foot in Greece during his days as a youthful wanderer – the distance by sea from southern Italy is not great. Alternatively, and more plausibly perhaps, he could have built up his knowledge of Greek steadily over the years since settling in England as part of his interest in the humanities.

How well he knew the other Biblical language is less certain. In 1529 Stephen Vaughan, in Flanders, was intending to buy a dining table for himself or for Cromwell, and on its borders were Scripture texts in Hebrew, Greek and Latin. This is not enough to prove that Cromwell knew Hebrew well, though he may have had some rudimentary knowledge of it.[6]

There is no evidence that Cromwell spoke German. He did not become a Lutheran councillor until 1531. After this the demands of his office would have ensured that he did not have the time to learn the language of Luther.

Cromwell's interest in the arts and humanities was wide-ranging. Sometime in 1533 or 1534, Hans Holbein painted the famous portrait (see plate 3). Like Erasmus and Melanchthon, though unlike many famous Tudors, Cromwell preferred to be painted sideways on. Holbein later produced the frontispiece for Coverdale's Bible and the design for Cromwell's Great Bible (see plate 2). Cromwell may have been Holbein's patron, and he certainly helped the young artist in his career. His collection of works of art, both sacred and profane, was one of the most varied and impressive of his time, including painted tables of the Nativity, the Magi, Christ's Passion, the 'Pity of our Lady' and the 'Salutation of our Lady', along with Lucretia Romana, coats of arms, a painting of King Francis I at Pavia, and much more.[7]

History was another of Cromwell's passions. A close friend of his was Edward Hall, the leading historian in Henry's reign. In 1535 Cromwell asked for, and duly received, a copy of Bede's *De Ecclesiastica Historia* and other historical works to add to his already expansive library. A year later Thomas

Bedyll told Cromwell of a discovery he had made in Ramsay Abbey – a 'charter of King Edgar', which 'I am sure you would delight to see for the strangeness and antiquity thereof'. Edgar had signed himself 'emperor' of England (*incliti et serenissimi anglorum imperatoris*). Bedyll had also found a charter of King Edward 'written afore the Conquest' in which Edward, 'by his kingly power could exempt this monastery of Ramsay from all the bishops' powers'. These findings, as Elton noted, prove Cromwell's interest in history *as* history, because ancient claims of royal authority over the church were no longer required solely for political or propaganda purposes. By 1535 that point had already been amply proved, at least to the satisfaction of reformers. Similarly, two years later, Cromwell asked Christopher Mont to translate German chronicles into English because he wanted to understand the history and reformation of Germany better.[8]

Another of Cromwell's friends was Thomas Wyatt, one of the foremost Tudor poets before the culturally peerless age of Elizabeth. Wyatt, it was said, once had a crush on Anne Boleyn, and Cromwell's intercession was called upon to persuade Henry that Wyatt was not one of her lovers. Cromwell may have known the leading musicians and composers of his time, like Thomas Tallis and Christopher Tye, but there is no firm evidence for this. He did, however, keep his own small orchestra of around twelve young musicians, and his accounts include references to 'Mr Bryan's minstrels' and a gift of something variously described as a 'lutte', 'lowtt' and 'lwwtt' – probably a lute.[9]

As well as Hall and Wyatt, Cromwell's circle of friends included two of the most talented Henrician humanists. Neither man was a devout evangelical. Thomas Starkey came to Cromwell's attention soon after returning to England in 1534 from Padua, where he had been studying for his law degree. An abiding friendship quickly developed.[10] Starkey, however, had misgivings over the suppression of the smaller monasteries in 1536, fearing that it might defraud the departed, especially the monastic founders, 'of the benefits of prayers and alms ... appointed to be done for their relief'.[11] Starkey was one of those – Robert Barnes was another – who urged that monastic revenues should be used for the common good. Although he became slightly disillusioned with some of Cromwell's reformist policies, the mutual respect and friendship continued.

The accolade of the greatest pre-Elizabethan Tudor humanist may well belong to Thomas Elyot, whose friendship with Cromwell began around 1519, and endured as long as Cromwell lived despite differences of opinion over religion and politics. Like Starkey, Elyot was not altogether happy with the direction in which Henry and Cromwell were leading the country. He was grieved by Henry's divorce from Catherine, by his subsequent marriage to Anne and the ensuing schism. Cromwell had also shown sympathy for Catherine on a personal level, so maybe he was able to identify to some degree. Once he gave Elyot a friendly warning against 'superstition', by which he meant the medieval religion to which Elyot's heart remained attached. Employed by Cromwell in his national survey of the monasteries in 1535, Elyot took the opportunity to ask for some recompense for the losses he had suffered as Henry's ambassador to Charles V two years earlier; he was not the only one sent on Henry's service to complain about unpaid expenses. After some delay, it seems that Cromwell did manage to persuade Henry to grant Elyot some lands in Cambridgeshire.[12]

Inevitably a minister like Cromwell would attract the attention of aspiring as well as established scholars. Elton has given several examples of more or less hopefuls sending their works to Cromwell, either applying for a post somewhere or seeking his favour. They include a former monk, who, after converting to the Lutheran faith, had decided to learn Hebrew and Greek. This done, he offered his services to Cromwell, quoting Richard Morison as a referee. Qualified teachers like Walter Graver and Thomas Hampton asked Cromwell's help to grant them suitable posts. Less welcome for a busy minister, and hardly necessary for a man of Cromwell's theological insight, was a long, dull essay on biblical hermeneutics from one Thomas Swinnerton. Welcome or not, evidence exists of a courteous reply to many of these unsolicited applicants.[13]

So much for Cromwell as Henry's Maecenas, and the appellation, if generous, is far from being grossly inflated. The rest of the chapter will try to give the reader a glimpse of the personality of Thomas Cromwell, all the while recognising that from a distance of 500 years, a glimpse is about all that can be offered.

Contemporary evidence is liable to be coloured by partisanship, but foreign ambassadors, more likely to be measured in their judgement, generally spoke well of him. The Venetian ambassador's reports reveal disappointingly little, but Chapuys called Cromwell a 'man of wit, well versed in government affairs, and reasonable enough to judge correctly of them'. Despite differences and occasional difficulties, their working and personal relationships were generally good, and Chapuys made a point of mentioning to Charles that when a fire destroyed much of his house, Cromwell had been generous with offers of assistance. A sour note was struck by the French ambassador, Castillon, who knew 'no more hypocritical men' (*plus feintes personnes*) than Henry and Cromwell. But Castillon harboured a particular aversion to England. To punish Henry for his schism and heresy, he once dreamed of a threefold alliance comprising of Francis, Charles and the Scots to invade and conquer England, and carve the country up between them. The idea failed completely to elicit any consideration from King Francis. The despatches of Marillac, Castillon's successor, are altogether more balanced, besides being enlivened by a dry Gallic wit – he once observed that if only Cromwell were as 'valiant in keeping promises as he is bold in making them', prospects for Anglo-French relations would be distinctly promising. Elsewhere Marillac described Cromwell as 'very assiduous' and 'willing to do justice to all, including foreigners'.[14]

John Stow was a Tudor writer, born in 1525, whose works give two sides of Cromwell. First, Stow describes Cromwell, sometime in 1533, building a house in Throgmorton Street by the Austin Friars Church. When the house was finished and space remained for a garden, Cromwell ordered the pales of the gardens adjoining on the north side to be taken down. He then measured twenty-two feet into his neighbour's gardens, ordered a 'line there to be drawn, a trench to be cast, a foundation laid, and a high brick wall to be built'. Stow's father had a house and garden there, and 'this house they lowsed from the ground' with a minimum of notice. When Stow senior remonstrated with the surveyors, they replied that they were carrying out Cromwell's orders, and 'no man durst go to argue'. Stow notes that 'the rising of some men causeth them to forget themselves'.[15]

This unappealingly overbearing behaviour is then counterbalanced by the same author in other parts of his book, where he speaks very well of Cromwell, especially his charity to the poor. 'I myself', he avows, 'in that declining time of charity, have oft seen at the Lord Cromwell's gate in London, more than 200 persons served twice every day with bread, meat and drink sufficient, for he observed that ancient and charitable custom'. Stow also recalled another ancient custom, during which the great and powerful 'did without grudgingly bear their parts in charges with the citizens', and how Cromwell 'bare his charges to the great muster', his men and servants marching 'among the citizens without any difference'.[16]

It may seem a little one-sided to take the testimonies of Cromwell's charity on trust, and then quibble over the story about the house, but there may be good reason to do so. As the editor of Stow's work notes, a memorandum of Cromwell's includes items about the purchase of St James in the Fields and certain old tenements in Westminster; it also has references to a new garden, a tennis playing area, another area for cockfighting, and a big wall. The same memorandum mentions the building of the *Mary Rose* and Hampton Court, repairs to the Tower of London and walls of Calais, wars in Scotland and Ireland and Queen Anne's coronation. None of these were Cromwell's personal projects. In fact, the memorandum is a list of undertakings authorised not by Cromwell, but by *Henry* since Cromwell entered the king's service. This may not clear up entirely the matter of Stow's house and his unfortunate neighbours, but it does cast some doubt on Stow's implication that Cromwell was acting entirely from personal, selfish reasons, and not in some way carrying out the king's business. Besides, under Tudor law no one could seize land rightfully belonging to another as arbitrarily as Stow describes.[17]

Other witnesses besides Stow spoke of Cromwell's hospitality. One grateful guest told him that no one except the king 'doth keep and feast Englishmen and strangers as you do'. Foxe has a number of anecdotes about Cromwell, some from people still alive in Foxe's time who may have known Cromwell in their younger days. One story concerns an old woman whom Cromwell owed a sum of money that he had apparently forgotten to pay; when reminded of it he not only repaid the debt, but gave her a yearly pension of four pounds and a livery. An old man whose father had helped Cromwell in times past received similar treatment. Rowdies and criminals liked him a lot less, and a gang of ruffians once scattered at the news that the Lord Cromwell and his train were nearby. On another occasion Cromwell saw a Friar Bartley still wearing his cowl, even after the suppression of religious houses. 'Will not that cowl of yours be left off yet?' Cromwell demanded. 'If I hear, by one o'clock, that this apparel be not changed, then shalt thou be hanged immediately'. The cowl disappeared at once. Either this was a bluff or the story has got a little stretched, because Cromwell did not have the authority to hang anyone on his own say so.[18]

Cromwell was not a man to hold a grudge. Once he was displeased with Lord Lisle over a minor matter, but John Husee assured Lisle that Cromwell's anger lasts only a 'little while'. Following the successful end of the northern risings, Cromwell's remembrances include a note to provide for 'wives and poor children of such as have suffered, to the intent that his grace may extend his mercy to them for their livings'.[19]

Passages from his letters suggest that Cromwell possessed a dry, ironic sense of humour. To Thomas Wyatt, after long and fruitless discussions with imperial ambassadors – 'I never heard so many gay words and saw so little effect'. Again to Wyatt, this time on Wyatt's brother and his poor record of attendance at court – 'I never saw a man that had so many friends here, leave so few perfect friends behind him'. On Wyatt's diplomatic mission and matters of expense claims – 'Other men make in manner of their debts mine own, for very oft where they have borrowed, I am fained to pay'.[20]

Cromwell's recreations included walking, riding and hunting. A friendly abbot in York once sent him gifts of hawks and falcons. He also enjoyed a game of bowls and dice, and would occasionally play for money, though not large sums. He remained devoted to his surviving family, frequently sending gifts to Gregory and his friends. He helped his nephew Christopher Wellyfed fulfil his wish to enter the church, and he arranged an advantageous marriage for his niece, Alice.[21]

Gregory Cromwell studied at Pembroke Hall in Cambridge in 1531, and later under the vigilant eye of Cromwell's friend and ally, Rowland Lee. Tutors spoke fairly well of Gregory's progress, though a school report by one of them, Henry Dowes, suggests that a little pressure had to be applied – Gregory was now 'somewhat in awe and dread, ready to give himself to study', and 'things which have heretofore alienated and distracted his mind ... are now subdued and withdrawn'. Gregory's range of studies included French, Latin, English, accounting, music and Roman and Greek history. Tutors and others who came into contact with him were not slow to take advantage; we find, for example, Gregory writing to his famous father commending one Sir John Clerk for his kindness, and asking a favour for Clerk's wife's regarding her business interests. The youngster also developed a love of hunting, and as a treat he and Wellyfed were allowed to indulge this pastime during breaks in schooling. Dutiful son that he was, Gregory promised his father that he would do his best at all times.[22]

In August 1537 Gregory married Lady Elizabeth Ughtred, widow of Sir Anthony and a sister of Queen Jane. Lady Elizabeth seems to have been a woman of some spirit. Before marrying Gregory, and not long after her first husband's death, she had been a suitor to Cromwell for one of the abbeys due to be suppressed. She reminded him of his promise to help her when they last met at court. As she put it, she was a 'poor woman alone'. Feminine wiles are discernible here because by now Sir Arthur Darcy had set his sights set on her, wooing her with offers of gifts, lands and more. 'I would have been glad to have you likewise' he confessed to her, but he ruefully conceded that 'some southern lord shall make you forget the north'. It is not known whether Cromwell played match-maker for Gregory and Elizabeth, but what little is known about the marriage suggests that it was a happy one. By November 1538 Thomas Cromwell was a grandfather, and doubtless to his delight, the child was christened Henry.[23]

Cromwell's relations with the ranks of evangelicals were, predictably, uniformly good. Nevertheless, his friends were not afraid to speak their minds to him. Stephen Vaughan was an angry man when, in his judgement, Cromwell secured the appointment of a 'Papist, an idolater and a fleshly priest' as bishop of Chester. This would be Rowland Lee, also bishop of Lichfield and Coventry. Obviously Vaughan did not share Cromwell's good opinion of him. 'Remember God in all your facts', Vaughan warned. Cromwell should know better than anyone the iniquity of this crop of bishops. Vaughan was 'sorrier for this deed done by you than for all the things that ever I knew you do'.[24]

Nor were Cromwell's men afraid to ask him to change his mind when they disagreed with him. Lee again, sometime in July 1534, had caught and convicted a bunch of felons, and Cromwell wanted the lot of them hanged, including one who had turned king's evidence. Lee remonstrated, and asked that the informer be spared because his evidence had led to the arrest of many. The outcome is not known.[25]

A surprising exception to the general rule, however, was Nicholas Shaxton. At first an immaculate evangelical, appointed bishop of Salisbury on Cromwell's recommendation, Shaxton later became embittered and disillusioned with the Vicegerent.

It was in February 1537 that Shaxton's chaplain, John Madowell, provoked complaints from local people on account of his fiery preaching. The city authorities, apparently unsympathetic to the Reformation, were planning to use the opportunity to prevent Shaxton renewing his charter, partly because of his Protestant beliefs and partly for legal reasons which Cromwell, as Principal Secretary to the king, could not ignore. Cromwell ordered an investigation (probably a stalling tactic), but the issue was not properly resolved until Shaxton resigned his bishopric in summer 1539.[26]

While this dispute was dragging on, Shaxton became involved in a squabble with the abbot of Reading when he ordered one of the abbot's monks, Roger London, to stop reading divinity lectures. During arguments between them, London had provoked Shaxton's anger on various points: he denied that Scripture alone would suffice for the Christian life, he insisted that that faith without works would never justify before God, and maintained that that a person may 'deserve grace' through works. Unwilling to suffer this popish talk any further, Shaxton asked Cromwell to let his own chaplain perform the service of reader. Shaxton was mystified when his request was declined. What had happened was that Cromwell had also received complaints from the abbot against Shaxton, and he was taking time to think the matter over. Quite arbitrarily, Shaxton then issued an order forbidding London to read, only to be defied by the abbot.

Shaxton's real wrath, however, was reserved for Cromwell, whose attitude struck him as inexplicably even-handed. Shaxton admitted that the king's Injunctions commanded a lecture in divinity to be given, but surely, he argued, 'if the reader readeth not well ... it longeth to mine office to inhibit him'. Why Cromwell had any time for the abbot, Shaxton could not understand. Judge for yourself, the bishop demanded, whether you have 'exercised your office for edification and not for destruction'. He then assailed Cromwell with texts from Scripture on the Judgment Day to come – 'the Judge stands before the door' (James 5:9); 'The day of the Lord will come as a thief in the night' (2 Peter 3:8–10). Cromwell should never forget that he would have to account for all he has done. Cromwell should have sacked the abbot rather than 'take the matter from me by your authority'. Neither was this the first time that Cromwell had offended him; so 'Our Lord have pity on you, and turn your heart to amendment when it shall please him'. After consoling himself with other Bible verses on patiently enduring adversity, Shaxton reminded Cromwell that he had 'no power over me except it were given thee from above' (John 19:11, taken slightly out of context). He feared Cromwell had some grudge against him, but even if 'all the devils in hell incite and stir you against me' he remained sure that not a hair on his head would perish. He was also upset that Cromwell 'seemed to bear' the mayor and citizens of Salisbury in their action against him. A most indignant letter ends with an appeal to Cromwell to treat him more favourably in future.[27]

Cromwell's reply, in March 1538, is a masterclass in calming troubled waters. He was, he said, deeply pained to hear Shaxton's harsh judgement of him. What had he ever done to suffer such reproach? He merely 'took a matter out of your hands into mine', and if 'mine office bid me to do so, what cause have ye to complain?' Cromwell was unconvinced by Shaxton's use of Scripture texts, for 'I trust to God, as great a clerk as ye be, ye allege them out of place'. This was not the first time that Cromwell told a bishop that he had misapplied verses from Scripture; he said the same to John Fisher three years ago as we saw in on pages 102–4. Cromwell would not boast, for 'I know who worketh all that is well wrought by me'; and as 'it hath pleased His goodness to use me as an instrument, and to work somewhat by me, so I trust I am as ready to serve him in my calling to my little power'. Shaxton had written 'worse of me that ye ought to think', but 'my prayer is that God give me no longer life than I shall be glad to use my office in edification and not in destruction'. Cromwell denied Shaxton's charge that he abused his power – 'I did not intend to let your just doing, but rather to require you to do justly'.

He also denied showing undue favouritism to the abbot. However, 'I am much readier to help him that complaineth of wrong' than to hasten to punish one 'whom I am not sure hath offended'. Cromwell denied taking the monk's cause, and he protested his zeal for the evangelical faith. God will be his judge. 'I willingly bear no misdoers. I willingly hurt none, whom honesty and the king's laws do not refuse'. He assured Shaxton of his goodwill, and pointed out that 'you might have provoked some other in my place, that would have used less patience with you'. Nevertheless, 'I can take your writing and this heat of your stomach, even as well as I can, I trust, beware of flatterers'. Gently but firmly, Cromwell insisted that he would continue his enquires regarding the abbot of Reading and his reader, 'and if I find them as ye say they are, I will order them as I think good'. But no hard feelings – Cromwell would 'let pass all that is passed, and offer you such kindness as ye shall lawfully desire at my hands'.[28]

Shaxton's anger was not fully assuaged, especially when, a few weeks later, Cromwell asked him to give one Sir John Purches priority over Shaxton's own chaplain, John Madowell, in a nearby parsonage. Shaxton raised various objections, including his opinion that Madowell could preach better than this Purches.[29]

The letters of Cromwell and Shaxton to each other both refer to other letters that have been lost, so we do not know all the facts or even the immediate outcome. However, the exchanges are quite revealing nonetheless. First, this Madowell was one of those who, in earlier and unrelated correspondence, addressed Cromwell as Maecenas; so Cromwell was not the type to be swayed or puffed up by the praise of men. Second, though Cromwell was the principal reformer in England, he was not prepared to trample at will over the lawful rights of men of the old faith like the abbot or his reader. Because he was an evangelical, Shaxton seems to have expected that Cromwell would automatically approve his actions against this alleged Papist reader; but when Cromwell decided to investigate the facts himself, and when he saw the matter in a different light,

Shaxton became aggrieved. Nor does Shaxton seem to have appreciated the point that evangelising in England had to be carried out with prudence and discretion. It was rash to take the abbot's reader so severely to task for denying justification by faith alone, as if this disqualified him from carrying out his entirely lawful service. And one of the readers Shaxton wished to advance was, in Shaxton's own words, 'a former priest, and for his marriage degraded' – a staggeringly tactless selection given Henry's well-known aversion to priests who broke their vows and got married. This brash evangelical over-confidence could all too easily derail the Reformation that Cromwell was trying to steer through thoughtfully and discreetly. In the circumstances, only a man of exemplary patience, who could master his spirit, would have replied to Shaxton's ill-tempered letter as Cromwell did.

With his main rivals, Cromwell showed restraint and good sense. The man who had most reason to resent his authority was Stephen Gardiner, bishop of Winchester, who might, but for some ill-timed resistance to the king's Supremacy, have become Principal Secretary himself and even Vicegerent. Cromwell made some effort to soothe Gardiner's wounded pride, and Gardiner even managed to thank Cromwell for interceding with Henry on his behalf in a minor disagreement he had with one Master Cook. But Cromwell and Cranmer too were wise to Gardiner and the threat he posed both to them and to reform. When Gardiner started to quibble over the technicalities of Cranmer's title as 'Primate of all England' around May 1535, Cranmer gave Cromwell some words of advice about the bishop. 'As ye know the man lacketh neither learning in the law, neither witty invention, nor craft to set forth his matters ... that he might appear not to maintain his own cause, but the king's'. Cranmer had known Gardiner better and longer than Cromwell, and 'I cannot persuade with myself that he so tendereth the king's cause as he does his own'.[30]

Whether Cromwell influenced Henry's decision to send Gardiner to France as his ambassador is not known. The posting certainly worked to Cromwell's advantage, and others have already noted that the prospects for the Reformation looked most promising during the three years that Gardiner was out of the country. Relations between Cromwell and Gardiner remained strained. In April 1538 Cromwell sent the bishop a conciliatory letter to try and end the coolness between the two. There had been a disagreement over something (the details are unclear) and Cromwell's letter was a peace offering, desiring that differences between them might be forgotten. Unfortunately they were not, and Gardiner will feature again, prominently and antagonistically, later in Cromwell's life.[31]

Although Reginald Pole was the author of Cromwell's Machiavellian image, these two men could, during the mid 1530s, show at least outward civility one to another. Pole was of royal blood, grandson of the duke of Clarence, the younger brother of Edward IV. He was treated well by Henry in younger, happier days; but when Pole opposed the schism and the Boleyn marriage, he decided for his own safety to live abroad. Nevertheless, Thomas Starkey assured the exiled Pole of Cromwell's goodwill, and Pole thanked Cromwell for his efforts to mediate between him and Henry. In 1537 – two years after the executions of More, Fisher and the Carthusians – Pole was still expressing regard for Cromwell. When Pole planned to go to Flanders, he hoped that if Henry were minded to send anyone to meet him there it would be Cromwell. Pole would have been glad to talk with Cromwell, he said, since both men claimed to be defending the king's honour.[32]

But relations soon became much more fractious, especially after the pope infuriated Henry by making Pole a legate. Pole was soon protesting angrily to Cromwell about Henry's attempts to have him arrested. He began blaming Henry's councillors for enticing the king to break with the Holy See. Then to Pole's chagrin, King Francis in France and Regent Mary in Flanders both declined a personal meeting with him in order not to enrage Henry any further. Pole was now musing on the possibility of stirring up another rising against Henry, more successful than the failed Pilgrimage of Grace.[33]

As late as September 1537, reconciliation remained theoretically attainable when Cromwell issued instructions to Drs Wilson and Heath for a meeting with Pole. Probably at Henry's insistence rather than Cromwell's, they were strictly enjoined to address him merely as 'Mr Pole'. More seriously, they were to press him to repent and wait on the king's mercy. Should he yield, then Cromwell promised to be a 'humble suitor' to the king on Pole's behalf.[34]

However, when Henry and Cromwell were apparently tricked by Michael Throgmorton, supposed to be an intermediary between the king and Pole, Cromwell gave a manifestation of that anger which, though it might last only a little while, nevertheless blazed fiercely once kindled. Cromwell lambasted Throgmorton as a man with 'no fear of God', who had deceived his 'natural prince' and served 'an enemy of God' and a traitor to his king. Pole was condemned for maintaining the 'religion that hath been the ruin of all religion', and for his foolish writings, in which 'one lie leapeth in every line'. 'Pity it is that the folly of one brainsick Pole, or to say better, of one witless fool, should be the ruin of so great a family'. Cromwell attacked Pole's 'ingratitude', warning ominously that 'there may be found ways now in Italy, to rid a traitorous subject'. For 'let him not think, but where justice can take no place by process of law at home, some times she may be enforced to seek new means abroad'. Cromwell also attacked the 'wily bishop of Rome', who 'intendeth to make a lamentation to the world, and to desire every man to pray that his old gains may return home again'. Let Rome rather lament that many will follow the lead of King Henry, who 'hath pulled his realm out of thraldom'. Rome should 'not pray so fast that we may return to error'. Even in this wrathful mood, however, Cromwell was still urging both Throgmorton and Pole to repent, 'and be good witnesses of the king's high mercy'. But if they refused, then 'doubt ye not, but your ends shall be as of all traitors for the most part is'.[35]

Henry and Cromwell began to discuss a plan to kidnap Pole and bring him back to England to face trial. 'We would be very glad to have the said Pole by some means trussed up and conveyed to Calais', Henry directed Gardiner and Sir Francis Bryan, his ambassadors at the French court; 'and we desire and pray you to consult or devise between you thereupon'. There is also some evidence, though sketchy, that the cardinal's assassination was considered. Under examination, a certain Hugh Holland claimed he heard Pole's brother, Geoffrey, say that Cromwell 'said openly in court that he, speaking of the cardinal, should destroy himself well enough, and that Mr Bryan and Peter Meotes were sent into France to kill him with a hand gun or other wise as they should see best'. Because this is a third hand report of what Cromwell is supposed to have said, it must be less than wholly convincing. Cromwell was unlikely to have spoken openly on such a subject. Besides, a kidnap would be a spectacular success, but an assassination a crude blunder. If Pole were found dead in mysterious circumstances one day, all of Europe would guess the explanation instantly. Rumours that his life might be in danger did not concern Pole unduly. 'Would my Lord Privy Seal so feign to kill me?' he is quoted as saying. 'Well, I trust it shall not lie in his power'.[36]

Cromwell's relations with the duke of Norfolk, the second most powerful figure on Henry's council, are somewhat more difficult to gauge accurately. On the surface, they seem to have been markedly different from those he had with Gardiner and Pole. Following Wolsey's fall, the duke may have coveted the first place beside the king, and because he and Cromwell were on opposite sides in religion, disagreements were inevitable from time to time. Nevertheless, real evidence of recurrent, simmering bad blood is elusive. Norfolk remained Henry's foremost soldier, and, as Lord High Steward of England, he had presided at the trial of Anne Boleyn. He also undertook important diplomatic missions. None of this was threatened by Cromwell's rise to power. Norfolk, therefore, was less likely than Gardiner to resent Cromwell's appointments as Principal Secretary (running the government administration) or Vicegerent (overseeing church affairs on behalf of the king). Neither of these roles would normally appeal to a military man accustomed to the raw excitement of soldiering. Consequently, relations between the two do not seem to have been particularly bad, at least not until the last year of Cromwell's life. If the nobility were miffed at the pre-eminence of a man of obscure and humble birth, they were by now accustomed to such rebuffs – Wolsey had been a butcher's son.

In May 1535, Norfolk promised Cromwell his friendship. A year later, when he drew up his will, Norfolk made Cromwell the principal executor, trusting him next only to the king, so he said. After Henry's illegitimate son, the duke of Richmond, died in summer 1536, Norfolk was given responsibility for organizing the funeral arrangements; but when he heard to his horror that Henry was displeased that Richmond had not been buried with sufficient honour, Norfolk begged Cromwell to intercede for him with the king. The following year the duke was charged with suppressing the Pilgrimage of Grace, and his letters from the northern parts were full of thanks and good wishes to Cromwell. In one of these, after a few details about the situation in the north, Norfolk went on to give his very frank, personal assessment of Franco-Scottish matters. The tone and content of the letter suggest that two men were wont to discuss affairs of the world together unofficially from time to time. According to one witness, Norfolk strongly upbraided the northerners for their hatred of Cromwell.[37]

However, a little wariness is needed with flowery Tudor felicitations. Seldom do they mean exactly what they say. During his time of service in the north, Norfolk solemnly promised Cromwell, in writing, his friendship for life.[38] He did not keep this promise, but there is no evidence that he was tempted into breaking it until he saw that Cromwell was falling out of favour with Henry, something we will discuss in Chapter 16. Until then, Norfolk more or less accepted him. The duke might also have had the brains to see that the place occupied formerly by Wolsey and now by Cromwell – right next to the king – was the most dangerous place on Henry's council.

Norfolk's wife also knew Cromwell, though not romantically. Norfolk had married Elizabeth Stafford, daughter of the duke of Buckingham, in 1513. She may have had little choice, for she claimed she was in love with Ralph Neville, heir to earldom of Westmorland. The marriage of the Norfolks, never a blissfully happy one, tumbled downhill dramatically when Norfolk took a resident mistress called Bess Holland and sent his wife away to live in Hertfordshire. It is not clear how or why Cromwell became involved in the Norfolks' marital difficulties, but in May 1533 he asked Lord Stafford, Elizabeth's brother, to take her into his house and help bring about reconciliation between her and her husband. Stafford comes over as a less than sympathetic brother; he thought his sister was at least partly to blame for the breakdown in the marriage.[39]

Apparently despairing of her brother, the duchess appealed to Cromwell, bitterly complaining about her husband's illtreatment. No letters from Cromwell to her have survived, but he must have done something to console her because she warmly thanked him for his kindness, sent him a pair of quality carving knives as a gift, and promised her prayers and friendship for life. Norfolk knew about this correspondence, but it did not trouble him much. He even asked Cromwell if he could provide a home for his unhappy wife, because if she continued with 'her most false and abominable lies and obstinacy against me', Norfolk threatened to have her locked up somewhere.[40]

In June 1537, after years of estrangement, the duchess, the forsaken wife, poured her heart out to Cromwell. Her husband had poorly provided for her, and 'forgotten now he hath so much wealth and honour, and is so far in doting love with that queen that he neither regards God nor his honour'. His unfaithfulness is known 'far and near'. Yet he 'chose me for love', even though she was twenty years younger, 'and he hath put me away four years and a quarter this Midsummer'. King Henry himself will witness she has lived like a good woman. Bess Holland was the object of the duchess's fury: 'that harlot ... but a churl's daughter and of no gentle blood ... that drab Bess Holland ... yet he [Norfolk] keeps her still in his house'. She had heard how Cromwell helped Mary in her troubles, and she begged him to do the same for her.[41]

In vain Cromwell persevered in trying to bring the unhappy couple back together. The duchess vowed never to return to her husband; she would rather be sent to the Tower. To add to her miseries, she apparently lost the sympathy of much of her family, and lamented to Cromwell that no woman ever had 'so ungracious an eldest son and so ungracious a daughter and so unnatural'.[42]

The trust the duchess placed in Cromwell may shed light on an unusual letter from Norfolk to Cromwell in June 1537, when Norfolk was at York. Expecting the king and his court to travel north that year, Norfolk invited Cromwell to stay in his house at York; and, he added, 'if ye lust not to dally with my wife', he could promise the services of a wench with 'pretty proper tetins', meaning breasts. This does not prove that Cromwell kept mistresses. All it proves is that Norfolk, besides a bawdy sense of humour, had other mistresses besides Bess Holland, and assumed that other men did likewise. Actually nothing came of it, because Henry did not go north that year. Norfolk bore Cromwell no ill will for listening to his wife with a sympathetic ear, and he carried on sending friendly letters and thanks for kindnesses rendered – nothing to do with wenches or tetins.[43]

Since 1528 Cromwell had been a widower, and because of his heavy workload he does not seem to have seriously considered marrying again. Occasionally rumours surfaced to the effect that he was hoping or scheming to marry Mary or Lady Margaret Douglas, the king's niece. It was all unfriendly gossip, with no proven substance to it. His relations with Mary remained cordial, and his accounts indicate that he regularly sent her a New Year present.[44] There is probably nothing suspicious or untoward in this, though it is noticeable that the same accounts do not mention New Year gifts to fellow councillors, or to other prominent men and women. It is, however, highly unlikely that he ever imagined he would become her husband. He was now in his fifties, and Mary was only twenty when she made her submission to the king in 1536. Such an age gap would not make a marriage impossible, but Cromwell was pragmatic enough to recognise that in the game of dynastic marriage-making, Mary was far too valuable to Henry to waste on a middle-aged councillor of humble birth, however good a servant he was to the king. The likeliest explanation for Cromwell's goodwill towards Mary is that he hoped, by personal kindness and considerate behaviour, that he might win her not for himself, but for the Reformation. If this sounds fantastically far-fetched, that is only because we know her subsequent history and reputation as Bloody Mary, the persecutor of Protestants. All this was unknown to Cromwell. So far as he was concerned, Mary was no more a medievalist in religion than he had been a few years ago when he wished that Luther had never been born (p. 47). In the 1530s it was imaginative, not fanciful, to hope that Mary might yet become a huge evangelical prize.

There is no evidence that Cromwell, in his years as a widower, kept a mistress. Ever since he made his will, in which he had requested a priest 'of continent and good living' to pray for his soul, he seems to have been a man of upright living and known for it. During the Dissolution, when Thomas Legh was visiting monasteries he found 'certain of the knights and gentlemen' with 'concubines openly in their houses ... putting from them their wives', to the great offence of many. Legh ordered them to put away their 'whores' and take back their lawful wives, else they would have to appear before Cromwell and answer for themselves.[45]

However, Cromwell did not live apart from women entirely. A letter survives from his friend, Rowland Lee, telling him that 'my good lady Oxford, who came to court on Sunday, intends to be merry with you on Monday or Tuesday at supper ... she is a woman of high wit and loves her friends'. Cromwell himself once addressed the countess of Oxford self-effacingly as 'your poor friend'. Another letter from Vaughan to Cromwell has a reference to 'your great friend Mrs. Addington', to whom Vaughan was also 'much bound'. But there is nothing here to nourish scandals. All it shows is that Cromwell, now well into middle age by Tudor standards, was an affable, expansive fellow, who, when affairs of state granted him the time, enjoyed the company of his friends, both ladies and gentlemen.[46]

Women seem to have found Cromwell an approachable man. Examples seen already include Catherine of Aragon, Alice More, the duchess of Norfolk and the petitions in the previous chapter. Another woman with an ungrateful husband, Lady Hungerford, also sought and received his help – Cromwell knew Lord Hungerford and told him he should give his wife a yearly allowance. Ironically, Hungerford ended his life on the same scaffold as Cromwell, though for widely different reasons. He was attainted for a grim litany of offences including supporting a Papist priest, incest, sodomy and trying to divine the king's death by sorcery.[47]

Anne Boleyn may have wished to see Cromwell's head cut off, but her sister Mary looked on him far more graciously. Sometime in late 1534, Mary was banished from court when she became pregnant by her new husband, William Stafford, a commoner she had secretly married. Like other distressed women, Mary turned to Cromwell for help. She was appalled that her marriage had caused such anger to Henry and Anne; but 'good master secretary', she pleaded, 'consider that he was young, and love overcame reason'. It is intriguing how she knew that Cromwell, of all men, would show understanding in an affair of the heart. She valued her husband's simple honesty, and 'I loved him as well as he did me'. Feeling rejected by the world, she chose to 'live a poor honest life with him'. She 'might have had a greater man of birth, and a higher, but I assure you I could never have had one that should have loved me so well, nor a more honest man'. She urged Cromwell to intercede for them to Henry and Anne. 'For God's sake help us', she implored; she had 'rather begged my bread with him than to be the greatest queen christened'. Would Cromwell also 'pray my lord my father and my lady … and my lord of Norfolk and my brother' to be good to them. She 'dare not write to them, they are so cruel against us'. There is no surviving letter from Cromwell in response, but fortune smiled on William and Mary Stafford. They did not return to court, but they did live quietly and contentedly in the country together until Mary's death in 1543.[48]

Cromwell also listened attentively to Lady Bryan, appointed governess to Princess Elizabeth after Anne Boleyn's death. She was sufficiently concerned to write to him about the young lady's upbringing now that she was 'put from that degree she was afore'. But this was not just a routine request for instructions, and Lady Bryan was quite unabashed at giving the king's chief minister a few candid facts about her royal charge. Elizabeth needed clothing, for she 'hath neither gown nor kertel, nor petticoat ... nor hankerchiefs' – Would Cromwell please ensure that she had all that was needful? The child 'hath great pain with her teeth, and they come very slowly forth; and this causeth me to suffer her Grace to have her will more than I would'. She was annoyed with a Mr Shelton, now claiming to be 'master of this house'. He and Lady Bryan were quarrelling over household affairs, including arrangements for Elizabeth's meals. She hoped Cromwell would not forget or despise her, and nor did he. He had words with Shelton, and it seems that her ladyship's wishes prevailed.[49]

It should not be too difficult to imagine what a really ruthless Machiavellian would have done with this letter, or with oversensitive evangelicals like Nicholas Shaxton, or rivals on the loose like Stephen Gardiner; or how much time, patience and sympathy he would have spent on the sorrows of Elizabeth, duchess of Norfolk, or all those entreaties from ordinary folk of the previous chapter. But Cromwell's approachability and his understanding heart were widely appreciated and taken advantage of by a variety of his fellow countrymen and women. Revisionists and others will doubtless claim that not everyone in England felt the same way towards him as those we have met in these chapters. That is true, so far as it goes. Cromwell certainly had enemies besides admirers at court and in the country, and those who resented his authority or opposed his policies knew better than to express their feelings in letters that could be used to incriminate them. In that sense, a one-sided survey has been given. However, it is not an entirely invalid survey. No chief minister of the crown expects to be universally loved. Opponents and controversy are no more than routine occupational hazards for anyone holding high offices of state, especially in times of great constitutional and spiritual change. We cannot, unfortunately, conduct an opinion poll to discover Cromwell's true overall approval rating; but the short case studies summarised here prove that alongside the detractors and the malcontents, he enjoyed a sizable reservoir of trust, admiration and even warmth among the Tudor populace.

And it takes an extraordinary kind of man to attract, apparently effortlessly, the attention of such a disparate group of men and women. Unsolicited letters arrived on his desk from hopefuls looking for employment, from monks disillusioned with their religion who were turning to the Gospel, from budding writers and scholars seeking his patronage, and from merchants canvassing government support for commercial ventures. Men and women including 'poor widows everywhere', whether frustrated by insensitive local officialdom, or weighed down by the cares and worries of life, sought his help. Wronged and broken-hearted wives like the duchess of Norfolk, victims of family feuds like Mary Boleyn turned to him to unburden themselves. There they found a strong shoulder to lean on and cry on. Their own kith and kin failed them, so they spoke to Cromwell from the heart with the candour and trust that no cold, callous, unprincipled politician could ever inspire. All these people knew, somehow, that he would listen understandingly and do what he could. Even prominent religious and political opponents could speak well of him. Rarely during the Reformation can Protestants and Papists be found paying each other compliments, but we have seen Catherine of Aragon, Princess Mary, Thomas More and his wife Alice all thanking Cromwell for his personal kindness and consideration. There may be a single word to describe such a man – but Machiavellian will hardly do.

PART IV

How Have the Mighty Fallen

14

The Vicegerency in Eclipse

In January 1538, Cromwell sent his friend and emissary, Christopher Mont, to the Lutheran Landgrave Philip of Hesse. For the sake of the cause of the Gospel in England, Cromwell was trying to encourage the Germans to send the embassy they had been half promising. In spring Cromwell was also preparing royal injunctions. Justices and local officers were commanded to ensure that priests and curates preach the Word of God and let the people hear the Bible in English; for here is the 'undoubted will, law and commandment of Almighty God, the only straight mean to know the goodness and benefits of God towards us'. (It is very Lutheran.) Should any difficulties arise from readings of the sacred texts, the people were to avoid contentions, and seek guidance from 'such learned men as be or shall be authorised to preach and declare the same'. Neither the Coverdale nor the Matthew Bible was specified, so presumably either was acceptable. Evangelical bishops enthusiastically complied, Shaxton insisting that all clergy in his diocese should read a chapter a day, and learn by heart the equivalent of one chapter every fortnight.[1]

More aggressively, Henry was determined to crush what little resistance remained to the Royal Supremacy. John Forest, the Observant Friar, or 'obstinate friar' as Hall unsympathetically called him, was the prominent, ill-fated victim, burned at Smithfield in May. Forest's papal loyalties had been known to Cromwell for nearly five years, and it was Cromwell who arranged for Latimer to preach at his execution in an attempt to persuade him to repent, confess Henry's headship of the church and accept the royal pardon that was dangled in from of him. Forest had made a submission once before only to retract it later. However, if the government hoped that the sight of the gibbet and the wood ready to be lit would induce another climb-down, it would be disappointed. Latimer delivered his lengthy sermon in vain. Forest then perished miserably along with an image of Derfel Gadarn taken from a Welsh shrine, which, according to semi-religious folk lore, contained miraculous powers that could even rescue of the souls of the damned from hell.[2]

A grim curiosity of Forest's case is that those who refused to submit to the Supremacy were normally hanged, drawn and quartered as traitors, not burned as heretics; but because the formal proceedings against Forest have been lost, it is not clear why an exception was made of him. Rather predictably, it has been insinuated that this double burning of Forest and a medieval image was another of Cromwell's nefarious deeds.[3] Besides being based on circumstantial evidence only, this argument ascribes to Cromwell powers that he never had. He did not have the authority to change the method of execution that had been in force for centuries. Only Henry could do that. From the incomplete evidence that is available, it could just as easily be argued that Cromwell and Cranmer, who was also involved, suggested the idea of Latimer's sermon in order to offer Forest a reprieve.

Diplomatic developments on the continent also demanded attention. Henry's attempts to put himself forward as a mediator between Francis and Charles were made redundant in summer when the two hitherto warring monarchs concluded a truce. Henry affected to be unconcerned, but Cromwell began probing Chapuys about the emperor's plans, particularly his forthcoming visit to France. Nevertheless, the threat of a Franco-Imperial alliance, and the danger that it might pose to England, was not enough to persuade Henry to abandon his interest in the Lutheran princes. Despite hold-ups and delays, a German embassy eventually arrived in June. Henry and Cromwell had hoped to see Philip Melanchthon leading it, but Elector John Frederick disappointed them both by deciding that Melanchthon could not be spared from his duties as lecturer in philosophy and theology at Wittenberg University. Instead the delegation was headed by Francis Burkhardt, Vice Chancellor of the Elector of Saxony, Dr George Boyneburg, a Hessian nobleman, and Frederick Myconius, overseer of the church in Gotha. Theological discussions then began between the Germans and English divines, and a document known as the Thirteen Articles was soon prepared. As in the earlier Wittenberg Articles, agree-ment was reached quite quickly on a number of points, including the central issue of justification – 'through faith freely for Christ's sake' – but with the rider that good works were 'necessary to salvation' in the manner Melanchthon had laid out in his *Loci* dedicated to Henry in 1535 (necessary as a consequence, though not a cause). The statement was consistent with Cromwell's Ten Articles, though significantly different from Henry's collection of ramblings in the Bishops' Book. Despite this anomaly, Henry let it pass.[4]

But the absence of Melanchthon may have nettled Henry, because when the Germans arrived in June the king sum-moned Bishop Cuthbert Tunstall from Durham to London to be his personal theological adviser that summer. Though Tunstall had accepted the Royal Supremacy, he had long been a bitter opponent of Luther; and, unlike Henry, there is little evidence that he had warmed to the more soothing voice of Melanchthon. Tunstall's journey south boded ill for the evan-gelical cause in England, especially as the Lutheran Elector John Frederick had directed his delegation to deal with three problematic issues – communion in one kind, private masses and clerical celibacy – on which both Henry and Tunstall held very medieval views.[5]

Cromwell was not involved in the day-to-day discussions with the Germans. He was, however, being lobbied by evangelicals to take stronger action against pilgrimages, images and shrines. Sir John Hercy urged him to take away a prominent image at Doncaster and to send some good preachers up there. Some of Cromwell's enthusiastic supporters, like Hercy, expected him to conjure evangelical preachers out of thin air. Latimer was also pressing him to put at end to 'our great Sybil', an image of Our Lady in Latimer's Worcester diocese, and 'the devil's instrument to bring many, I fear, to eternal fire'. Latimer demanded similar treatment for 'her old sister at Walsingham', and other wicked sisters at Ipswich, Doncaster and Penrice in Glamorgan; and he looked forward to a 'jolly muster at Smithfield' for the lot of them. In July the Walsingham image was unceremoniously disposed of, but for her sisters Cromwell had something even more dramatic in his mind than a mere 'jolly muster' in Smithfield.[6]

On 18 August he received a letter from Cranmer, informing him that the Germans wanted to discuss the 'abuses' (by this he meant communion in one kind, private masses and clerical celibacy). Then Cranmer introduced the name of Thomas Becket, the twelfth-century archbishop and medieval saint, famous as the defender of papal authority against the claims of Henry II to extend his control over the church. As if in defiance of four years of schism and evangelical advance, Becket's shrine was still standing, proudly and provocatively, in Cranmer's Canterbury. Cranmer gave his opinion that Becket's blood in Canterbury cathedral might be 'feigned'. Reading this letter it is easy to suspect that he and Cromwell had been discussing Becket before, and how they might get rid of him. A few days later Cranmer wrote again to say that talks with the Germans had run into difficulty. Knowing Henry's strong views on the three disputed points, the Germans had written directly to the king in an attempt to persuade him. Henry, with Tunstall by his side, had now decided to enter into a theological debate with the Lutherans.[7]

The medieval church normally administered communion in one kind only – that is, the laity received the consecrated bread but not the wine. Luther denounced this practice as a violation of the Lord's Supper and the Words of Institution (Luke 22:19–20), according to which the laity should receive both bread and wine. Henry, as if trying to arbitrate from a perch of lofty neutrality, argued that either one kind or two kinds may be permitted.

Henry then turned to private masses. Again he appeared to be trying for some sort of compromise. The Roman mass as a propitiatory sacrifice for the living and the dead was rejected by Luther for two main reasons. It was another perversion of the Words of Institution – *This is my Body … this is my Blood given for you.* The Sacrament is a divine gift to the church, not a sacrifice to be offered *by* the church, and moreover, it is a gift for the living, not the dead. Besides, the whole concept of a sacrifice performed by a priest for the soul's salvation clashed irreconcilably with the Gospel of God's grace freely given and received by faith alone. These points were made afresh by the German delegation as gently as possible. Henry's reply suggested that the Lord's Supper may yet be called a sacrifice because Christ, once sacrificed for our sins on the Cross, was present on the altar. But he disingenuously avoided the real issue, the *propitiatory* sacrifice, still in practice in England. Consequently, the fundamental difference between Luther and the medieval church remained unresolved.

The third disputed point – clerical celibacy – contained all the elements of a Tudor farce. For Luther, priestly marriage enjoyed Scriptural sanction, though it was not commanded. It was a matter of Christian liberty, and a most welcome one especially for those who could not cope with the demands of a strict celibate life, which were well nigh impossible anyway. The issue brought out the religious legalist in Henry. He insisted that priests *ought* to be able to cope with the celibate life. On this point, Henry sought neither a compromise nor a middle way. Blissfully unaware of his own archbishop's secret marriage six years ago, he quoted abundantly from the church fathers on the virtues of celibacy. Lutheran ideas about Christian liberty were brushed aside. All fleshly temptations must be resisted. Priests who could not keep their vows should be defrocked. Henry would never know that it was a married clergyman who had confirmed his own marriages and divorces, as well as his Supremacy in the English church.

Despite his strong views, however, Henry did not mean to shut the door on the Lutherans entirely, or send them away empty-handed. He was simply indulging his love of arguing and debating. His replies to the Lutherans were more a set of counter proposals than a final rejection. When they took their leave of him, he commended their piety and learning to the Elector, and he looked forward to hearing further from them after they returned to Germany for consultations. Nevertheless, English evangelicals hoping for a breakthrough had suffered a setback, and a response was called for.

Cromwell rushed through a second set of royal injunctions, issued on 5 September. Besides reinforcing the earlier set, they specified that a Bible was to be placed in every church, and that persons were to be examined on the 'articles of our faith and the *Pater Noster*'. A more vigorous line was taken against images, relics, saints and 'wandering to pilgrimages'. Registers of baptisms, marriages and burials were also required.[8] A few days later Becket's shrine was ceremonially destroyed in the presence of the king. This strike against that great symbol of papal power in England, almost certainly organized by Cromwell, served to soften the disappointment of the failure to persuade Henry on all the disputed theological points. The Germans took the news home with them, where it was well received. Prominent medieval shrines had now become a target for the government, though under Henry and Cromwell, unlike Edward's reign later, images and paintings in churches were left largely untouched. When Stephen Gardiner returned to England from his ambassadorial service in France on 28 September, one of the first things he learned was that the famous shrine in his own Winchester diocese had been smashed up just like Becket's. It is more than likely that Cromwell, who might have preferred to keep Gardiner out of the country if he could, had staged this welcome home for his most formidable rival.[9]

However, Cromwell's grip on power and his influence on Henry were slowly but perceptibly beginning to loosen. Even if all the shrines in England were razed to the ground, it would still not be enough to induce Henry to take the *Augsburg Confession*, and from now on much of Cromwell's efforts would be directed at trying to prevent evangelical fortunes going into reverse. He may have hoped by now to be super-intending the Lutheran Reformation in England, but instead he was required by the king to set up commissions to investigate religious radicalism, particularly the Anabaptists. Besides rejecting infant baptism, some extreme members of this sect were now denying more fundamental Christian doctrines such as the Trinity and the Deity of Christ. Then a king's proclamation on 6 November, though condemning Becket and alleged superstitions, also declared – Henry insisted on this – that clerical marriage was contrary 'to the wholesome admonitions of St Paul to Timothy and Titus and to Corinthians ... and many of the old fathers'. Getting carried away with his crusade against married clergy Henry was now talking utter nonsense, because these epistles of St Paul clearly state that priests are permitted to marry (1 Corinthians 7:28; 1 Timothy 3:2; Titus 1:6). Cromwell carried on his campaign against superstition and Becket, and he managed to modify some statements on religious ceremonies in a slightly reformist direction; but he was a long way from persuading Henry to become a Lutheran.[10]

Another distraction for Cromwell was that although he had succeeded in making Lutherans acceptable in some ways to Henry, many English evangelicals were now drawn to the ideas of the Zürich reformers, who, following their deceased founder, Huldrych Zwingli, denied the real presence of Christ in the sacrament. They emphasized instead the Lord's Supper as a distinctive expression of the bond among Christians, and they admitted a spiritual, but not a substantial, divine presence. In England Zwingli's supporters were commonly referred to as sacramentaries. In the 1530s Cromwell, Cranmer and most leading English reformers all held the Lutheran view of Christ's real presence in the sacrament, which was fortunate for them because Henry detested the sacramentaries almost as must he detested the Papalists. In July 1533 John Frith and Andrew Hewitt had been burned for this heresy despite the efforts of Cromwell and Cranmer to persuade them to repent and recant, but the fires had failed to extinguish Swiss ideas from the hearts and minds of some in the English evangelical movement. During 1538 attempts were being made on the continent to reconcile Wittenberg and Zürich, and during this pleasant thaw in relations Luther and Bullinger were writing civilly and understandingly to each other. Cromwell knew of these developments and welcomed them, and he may even have authorised his own agents to make discreet contacts with the Swiss, but there is nothing to suggest that he had undergone a change of heart on the Eucharist.[11]

In summer 1538 a voluble and radical sacramentary called John Lambert was questioned by Cranmer, following complaints made against him by Robert Barnes and Rowland Taylor. Cranmer tried to reason with Lambert, just as he had tried with Frith five years earlier. But then Lambert did a very odd thing – he appealed over the gentle Cranmer's head to the king. Why Lambert did this is a mystery. He must have known of Henry's aversion to the sacramentary heresy. He was, unfortunately, the kind of man who rushed in where angels fear to tread; he now found himself at the centre of a prominent public trial in November, presided over by Henry, robed augustly for the occasion in solemn white. On Henry's orders the assembled bishops – including Cranmer, Gardiner and Tunstall – all tried to turn Lambert back to more orthodox views. After five arduous hours of arguing and debating had failed to convert Lambert, Henry then turned to Cromwell, who had sat silently through it all thus far, and ordered him to read the sentence.[12]

Reporting the trial to ambassadors abroad, Cromwell commended Henry's 'excellent gravity and inestimable majesty' in his proceedings against the 'miserable man' Lambert. It was, of course, part of Cromwell's duty to present a favourable image of Henry at all times. There would be no reason to suspect that Cromwell had any sympathy for Lambert except for a passage in Foxe, which, in view of the later accusation that Cromwell supported sacramentaries, calls for some notice. On the morning of his execution, says Foxe, Lambert was led to Cromwell's house, where he had a private meeting with him, and then took his last breakfast before going to die. 'It is reported of many', Foxe adds, that Cromwell asked Lambert's forgiveness for his part in the trial. The somewhat non-committal 'it is reported' suggests that Foxe was relying on hearsay and not entirely sure. Besides, executioners customarily asked forgiveness of those they were about to send out of this world, but it did not mean that they agreed with them, or with what they had done. [13]

A possible explanation of this last meeting between Cromwell and Lambert may lie in Foxe's account of Lambert's death. Rather like the unfortunate Forest a few months earlier, Lambert was burned deliberately slowly. After his legs were burned 'up to the stumps ... two that stood on each side of him with their halberts pitched him up on their pikes' before letting him down again, after which he 'fell into the fire, and there gave up his life'. This added torment was unusual, and unlikely to have been carried out on the whim of those supervising the execution. Someone must have given an order that an example should be made of Lambert as a warning to other sacramentaries. Given Henry's loathing of this particular heresy as well as his judicial role in Lambert's trial – for seldom did a king preside over a heresy trial as Henry had done – the likelihood must be that the order had come from the king. So Foxe's story may have a fairly simple explanation: Cromwell met Lambert that morning to warn him that his death in the fire would be even more ghastly than normal, and he was trying to persuade Lambert to see sense and recant at the last moment. But Lambert, a rash and foolhardy fellow apparently, took no more notice of Cromwell than he had done of Cranmer a few months before. [14]

About the same time as the Lambert affair, the so-called Exeter conspiracy was unravelling. Henry Courtenay, marquis of Exeter, was the son of Katherine, daughter of Edward IV. As such he would have had a claim of sorts to the throne if Henry died without an heir. Exeter's close circle of friends included Lord Montague, Sir Edward Neville and Geoffrey Pole, brother of Reginald the cardinal, the man hated by Henry above all others. Montague and the Poles, like Exeter, were of the house of York. They also followed the old faith and opposed Cromwell's reformist policies. They were tried for treason in December 1538. Exeter, Montague and Neville were beheaded, while Geoffrey Pole was pardoned, mainly because he supplied much of the incriminating evidence. Reginald Pole's elderly mother, the Countess of Salisbury, was imprisoned and attainted in 1539, but not executed until two years later.[15]

The main work on the Exeters remains the one by the Dodds sisters. According to the Dodds, although the Exeters were opponents of Cromwell, and had even become estranged from the king, they were guilty of no treasonable conspiracy. Their downfall is explained by the ruthlessness of Henry and Cromwell in pursuing to the end anyone remotely likely to be a threat to the regime.[16]

Naturally, Henry and Cromwell saw things differently. Cromwell told Thomas Wyatt that the Exeters were convicted not 'by light suspicion, but by certain proofs and confessions'. His assistant, Wriothesley, told foreign contacts that Exeter 'had been a traitor these twenty years and ever studied how to take his master's place from him, and to destroy all his children'. Via Ambassador Wyatt, Henry told Charles V that the Exeters had conspired to destroy not only Henry but Edward, Mary and Elizabeth as well – this is according to Geoffrey Pole's confessions. The government told the French ambassador, Castillon, of the Exeters' plot to chase out the king and receive Reginald Pole back. Exeter's treason, added Cromwell, was amply proved by copies of letters between him and Pole, found among the possessions of Exeter's wife (the originals had been burned) and Exeter had been scheming to gain control of England by marrying his son to Mary and destroying Edward. Neither Castillon nor Chapuys were entirely convinced, while the Misses Dodds suspect that these letters were largely imaginary.[17]

The Exeters were convicted when Geoffrey Pole, at first one of their party, turned informer. What motivated him to do so is not known, but even the Dodds concede that no evidence exists of torture. It may be accepted, therefore, that Pole confessed more or less freely. He was no longer the same man Chapuys had known so well a few years before. Back in 1534, Chapuys told Charles that Geoffrey Pole 'ceases not, like many others, to importune and beg me to write to your Majesty, and explain how very easy the conquest of this kingdom would be, and the inhabitants are only waiting for a signal'. Chapuys was being 'daily assailed on every side' by people 'soliciting the execution of the apostolic censures against Henry'. Many were convinced that 'such a resolution of Your Majesty's [Charles's] part would be a sufficient remedy, considering the great discontent prevailing among all classes of society at this King's disorderly life and government'.[18]

So Geoffrey Pole was one of a number of influential people begging a foreign power to attack and conquer England. If this is not treason, the word has lost its meaning. Chapuys does not incriminate Exeter or Montague directly, but who else could Pole's co-conspirators have been? Not Cromwell, or Cranmer or Audley. This question alone may not be enough to convict Exeter, but it would be mightily strange if Geoffrey Pole had often talked about the subject with Chapuys without ever mentioning it to his friends the Exeters.

Here now are some of the things that Exeter and Montague said, according to Pole's confessions. First, 'knaves rule about the king', and Exeter hoped to 'give them a buffet one day'. This is not necessarily treasonable, though a lot might depend on what 'buffet' really meant.[19]

Then this: 'The Turk was more ch ... h ... su ... than the king being a Christian prince'. Unfortunately the document is too badly damaged to be more accurate, but it is plain that Henry was being compared, somewhat less than favourably, with the Turk.

Now this: 'Even though we have a prince [Edward] ... the king and his whole issue stand accursed'. And this: 'knaves and heretics and smatterers of small learning were the king's assisters [in Henry's divorce]'. And especially this, which the Misses Dodds have curiously declined to quote:

> Yet we should do more, and here when the time should come, what wt [sic] power and friendship, nor is it the plucking down of these knaves that will help the matter; *we must pluck down the head*.[20]

Other evidence has Montague calling Darcy a 'fool' during the Pilgrimage of Grace; for 'he went to pluck away the council: he should first have begun with the head, but I beshrew them for leaving off so soon'. Montague had also recalled Henry saying to his lords that 'he should go from them one day'; to which Montague added: 'if he will serve us so, we shall be happily rid.'[21]

Then, according to Exeter's wife, when her husband joined Norfolk against the Pilgrims, Sir Edward Neville, a family friend and brother-in-law of Montague, visited her one day. She was downcast, and Neville tried to raise her spirits. 'Madam', he told her, 'be not afraid of this, nor of the second, but beware of the third'. Neville's words are a mystery to the Misses Dodds, but they were no mystery to the government, especially in view of what has been seen above. Cromwell's personal files include a note that the 'words touching the insurrection, which was "beware of the third", were spoken at Windsor'. The government obviously took Neville's words to be evidence of a conspiracy of a future, more successful rising than the Pilgrimage of Grace.[22]

There are other quotes from various people, mostly servants of Exeter, to the effect that Exeter would be king one day, though this does not prove that he encouraged such words. Servants of Exeter and Montague also told investigators that they saw many letters being unaccountably burned on the orders of their masters. Cromwell was convinced that these letters were destroyed to get rid of treasonable evidence.[23]

So was this a dangerous conspiracy, or was it a Tudor despotism determined to destroy all opposition and every conceivable threat to the throne, if necessary on the lightest of pretexts? There is a certain similarity between the fall of the Exeters and that of Anne Boleyn. In both cases evidence exists against the accused, though whether it is decisive may have to remain debateable. History can only record an open verdict. It is, however, far too naïve to imagine that Montague was simply injudiciously letting off steam with his threats of 'plucking down the head'. This kind of talk, even if it progressed no further, could easily have been construed as treason even before the Treason Act of 1534. The same applies to the unflattering comparison of Henry with the Turk, to say nothing of the solicitations to Chapuys urging the emperor to invade England. The Dodds are quite right – Cromwell did indeed pursue the Exeters relentlessly – but the man responsible to king and country for the security of the realm could scarcely have done less. The previous century had shown what havoc and misery frustrated, grasping noblemen could cause. If the Exeters were not traitors, neither were they spotless innocents. According to Castillon, Henry had wanted to eliminate the White Rose Yorkists for some time. If so, then the Yorkists, like Anne before them, had rather obligingly supplied him with every excuse he needed.[24]

Besides the fall of the Exeters, the old order in religion was now about to suffer a further, heavier blow. The establishment of the Court of Augmentations in 1536, to administer the suppression of the smaller monasteries, had sent signals around the country that government action against the remaining, larger religious houses would follow soon. Cromwell was receiving letters from all kinds of people eager to acquire monastic lands or keep a certain house intact. A payment accompanied most letters, but other inducements were tried as well. The abbot of Croyland sent Cromwell a supply of locally caught fish, 'right meekly beseeching your lordship favourably to accept the same fish, and to be good and favourable lord unto me and my poor house'. Some monasteries that had received a bad report from Cromwell's commissioners for their 'misorder and evil life' were already surrendering, theoretically voluntarily.[25]

Nevertheless, concerted government action on a national scale was a little slow in coming, and the period 1536–7 even saw a few refoundations. These, however, were exceptional. Richard Layton had sensed that something was in the air when he wrote to Cromwell back in June 1537. His letter begins with 'whereas ye intend shortly to visit'. Pointing to his past experience as a visitor, Layton's letter was effectively an application to be appointed a commissioner in future; he asked that he and his friend, Thomas Legh, might 'have committed unto us the north'.[26]

Layton's request was not granted immediately, because he was in Cambridge in January 1538, telling Cromwell about widespread fears that Henry intended shortly to suppress all houses. Layton assured the people this was not so; they should not listen to such 'vain babbling' that 'utterly slandered the king'. He warned that such 'babblers' from the ranks of commoners would be set in the stocks to teach them a lesson, while gentry babblers would have to answer to Cromwell personally. Actually thirty-five monasteries surrendered during the first few months of 1538, though in March that year Cromwell sent a circular letter to the heads of religious houses, promising that no well-run community need fear any government action against it. Henry, Cromwell assured them, would not accept any surrender 'unless overtures had been made by the houses that resigned'. Henry intended no suppression of any house 'except they shall desire of themselves with one whole consent ... or else misuse themselves contrary to their allegiance'. Cromwell urged the religious to live in a godly manner and provide for the poor, and they would come to no harm.[27]

Scholars who have examined the subject suggest that it was chiefly for financial reasons that the major dissolution of the monasteries began in late summer 1538.[28] This, it will be remembered, was when the Lutheran talks failed, or rather stalled, and when Cromwell intensified his assault on medieval religious shrines, especially that of Becket. It could be the case, therefore, that he had also decided that the time was now ripe to proceed more aggressively against the monasteries. A double strike against the shrines and monasteries would provide some compensation for the failure to achieve any real breakthrough with Lutherans.

If so, the offensive started tentatively. In August the bishop of Dover reported to Cromwell that whereas he had taken some houses 'into the king's hands', he could 'find no great cause' for suppressing a house in Shrewsbury of the black friars, and he did 'not suppress the houses except such as give up'. In September the abbot of Vale Royal received a demand to surrender, but he protested to Cromwell that he had not consented to do so, nor would he unless commanded by Henry; and he appealed to Cromwell to intercede with the king to let his monastery stand. In October, when Dr London arrived at Coventry to suppress two friars' houses, the mayor and aldermen first tried to dissuade him, and when this failed they too appealed to Cromwell.[29]

There is a suspicion here of some Cromwellian gamesmanship in the choice of visitors, who were hardly acting on their own authority. The bishop of Dover and Dr London were men of the old faith. So Cromwell may have been testing the water to see how pliant the religious orders might be, and also – typical of him – sending out religious traditionalists rather than eager evangelicals to do this rather delicate work. Only a few weeks earlier he had stung the bishop of Dover by implying that he had changed his habit but not his 'friars' heart'. 'Good my lord, judge me not so', the shocked bishop pleaded, for 'my friars' heart was gone two years before my habit'. It reads as though Dover was made to feel a bit suspect, and that he may have been 'volunteered' by Cromwell to do something to prove his loyalty.[30]

On 3 August Cranmer recommended a Master Hutton to Cromwell, suggesting that he might be made 'an abbot or a prior, and his wife an abbess or prioress' in one of the houses in Hutton's county of Warwickshire. Actually Hutton died the following month so the idea was not followed up; but

Cranmer's letter shows that he and Cromwell were still seeking opportunities to put their own men in the monasteries. They had not settled on dissolution – not yet.[31]

Infiltration, incidentally, did not always work as planned. In October the prior of Gisburne, with a certain Tristram Teshe, were sent by Cromwell to the monastery of Whitby to supervise the election of a new abbot – 'him that your lordship commanded us in your letters' – but the plucky monks refused to accept and planned to appeal. So Cromwell did not always get his own way with clerical appointments; but it is not clear why, as late as October 1538, he was even trying, *if* a decision had now been made to proceed with a national suppression.[32]

These may be exceptional cases, however, because government pressure on the religious was steadily increasing. On 6 November, Cromwell told Legh that it was Henry's pleasure to dissolve the monasteries at St Osyth and Colchester. Many houses complied with similar 'voluntary' – in the army sense – surrenders, though not all. One awkward abbot of St John's boasted that 'the king shall never have my house but against my will and against my heart, for I know by my learning that he cannot take it by right and law'. For this he was reported to Cromwell. In December Legh and Dr Peter, another servant of Cromwell's, were sent to accept the surrender of a house in St Albans. After examining the monks they told Cromwell of 'just cause of deprivation' against the abbot for 'breaking the king's injunction' as well as negligent administration, but the abbot still refused to comply. Dr Tregonwell was just as unsuccessful with the abbess and convent of Shafton. When the prior of Henton also proved unyielding, the visitors did not force surrender, though Henry was particularly displeased with this prior, who later wisely conformed.[33]

The dissolution would also apply in Ireland, where Archbishop Browne, Chancellor Alen and the Treasurer Brabazon were commissioned to act in Cromwell's stead as Vicegerent to take the surrender of all religious houses. The Irish had been anticipating something like this, and many of the clergy were already selling their lands to cheat the government. One of the speculative buyers of church lands was, allegedly, the deputy Lord Grey.[34]

A full dissolution, however, would run slightly counter to Cromwell's earlier infiltration policy, which continued to bear fruit (see Chapter 6). Friar William Oliver of the Bristol friars caused a stir among the religious for preaching justification by faith alone, and he startled his fellow monks with the information that 'nor a whole ship laden with friar's girdles, nor a dung cart full of monk's cowls' would avail for justification. Cromwell himself asked Bishop Latimer, in November 1537, where he could get 'good monks' from – this would mean evangelical monks. Latimer recommended two from 'my brother abbot of Westminster'. Latimer had his own contacts among the religious, and he endorsed the abbot of Evesham as a 'very civil and honest man'. In October 1538 Latimer urged Cromwell to be favourable towards the prior of the Black Friars in Worcester, who had surrendered his house, and he passed on the abbess of Malling's thanks to Cromwell for his 'goodness towards her'.[35]

Latimer was the man who, on Cromwell's instructions, had investigated the 'blood of Hailes', a famous relic said to contain the true blood of Christ. The relic turned out to be nothing but 'unctious gum' coloured red, snorted Latimer contemptuously after pretty quickly wrapping up his examinations. This evangelical triumph was made all the sweeter by the conversion of a local abbot, who thanked Cromwell that God's truth was now 'perched in my very heart' after reading the Scriptures in English. But even Latimer was not yet campaigning for an indiscriminate dissolution. As late as December 1538, he was petitioning Cromwell on behalf of the prior of Great Malvern, now fearful of losing his house. Latimer supported the prior's appeal to allow 'for the upstanding' of his house: 'not in monkery, he meaneth not so; God forbid! But ... to maintain teaching, preaching, study, with praying'. Coming from Latimer, this means evangelical teaching, preaching and study, further proof of Cromwell's considerable success in introducing the new learning into the monasteries. The prior was well known for his good housekeeping, his hospitality and goodness to the poor, commended Latimer, and he proposed 500 marks for Henry and 200 for Cromwell, which 'for your goodwill might occasion the promotion of his intent'.[36]

It is time now to meet one of Cromwell's women. She was Katherine Bulkeley, and, thanks to Cromwell's recommendation to the king, the Lutheran abbess of Godstowe. She gratefully offered Cromwell the stewardship of her house, sent gifts of fresh apples and Banbury cheeses, and promised him her daily prayers for his well being. When Dr London turned up in Godstowe in November 1538 seeking surrenders, the indignant abbess knew where to turn. She wrote straightaway to Cromwell; as she owed her position to him, she would make no surrender except 'at the king's gracious commandment or yours'. But Dr London, 'which as your lordship doth well know, was against my promotion, and hath ever since borne me great malice and grudge, like my mortal enemy', has turned up as an unwelcome guest and 'doth threaten me and my sisters', demanding that she surrender her house. She besought Cromwell 'to continue my good lord, as you have ever been', and 'remove him hence'. She assured him of her loyalty, and wished 'the grace of almighty Jesus' may preserve him.[37]

Soon the abbess wrote again, on 26 November. She thanked him for the 'stay of Dr London', who was 'ready to suppress this poor house, against my will and all my sisters' until Cromwell 'so speedily sent contrary commandment'. This 'poor maiden' promised to pray daily for Cromwell, as 'I have no other riches to recompense you'. 'Be assured', she went on, 'there is neither pope nor purgatory, image nor pilgrimage, nor praying to dead saints, used or regarded among us; but all superstitious ceremonies set apart, the very honour of God and the truth of His holy words ... is most tenderly followed and regarded with us'. Abbess Bulkeley was as Lutheran as Luther, especially with her 'dead saints' – that very Protestant scorn for the sheer pointlessness of praying to the dead. 'This garment and fashion of life', she confessed, 'doth nothing prevail toward our justifying before God, by whom, for His sweet

Son Jesus' sake, we only trust to be justified and saved, who ever preserve your honour'.[38]

Abbess Bulkeley, the prior of Malvern and those like them must be distinguished from others who surrendered willingly enough, but more out of routine obedience than any Lutheran conviction. Take the warden of the Grey Friars in London, for example. He was going to 'cast off this Papistical slanderous apparel', not quite because he thought it unscriptural or morally wrong, but because 'it hath not been rightly used many years'. The warden quoted Hezekiah destroying the brazen serpent that Moses had made by the command of God (2 Kings 18:4), thereby showing that 'princes may change a thing that God did institute, when it is not used to God's intent'. He offered his services to Cromwell. Though Cromwell may have made use of arguments like this, it is unlikely that he rushed to take the warden into his service. His letter implies that monasticism *was* something divinely commanded at one time. There is nothing Lutheran about this; nothing about dead saints either, or justification by faith alone.[39]

The existence of these religious evangelicals may partly explain the cautious, hesitant and occasionally contradictory approach of the government and of Cromwell personally around late 1538. Nevertheless, the end was not long in coming. In May 1539 an act of parliament secured all religious houses and lands for the crown, and within two years, monasticism in England had virtually disappeared.[40]

Any assessment of Cromwell's policy, motives and role in the dissolution must begin by recalling that Henry had had his eyes on church property before Cromwell became a councillor, let alone Vicegerent (see Chapter 6). I have suggested, however, that the failure of the Lutheran talks in August 1538 may have been the stimulus that made Cromwell decide to act more forcefully against the monasteries as well as the shrines. Having sought to reform them by planting evangelicals in key places, he may have decided that infiltration, though it had enjoyed some success, had now run its allotted course, and that the time had come to wrest the initiative from the opposition party after the disappointing end of the Lutheran visit. The financial motive cannot be ignored, but on its own it does not explain the timing of the dissolution. The evidence is not conclusive, but from August–September 1538 there was a perceptible increase in activity, beginning with a softening up of the monasteries in preparation for the act of May 1539. But for Abbess Bulkeley and those like her, action may have been swifter and more ruthless. Cromwell certainly showed his loyalty to his own men and women by making sure that they received generous pensions. Few if any of the religious were cast out of their orders with no compensation and pensions were generally adequate, usually four or five pounds a year, but Katherine Bulkeley, due doubtless to Cromwell's patronage and influence, received a handsome £50 a year.[41]

By general consent, the administration of the dissolution was a huge success, and yet another example of Cromwellian efficiency. More interesting, however, is Cromwell's desire to see dissolved monasteries converted into colleges, universities, schools and hospitals. He listened sympathetically to Richard Lee, who hoped to preserve the cathedral church at Coventry, 'if by your goodness it might be brought to a college church'. The Vice Chancellor of Cambridge University was glad to hear Cromwell say that monasteries should be transformed into places of learning and true doctrine. The evangelical abbot of Evesham asked Cromwell if his house might be made into a college to preach the Word of God, provide education for the young, and relief for the poor and lame. The mayor and aldermen of Carmarthen petitioned Cromwell regarding the mansion of Grey Friars. Fearing that it would go to ruin after its surrender, they sought a grant to maintain the building as a grammar school.[42] Ambassador Marillac told King Francis, in May 1539, that parliament was discussing the possibility of turning suppressed monasteries into bishoprics, schools for children and hospitals for the poor. On 23 May, Cromwell introduced a bill to allow the king to establish new bishoprics. The bill's preamble recommended putting monasteries to better use, 'whereby God's word might be better set forth, children brought up in learning, clerks nourished in the universities, old servants decayed to have livings, almshouses for poor folk to be sustained in, readers of Hebrew, Greek and Latin to have good stipends, and daily alms to be administered'.[43] One year later Henry Bullinger in Zürich heard from a contact in England that 'some of the principal monasteries are turned into schools of studious men'. Nicholas Partridge reported that Henry has 'desired certain bishops to consult with respect to the selection of twelve monasteries, where boys might be piously and holily brought up in all kinds of useful learning'. An anonymous proposal, possibly dated March 1540, hoped that the priory and convent of Rochester could become a grammar school for poor men's children.[44]

In the event, as others have pointed out, neither education nor public welfare gained appreciably from the dissolution.[45] The main reason for this is that little more than a year after the dissolution act, Cromwell was condemned to die. Responsibility for the horrendous mismanagement of monastic revenues does not lie with him. So long as he was alive, expectations were high that benefits would flow to learning and the common good from the passing of monasticism. Some positive measures in that direction had already been taken.

Running parallel with the dissolution was arguably Cromwell's major evangelical initiative – to provide every parish in the land with an English Bible.

By the late 1530s, two Bibles were already available, the Coverdale and the Matthew. Coverdale's was not entirely a direct translation from the original Hebrew and Greek, for he had made extensive use of the Vulgate, Erasmus, Luther and Tyndale. The Matthew had aroused resentment in some quarters for supposedly being too dependent on Luther and Tyndale. At some point, perhaps to diffuse such criticism, Cromwell decided that a revised version translated directly from the original languages would be desirable, and he entrusted the work to Coverdale. Grafton and Whitchurch were chosen to be the publishers. The Bible would be produced at Paris, where the printing was reputed to be of the finest quality. To ensure that everything would proceed without hindrance, Cromwell persuaded Henry to secure the approval of King Francis.[46]

By early summer 1538 Coverdale and Grafton had begun work in Paris. At Cromwell's request they sent him samples of what they called 'your lordship's work' – a telling phrase, proving that Cromwell was the man directing the Great Bible project. What Cromwell received from Paris, however, was not just a routine progress report. 'We follow not only a standing text of the Hebrew with the interpretation of the Chaldee and the Greek', the writers explained; 'but we set also, in a private table, the diversity of readings of all texts, with such annotations ... as shall doubtless elucidate and clear the same'. They explained the different annotations they were using. One would indicate a 'diversity of reading among the Hebrews, Chaldees, Greeks and Latins'; another a sentence 'not in the Hebrew or Chaldee, but in the Latin and seldom in the Greek'; while a cross would point out Old Testament texts 'alleged of Christ or of some apostle in the New Testament'. So Cromwell, apart from organizing things, was taking a close interest in the technical and linguistic details as well. But these reports also contained a note of anxiety: 'We be daily threatened', they told him, though frustratingly they gave no details. The problem soon worsened. On 7 October the English ambassador in Paris, Edmund Bonner, reported 'a stay' in the printing of the Bible, though he had petitioned the Grand Master to allow the work to continue. In December Grafton told Cromwell he feared the opposition of 'these men' and their 'cruelness against us', and that the work might be confiscated; but again, he named no one.[47]

Then on 17 December, the French Inquisitor General formally ordered the work to be halted. He further ordered that all Bibles produced thus far – approximately 2,500 – should be confiscated. According to Foxe, the opposition originated from English bishops opposed in principle to an English Bible. Such opposition undeniably existed, but it is a little unlikely that a few disgruntled bishops could, unaided, have foiled a project authorised by the king of France at the request of the king of England.[48] More serious opposition was coming directly from Rome, by now renewing attempts to forge a continental alliance against England, and demanding that the Bible 'corruptly translated into the English tongue should either not be published, or else burned' (*che la Biblia tradotta in lingua Angla corrottamenti o non si divulghi o si abbruci*).[49] Pope Paul III had renewed his bull against Henry, especially in view of his impenitence and his most recent crimes like the destruction of Becket's shrine, seen abroad as a calculated attack on the spiritual authority of the papacy. The pope and Cardinal Pole were pressing Francis, Charles and the Scots to enforce a united trade embargo against England. Fearing that Charles's proposed expedition against the Turk would delay such action, Rome was even willing to consider a temporary truce with the Turk so that Christendom's continental princes could marshal their combined resources to reduce Henry, and if possible the Lutherans as well, to submission.[50]

Cromwell had a personal as well as a religious interest in the Great Bible, because he had invested his own money to finance it. To try and get the printing re-started, he appealed to the French ambassador, Castillon. He also urged Bonner to appeal to the French authorities, including Francis personally. Castillon was uncompromising. The French Inquisitor, he claimed, had found many things corrupt and false (*vicieuses et fascheuses*) in the work, so any more printing in France was unthinkable. The dexterous King Francis, however, desirous of keeping good relations with Henry as well as with Rome, dropped a subtle hint that the English might be able to buy the necessary types, printers and paper, and carry on the printing in England.[51]

After being 'well comforted and encouraged by the Lord Cromwell', says Foxe, the Englishmen were allowed to collect presses and printing equipment from France and bring them to England, where printing resumed in April, 1539. Cromwell's next task was to try and recover the Bibles that the French had confiscated. At first the French refused, again on the grounds that the translation was faulty, though they declined to give examples of defective work. To put pressure on the French, Cromwell used the Rochepot Affair – a maritime dispute involving a French raid on German merchant vessels in the English Channel – as leverage in negotiations. The fate of these confiscated Bibles, however, presents a puzzle. Foxe says that the Englishmen never could recover any of them, but then he has this intriguing passage:

> Saving that the lieutenant-criminal having them delivered unto him to burn in a place of Paris (like Smithfield) called Maulbert Place, was somewhat moved with covetousness, and sold four great dry-fats of them to a haberdasher, to lap in caps, and those were bought again, but the rest were burned.[52]

But why would a French haberdasher buy a large consignment of *these* Bibles? Not only were they banned by the French authorities; they were also printed in the English tongue. Who could this strange buyer be? And where could he sell his illicit goods – except in England?

Ambassador Chapuys, still monitoring English affairs with interest, has a cryptic note to the effect that Francis, still seeking to be all things to all men, had dropped another of his discreet hints. He had implied that printed copies might after all be delivered to English ministers in certain circumstances. Chapuys had no details of how, when or even if this was done, but he has given us a useful clue to the riddle of the missing Bibles.[53] Because they were no use to anyone else, only one explanation seems possible. Cromwell must have struck a secret deal with the French, and Foxe's mystery haberdasher was an agent of Cromwell's paid to buy up the Bibles in France and then ship them back to England. The entire operation must have been funded by Cromwell. Nobody else would have put up the money, certainly not Henry or the French government. So not for the first time in his career, Cromwell had to resort to bargaining and haggling in his evangelical endeavours.

The title-page of the Great Bible is a fascinating piece of religious art and can be seen in the illustrations section (plate 2). In the centre is the Word of God itself, 'The Byble in Englyshe'. Then there are three distinct frames. In the first (top) frame Henry sits on his throne. On his right stands Cranmer at the head of the clergy. On Henry's left is Cromwell, and behind him the privy councillors. Cranmer and Cromwell each receive a Bible from the king, though Henry's gaze is directed at Cranmer. Then in the second (middle) frame, Cranmer hands the Bible to the clergy, while Cromwell on the left does the same to the laity. In the third and lower frame we see on the right, below Cranmer, a congregation listening attentively to a sermon. On the left, below Cromwell, another group of godly, contended Tudor citizens are doing nothing specific apart from going cheerfully about their daily lives.

It is believed to be a work of Hans Holbein, but the brain behind it was probably Holbein's patron, Thomas Cromwell. Its message is that the English Bible is the king's gift to the English people, and it therefore behoves all loyal subjects to read it. But they are not only to read it, or have it read to them, in church by their priests. The Bible is for the nation as a whole: church and state, clergy and laity. Another example of Cromwellian evangelical strategy, it is designed to encourage Bible-reading among an increasingly literate laity, with the aim of weaning them further away from the medieval religion, and directing them instead to the more Scripture-based faith of the Reformation.

The royal proclamation regarding the Bible declared that Henry had appointed 'our right trusty and well beloved coun-cillor the Lord Cromwell, Keeper of our Privy Seal' to be responsible for licensing Bible translations. One small curiosity of this royal edict is that in this undeniably spiritual project, Cromwell was not referred to as Vicegerent. In fact, his exact terms of reference as Vicegerent are unclear. Four years before, he had drawn up plans for a Vicegerential court and office, but unfortunately no useful details have survived.[54] Nevertheless, some idea of the vicegerency in practice may be gauged from letters to Cromwell from Cranmer. Though Cranmer usually addressed his friend and ally as Lord Privy Seal, the letters discussed below all relate to church affairs of one kind or another during 1537–9.

Beginning in May 1537, Cranmer reported that the bishop of Norwich, William Rugge, a man of the old faith 'doth approve none to preach in his diocese that be of right judgment'. Cranmer asked Cromwell to grant the king's licence to one Mr Gounthorp of Norwich, of whom Cranmer approved. Cranmer also knew of three or four good men in that diocese 'to whom, if your lordship would give the king's licence, I doubt not but you should do a deed very acceptable to God'.[55]

Next summer Cranmer reported the case of a sacramentary called Atkinson, commanded to do penance at Paul's Cross. Atkinson then asked if he could do penance at his parish church instead. Cranmer would have preferred Paul's Cross, 'where the most people might be present ... and be ware of like offence'; but apparently this was not a decision that he as archbishop was able to make, so he asked Cromwell 'what answer I shall make unto him at this behalf'.[56]

Cranmer then took up the cause of an old unnamed friend from his days as a scholar at Cambridge. The man wished to leave the priesthood 'for causes moving his conscience', but feared he might lose his livelihood due to the hostility of certain people in Ludlow, where he now lived. Cranmer asked Cromwell to write to the warden of the guild in Ludlow, so that the man would be allowed to carry on teaching at the school there, even though he had left the priesthood. Cranmer admitted that 'there is no foundation or ordinance, as he sheweth me, that the schoolmaster thereof should be a priest', but Cromwell's help and patronage were requested in view of the man's background.[57]

When the dean of Tamworth died in August 1538, Cranmer asked Cromwell if 'you will have in remembrance Doctor Barons unto the king's majesty, for his preferment thereunto'. This indicates that even Cromwell did not actually make appointments himself, but that he, not Cranmer, made recommendations and representations to the king.[58]

In October Cranmer received reports from a scholar of Oxford about suspicious words and activities. A certain Mr Don had been defending papal primacy, while others tried to 'keep the youth of this college from the knowledge of God's word'. Nor were the king's injunctions being kept, and Bible-reading was suppressed. Cranmer sent full details and a report to Cromwell 'to be examined by you'. In the same month he recommended Dr Champion, his chaplain, for a vacant benefice in Somerset by Cromwell's 'favour and aid'. Once again the suggestion is that Cromwell had to refer the matter to Henry for final approval.[59]

Then Dr Cave, a servant of Cromwell's, was 'right willing to leave a prebend, which he now hath in the king's majesty's college at Oxford', to Dr Barber, Cranmer's chaplain. Cranmer, 'having no other mean to the king's highness ... was compelled in this, as in all other my business, to have resource to your lordship' to secure this favour for Barber. In January 1539 Cranmer detained two priests in Kent for breach of injunctions, and commanded them to give alms of forty shillings to the poor. He then asked Cromwell to 'send me word, how I shall behave myself hereafter in punishing of such offences'.[60]

Another short case study concerns a priest, Sir William Swerston, who was reported to the bishop of Norwich for heresy. Swerston refused to answer the charges laid against him, and appealed to Cromwell as vicar-general. The bishop kept him in custody until he knew what Cromwell wished to do. Unfortunately, neither the details nor the outcome are known.[61]

At the time of the Germans' visit, and with Cromwell's encouragement, Cranmer was beginning the first drafts of a revised order of service for church offices – daily readings of Scripture, prayers and worship, though not the main Eucharist service. It is possible that this initiative came from Cromwell. Besides being technically superior to Cranmer in ecclesiastical affairs, he was also by nature more energetic and innovative, and liturgical reform might well have come under his Vicegerential remit, though this cannot be proved. However, there is nothing to suggest that he was seriously thinking of a full English, evangelical liturgy at this stage. Had he done so, the most likely blueprint would have been Luther's German mass. Frustratingly, not much more can be said on this point because Cranmer appears to have stopped work when the evangelical program ran into difficulties, and he did not return to it during Cromwell's lifetime.[62]

The prestige and authority of the office of Vicegerent is impressively declared in the act for the placing of lords in Parliament in 1539. It confirms that Henry appointed 'Thomas, Lord Cromwell and Lord Privy Seal, his Vicegerent, for good and true ministration of justice to be had in all causes and cases touching the ecclesiastical jurisdiction, and for the godly reformation and redress of all errors, heresies and abuses in the said church'. According to this act the office would be permanent, and Cromwell 'and all other persons which hereafter shall have the said office of the grant of the king's highness, his heirs or successors, shall sit ... upon the same form that the Archbishop of Canterbury sitteth on, and above the same archbishop and his successors'.[63]

It reads grandly. However, it is worth recollecting that when the Lutheran delegation arrived in summer 1538, Cromwell was sidelined in favour of Bishop Tunstall. Presumably Henry guessed that Tunstall would be more sympathetic than Cromwell to the king's views on masses and priestly celibacy. So the imposing title of Vicegerent, and the theoretically sweeping powers accompanying it, could be just a little misleading, because without Henry's approval there was not a great deal that Cromwell could safely do. The vicegerency existed chiefly to enforce the *king's* will in the church, and herein lay Cromwell's dilemma. With Henry hardening on priestly celibacy, determined to hold on to private masses, and all at sea on justification by faith, Cromwell's ability to further the Protestant cause was becoming increasingly limited, as reports reaching him on the state of reform in England made uncomfortably plain.

As he probably expected, not everyone was delighted to receive his new injunctions. 'By God's bones', grumbled Robert Mawde, a Warwickshire curate to his congregation one day, 'I have read this out to you a hundred thousand times and yet ye be never the better'. Mawde also complained about their wordiness – 'here is a hundred words in these injunctions where two would serve'.[64]

Nottinghamshire and Lincolnshire were generally quiet, according to John Marshall. When people heard about reforms, they 'whisper a little but it is soon forgotten'. The English *Pater Noster* was well received, and the abbeys were 'nothing pitied'. Some were surprised at the recent legal requirement to register births, marriages and burials, fearing that a new tax will soon be imposed. Following the deaths of Exeter and Montague, many wondered whether Reginald Pole 'should make business one day to all the power he may'. A stained glass window of Becket had been removed, and people were uncertain about what was expected of them on traditional feast days. A few weeks later Marshall had to admit that, whilst there was no open opposition to Henry in Nottinghamshire, there was little enthusiasm for reform either, and few priests were preaching according to the injunctions.[65]

In Newbury, Miles Coverdale found some prohibited popish books, and he promptly ordered the local curate to call all such books in. A lingering fondness for forbidden images of Becket among church goers in Kent was discovered by John Fogges and Henry Goderick. Injunctions were only grudgingly obeyed in much of Kent, and apart from Cranmer and his chaplains, few preached the Gospel sincerely. In a Barking parish, Robert Ward reported that the injunctions were not being read at all.[66]

Robert Ferrar, evangelical prior of St Oswald's in the north, advised Cromwell that whilst Yorkshire folk were eager to learn the Gospel, very few were willing to preach it. In Northumberland, too, people were glad to hear the Word, while law and justice were in better order and crime was down. But Ferrar added sadly that he knew of only one good preacher between the Tyne and the Tweed.[67]

A sample as short as this is nowhere near representative enough to draw definite conclusions on the reception of the Reformation in England. However, it is probably fairly typical. Although it is interesting that there were encouraging signs even in the north, the overall picture was a disappointing one for evangelicals. Progress towards reform was somewhat pedestrian, and no decisive breakthrough appeared in prospect. There was even the danger that the Lutherans might now give up hope on Henry. To forestall this, and to keep Protestant hopes alive, an idea had entered Cromwell's mind to cement the Anglo-Lutheran relationship in a time-honoured way – by a diplomatic, royal marriage.

15

The Affairs of Kings

The 'displeasure and sorrow' of Queen Jane's death in October 1537 was reported to English ambassadors abroad by Cromwell. The official announcement added that although Henry was not minded to marry again, the council had urged him to re-consider for the sake of the realm. Ambassadors were soon being asked to make discreet enquiries about eligible ladies on the continent. Cromwell also sounded out John Hutton, governor of the Merchant Adventures in Antwerp, who was also an English agent in Flanders. Hutton praised the duchess of Milan, who had just arrived there – 'a goodly personage of body and competent of beauty, of favour excellent, soft of speech and very gentle on countenance'. He also mentioned the daughter of the duke of Cleves; he had not seen her, but he had heard 'no great praise neither of her personage nor beauty'.[1]

Christina, duchess of Milan, was the second daughter of the deposed King Christian II of Denmark. She was a niece of Charles V, and, though only sixteen years old, already a widow. The duchy of Milan, prized by both Francis and Charles, could have given Henry enviable diplomatic leverage in European power politics. Cromwell was soon involved in the marriage talks, and he raised with Chapuys the possibility of a multiple alliance: Henry to the duchess, Edward to the emperor's daughter, Maria, and Elizabeth to the son of the duke of Savoy or the son of the king of the Romans. Chapuys was cautious. Probably rightly, he suspected that Henry was coveting Milan mainly to 'sow suspicion' between Charles and Francis, who were now on more amicable terms.[2]

According to the French ambassador, Castillon, Cromwell must have carried his traditionally pro-Imperialist preferences a little too far. For this he received a royal ticking off from Henry, who told him that whilst he was a good secretary he had no right to interfere in the affairs of kings (*Il estoit bon pour le mesnaige* [sic], *main non pour entremettre des affaires des roys*.) *Le ménage* usually means 'housework', but it is unlikely that Cromwell was being assigned household chores from now on. The *Letters and Papers* translates it as 'manager', but I have rendered it as 'secretary' because it seems that Henry was reminding Cromwell that he was the king's Principal Secretary, appointed to run the government administration, and not get ideas above his station. It was nothing serious – just an example of Henry getting testy.[3]

Cromwell's enthusiasm for the duchess may have irritated Henry because at this stage the king was rather keen on a French marriage. His interest focussed on Madame de Longueville until, to his intense annoyance, he found himself in competition with King James of Scotland. Madame's ample figure had appealed to Henry – 'we are big in person and would like a big wife', he informed bemused French envoys. With some difficulty the French tried to persuade Henry that whilst they would be delighted to oblige him wherever they could, Madame was already promised to the Scottish king and the promise could not be broken. Trying to be helpful, the French suggested other names that might be suitable, though they were less than enamoured with Henry's idea that these titled Gallic ladies should present themselves to him at Calais for inspection. Why, French envoys asked diplomatically, could Henry not send a dependable representative to see the ladies and report back? 'By God', replied Henry, 'I trust none but myself, for the thing touches me too dear'. Though Henry did relent a little, these words are crucial to understanding the later, ill-matched Cleves marriage correctly: Henry, not Cromwell or anyone else, would choose the new queen of England, and Cromwell was not so stupid as to imagine that the king could be forced against his will.[4]

In summer 1538, Chapuys heard that a painter would be sent to Germany, and he was probing Cromwell for more news. Cromwell assured him that Henry was 'not one to marry without having first seen and known' the lady. Chapuys suspected a German marriage alliance was being considered, but he wasn't sure of the details. His despatches mention the young duke of Cleves for Mary, and a relative of Cleves' for Henry. Castillon has a similar report of Mary being considered for young Cleves. The name Anne of Cleves now began to appear in diplomatic despatches; but Castillon, like the English, expected her to marry the son of the duke of Lorraine because a pre-contract was believed to exist between them. In August Cromwell put forward the possibility of a marriage between Mary and young Cleves to the German delegation in England. The response was encouraging, and Elector John Frederick subsequently wrote to Cromwell about it.[5]

The Cleves connection, almost certainly Cromwell's idea, was entirely safe and timely. The Cleves family was a bit like Henry – neither wholly Catholic nor wholly Lutheran – but they were related by marriage to the Lutheran Elector John Frederick of Saxony. The Lutherans had come to England at Henry's invitation, and, although Henry disagreed with them over private masses and priestly marriage, he would have preferred to negotiate further on these points and not end the Lutheran dialogue completely. So an indirect connection with the German princes, one which would not bind Henry to the *Augsburg Confession*, easily commended itself to the king.

According to ambassadors' letters from October to December 1538, however, the duchess of Milan was still the government's preferred choice, and negotiations were proceeding accordingly. Nevertheless, it must have been during this period that Anne of Cleves was first considered as well, maybe in case the Milan talks failed.[6]

On 10 January, 1539 Christopher Mont was sent to Germany to press John Frederick for replies regarding the theological discussions of the previous summer; but he also took with him quite specific instructions from Cromwell regarding the Cleves ladies. Besides a match between Mary and young Cleves, Mont was to – 'diligently but secretly' make enquiries about the 'beauty and quality' of Anne, including her 'shape, stature, proportion and complexion ... her learning, activity, behaviour and honest qualities'. If Mont was satisfied that she was 'such as might be likened unto his majesty', then Mont should assure the Germans that Cromwell was 'much tendering the king's alliance in Germany ... and would be glad to employ himself earnestly to induce and persuade the king's highness, his sovereign lord, rather to join with them than otherwise'. Cromwell did not yet know whether any conclusion had been reached regarding the prospective French or Milan marriages, but he stressed that 'his grace is not of light proceeding in a matter of such importance'. If the Germans were willing, and if Anne was suitable, 'he thinketh that it should be most expedient they should send her picture hither, so that his lordship might the better persuade his Majesty thereby'. (Here, 'he thinketh' refers to Cromwell – he refers to himself in the third person throughout the letter.) What is not absolutely clear from this letter, however, is whether Cromwell had discussed the idea with Henry. The probability must be that he had, because it would be uncharacteristically indiscreet to ask for a picture of Anne to be sent to Henry without talking the matter over with Henry first, especially when a marriage to the duchess of Milan or a French lady was still a possibility. Then, to Cromwell's satisfaction, Mont replied quickly; he had seen John Frederick, who was supportive.[7]

Sometime in late 1538, therefore, Cromwell had floated the suggestion that Henry might consider Anne as well as the duchess of Milan. Nothing was decided on, but Cromwell was willing to promote a marriage to Anne *provided* the emissaries considered her a suitable candidate. Cromwell's idea was to forge an Anglo-German bond that did not require Henry to formally accept the *Augsburg Confession*. This was entirely in accord with the king's own wishes, a point that popular accounts of Henry and his wives miss completely. There was absolutely nothing reckless or foolhardy in it.

Prospects for the Cleves marriage then received a boost. Because the duchess of Milan was a niece of Charles V, she was also great-niece of Catherine of Aragon, so a relation of affinity, albeit a distant one, existed between her and Henry. A papal dispensation might therefore be needed to sanction this marriage. The English had known about this potential sticking point all along, but negotiations had continued in the hope that somehow they might be able to resolve it amicably. At Toledo in February 1539, however, Charles told the English that he would insist on a papal dispensation. He rejected outright any suggestion that Henry, just because he had made himself Head of the Church in England, could issue a dispensation on his own authority; from this it sounds as though Charles was never especially keen on this marriage. Then on 10 March, Henry sent a message to Charles via Ambassador Wyatt: Henry, it stated bluntly, would never accept papal interference or ruling in his affairs.[8]

So the Milan marriage was moribund, and not because Cromwell had lured Henry away from the duchess against his will. It was Henry who ruled it out by refusing even to consider any involvement on the part of the pope. The door was now open to Anne of Cleves. On the same day – 10 March, 1539 – Henry sent emissaries Carne, Wotton and Birde to the duke of Cleves, promising his good will and inquiring about the possibility of a treaty by marriage. Carne and his companions were to ask to see the Lady Anne and obtain permission for a portrait. Cromwell separately instructed Christopher Mont to ask what 'contribution and aid' might be available from Cleves and the Germans if England were threatened with attack from either Francis or Charles. Cromwell was also pressing for another Lutheran embassy to England.[9]

On 18 March, Cromwell was able to report to Henry that John Frederick might support a marriage with Anne, and that a portrait of her could be ready soon. Cromwell then gave a very glowing description of Anne: 'Every man praiseth the beauty of the same lady as well for the face as for the whole body above all other ladies excellent'. According to one witness, she 'excelleth as far the duchess [of Milan] as the golden sun excelleth the silver moon'. These are Cromwell's words based on a letter he had received from Mont, now frustratingly lost, so the theory that Cromwell was exaggerating is pure guesswork. Cromwell added that John Frederick, despite being pressed by Mont to continue talks on theology, had not yet made any firm promise.[10]

We will leave Mont and his companions on the continent for now, because while romantic affairs were being conducted abroad, at home England was virtually on a war footing. King Francis and Charles V had made peace, a dangerous peace for England, and Rome renewed her determination to bring Henry to his knees. Cardinal Pole and the pope were urging Franco-Imperial action against England, beginning with a trade embargo in the hope of stirring up unrest and possibly a rising against Henry.[11]

Cromwell began England's diplomatic counter-offensive in Italy, the land he knew well and still loved. He instructed Edmund Harvell, a merchant friend and agent in Venice, to open exploratory talks with the duke of Urbino and other Italian states in dispute with Rome, to see if any alliance with England might be made. He may have heard reports of Lutheranism penetrating Italy, so he decided to sponsor some undercover evangelising there. Harvell was to seek out 'notable and honest persons ... that like to have a sincere zeal for the truth', and who oppose the bishop of Rome. He should then 'employ his wit to power in some smack of the pure learning of Christ's doctrine among them', and wean them away from the 'abuses of pardons, relics and other superstitions of the bishop of Rome's see, contrary to the Gospel'. If Harvell found any willing hearers, then let him 'proceed from step to step, further and further … if he shall find any inclined to the Protestant religion or averse to the pope, he shall soberly explain to them the vanity of the Romish doctrine'.[12]

This was the year (1539) of Reginald Pole's *Apologia to Charles V*, in which he cast aside his former reasonableness towards Cromwell. Pole's work begins with a savage attack on Henry for the dissolution of the monasteries, the executions of More, Fisher and the Carthusians, the destruction of Becket's shrine and the Exeters. Pole then urged Charles to fight Henry rather than Turk, for the English king had sunk so low that he was worse even than the 'infidel'. The *Apologia* recalled the early days of Henry's first divorce, how Henry expected Rome would approve, and when she did not, the king at first decided to proceed no further. But then 'a messenger of Satan' approached Henry to make him suspect the wisdom of his loyal councillors. This messenger, Pole continued, beguiled the king, flattering him that he was 'above all law', and that all who opposed him deserved death. If, therefore, the pope refused to grant his divorce, then Henry should renounce Rome and make himself Head of the Church in England. The messenger led Henry to the 'pinnacle of the temple', from whence he showed him all the alluring riches that the king would gain by seizing the possessions of the church and commanding the clergy's submission. All opposition would be made treason. Pole then revealed the identity of this satanic envoy – *Cromwell* – a creature 'more like the demons in the tombs than a man, without conscience or any sense of right'. Pole described Cromwell lecturing him one day on a minister's duty to his prince. Cromwell told Pole he should forsake the insipid scholastic theologians and learn the practical, if brutal, art of government. He promised to send Pole a book on the subject. The book was Machiavelli's *The Prince*, in Pole's view a 'satanic work'.[13]

As noted already, Pole's account of the English schism, and of Cromwell's allegedly decisive role in it, has not convinced Elton or Mayer, Pole's most recent biographer. Such scepticism is understandable. Henry's wish to divorce Catherine, his aim of supremacy over the church and his desire for monastic acquisitions all pre-dated Cromwell's rise to power. The point about Machiavelli and the *Prince* is probably true, though over-dramatised. The timing of the *Apologia* is also a little suspicious. It was written when Francis and Charles were, for once, at peace, and the dream of a crusade against schismatic England might at last be realised.[14]

Charles's reaction to this assault on Cromwell – a man he and Chapuys had previously looked on with some regard – is not known. However, the position of foreign ambassadors in England was now uncertain. Castillon feared for his safety and asked to be recalled. Henry and Cromwell were more concerned about the departure of Chapuys in March 1539. Castillon was soon replaced by Charles de Marillac, but Chapuys did not return until after Cromwell's fall.[15]

The English government now mobilised the nation to prepare for war. In March writs were issued to summon a new parliament, the first for three years. Then, in response to an order from Charles to detain all ships in Antwerp, Henry issued a similar order for ships in English ports. Cromwell instructed Ambassador Bonner in France to apologise to Francis in case any French vessels were affected, and to try and find out whether Francis 'would be our enemy if the emperor would declare himself against us'. Bonner should let Francis know that 'from time to time and by little and little, his ships shall be delivered, and no damage done unto them'. Cromwell urged Ambassador Wyatt to find out more about Charles's intentions. Henry appealed to Francis to arrest Cardinal Pole should he enter French territory. Concerned but undaunted by the emperor, Cromwell was now rallying anxious English hearts: 'We trust to God', he urged his servant Wriothesley. 'He is our hope. What should we fear? He will defend His own cause; how and after what fashion, we leave it to His divine providence. Be ye always of good comfort. We lack neither heart nor courage'.[16]

Preparations for defence against an invasion, begun the previous autumn, continued apace throughout 1539. All along the south coast, the Thames, in Calais, on the coasts of Essex and Suffolk, and as far north as Berwick, officers appointed by Cromwell were superintending defence fortifications. From Calais Cromwell heard reports of hoarding, and he magisterially rebuked the deputy, Lord Lisle. In almost every county, including Wales, plans were laid to raise able-bodied men for war, and provide training and arms. Cromwell directed that a warrant be made for the order of beacons throughout the country. The people's response was heartening. At Harwich, wrote one officer to Cromwell, 'ye should have seen women and children work with shovels in the trenches and bulwarks there'.[17]

Cromwell made sure that ambassadors Chapuys, Castillon and Marillac saw for themselves the resistance that an invading army would have to face. Before he left, Chapuys warned Charles how well prepared England was. Marillac received a guided tour of coastal defences at Portsmouth and Southampton, and his despatches to Francis and Montmorency give vivid accounts of life in England during spring and early summer. In April Cromwell mustered 10,000 men, with another 50,000 expected imminently. No one was exempt; even strangers living in England were called up. Five or six ships sailed round the country as patrol boats, sending messages to each other and to coast guards by fires. If any foreign vessel approached the shores of England, the whole country would be alerted instantly. Henry had nearly 150 warships; at least 90 were well equipped, and thirty more would be soon. The government had taken the names of all French subjects in England. All this and more was dutifully reported to King Francis.[18]

Intelligence and security were also tightened. In March, the earl of Westmoreland advised Cromwell that he had detained a priest for speaking ill of Henry, and two Irishmen, a monk and a friar. The Council of the North confirmed the facts. The priest was Robert More, and letters for the pope and Pole were found on the Irishmen. The monk was questioned but refused to co-operate, so on Cromwell's orders he was sent to the Tower to 'see him set in the brakes, and by torment compelled to confess the truth'.[19]

In April Cromwell received an intelligence report from Thomas Cheyne that fifty great ships of war were ready to sail from Holland. Cheyne asked for instructions, because Henry had ordered that people should not be levied unless the danger was real, for fear of wearying them with too many false alarms. Cromwell instructed Cheyne to put two patrol boats to sea. Two days later the ships were sighted, anchored at the North Foreland. Cheyene sent another vessel to watch them. Next day he suspected that the ships were really bound for Constantinople. Four days later Stephen Vaughan, in Flanders, heard that Charles was about to recall the ships, and he dashed off a letter to London. Soon Cromwell was able to tell Henry that Charles's fleet had been 'undoubtedly prepared for Barbaria'. The danger had passed – it may have been a false alarm – but the intelligence network was working well.[20]

Not surprisingly in view of the reports being sent out of England, foreign enthusiasm for an invasion quickly subsided. Cromwell heard from Norfolk, in Berwick during spring, that King James of Scotland had promised not to break his truce with Henry, even though the Scots clergy were eager to see England invaded and conquered. The prelates feared that James, urged on by lords and gentry, might follow the example of Henry in England and bring the clergy into submission. However, Norfolk remained suspicious of Scottish intentions.[21]

On the continent, Cardinal Pole had to report sadly that Charles was unlikely to take action against England. Charles confided to the Venetian ambassador that he had little appetite for an invasion, despite appeals from Rome and Pole. Neither was the emperor, to Pole's chagrin and Cromwell's delight, keen on a trade embargo; and he had even refused Pole's requests to detain Englishmen living in his dominions. The pope continued to try, but Charles pleaded that unresolved issues in Germany had to be dealt with before he could turn his mind to England. With King Francis, Pole had even less joy. Stalling just as adroitly as Charles, Francis purred piously about sending a joint Franco-Imperial embassy to England, which would urge Henry to return to the obedience of the church. Nothing came of it.[22]

If a nation's military strength is measured by the successful conquests it makes, then England under Thomas Cromwell had little to boast of. If, however, another criterion is applied – if the test of strength is the ability of a nation to defend itself against all dangers – then Cromwell's England was as powerful as any country in Europe. Cromwell had always been opposed to English involvement in foreign wars, because he had grasped one of the fundamental tenets of military strategy. On paper and on the continent England was weaker than France and the empire. At home in the Channel, properly defended, she was stronger than both.

Ironically, Cromwell enjoyed more success as Henry's all-embracing minister for foreign affairs, national defence, intelligence and security than he did with his German Lutheran brethren. He was increasingly concerned at the Germans' apparent lack of enthusiasm to persevere with Henry, especially when news reached England that, at the Frankfurt Interim, the Schmalkaldic League had promised Charles that it would admit no new members for eighteen months. Theoretically, therefore, England could not have joined the League even if Cromwell had managed to persuade Henry to accept the *Augsburg Confession*. Cromwell urged emissaries Christopher Mont and Thomas Parnell to stress to the Germans how Henry, 'being a prince that favoureth the Word of God above all other things', still earnestly desired an alliance with them. Mont was to press for an answer, to remind them that Henry was the first prince in Europe to cast off papal authority in his realm, and urge them to consider an alliance in the face of hostility from Rome and now the emperor as well. The result was a huge disappointment. Letters from Germany regretted Henry's refusal to endorse the *Augsburg Confession*, and, when a delegation eventually arrived on 23 April 1539, it was a minor one compared with the previous year. Led by Franz Burkhardt and the Hessian noblemen, Ludwig vom Baumbach, the League's answer to Henry contained the news that English evangelicals had dreaded. In view of Henry's support for private masses and clerical celibacy, the Germans saw little point in any further negotiations on theology. Some sort of relationship between Henry and the League might still be concluded, though not full membership. Even for this uninviting offer, the League's terms were derisorily one sided. Henry would have to pay 15,000 crowns a year for eight years, and an extra 30,000 crowns if war broke out; Henry could also recruit mercenaries from Germany if necessary. Henry was hugely displeased, and a crisis point in Anglo-Lutheran relations had now been reached.[23]

Cromwell could not meet the Germans on their arrival because he was ill with tertian fever. Desperately trying to salvage something from the wreckage, he wrote to Henry from his sick-bed, and this letter affords some insight into the tactical approach that Cromwell was likely to use in trying to reason with Henry. After profuse regrets that he was unable to attend on the king, Cromwell assured Henry that Melanchthon and the German princes remained well disposed towards him, though they were saddened by his stance on private masses and priestly marriage. Cromwell quoted Melanchthon on the subject, knowing Henry's admiration for him. He reminded Henry that some nuns discharged from monasteries in England were not forbidden to marry. Then he brought in the prospect of the marriage to Anne, confirming that John Frederick remained supportive. At this point the letter takes a subtle turn. The Schmalkaldic League, said Cromwell, was 'steadfast and constant'; but the German princes expect a crisis in Europe at any time, so that 'either the evangelicals must destroy the Papists or else the Papists them'; and we trust 'it shall no more be in their power than in the devil's power to overcome Christ, the true Protector of the Gospel'. The Anglo-German alliance was 'very formidable' to Rome and the Papists, and 'if your Majesty shall happen to join with them, the Papists in my judgement shall be half desperate'. This was the reason why, at the Frankfurt Interim, Charles was so anxious that the League should admit no new members.[24]

Perhaps a paraphrase of this letter may be offered. Behind Cromwell's deferentially couched language lay an urgent appeal to Henry to put aside his bickering and make up his mind. Why make such a fuss over priestly celibacy when you let some of our own nuns marry? See what Melanchthon – the reformer you really and genuinely admire, and who dedicated his *Loci* to you – says about it. Accept, therefore, the *Augsburg Confession* and make a treaty with the League, for Rome and the emperor are seeking to destroy England. Do not be angry with the League for agreeing not to receive any more members for now – they did this only under pressure because the Papists and the emperor are afraid of the growth of the Gospel.

Had Cromwell been able to meet Henry face to face and argue thus, the English Reformation might have taken a different turn at this critical juncture. But his fever persisted; he was unable to attend the opening of parliament on 28 April, and a meeting with the Germans scheduled for the following day had to be postponed. Cromwell did eventually see them on 2 May at his home, though while still unwell. Norfolk, Suffolk, Audley and Tunstall were also present – three of the old faith and one of the new. No report of that meeting has survived, but on 5 May Audley announced to the Lords that Henry would be setting up a committee to discuss religious differences. On it would be Cromwell, presiding as Vicegerent, and a selection of senior clergy fairly evenly divided between evangelicals and Catholics, which suggests that the balance had not yet swung too far against the reformers. One name notably absent from the proposed committee was Stephen Gardiner, probably a small Cromwellian victory. By the time that Cromwell had recovered from the fever on 10 May, Nicholas Hare, a Norfolk supporter, had been elected Speaker of the House of Commons.[25]

About this time the possibility of the king's marriage to Anne of Cleves surfaced again. One potential problem was Anne's pre-contract with Lorraine's son, and this was dealt with in a report from Wotton and Birde, Henry's envoys in Germany, to Cromwell dated 3 May. During preliminary discussions with Cleves, they had feared that the whole matter was 'made and sealed up'; but then Cleves's Chancellor assured them that the contract had been made between the parents, and 'the parties as yet have not given their consents, but are at their liberty to do what they will'. If Anne did not marry Lorraine, however, Cleves might have to make a compensation payment. Cromwell discussed this with Henry, and it was decided to send Wotton and William Peter, another agent in Cromwell's service, to Cleves to settle the matter once and for all. Instructions signed by Cromwell directed Wotton and Peter to personally inspect all the relevant documents and be sure of the facts. If Anne really was promised to Lorraine's son, and if it was impossible now to break that promise, then a marriage with her sister might be feasible; but Cromwell insisted that Peter and Wotton must report back to Henry before making any commitment, and that no further marriage talks should take place until Henry gave his approval. They were also ordered to ask permission to see the Cleves sisters themselves, and arrange for portraits to be sent to England.[26]

Two significant facts emerge from these discussions. The first is that Henry, despite his disappointment with the Lutheran delegation, did not cancel the Cleves negotiations, even though he had ample reason and opportunity to do so. This will prove that he was seriously interested in Anne, and not being led along unsuspectingly by a devious Cromwell. The second point is that, on Cromwell's own orders, negotiations regarding Anne would have to stop if it turned out that the pre-contract was a serious problem, at least until Henry had decided what to do next. This, hopefully, should to be enough to answer fanciful theories that Cromwell was rashly determined on this marriage at all costs, or that he ordered his agents to exaggerate Anne's qualities to Henry, or that Hans Holbein was bribed by Cromwell to produce a flattering portrait of Anne in order to deceive Henry. Which of Henry's ministers, unless he was completely mad, would have dared to play such a crude trick on his king? The argument dismisses itself. Despite his hopes for the Cleves marriage, Cromwell applied no undue pressure to anyone, except to establish all the facts and report them to Henry.

As Peter and Wotton were setting off for Germany, Cromwell was carrying on the evangelical struggle at home. On 10 May the posthumous attainder of the Exeters was presented to the Lords, and during the debate a silk tunic was held up to view. The striking scene is described in a letter from John Worth to Lord Lisle. 'On the side of the coat there was the king's grace's arms of England, that is the lions without the flower de lys, and about the whole arms was made pansies for Pole, and marigolds for my lady Mary'. In between the marigold and the pansy 'was made a tree to rise in the midst, and on the tree a coat of purple hanging on a bough, in token of the coat of Christ, and on the other side of the coat all the Passion of Christ'. The propaganda message was that Pole intended to marry Mary, 'and betwixt them both should rise again the old doctrine of Christ'. Worth had received his information from a certain Sir George Speke. Many have assumed that it was Cromwell who held up the tunic. This could well be so, though Worth does not confirm it. The words seem to be Worth's summary of what was said, because it is a bit unlikely that Cromwell would have referred to the papal religion so nostalgically, even affectionately, as the 'old doctrine of Christ'. Nevertheless, the theatrical gesture was clearly designed to remind parliament that the threat from abroad, though it had receded of late, had not disappeared entirely.[27]

Still in May 1539, Cromwell received further encouragement from the Lutheran King Christian III of Denmark. Cromwell had persuaded Henry to send Robert Barnes to Copenhagen to discuss Anglo-Danish relations. Assuring Henry of his goodwill, Christian suggested a meeting of English and Danish diplomats and representatives of the Schmalkaldic League, possibly in England. Helpfully for Cromwell, Christian was urging Henry to accept the *Augsburg Confession* and join the Protestant alliance. Henry, however, was unyielding. On 16 May Norfolk introduced the infamous Six Articles to the House of Lords, and Henry's last meeting with his German visitors on 26 May ended with a bad-tempered row over clerical celibacy.[28]

The Act of Six Articles enforced by law the doctrine of transubstantiation, though the word itself, possibly because of its connotations, was left out. It affirmed the medieval practice of communion in one kind only, but it did not condemn both kinds outright. Vows of chastity and private masses were defended. Clerical celibacy was declared to be a 'law of God', not some mere church law or tradition, and with this sweeping dismissal of Lutheran arguments, Henry showed himself more resolutely opposed to the marriage of priests than any medieval pope had ever been. Auricular confession was also upheld, though this time as a commendable practice and not a divine law. However, the act failed to assert the propitiatory sacrifice of the mass, and, much to the chagrin of Bishop Tunstall of Durham, it also watered down somewhat the medieval teaching on confession. Henry had achieved the uncommon feat of producing something very anti-Lutheran, but at the same time inadequately Catholic.[29]

Cromwell had already realized that this was a battle the evangelicals had lost. He even advised his supporters to restrain their opposition to it during debates in parliament.[30] His reasons have puzzled some writers, but Cromwell knew Henry's convoluted psychological make-up better than most men did, and he had read the situation with his customary shrewdness. Though Henry enjoyed debating theology, the Lutherans were not interested in wrangling with him over communion in one kind, private masses and clerical celibacy. Earthy, no-nonsense Saxons like Martin Luther and John Frederick had little time for Henry's home-grown, half-baked so-called 'middle way' religion. (It should really be called the 'muddled way' because there is so little coherence or purpose in most of it.) Henry took umbrage at this disinterest, so he responded by enforcing his peculiar opinions in law. Wounded pride as much as religious conviction brought the Six Articles onto the statute books of England. As Cromwell knew, Henry did not want to end all dealings with the Lutherans, because unless Henry chose to humble himself before the pope, the Germans were the only religious allies he could hope to have. What Henry wanted was for the Lutherans to treat him with more respect, to send Melanchthon to England and conclude a settlement more congenial to him than the *Augsburg Confession*. Better, therefore, to humour the prickly king and let him have his Six Articles; and then, maybe after a short cooling off period, Cromwell could try to soften the effects of the act somehow and even get it modified. It was an illustration of discretion proving the better part of valour. Besides, though the act was a bitter pill for evangelicals to swallow, it did not actually overturn any Cromwellian reformist measure thus far, and it was only one part of a broad picture. The shrines were crumbling and the monasteries dissolving, evangelical preachers still enjoyed access to the pulpits and Cromwell's protection, and progress on the Great Bible was encouraging. The Six was a setback for sure, but the Protestant cause was far from beaten.

However, the act was too much for Latimer and Shaxton to bear, and both resigned their bishoprics. According to one report, Latimer was induced into this. Cromwell is supposed to have told Latimer that Henry wanted him to go, though Henry later denied this and took pity on the bishop. It is not especially convincing. Latimer had developed a habit of inveighing against adultery in high places in his sermons, so the tale that Henry missed him and felt sorry for him takes some believing. What probably happened is that Cromwell had a quiet word with Latimer to tell him of the king's displeasure on certain points, and this, plus the shock of the Six, persuaded him to quit.[31]

Shaxton's relations with Cromwell were still under some strain following the affair of the abbot of Reading (see pp. 290–3). Another awkward incident had occurred in April, just before the Six was discussed in parliament. John Goodhall, a junior to Shaxton, had clumsily removed an image that people were kissing and venerating, unaware that it contained the sacrament. The people were outraged, and the mayor's report of the matter to the council hinted that Goodhall might be a sacramentary. Shaxton and Goodhall denied this, and appealed to Cromwell for help. No harm came to either man, but this was just the sort of distraction that Cromwell could have done without at a difficult time. He may not have been unduly sorry to see the accident-prone Shaxton depart.[32]

Cranmer was mortified by the passing of the act. He had led the Protestant fight against it in the Lords, and but for his unwavering loyalty to Henry, he might have considered the prospect of a peaceful exile. Not the least of his problems was how to provide for his still secret wife. His misery was cruelly compounded by acute embarrassment when the requirements of the act compelled him to examine a priest and a woman in his diocese 'very suspiciously taken' by a constable. As there was no 'commission out as yet' for the punishment of such offenders, Cranmer passed the details on to Cromwell, asking him 'to advertise me with convenient expedition of the king's grace's pleasure, how and in what manner they shall be ordered'. Cranmer suggested that favour should be shown to the woman if, as he believed, she had confessed honestly. The outcome is not known.[33]

Foxe and Burnet both have a short passage in their volumes saying that Henry, out of sympathy for Cranmer, organized a dinner for him, attended by many leading lights of the realm. Around the table one of the guests, unnamed in Foxe but Cromwell according to Burnet, compared Cranmer favourably with Wolsey. Then Norfolk reminded Cromwell that he had been Wolsey's servant, half implicating Cromwell with Wolsey's ambitions and misdeeds. Cromwell conceded that he had been in the cardinals' service, be he denied that he would ever have gone to Rome with Wolsey had the latter been made pope. At which Norfolk accused Cromwell of lying, and 'upon this, great and high words arose between them'. Elton half believed this story. The difficulty with it is not with the dinner, but the slanging match during it. If any comparisons should be made, we would expect Cromwell to Wolsey and Cranmer to Warham. Nor is there any evidence apart from this that Cromwell was ever suspected of being party to Wolsey's papal aspirations, even though his knowledge of Italy and its language would have fitted him well for a position in Rome. There is, however, some evidence of tension between Norfolk and Cromwell around this time. Anthony Rouse of Denington in Suffolk, once a servant of Norfolk's, was seeking Cromwell's support to marry the daughter of a wealthy squire, Sir Edward Ichingham, but Norfolk resented Cromwell's involvement in affairs in his part of the country. Whether this has any relevance to the altercation reported by Foxe and Burnet is unclear. However, it does seem highly unlikely that at a dinner laid on by Henry to cheer Cranmer up, Cromwell and Norfolk would have been so careless as to get into an undignified public row.[34]

Whatever actually happened, it now fell to Cromwell to help evangelicals escape the worst rigours of the new act. He began by stalling with his customary consummate skill on the setting up of commissions that were supposed, under his direction, to enforce it. His opponents of the old faith, sensing that here was a golden opportunity to embarrass him, tried to press home their advantage. The bishop of Lincoln reminded him of a group of Oxford evangelicals reported to him in the spring for eating meat during Lent. Again Cromwell stalled, again apparently successfully. Then Richard Bush, parish clerk at Hastings, took an indirect shot at Cromwell with the claim that the Matthew Bible in his church – a Cromwellian reform measure – had mistranslated 1 Corinthians 9:5. The Matthew read: 'Have we not the power to lead about a sister as wife'; and, with a wonderful turn in logic, Bush argued that this contradicted the prohibition on clerical marriage in the Six, so the translation had to be false.[35]

Despite the disappointments and the problems that the act brought, there is no evidence that Cromwell considered resigning, or that he shared the prevailing evangelical despondency. Years of hard experience had forged a steely, resilient character, cheerfully solid in times of adversity, which did not know the meaning of giving up. Besides, delicate affairs of kings needed attention, which could still help preserve the Lutheran connection.

In August Henry received a letter from emissary Wotton, now in Germany with Dr Peter investigating the matter of Anne's pre-contract with Lorraine's son. Cleves and his council had assured Wotton that all relevant documents would be sent to England to confirm that no impediment existed to a marriage between Henry and Anne. Then Wotton gave some interesting details about Anne. She had been educated with the lady duchess, a 'wise lady, and one that very straightly looketh to her children'. All in Cleves's court said that Anne was 'lowly and gentle'. Much of her time she spent 'with the needle'. She did not speak French or Italian, or play a musical instrument; 'for they take it here in Germany for a rebuke and an occasion of lightness that great ladies should be learned or have any knowledge of music'. However, Anne's 'wit is good', and Wotton was sure she would be able to learn English soon enough. He went on: 'I could never hear that she is inclined to the good cheer of this country, and marvel it were if she should, seeing that her brother, in whom it were somewhat more tolerable, doth so well abstain from it'. Holbein, meanwhile, had painted Anne and her sister, and 'expressed their images very lively'.[36]

This letter to Henry is another significant document in the Cleves story, because Cromwell is supposed to have embellished accounts of Anne's qualities, while keeping his king in the dark about less appealing reports of her, like this one. It will be obvious from this lengthy extract, however, that Wotton's letter was not intended critically. In her education and pastimes, including her inability to speak languages or play music, Anne simply followed the custom of leading ladies in Germany. The same goes for the rest of the letter. Certain sections do not read very well, but all it means is that Anne and her brother were serious minded, not frivolous. This letter can hardly be taken as a warning to Henry to withdraw now while he had the chance. There is no hint from Wotton that Anne was unworthy or unsuitable. If anything the reverse is true, because after the traumas of Anne Boleyn, why would Henry want a wife who could sing and dance and play? It would increase, not dampen, Henry's desire for Anne of Cleves to hear that she resembled nice, comfortable Jane Seymour rather than her troublesome namesake. There was no reason, therefore, why Cromwell would have kept these details hidden from Henry. Besides, the letter was addressed to the king, and the idea that Cromwell intercepted and doctored letters to his prince – when he knew how determined Henry was to see and hear of Anne and decide for himself – is too ridiculous for words.[37]

On 1 September Marrilac wrote to King Francis to tell him that Henry was well satisfied with Holbein's portrait of Anne, and that an embassy from Cleves was on its way to conclude the marriage treaty. It was *Henry*, therefore, not Cromwell, who had decided to go ahead with the marriage, even though the pre-contract papers had not yet arrived in England. Cleves's assurance that no legally binding pre-contract existed between Anne and Lorraine, and that documents to prove it would be sent to London in due course, was taken on trust by the king.[38]

On 20 September, German ambassadors landed in England and met Cromwell, who gave them an effervescently upbeat assessment of church affairs. Reports quickly went back to John Frederick saying that the Six Articles were not being rigorously enforced, that the bishops who supported the act were now out of favour, and that Cromwell had re-asserted his authority and influence with the king. The ambassadors then hunted and dined with Henry. He assured them he still wished to have good relations with the League, including an agreement on religion. Within days, arrangements were being made for Anne's journey to her new country. On 6 October Henry signed the marriage treaty. And still no pre-contract documents had arrived.[39]

Ambassador Marillac, following a personal meeting with Henry, gave King Francis a very perceptive analysis of Henry's strategy and thinking. Henry still wanted an alliance with the Schmalkaldic League, Marillac explained, and the Cleves marriage was arranged mainly for that reason. Henry hoped that the 'intercession' of Cleves would help to 'soften' certain aspects of Lutheranism that Henry found too 'harsh and sharp', and that an acceptable agreement or compromise might yet be found on outstanding points, meaning priestly marriage and private masses. Henry, the ambassador continued, had only one son and was hoping for more, and the king had spoken highly of Anne in conversations with Marillac. Meanwhile, England eagerly awaited her new queen.[40]

Marillac wrote well, as usual. Despite the Six Articles, Henry still clung to the belief that substantial areas of agreement existed between him and the Lutherans, especially regarding the rejection of papal authority. He felt that the Germans had gone too far on certain points, but he did not want to cut his ties with them completely. They could yet make useful allies. Knowing the way Henry's mind operated, Cromwell advocated the Cleves marriage as being in the king's interest. Henry approved it, and readily. The king was not tugged, tricked or enticed into an unwanted marriage or an unwanted Protestant alliance against his will. The idea was Cromwell's, but he made sure the decision was Henry's.

There was, however, a subtle difference between the king and the minister. Whereas Henry wanted the Lutherans to 'soften', as Marillac says, Cromwell was hoping that *Henry* might soften, especially when he was happily married to Anne. If the marriage could repair the bruised relationship between Henry and John Frederick, then a new German delegation, headed this time by Melanchthon, might finally achieve Cromwell's aim of winning Henry for the Reformation. Thus Henry and Cromwell each had his own slightly different hopes and expectations regarding the Cleves alliance. Cromwell knew, even if Henry did not, that the Germans would never alter the *Augsburg Confession* to suit Henry's 'middle way'. Cromwell knew his master's mind thoroughly, but whether Henry fully understood the workings of the more finely developed mind of his minister is less certain.

While England was waiting for Anne's arrival, Cromwell enjoyed another success. Having recovered many if not all the Bibles confiscated in France, printing of the Great Bible had now begun in England. Cranmer composed the preface, and a royal proclamation made Cromwell responsible for licensing Bible translations for the next five years. Another circular from Cromwell in late 1539 powerfully echoed Luther's Reformation rallying cry of *sola Scriptura*, 'Scripture alone'. It stressed the king's personal commitment to the English Bible, and commanded preachers to declare that 'all things contained in this book is the undoubted will, law and commandment of Almighty God, the only straight way to know the goodness and benefits of God towards us, and the true duty of every Christian man to serve Him accordingly'. It provided further heartening news for evangelicals still smarting from the Six Articles.[41]

Meanwhile, Anne's entourage set off from Germany in November. Accompanying the Cleves delegation were representatives of the Schmalkaldic League. Their instructions were to report back on the state of religion in England, and if it appeared favourable, a further embassy to England, maybe including Melanchthon, might be considered. Among those waiting to welcome Anne at Calais were Lord and Lady Lisle, Nicholas Wotton, the earl of Southampton and Gregory Cromwell. Lady Lisle was glad to hear from a friend who knew Anne that she was 'so good and gentle to serve and please'. On 13 December, Southampton and Wotton reported Anne's safe arrival to Henry. She was happy with her reception, they said; she enjoyed the banquet and watched the jousts. Because the channel crossing had to be delayed a day by bad weather, she played cards with her hosts 'as pleasantly and with as good a grace and countenance as ever in all my life I saw any noble woman'. She then invited Southampton and others to supper, where 'her manner, usage and semblance', beamed the admiring earl, were 'such as none might be more commendable, nor more like a princess'. Southampton innocently expected Henry to read his report with benign approval. Later, when he learned that Henry was less than delighted with Anne, he tried ungallantly to wriggle out of these kind words.[42]

Henry and his train, including Cromwell, were now at Greenwich waiting expectantly for Anne to arrive. What follows here is taken from Hall's narrative of that first encounter, and of the public ceremonial of the marriage. Interspersed with this I give Cromwell's recollection of his private conversations with Henry. Though written six months later, this is the fullest record available of what happened behind the scenes, and of Henry's confidential reaction to that fateful meeting.[43]

Henry was impatient to see his bride. Rather than wait for Anne to arrive at Greenwich, he hastened down to Rochester on New Year's Day to surprise her with gifts and 'to nourish love'. Cromwell stayed at Greenwich. Henry's sudden arrival (says Hall) astonished Anne, but:

> After he had spoken and welcomed her, she, with most gracious and loving countenance and behaviour received and welcomed him on her knees, whom he gently took up and kissed: and all that afternoon commoned and devised with her, and that night supped with her, and the next day he departed to Greenwich.

We revert now to Cromwell's account. When the king returned to Greenwich, Cromwell asked him how he liked the lady Anne. 'Nothing so well as she was spoken of', growled Henry. If he had he known the truth about her, 'she would not have come within this realm'. He asked what remedy there was. Cromwell was stunned; he replied that he knew of none, and then lamely added that he was 'very sorry' for this 'hard beginning'.

Next day Anne reached Greenwich. Hall describes her reception by all the lords and ladies, and her 'most goodly demeanour and loving countenance'. In public at least Henry played the part of the joyful bridegroom: 'With most lovely countenance and princely behaviour, he saluted, welcomed and embraced her, to the great rejoicing of the beholders'. To this courtliness Anne responded 'with most amiable aspect and womanly behaviour'. Then the royal couple talked together, rode together, and 'O what a sight was this to see so godly a prince and so noble a king to ride with so fair a lady of so goodly a stature and so womanly a countenance, and especially of so good qualities'. When they reached court they

dismounted, and Henry 'lovingly embraced and kissed her ...
and led her by the left arm up to her privy chamber, where he
left her for a while'.

The king then summoned Cromwell, who had been watching the spectacle, hoping against hope that his master's opinion
of Anne had mollified overnight. Alas, it had not. 'She is nothing so fair as she hath been reported', grouched Henry, though
in a rare display of chivalry he strained himself to concede that
Anne looked 'well and seemly'. Cromwell agreed – he could
hardly do otherwise. But he also dared to suggest, and Henry
did not contradict him, that Anne had a 'queenly manner'.
Then Henry ordered Cromwell to summon the council to
consider afresh the legality of the marriage, especially in view
of Anne's pre-contract. The Cleves delegation was 'much
astonished and abashed' at this unexpected turn of events, and
embarrassed officials promised that pre-contract documents
would be sent soon. 'I am not well handled', grumbled Henry,
though he appears to have overlooked the fact that *he* had
signed the marriage treaty without seeing these pre-contract
papers. Henry then muttered something about cancelling the
wedding, but he drew back for fear of 'making a ruffle in the
world' that would 'drive her brother into the hands of the
emperor and the French king'.

Henry then made a blunder. He demanded that Anne
state before the whole council whether she was 'free from
all contracts'. This she obediently did, finally cutting off all
possibility of escape for her reluctant bridegroom. 'Is there
no other remedy, but that I must needs put my neck in the
yoke?' groaned the unhappy king. Not now there wasn't, and
on the morning of the marriage Henry took Cromwell aside
and unburdened himself: 'My lord, if it were not to satisfy the
world and my realm, I would not do that I must do this day for
no earthly thing'.

Hall then describes the marriage itself, the pomp and
splendour, all the leading lords and ladies in gorgeous apparel,
followed by banquets, masks and 'diverse disports' that evening.
The ceremony and the bridal night over, Cromwell again

called privately on the king, where a sorry sight awaited him. 'Surely my lord', said Henry, 'as ye know I liked her before not well, but now I like her much worse'. Henry then went over his loveless first night with his new queen. 'I have felt her belly and her breasts, and thereby as I can judge she should be no maid, which struck me so to the heart ... that I had neither will nor courage to proceed any further'. He then left her 'as good a maid as I found her'.

Henry would later repeat, to Sir Anthony Denny, that he 'somewhat suspected' Anne's virginity. It is puzzling to hear such a claim about a piously brought up sixteenth century duchess. It also sits uneasily with stories of Anne's supposed sexual innocence, though these are admittedly based on statements taken from gossipy ladies at court. It is tempting to somewhat suspect that Henry made this up. But this is by the by.[44]

Too many writers simply take it for granted that because Henry did not find Anne desirable, she must have been unattractive and unsuitable. Contemporaries saw her differently. In her native Germany, and among her own people, she was described as beautiful and elegant. One of Cromwell's overseas contacts, Sir Michael of Grave in the Low Countries, waxed eloquently over her, calling her 'beautiful, illustrious and noble', with a 'great gift from God, both of sense and wit'. Hall admired her, and his favourable view was shared by the English people. The duke of Suffolk told Cromwell how delighted Anne was at the joyous welcome she received from the mayor and people in Canterbury. Nor was this a performance stage-managed by Cromwell, or put on out of fear of the king, because Henry's people had not been afraid to tell him that they did not love Anne Boleyn. Then at festivities and jousts a few days after the marriage, Hall describes Anne looking on dressed 'after the English fashion, with a French hood, which so set forth her beauty and good visage that every creature rejoiced to behold her'. Marillac was slightly more reserved, though still complimentary: She is 'tall and slim, of medium beauty, and of very assured and resolute countenance' (*de corps haute et gresle, de beaulté moyenne et de contenance fort asseurée et résolue*); but if she was not quite as young and lovely as some had expected, the 'turn of vivacity and wit supplies the place of beauty'.[45]

Opinions may differ between Marillac's 'medium beauty' and some of the more ardent descriptions – this is largely a matter of taste – but Holbein's portrait shows a face far from ugly, and at least as attractive as any of Henry's other wives. As this view is borne out by so many contemporary witnesses, it is pointless to pretend that Holbein painted an unduly flattering picture designed to deceive Henry about Anne's attractiveness. If that were true, why was no action taken against him? Why was he not summoned to court to account for himself? Why, moreover, was no action ever taken against Peter, or Wotton, or Mont, or Parnell, or Southampton, all of whom had spoken well of Anne to the king, and were liable to the king's laws and punishments for any misleading reports or unfaithful service rendered to him?

Just as important as Anne's appearance – for royal marriages were invariably more diplomatic than romantic, and few kings married solely for love – was her character. Anne was young without being girlish, regal but not flirtatious. There would be no royal scandals this time. She had a natural dignity, and if she was perhaps a little serious in her manner, she was also gentle, gracious and meek-spirited. She would remind Henry of his beloved Jane, not the wilful, wayward Anne Boleyn. Even Henry admitted she had a 'queenly manner'. From accounts of her reception, the English people took her instantly to their hearts. She was willing to learn English and adapt to English life and customs. She gave Henry a connection with the Cleves duchy and the Lutheran princes that did not require him to commit himself to the *Augsburg Confession* – just what Henry was looking for. This marriage antagonised neither Francis nor Charles; and it would allow Henry to continue his policy of detached neutrality in European politics, playing the one off against the other as it suited him. It would bring England new allies and no new dangers. Yet on and on the story goes that Cromwell saddled his king with an unsuitable wife!

Marriage introduction agencies could tell dozens of stories similar to this one, albeit on a humbler level and without the same sort of ramifications for affairs of state. A couple read each other's profile, correspond briefly, speak on the phone, exchange photos; everything goes swimmingly until they meet in the flesh, and then things do not work out as happily as expected. What happened to Henry was one of the attendant risks of an arranged marriage. There was nothing wrong with the choice of Anne as queen, at least on paper. Besides the diplomatic advantages to Henry, she was by all accounts a pleasant and attractive lady. Henry meant no malice towards her personally; he had genuinely looked forward to seeing her, and in the subsequent divorce settlement he made sure that she was well provided for. Without wanting to indulge in amateur psycho-analysing, however, it is worth noting that neither diplomatic nor dynastic calculations had featured in Henry's previous two marriages, and nor would they in the two yet to come. Consequently, he seemed unable to consider marriage in purely dynastic terms. This made him unique among fellow princes of his age. Henry needed a love match, and he did not find one with Anne. Maybe his expectations were just a bit too high. Henry was now well past his physical prime, uncomfortably overweight, bothered with gout and with two failed marriages behind him; many a man in his position might feel that he had done rather well with the Lady Anne. But in all the testimonies about her, Henry's was the only disagreeable, discordant note. Unfortunately, his was the only opinion that really mattered, so yet another royal marriage crisis was now looming.

16

A Treacherous Place

According to the traditional popular story, Henry's acute disappointment when he met Anne sounded the fateful knell for Thomas Cromwell, whose demise was now inevitable. Not for the first time in the life of Cromwell, however, the traditional story, even on the surface, is wrong. Henry first set eyes on Anne on New Year's Day, 1540, but Cromwell was not arrested until June six months later, and on the lengthy indictment against him not a word can be found about Anne of Cleves. After this his fourth wedding, Henry treated Cromwell as a confidant, not a scapegoat, and Cromwell acted his part dutifully and patiently. Vengeance was not on Henry's mind. He was not happy, but there were no royal tantrums or rages, and no accusing fingers pointed at Cromwell or any other minister. Neither in January nor in June was he blamed or held accountable. Nevertheless, 'treacherous is the first place with kings', as Bishop Tunstall of Durham was quoted as saying around this time, and sooner or later Cromwell was the man who would be expected to sort out the latest royal marriage fiasco. Well aware of Henry's unpredictability, Cromwell would have to be discreet, circumspect and more than usually astute in the coming weeks and months. With all this on his mind he told the visiting Germans that although he was with them in the faith, 'the world standing as it now does, whatever his lord the king holds, so too will he hold'.[1]

Fortunately for Cromwell, his lord the king was still in a pro-German mood. Henry urged the delegation from the Schmalkaldic League to carry on talking theology with him, with a view to settling their differences and concluding a religious and political alliance. Confident of Henry's support, Cromwell also appealed to the Germans to send another embassy before parliament convened, this time headed by Melanchthon. But the Germans were stiff and correct as ever; they could make no promises until they had consulted with their authorities back home.[2]

On the diplomatic front Henry's relations with Charles remained chilly, and the king turned his attention to wooing the Scots and the French. In January 1540 Henry sent Ralph Sadler, Cromwell's assistant, to Scotland with gifts and discreet suggestions that James might care to fill up his coffers with revenues from the Scottish monasteries, just as Henry was doing in England. Henry proposed an end for ever to the ancient enmity between the two kingdoms, and hinted that James might one day be included in the line of succession to the English crown. The result was encouraging. James assured Sadler that he never intended to be part of any continental invasion of England, and promised he would not break his friendship with Henry. The influence of Cromwell, who had consistently argued for an Anglo-Scottish accord, is easily discernable in all of this. He heard from Sir William Eyre, one of his contacts north of the Border, that James and his council were 'greatly given to the reformation of the misdemeanours' of the clergy, a reformation that might yet follow the English model. Sadler also advised that many Scots were inclined to the Reformation, and wished their king had a Cromwell beside him.[3]

Relations with France were a little more difficult, partly because Edmund Bonner, the new English ambassador in Paris, had offended King Francis with his abrasive manner. To try and placate Francis, and also to wean him away from his friend-

ship with Charles, Henry sent Norfolk to France with the
not too subtle suggestion that Charles had gained more than
Francis from the recent Franco-Imperial treaty. Henry told
Francis that a private conversation between them had come
to Charles' attention – Charles had reported it to Ambassador
Wyatt, and Henry suspected someone in the French council
was responsible for the leak. Henry also hinted that pensions
owed by France might be reduced, and that Francis might
consider joining an alliance with England, the duke of Cleves
and the German Lutherans against Charles and Rome.[4]

Norfolk did manage to sow a few seeds of doubt in Francis'
mind about Charles's good faith. Norfolk also spoke with
the queen of Navarre, who sent good wishes to Henry. In a
separate letter to Cromwell, Norfolk did not believe that the
French wanted war against England, and he suggested that
Francis secretly held more goodwill towards Henry than to
Charles. The queen remained favourable to England, Norfolk
added, but the Constable of France 'is too much Papist to do
good to us'.[5]

Henry ordered Norfolk to keep up the good work. He
repeated his invitation to Francis to join England, Cleves
and the Schmalkaldic League and thereby 'redubbe all things
past'. It was a bit rich from Henry, still not a member of the
League himself, and it was too unsubtle for Francis. Norfolk's
next letter to Cromwell, dated 21 February, doubted whether
Francis would break his pact with Charles, a prediction Francis
quickly confirmed. Nevertheless, Henry and Cromwell
instructed Ambassador Wallop in France to maintain contacts
with the queen of Navarre, in the hope that Francis might yet
be enticed away from the emperor.[6]

Two interesting points emerge from these dealings. The
first is Norfolk's habit of sending candid and almost friendly
reports to Cromwell as well as more official ones to Henry.
The second is that Henry still saw useful diplomatic mileage in
his marriage to Anne. There is no hint that Henry was thinking of a divorce, no sign that Cromwell was in danger, no sign
either that, in the first weeks of 1540, Norfolk had begun plot-

ting the destruction of Cromwell. Relations between Henry and Cromwell and Cromwell and Norfolk were, so far, carrying on much the same as before.

Meanwhile, the Schmalkaldic League had heard from their envoys that the 'beginning of the marriage' between Henry and Anne was 'joyful and prosperous'. Cromwell received two puzzling letters from Stephen Vaughan (15 January) and Nicholas Wotton (22 February), both on the continent. Vaughan's deals mainly with miscellaneous diplomatic affairs, but at the end he added this: 'I read your lordship's letter signifying the king's majesty's marriage, and became exceedingly glad that your lordship found my judgement true of the queen's grace'. Then Wotton, sent by Henry to Germany on a diplomatic mission, told John Ghogreve, Cleves's chancellor, how well Henry and Anne liked each other; he also passed on Ghogreve's gratitude to Cromwell for writing to him.[7]

It is difficult to know what to make of this evidence, especially as Cromwell's letters to Vaughan and to Ghogreve are, unfortunately, both missing. The best guess is that Cromwell had managed to persuade Henry to make some effort to get used to, and maybe even to like, his new wife.

So not for the first time in his career, Cromwell had recovered well from a major setback. He was also bringing the Great Bible project to completion. The number of printed copies stood at 3,000, and a further 3,000 were scheduled for March or April. With these, and the Bibles recovered from France, Cromwell would soon have enough, or nearly enough, to fulfil his cherished ambition of providing every parish in England with a Bible translated directly from the original Hebrew and Greek. However, this project did not proceed unopposed. The evangelical William Turner would later say that the Bible had been brought into England's churches 'in the spite of your teeth', by which he meant the bishops. Foxe agrees, and unless these men were being slanderously polemical, then Cromwell's opponents must have been unusually hostile to his Bible mission, even though Henry had been cautiously favourable to the principle of a vernacular Bible for some years. What may have particularly rankled with bishops of the old faith was the prospect of the Scriptures translated by Lutheran men like Rogers and Coverdale, acting under Cromwell's direction and leadership. But Cromwell's victory over the Bible was not a decisive one, because invariably in theological disputes it is not the Scriptures themselves that are contentious, but the interpretation of them, especially on key doctrines like justification. This calls for a brief review before going further.[8]

Justification by faith alone, not through good works or human merits, formed the core of Luther's Gospel and the Reformation. Casual observers may have imagined that Henry had reconciled himself with Luther on this point because at the recent Cleves wedding Henry confidently assured his German guests that 'we are agreed on justification and the essential points'. In that case, he argued, agreement should also be possible on private masses and clerical celibacy if the theological dialogue could be restarted. Yet Henry's own personal notes on justification in the Bishops' Book, penned in his own hand, were completely at odds with Luther. Henry, in short, was in a muddle. Obsessed with private masses and keeping his priests celibate, the Defender of the Faith had not fully thought through the most fundamental subject at stake in the Reformation.[9]

What had most likely confused him was the slightly intricate relationship between faith and good works. In his *Loci Communes* dedicated to Henry in 1535, Melanchthon had said that good works were 'necessary to salvation', by which he meant a necessary *consequence*, not a cause or contribution. Luther accepted this, and so did Cromwell. Cromwell's Ten Articles declared that justification was attained by 'contrition and faith joined with charity'; but then, a little further on, only 'through the Father's grace and mercy, and for Christ's sake'. This adroitly worded passage left open the key question – exactly how was charity joined to faith? Does charity come before, with or after faith? Is charity an essential prerequisite to justification, or an inevitable result of it, a virtue flowing naturally from it? Cromwell's studied vagueness allowed evangelicals to understand the article in a Lutheran way, and others in a medieval way if they wanted to. The Thirteen Articles in summer 1538 were similarly phrased. The passing of the Six Articles the following year had done nothing to alter this, because justification was not a point that Henry chose to dispute with the Germans. So all through the controversy about clerical celibacy, private masses and communion in one kind or two, Protestant men backed by Cromwell were preaching justification in very Lutheran fashion, with virtual impunity. Cromwell had also inspired Richard Taverner to translate Melanchthon's *Apology* in 1536, and yet more Lutheran works during 1538–40. As another has already noted, these translations were doubtless timed to coincide with the Bible project, so that key texts might be understood evangelically. All this was going on, under Cromwell's direction, and with Henry's apparent consent.[10]

Watching these Lutheran advances with smouldering fury was Cromwell's chief adversary, Stephen Gardiner, bishop of Winchester. Since his return from France eighteen months ago, tensions had arisen between these two men over the activities of reformist preachers in Gardiner's diocese. Now Gardiner had fixed his eye on Robert Barnes, one of Cromwell's closest allies and the foremost Lutheran preacher in the country now that Latimer was detained following his resignation after the Six Articles. Barnes, an old enemy of Gardiner's, was especially lively in proclaiming justification by faith when the Bible was rolling off the printing presses and into the parishes.[11]

In Lent 1540 a series of preachers were commissioned to speak at Paul's Cross. Among them were Barnes and two close friends, Thomas Garrett and William Jerome, the vicar of Stepney, where Cromwell lived. On the first Friday of Lent, however, Gardiner preached before the king. No record of that sermon has survived, but it seems to have made a most favourable impression. Two days later on Sunday, Gardiner also preached at Paul's Cross, even though he was not on the original list of speakers. Preaching arrangements were altered at the last moment, possibly with the help of Richard Sampson, the dean of St Paul's and an ally of Gardiner's.

Gardiner began with the temptations of Christ, and he gave the Gospel texts (Matthew 4:5–7; Luke 4:9–12) a novel twist. The devil, thundered the bishop, is still tempting us, through this 'new teaching'. He tempts us away from fasting, praying and confession; he tempts us to live 'idle and void of good works'. Taking a tactical middle ground between Rome and Luther, cleverly calculated to appeal to Henry, Gardiner recalled how the devil used to tempt with 'pardons from Rome' and with friars as his 'ministers'. But now the friars have gone, so 'the devil was playing a new tune'. Now the devil tells us that gaining eternal life 'needs no works at all, but only belief, only, only, nothing else'.

What sounds like a caricature of justification by faith alone was really a challenge to some evangelical contestant to enter the fray under the Lutheran banner. Robert Barnes could not resist it. When his turn came to preach on 29 February, he hit back lustily. He picked his texts from Romans and Hebrews: 'whatever is not of faith is sin', and 'without faith it is impossible to please God' (Romans 14:23; Hebrews 11:6). Warming to his theme, Barnes stoutly proclaimed justification as Luther had done: man's salvation depends solely on divine grace and faith in Christ; good works were really fruits of true faith, and though necessary for godly Christian living, they play no part in justification; Christ alone, as Saviour and Mediator, can make us righteous in the sight of God. Then, unaware that Henry had recently listened appreciatively to a sermon by Gardiner, Barnes delivered a few ripe personal insults at the bishop. According to one report, Barnes stepped down from the pulpit to thunderous approval and applause. In quick succession, Garrett and Jerome preached in similar vein.[12]

However, when Henry heard of the sparring at St Paul's he was livid. He summoned Barnes and Gardiner to his presence and commanded each man to give an account of himself. Immediately Henry took Gardiner's side. With little more ado, he ordered Barnes, Garrett and Jerome to recant in public. This they did at the end of March. To many in the audience, however, these recantations sounded half-hearted and insincere, an impression quickly confirmed when the trio reverted to preaching justification by faith alone just as before. Henry was furious to hear that his orders had been treated so frivolously, and within days the three Lutherans were arrested and locked up in the Tower. If their behaviour seems breathtakingly indiscreet, it only shows how freely and confidently Protestant men in Cromwell's service had been proclaiming their message until now. But times had changed. Over two years ago in the Bishops' Book, Cranmer had tried his best to explain this faith-works issue to Henry; but for some reason Cranmer's comments had little effect, and Henry carried on with his policy of dialogue with the Lutherans, never realizing that his own views were quite different from Luther's. As a result, a theological time bomb had been lying around largely unnoticed until Gardiner spectacularly detonated it at Lent. Naturally, Gardiner knew in advance the effect it would have on Henry. As with private masses and clerical celibacy, the crisis proved that Henry remained a medievalist at heart, despite his personal animosity towards the pope. It also jolted Henry into seeing the Germans in a wholly new light. Believing that he had understood the Lutheran teaching, and found it worth negotiating over, he had, under Cromwell's influence, begun and persevered with his Lutheran policy. In furtherance of that policy he had also, again at Cromwell's suggestion, married Anne of Cleves. In fact he had all along completely *mis*understood the Lutheran doctrine on justification. When eventually he managed to grasp it rightly, thanks to Gardiner's good offices, he liked it no more than he liked his German wife.

No record survives of Cromwell's first meeting with Henry after these Lenten contests. Maybe the king's countenance, like Laban's to Jacob in olden times, was no longer 'toward him as before' (Genesis 31:2). Until now it had been a remarkable achievement of Cromwell's to get Henry to agree to do so much of what *Cromwell* wanted. Though never a Lutheran, it was Henry who kept inviting Melanchthon and others from Germany to England to parley with him on theology; it was Henry who signed the Cleves marriage contract for the sake of a German alliance; and it was Henry who authorised the Bible in English, though without fully appreciating that Cromwell's main purpose behind it was to draw the people more and more towards the new learning. Cromwell's success, moreover, was not that he had merely persuaded the king to go along with this or that suggestion. Cromwell operated in such a way that left Henry convinced that he (Henry) was actually carrying out his *own* policy. This is the really clever part of it. It is the highest and most resourceful form of the art of psychological manipulation. Put more simply, it is the knack of getting the boss to do what *you* want, and do it willingly.

But it can also be a risky strategy. What if the boss twigs? This is what happened at Lent – Henry finally twigged. The whole Lenten saga was, therefore, a consummately cunning stratagem of Gardiner's – 'wily Winchester' as Foxe called him. No longer was Henry interested in delegations from Germany for talks on theology. With a single sermon Winchester had threatened to destroy all that Cromwell had achieved during the past seven years. The Protestant Reformation in England now faced a crisis far more serious than the Act of Six Articles. The whole Lutheran policy was in shreds, and three of the ablest Lutheran preachers in jail. Cromwell's own fortunes had suddenly tumbled. For the first time since he became Principal Secretary, observers sensed he was in danger of falling. Cromwell and Cranmer 'do not know where they are', said Marillac, reporting the events to King Francis. Cromwell was 'tottering' (*en branle de trébucher*), and rumour had it that Tunstall would be made vicar-general, and the bishop of Bath appointed Lord Privy Seal. Cromwell might, but only if he was lucky, hang on to some administrative post.[13]

Marillac reflected the general mood of excitement pervading London. He may, however, have slightly underestimated Cromwell's ingenuity. Cromwell had certainly used his powers as Vicegerent to advance the Lutheran Gospel further than Henry, had he properly understood it, would have wished. But Cromwell had also covered his tracks carefully and skilfully. He had broken no law or royal proclamation. He had done nothing technically illegal. So he could not be arrested for any crime – not yet. Besides, he was just as shrewd an operator as 'wily Winchester'.

Cromwell's response to the crisis was diplomatic. He invited Gardiner to dine with him. The two men then 'opened their hearts' to one another, with the result that 'all displeasures are forgotten' and 'they be now perfect friends' – this from one Sir John Wallop. The customary handshake before the heavy-weight title bout might be more apt. The outward bonhomie and show of unity was laid on by Cromwell for Henry's ben-efit, to let the king see that Cromwell and the bishop were at peace. Gardiner could not refuse the dinner invitation, because Henry might ask why he had spurned Cromwell's hand of friendship. Gardiner would then risk losing the unpredictable king's favour that he had recently so expertly gained. Each man divined the mind of the other; each was trying to guess what his opponent would do next.[14]

Cromwell's ploy paid off. On 12 April, the new ses-sion of parliament opened with speeches from Chancellor Audley and Cromwell. Cromwell stressed the king's desire for unity in religion, regretting the 'rashness and licentious-ness of some, and the inveterate superstition and stiffness of others in the ancient corruptions'. In public, and chiefly for Henry's consumption, Cromwell was now taking the so-called middle ground. The king, Cromwell continued, 'leaned neither to the right hand nor to the left', but sought only the 'pure and sincere doctrine of the Christian faith'. To this end Henry had appointed one committee of bishops and divines to complete the *Institution of a Christian Man*, and another one to examine which religious ceremonies ought to be retained.[15]

Still in April, Cromwell resigned as Principal Secretary, trans-ferring his duties to two of his staff, Ralph Sadler and Thomas Wriothesley. The reasons for this governmental re-organi-sation are not stated in any surviving official paper, though Elton suggested that Sadler and Wriothesley each became joint Principal Secretary so that one could serve the king and the other Cromwell. It was not a demotion for Cromwell, however, because he retained his titles of Lord Privy Seal and Vicegerent, as well as his place on the Council. More honours quickly followed. On 18 April Henry made Cromwell earl of Essex, succeeding Henry Bourchier, who had recently died without a male heir. Cromwell was also appointed Lord Great Chamberlain, a prestigious hereditary office of the de Vere Earls of Oxford, whose family had Howard connections. At the ceremony, Henry personally presented Cromwell with the staff of the office. His full title now ran as Thomas Cromwell, earl of Essex, Vicegerent and High Chamberlain of England, Lord Privy Seal, Chancellor of the Exchequer, and (for good measure), Justice of the Forests beyond the Trent. From the near disaster of Lent, Cromwell now found himself in the most exalted ranks of the nobility; and he was 'as much favour with his master as he ever was, from which he was near being shaken by the bishop of Winchester and others', reported a surprised Marillac.[16]

This turnaround in fortunes can be partly explained by Cromwell's natural genius for survival, his show of unity with Gardiner and his cleverly tactful address to parliament, all of which had impressed Henry and deflected immediate danger. Besides this, however, there must have been something which the surviving evidence and official papers do not reveal, maybe a personal meeting between the king and his minister at which assurances were given and soothing words spoken. This can only be a suggestion, but it may also be the case that Henry took this opportunity to warn Gardiner that although he had rendered his king good services at Lent, he should not try and overreach himself. Henry valued Cromwell highly, but although he was closer to Gardiner on religious matters he never had any real warmth for the bishop, especially since Gardiner had been slow to accept the Royal Supremacy. Henry's trust in Cromwell may have been shaken, but not destroyed. The king was willing to keep his minister alongside him, at least for the time being. It is also worth noting that this ennoblement was more ceremonial than practical, and it did not grant Cromwell any additional power or authority. So its significance in the story of his last months need not be exaggerated.

The good citizens of Tudor England, meanwhile, as if oblivious to the intrigues at court, continued to petition Cromwell on personal affairs, and what a blessed relief humdrum routine tasks can be at times of danger and heightened tension. John, earl of Bath, wrote to him on 3 May. Bath's father had just died, leaving him with 'weighty charges without allowance by will or otherwise'. His mother-in-law, who had always been spiteful towards him, had persuaded his father 'no part of his goodness to bequeath me' when he made his will. Bath appealed to Cromwell for help, for 'other refuge than your good lordship I have none'. The aggrieved earl added that he was troubled by a chesty cough. The outcome is not known.[17]

To return to weightier matters, the parliamentary committee set up to deal with the *Institution* had an emphatic Catholic majority. Only three out of twenty – Cranmer, Cox and Barlow – were evangelicals. Cromwell did not sit on the committees himself, though regular reports were sent to him. He also had secular affairs to attend to. About the only one of real interest here is the subsidy. Not for the first time, Cromwell had to persuade the Commons that Henry needed money. As he habitually did on such occasions, Cromwell appealed to the loyalty of the Commons and their love of their king. Under Henry's blessed reign, England enjoyed peace, safety and prosperity, and, most important of all, deliverance from the power of Rome, idolatry and superstition. Grateful subjects, therefore, would surely not refuse this request. Necessary royal expenses included putting down the Pilgrimage of Grace rebellion, the defence fortifications of 1539 when danger threatened from abroad, the cost of councils in the North and West, repairing Westminster Hall, and maintaining the army in Ireland.[18]

The outcome was a most satisfying one for both Cromwell and Henry. The only dissenting voice was Tunstall's, who unwisely murmured against imposing the tax on the clergy, though he dropped his objection when it was pointed out to him that the clergy had contributed to previous taxes. The subsidy bill was quickly accepted by both Commons and the Lords. It was the largest tax of the century, and a grateful Henry made a point of thanking parliament. Marillac, too, was impressed. On 8 May he told King Francis that Henry might receive most of the money he wanted, but a fortnight later he reported that he had got all of it 'without contradiction'. Other secular business also went well, leaving religious matters the only outstanding problem, with the bishops in their customary state of almost complete disagreement on doctrine.[19]

This subsidy bill must count as one of Cromwell's most impressive achievements in parliamentary management. England was not at war, the threat of invasion that hung over the country the previous year had receded, money was pouring into the coffers of the crown from surrenders and sales of the monasteries; and yet Cromwell wrung a huge tax from parliament with barely a squeak of protest. Raising money has never been popular, especially in peacetime, but what is especially interesting on this occasion is Cromwell's reason for the new tax – it was primarily to keep England safe from Roman power, machinations and 'superstitions'. His policy in parliament may have been part of a wider strategy, and this leads to affairs in Calais and a necessary digression.

Relations between Cromwell and Lord Lisle, the Calais deputy, had been decidedly prickly for at least three years. Cromwell had reproved Lisle, in summer 1537, for the 'Papistical faction that is maintained' in Calais. Henry had heard of it too, and he warned Lisle that he might 'put others in the best of your rooms' if the situation did not improve. Cromwell, while promising Lisle his personal friendship, noted that some on the Calais council 'lean much to their superstitious old observations' and should be 'induced to bring their hearts inward to the conformity of the truth'. The following May Cromwell rebuked Lisle again, this time for not reporting information about sacramentaries in Calais. He demanded an investigation.[20]

Adam Damplip was an alleged sacramentary who had become involved in a tangle with Gregory Botolf, a chaplain to Lisle. Damplip was sent to England to be questioned before a commission, including Cranmer. However, the archbishop advised Cromwell that he could find nothing seriously wrong with the man. According to Cranmer, Damplip confessed Christ's presence in the Eucharist, but denied transubstantiation – which would, if correct, make Damplip a good Lutheran. Cranmer thought Damplip spoke 'but the truth', and he called the prior who had complained against Damplip a 'hindrance to the true Gospel and a teacher of superstition' (in other words, a Papist).[21]

As if satisfied with Cranmer's explanation, Cromwell may not have taken stories of sacramentary heresy in Calais too seriously. He was more concerned by a report that the deputy had refused to allow Bible-reading at mass and other services. When sacramentary allegations surfaced once again, Cromwell told Lisle he should use good sense and discretion; such charges should not be made lightly, so Lisle should make double sure that the evidence was valid. Lisle suspected that Cromwell was fobbing him off, and he clumsily threatened to write directly to Henry. But Cromwell easily outwitted Lisle. When a second set of complaints about Damplip reached London, Cromwell wrote to Lisle demanding to know why these charges, which seemed 'very pestilent', were not put to Damplip before 'when he was accused of the matter of transubstantiation'. In other words, it was all Lisle's fault. Having neatly got himself and Cranmer off the hook, Cromwell put the facts before Henry. Again the king was angry with Lisle. What was the point, Henry wondered, of having a governing council under Lisle if such scandals were allowed to continue unchecked? To resolve the matter the government decided it would set up its own commission to investigate and report back.[22]

A commissioners' report was produced on 5 April 1540, just after the Lenten crisis between Gardiner and Barnes. It confirmed the existence in Calais of heretics and sacramentaries. Adam Damplip, William Smith and Thomas Brook were among those named. Damplip's conduct during his examination by Cranmer two years earlier now appears disingenuous. If he really was a sacramentary, as the government commission claimed, he must have put on a plausible Lutheran face when questioned by Cranmer, hoping that this way he could count on the support of Cranmer and Cromwell. Or maybe Damplip just panicked and backed down under pressure and momentary fear. Whatever the truth, this was an awkward little matter for both Cromwell and Cranmer, which a clever opponent could have exploited. The offenders, meanwhile, were kept in ward until arrangements were made to send them to England. Henry was determined to deal vigorously with the heresies; but when the Calais prisoners arrived in London on May Day, Cromwell sent for them, ordered their chains to be removed, spoke kindly to them, urged them to be patient, and promised them that although they would have to go to the fleet for a little while, they would soon be free to return home. Cromwell was brimming with confidence once more. If he felt this way for the Calais men, he must also have had high hopes that he could secure the freedom of Barnes and his allies before long.[23]

Besides, Cromwell was now sharpening his arrows for a strike against Lisle. While these enquiries about sacramentaries were going on, Cromwell received an intelligence report on Gregory Botolf, Lisle's chaplain, and one of the original complainants against Damplip. Under the pretence of going to England in February, Botolf had set off for Rome via France to offer his services to the pope and Cardinal Pole. Botolf's ultimate aim, however, was even more ambitious – he would betray Calais into the hands of the king's two greatest enemies. He was back in Calais on 17 March, but unfortunately for him his conspiracy came to light thanks to a former comrade called Philpot, who, fearing he was under suspicion, panicked and confessed to the authorities. Investigations began quickly, and a report was sent to Henry and Cromwell.[24]

Lisle then paid an official visit to London, and he met Cromwell at the Garter Feast on 9 May. Ten days later the hapless deputy found himself directly implicated in the Botolf conspiracy: he was placed under arrest, accused of 'secret intelligence with Cardinal Pole, and of certain practices to deliver the town of Calais to Pole'. At approximately the same time, though in a separate incident, Richard Farmer, one of London's wealthiest merchants, was imprisoned for life because his chaplain, already in jail, was convicted of defending papal authority. Marillac understood that 'another great personage' would soon be taken, though he did not know the name or the cause. Although Henry thought Lisle may have erred through ignorance rather than malice, he was taking no chances. Henry was very sensitive to popish conspiracy theories, especially at Calais where the risk of invasion the previous year had been high. Like the rest of the country, Calais had been placed on a war footing.[25]

Meanwhile, Marillac learned that a book was about to be issued – presumably the revised *Institution* – which would grandiosely 'determine all that is to be held in religion'. Its confessional line would be 'not according to the doctrines of the Germans or of the pope, but of the ancient councils of the church, by which the king shall be known … as a searcher and lover of truth only'. A tract had belatedly been sent by Elector John Frederick from Germany in response to the Six Articles. It defended yet again the Lutheran view on communion in one kind, private masses, clerical celibacy and vows. However, Henry's interest in the Germans had now all but gone. He was hoping that the *Institution* would be ready by Whitsunday (16 May), but because the bishops had failed to settle the religious disputes in time, Henry prorogued parliament until the 25th.[26]

Despite the uncertainty hanging over the *Institution*, however, and despite Henry's present mood of indifference towards the Lutherans, Cromwell had staged an astonishing recovery since Gardiner's attack at Lent. He had deflected the attention of king, parliament and the country from heretical Lutheran preaching at home to the dangers from abroad, especially Rome. A commanding performance in parliament had earned him the gratitude of his king. With the arrest of Lisle, Cromwell had turned a potential thorn in his flesh to his advantage. His friends – Barnes, Garrett and Jerome – were still in custody, but no heresy charges had been brought against them, and so long as Cromwell remained Vicegerent, nothing worse than detention looked likely to befall them. If the Reformation was not exactly thriving, the danger that Gardiner might destroy it had markedly receded. Alas for Cromwell, one quandary remained, irremediable and unsolvable.

On May Day, Henry and Queen Anne watched the jousting at Durham House. After this they feasted with the lords and ladies of the court. But outward appearances were deceptive, the marriage was a failure, and Cromwell found himself cast in the role of marriage councillor, repeatedly compelled to listen to a litany of moans about the queen. After Candelmass and before Shrovetide, Henry confessed to Cromwell that his heart 'could never consent to meddle with her carnally', even though he 'used to lie with her nightly or every second night'. At Lent, Easter and at Whitsuntide, Cromwell heard the same depressing story. Henry feared he would never have more children, and he was convinced that Anne was not his 'lawful wife'. He had done all he could to 'move the consent of his heart', but the heart failed to respond. Cromwell promised to 'do my uttermost', whatever that meant, but by now he had given up hope that Henry would ever find love and contentment with Anne. Henry also consulted his physician, Dr Butts, on a matter of some intimacy – surely he could not be impotent, he enquired anxiously, because since his wedding he had had wet dreams. The doctor's reply is not recorded.[27]

There may be a fairly simple explanation for Henry's failure to be aroused by Anne, though neither Cromwell nor Butts would have dared to suggest it. The king was now 'much taken with another young lady', visiting her frequently 'by day and by night', according to Richard Hilles, the London merchant, writing to the Zürich theologian and divine, Henry Bullinger. Gardiner, Hilles continued, has been 'providing feastings and entertainments' for the ageing though amorous Henry and his child sweetheart at his episcopal palace. The young lady was Catherine Howard, niece of the duke of Norfolk. She was nineteen years old, and Henry nearly fifty.[28]

Hilles does not, unfortunately, say when these entertainments first began, though by the end of May they had become common knowledge to 'many citizens of London'. Henry first saw Catherine the previous August when Norfolk, eager to place some members of his family in the new queen's household, brought her to court. However, as Norfolk's biographer well notes, Norfolk could not have known then that Henry would dislike Anne when he met her; so Norfolk's intention, at least at that stage, was not to use Catherine to tempt Henry away from his German bride and injure Cromwell in the process. Though it was later reported that Henry 'cast a fantasy' to Catherine at first sight, it was not a strong enough fantasy to quench his desire for Anne, nor did it prevent him from rushing down to Rochester to see her on New Year's Day instead of waiting for the scheduled meeting at Greenwich. Apart from Hilles, the first real indication of anything seriously romantic is found in notes of Henry giving Catherine presents, including a set of quilts, in April and May 1540, which tallies with Hilles's letter.[29]

What may have happened is this, though admittedly it is a best guess. Henry did indeed take a liking to Catherine when he first set eyes on her in August, but he tried to put it out of his mind because at that time he was genuinely looking forward to his marriage to Anne. But little passions are not easily tamed, and this one had ample chance to ripen after Henry's loveless wedding. When, in January and February, Cromwell tried to persuade Henry to make the best of things, the king obliged for a while; but his heart was in it no longer. Memories of Catherine were proving irresistible. By May, Henry was well and truly smitten.

Catherine's entrance on to the stage inevitably raises questions about Norfolk's role in the power struggle at court, and many historians have assumed that Cromwell was overthrown by a Gardiner–Norfolk coalition. There is, however, little evidence that Norfolk had been an active co-worker with Gardiner during the bishop's Lenten intrigues. In March Norfolk was more concerned about the government's French policy and whether it might affect his gainful French pension, and he was asking Cromwell's advice.[30] It is also noticeable that Hilles named Gardiner, not Norfolk, as the host at those 'feastings and entertainments'. Nevertheless, Norfolk had always been a potential if not an active rival of Cromwell's, and he was an ambitious man with a ruthless streak. The glittering prospect of his niece being crowned queen of England, and a son born to the king with Norfolk blood in his veins, may have been the catalyst that induced the duke into an alliance with the bishop against Cromwell and Queen Anne. Maybe Norfolk recalled Henry's first sight 'fantasy' for Catherine, and now saw the opportunity to exploit it following Henry's unhappy marriage and Cromwell's subsequent bruising during Lent.

For most late medieval monarchs, a fairly obvious solution to the predicament existed. Anne would remain as queen and Catherine would be the royal mistress. But with Henry this was unthinkable – as with Anne Boleyn and Jane Seymour, the mistress must be queen. So this latest royal love affair, a wonderful boon for 'wily Winchester', was a devastating, seemingly incurable blow for Cromwell just when he was recovering from the Lenten crisis. It would only be a matter of time now before Henry demanded another divorce, this time with potentially disastrous consequences for the Vicegerent. Anne's removal would incur the odium of her brother and the German princes, and cut off any slender hopes that may have remained of an alliance with the Lutherans. With Catherine Howard on the throne, further advancement for Gardiner and Norfolk at the expense of the evangelical party looked certain. Four years ago Cromwell had not resisted the accession of Jane Seymour, another queen of the old faith, but the state of affairs in summer 1540 was radically altered. Now that Henry understood what justification by faith meant, the nightmarish vision loomed of an outright victory for the Catholic faction and utter defeat for the Protestant cause. Most galling for

Cromwell, he was the man who would have to arrange the divorce, preside over the effective collapse of the Reformation, and live out his days as a lame-duck Vicegerent.

Faced with such mounting misfortune, a Roman of old would have fallen on his sword. Cromwell, too, now realized that his days on earth were probably numbered. He began to set his affairs in order and to provide for servants, friends and dependents. Twelve young musicians received £20 each, according to Foxe, who had spoken to witnesses still living. But Cromwell was not the kind of man to offer his head on a charger to bishops and dukes, and, like Samson of old, he resolved to go down fighting and bring his enemies down with him. At the end of May, acting on an intelligence report, he sent a certain John Legh to join Farmer and Lisle in the Tower, and for the same reason – suspected contacts with Pole. Legh had just arrived back from Italy. He admitted meeting Pole while he was there, but in vain he denied any wrongdoing.[31]

Cromwell then raised the stakes with the arrest of Bishop Sampson of Chichester and Dr Wilson, a chaplain to the king, again on suspicion of secret communications with Rome. Both men were close allies of Gardiner. The sight of a prominent bishop being marched off to the Tower left the others 'in great trouble, some for fear of being found guilty of the same deed', reported Marillac. A climate of mistrust was pervading London, and 'every day new accusations are discovered'. According to an unnamed but 'trustworthy personage', Cromwell avowed that five other bishops ought to get the same treatment as Sampson. Marillac was not sure who these five were, though he suspected Cromwell's most active antagonists which would mean Gardiner plus four more, possibly including Tunstall. Marillac also heard that Barnes would soon be released and Latimer made bishop again – 'so great is the inconstancy of the English'. The bishops, the ambassador continued, were still locked in 'irreconcilable division' and the people hardly knew what to believe. Interestingly, Cranmer had preached a sermon at Paul's Cross quite contrary to the one Gardiner gave there in Lent, which had sparked off the

Barnes trouble. It is likely that this sermon was Cromwell's idea, because apart from Philip Melanchthon, Cranmer was about the only man in Europe who stood any chance of persuading Henry to accept justification by faith.[32]

Cromwell then ordered Wilson to state what contact he had had with Dr Hilliard (or Heylard), a former chaplain to Bishop Tunstall, now an alleged traitor and fugitive in Scotland. Wilson wrote to Cromwell on 4 June. An anxious man now, he protested his loyalty to Henry; he admitted conversations with Hilliard at Tunstall's house on various points, but nothing treasonable was said or concocted. He also admitted having helped three long-time prisoners and supporters of Catherine of Aragon – Abel, Featherstone and Powell – but he assured Cromwell he did not share their Papalist views. Meanwhile, again on Cromwell's orders, Lady Lisle was examined by Sussex and Sir John Cage, though nothing significant was wrung from her.[33]

Cromwell then sent two of his trusty agents, Dr Peter and Mr Bellows, to question Bishops Tunstall and Sampson about conversations between themselves and with Gardiner. Tunstall denied he had urged Sampson to 'lean and stick to the old usages and traditions of the church'. Sampson was stunned when he heard this – Tunstall and the late bishop of London were 'fully bent to maintain as many of the old usages and traditions as they might', he spluttered. Sampson, however, gave nothing away that might implicate Gardiner: he had said only that ceremonies 'were not to be broken without a great cause, and some of them were in no wise to be broken'. This apart, Gardiner had prudently advised Sampson to leave the matter of ceremonies and church traditions to the king. Prospects for the unfortunate Sampson now looked bleak, for his denials left Henry unimpressed. Ralph Sadler, after meeting Henry, reported that the king 'liked both him and the matter the worse, perceiving by the examinations that there were witnesses sufficient to condemn him'.[34]

So Sampson and Wilson were languishing and fretting in jail. Cromwell's men had also spoken to Tunstall, who by now must have regretted murmuring against taxing the clergy in parliament (see pp. 376–7). Cromwell was even closing in on Gardiner, though nothing had been unearthed to incriminate him – yet. 'Wily Winchester' had taken care with his words, even to his closest friends.

But Gardiner had reason to be nervous, as another short digression will show. As Henry's ambassador in France from 1536–8, Gardiner had some contacts with Rome about Reginald Pole, though always discreetly, through intermediaries, and with no commitments or treasonable words. Just after Pole was made papal legate, however, Henry was furious with Gardiner and Sir Francis Bryan for failing to apprehend Pole on a visit to France. King Francis – under pressure from Henry to hand Pole over, and from the pope to receive him honourably – compromised by asking Pole to leave France quietly and unharmed. Henry was enraged yet further when word reached him that Gardiner had connived at this.[35] Sometime later, Gardiner and Bryan quarrelled. When Gardiner returned from France in September 1538 the council received a report that, according to Bryan, 'my lord of Winchester should have said he could devise a way how the king's majesty might have all things up right with the said bishop of Rome and his highness' honour saved'. Ralph Sadler questioned Bryan on the matter, but Bryan then denied everything.[36]

The picture is a little confused. However, if Bryan's claim had contained any real substance, then Gardiner, like the Exeters, would have been speedily despatched to the Tower and the scaffold. So there was probably nothing much in it. But in the feverish climate of early June 1540 – with Cromwell on the offensive, Sampson and Wilson in the Tower on suspicion of Roman connections, Sampson questioned about what Gardiner had been saying to him, and even Cuthbert Tunstall interrogated by Cromwell's agents – with all this swirling around, Gardiner had every reason to fear that Cromwell might be about to produce something that would damage him.

Though Cromwell's exact plans will never be known for certain, it looks as though he had decided that attack was the best means of defence, indeed the only means now available to him. He was rooting for evidence – any scrap of evidence would do – that might fatally connect the bishops with Pole or Rome, both of whom Henry hated violently. In other words, Cromwell wanted to expose the bishops for what, in his eyes as a Protestant statesman, they really were – Papists in all but name. Though they had accepted the Royal Supremacy, they still remained attached to most Roman dogmas like clerical celibacy, the mass, transubstantiation and the saints. To have them condemned for popish connections would have been rough justice, but not, at least not by Tudor standards, a complete travesty of justice. Had this plan succeeded, then the king would see that the bishops were traitors, whereas the reformers, whatever their faults, were his true and loyal supporters. The Reformation might yet be saved.

Henry, however, badly needed Tunstall and Gardiner. Tunstall had been his special advisor on the disputed theological points with the Lutherans two years ago, while Gardiner had opened Henry's eyes for him on justification by faith. Whatever Henry felt about Sampson, he could hardly afford to lose the other two. Gardiner, moreover, unlike Cromwell, was now ready, willing and able to arrange a quick divorce for Henry so he could marry Catherine Howard. And if Cromwell's purge of prominent bishops had gone ahead unchecked, the result could have been the near obliteration of the Catholic party, and a triumphant Reformation party led by an all-powerful Lutheran Vicegerent. Henry would scarcely have countenanced such an imbalance of power even in the heady days of 1535–6, when Melanchthon was dedicating his *Loci* to the king, and Henry was looking forward to seeing Melanchthon personally. But now – now that the scales had fallen from his eyes on justification; now that he, at last, understood Lutheranism properly; now, besotted with Norfolk's voluptuous niece and desperate to be rid of his German wife – in these vastly changed times the prospect of Cromwell holding unlimited sway in government and parliament was unthinkable.

Yet despite the lure of Catherine and her faction, Henry drew back from the destruction of Cromwell. All too well the king knew what an outstanding chief minister he had. Cromwell's performance in parliament that spring was just one more reminder of how ably he could direct affairs of state in Henry's interests. No equal or no obvious successor lay in wait to replace him. Gardiner was a skilled lawyer and Norfolk a fine soldier, but neither was a match for Cromwell as Henry's chief minister, responsible for the entire gamut of government business ranging from church matters to foreign policy, security, finance and economics. If either of these two coveted the vicegerency or the chief place beside the king, he would be quickly disappointed. Furthermore, knowing the hostility of Pole and Rome towards him, Henry needed Cromwell and his efficient intelligence network to thwart and investigate these popish plot theories. Henry's attitude towards Lisle and Sampson strongly suggests that he suspected some mischief was afoot, and that Cromwell was not merely scare-mongering. So the king was caught in a dilemma. Perceptive as ever, Marillac read the situation well and summed it up with admirable succinctness – Cromwell and Gardiner were both in great favour with Henry, but 'things have come to the point where one of them must succumb'.[37]

An affair of the heart would decide the outcome. On 6 June Cromwell admitted to Secretary Wriothesley that 'one thing rested in his head, which troubled him – that the king liked not the queen, nor did ever'. When Wriothesley suggested that 'some way might be devised to relieve the king', Cromwell would only reply that it was a 'great matter'. Next day Wriothesley pressed him again, because if no solution could be found, then ere long 'they would all smart for it'. Again Cromwell merely replied that it was a 'great matter'. 'Let the remedy be searched for', begged Wriothesley. 'Well', said Cromwell – 'and then brake off from him'.[38]

This is Wriothesley's account of one of his last meetings with Cromwell, from which it is plain that Cromwell was not about to 'relieve the king' by ridding him of Anne and giving him Catherine. Other witnesses confirm this. Richard Hilles told a foreign correspondent that Cromwell, unlike Gardiner and others on the council, was known to be opposed to Anne's removal. Foxe has a story of Cromwell wishing 'his dagger in him that had dissolved or broken that marriage'.[39]

So this was Cromwell's 'great matter'. He was risking a clash not just with his enemies, but also with Henry. Cromwell would not actively rebel, or disobey a specific royal command; but he would oppose or stall on Anne's divorce even in discussions with the king's councillors, even though he, like everyone else, knew that Henry longed to be married to Catherine. No wonder this one thing troubled him more than any other. It does not sound as though he was unduly worried about the setback for reform, or the detention of Latimer and Barnes, prospects for both of whom had improved recently. Nor did he seem greatly concerned about the men from Calais still in jail. All this had become secondary. Even if Cromwell could rout his enemies and set his friends free once more, and reverse the setbacks the Reformation had suffered, he would still be left with one thing to trouble him – he could never force the king to love Queen Anne. And while Henry wanted a divorce, Cromwell could only stall and hedge. The search was on for something that would convict his rivals of illicit links with Rome, but his agents had yet to uncover anything damning. Never in his long, eventful life had he lived more dangerously. He could neither consent to Anne's demise, nor deliver the decisive blow against his foes.

Frustratingly, the surviving records give little useful clue to the flurry of conspiratorial activity between 7 and 9 June, though presumably Wriothesley reported his meeting with Cromwell to Henry. It must have been on 9 June that the king, egged on by Gardiner, turned fatefully against his minister. On the 10th Cromwell attended parliament along with Norfolk and Audley. Gardiner, still vulnerable in the face of Cromwell's onslaught against the bishops, stayed away. Cromwell's name appears on the parliamentary lists for the next six days, though without the 'p' ('present') beside it. After that it is gone. Which suggests that what followed that afternoon was sudden and hastily planned.[40]

Around mid-day Cromwell left parliament for the council chamber at Westminster to deal with affairs of state. At three o'clock the door opened, and in strode the Captain of the Guard with a royal warrant bearing the king's seal. The Captain announced the arrest of Thomas Cromwell, earl of Essex, on a charge of treason. Cromwell threw his bonnet to the floor, and fixed his eyes intently on the council members sitting at table. He appealed to their consciences to judge whether he was a traitor or not; but if this was the will of the king, he vowed he would renounce all pardon. All he would ask of Henry was a quick end. Some of his fellow councillors, emboldened now like never before, called him a traitor. Others said he should be judged by his own laws, words which themselves might be deemed to be treason. (Actually these were the king's laws, which all councillors, not just Cromwell, supported.) Norfolk rose from the table to reproach Cromwell for his villainies and snatch the order of St George from him. The earl of Southampton, soon to be made Lord Privy Seal in Cromwell's stead, tore off the Garter. Cromwell was then ushered into a waiting barge and rowed to the Tower, entering under the Traitors' Gate.[41]

17

The Pillar is Perished

'Many lamented, but more rejoiced'. So the historian, Edward Hall, noted in his chronicle as news spread through London and beyond of the arrest of Thomas Cromwell. Those rejoicing were mainly 'religious men'; they 'banqueted and triumphed together that night, many wishing that that day had been seven years before'. Others, fewer in number, 'lamented him and heartily prayed for him'.[1]

With entreaties and thanksgivings rising to heaven together, Marillac described how Cromwell's party, which lately had 'seemed the stronger', was thrown into turmoil by the downfall of its leader. Cranmer was still free, but he 'dare not open his mouth'. Marillac stressed the suddenness of it – 'the thing is the more marvellous as it was unexpected by everyone'.[2]

Henry had sent a special envoy to Marillac to tell him 'the truth' about Cromwell's arrest. The 'truth' went like this:

The substance was that the king, wishing by all possible means to lead back religion to the way of truth, Cromwell, as attached to the German Lutherans, has always favoured the doctors who preached such erroneous opinions and hindered those who preached the contrary; and that recently, warned by some of his principal servants to reflect that he was working against the intention of the king and the acts of parliament, he had betrayed himself and said he hoped to suppress the old preachers and have only the new, adding that the affair would soon be brought to such a pass that the king with all his power could not prevent it, but rather his own party would be so strong that he would make the king descend to the new doctrines even if he had to take arms against him.[3]

Henry had good reason to take Marillac into his confidence. Like King Francis, Henry's feelings towards the Lutherans had changed. Francis had long since abandoned his conciliatory approaches towards the Schmalkaldic League, and edicts had been issued to punish Protestant heretics throughout France. Francis was gratified to learn of Cromwell's arrest; his removal will 'tranquillise the kingdom to the common welfare of church, nobles and people', he replied to Marillac. 'Norfolk will remember what I said of it to him' when he was in France, Francis added intriguingly.[4]

Exactly what Francis said to Norfolk, and vice versa, is not recorded. If, as is likely, he expressed some sort of displeasure with Cromwell, then Norfolk would have mentioned it to Henry. With Henry in need of new allies following his rupture with Cleves and the Lutherans, he may have hoped that news of Cromwell's arrest would facilitate a renewed Anglo-French accord.

The drama of 10 June did not end with Cromwell's arrival in the Tower. The king's archers were soon at his house taking an inventory of his worldly goods, and certain valuables were taken away to the king's treasury. Then the news was formally announced to parliament and the European envoys as follows. Whereas Henry had ever sought to establish good order in religion for the glory of God, Cromwell had been 'secretly and indirectly' acting contrary to the king's will. Cromwell had said – this has been 'justified to his face by good witnesses' – that 'if the king and all the realm would turn and vary from his opinions, he would fight in the field in his own person with his sword in his hand'. Furthermore, Cromwell had been scheming to 'bring things to the frame that the king could not resist it'. For this treason and 'other great enormities', Cromwell had been committed to Tower. So the official version ran.[5]

When Richard Pate, Henry's envoy in Bruges, heard this he promptly wrote to Henry. He was appalled, he avowed dutifully, to learn that Cromwell could be so treacherously minded to 'pluck the sword' from the hand of the king, his benefactor. Cromwell should never have involved himself with religion, or tried to disturb the people with the 'false doctrine' which 'condemned good works, trusted too much in faith' and held that 'charity and the observance of the Ten Commandments could not be admitted as means to obtain the kingdom of heaven'. Cromwell should have obeyed his king, who had shown such exceptional patience in dealing with the 'adverse party in religion'.[6]

By the 'adverse party' Pate must have meant the party of hitherto acceptable reformers like Cromwell, Cranmer and their friends – those who were Lutheran or near enough. Pate was not referring to the sacramentaries, because they were arraigned and condemned under Henry, not dealt with 'patiently'. Like many, Pate interpreted Cromwell's fall as a sign that Henry's Lutheran experiment was over.

On the day after Cromwell's arrest (11 June), a full house gathered in Parliament hoping for more news, but there was none. Marillac then heard that a search of Cromwell's house had discovered several letters he had written to, and received from, the Lutheran lords of Germany. Marillac did not know the contents, but Henry was now 'so exasperated against him [Cromwell] that he would no longer hear him spoken of, but rather desired to abolish all memory of him, as the greatest wretch ever born in England'. Here is the first sign that an official disinformation campaign was getting underway: for it would be strange indeed if Cromwell, an astute man in a power struggle with his rivals, had been careless enough to leave incriminating letters lying around in his house.[7]

On 12 June Henry received two letters, one from Cranmer, the other from Cromwell. Cranmer, who might have been in some danger himself, admitted that Cromwell was his friend, whom he admired for his wisdom and diligence. If, however, it was true that Cromwell was a traitor, Cranmer was sorry he ever thought well of him, and prayed God devoutly to send Henry a counsellor he could trust. Because Cranmer was just as Lutheran as Cromwell – and everyone including the king knew it – this was a brave letter, though the spirit that composed it was a submissive one, always prepared, no matter how painful it would be, to defer to the king.[8]

Cromwell's letter was similar in tone, but markedly different in substance. He was made of sterner stuff. The charge of treason charge he rejected as utterly untrue. Never had he said, never would he have said, 'that thing which of itself is so high and abominable offence, as God knoweth, who I doubt not shall reveal the truth to your Highness' – this would be the claim that he was ready to 'fight in the field' against the king. 'Mine accusers your grace knoweth; God forgive them'. Calling God to witness, he protested his loyalty and service to Henry. Were it in his power, he would have made Henry 'so rich as ye might enrich all men ... so puissant that all the world should be compelled to obey you'. He thanked Henry for his past goodness, and denied saying those words to Rich and Throgmorton, thereby revealing the names of the chief witnesses against him. Cromwell continued:

> Your grace knoweth what manner of man Throgmorton hath ever been towards your grace ... and what Master Chancellor (Rich) hath been towards me, God and he best knoweth ... I would to Christ I had obeyed your often most gracious grave counsel and advertisements, then it had not been with me as it now is.

It is not completely clear from his involved prose whether he means that he wished he had heeded *Henry's* warnings about Rich and Throgmorton, or whether he regretted not being a more obedient servant to Henry. The context suggests the first, because he went on to repeat his denial of the charges against him, though he trusted in God and the king's mercy. He had never willingly offended Henry, and if he had offended unwillingly, he begged the king's pardon. He denied breaking a trust on a 'matter of great secrecy' – this would refer to Henry's feelings for Anne, which Henry had confided to Cromwell. He had, he admitted, sinned against God and the king, and had not always behaved as well as he should; but this was a very general confession, 'like forgive us our trespasses' and nothing specific. His offences towards Henry, 'God knoweth were never malicious or wilful'. He ended with a prayer for God's blessing on Henry and Edward. The letter was deferential in tone, full of appeals to the king's grace and mercy, all in the standard flowery, verbose Tudor style. But the spirit of its sender was defiant and unbowed.[9]

It is time now to consider the accusations against Cromwell more closely. The alleged crime was an unusual one, effectively religious treason. It was worse than heresy or holding heretical beliefs. Cromwell had been conspiring by all sorts of means, including the threat of insurrection, to defy Henry by bringing the Lutheran religion into the country against the king's wishes. He had been pursuing a religious agenda of his own, and because Henry was Defender of the Faith and God's anointed in England, this could be construed as treason, though there was no specific law against it.

We will deal with the charge of insurrection a little later, for it will feature again on the indictment. Meanwhile, regarding the more general charge that Cromwell had Lutheran ambitions contrary to the king's interest, the problem for his accusers was that he had a very obvious defence. Cromwell had indeed advocated the Lutheran policy – but Henry had willingly accepted it. Henry had been scarcely less eager than Cromwell to see Philip Melanchthon set foot in England; and, as recently as January, Henry was urging the Cleves delegation to carry on the religious dialogue. Moreover, though Henry had not committed himself to the *Augsburg Confession*, he and everyone else knew that Cromwell – like Cranmer, Latimer, Barnes and others – belonged to the Lutheran party in England. There was nothing treasonable about this *until* the Barnes–Gardiner clash at Lent, when Henry was brought forcibly face to face with the fact that an uncomfortable gap existed between him and Luther on justification by faith (see pp. 370–1). Had Cromwell been tried in a court, therefore, he would have run rings round the prosecution. His defence was impregnable – yes, he had indeed favoured the Lutheran policy, but he had always acted with the king's consent, and had broken neither the king's laws nor any royal proclamation. By definition, anything sanctioned by the king could never be treason.

So this aspect of the case against Cromwell was weak and badly thought out. It confirms the suspicion that his arrest, or at least the timing of it, was undertaken hurriedly, either as a panic measure in response to his own offensive against the bishops, or because Henry acted in a burst of rage on hearing from Wriothesley of Cromwell's unwillingness to make preparations for Anne's divorce. Most likely it was a combination of the two.

Cromwell's opponents quickly realized that they had made a hash of it. Anxious to cover up Henry's blunder over justification, they decided that the Lutheran charge would have to be ditched. They also decided to convict Cromwell by means of parliamentary attainder, not a formal trial. On 17 June a bill of attainder against him was brought into the Lords and read the next day. Two days later it received its second and third readings, and the Lords' unanimous assent. After this it went to the Commons. On 29 June the Commons returned its own version of the bill with the Lords' original. The attainder took the form of a petition to the king, an unusual though not unprecedented procedure. It implied that popular demand existed for Cromwell's removal, which cleverly deflected attention away from the real reason – Henry wanted to be rid of Cromwell so he could get divorced. Why the Commons had to produce a new version is not known because many of the relevant papers have been lost.[10]

Nevertheless, the substance of the attainder has survived. After opening with extravagant praise for the king's most beneficent rule, it deplores the fact that his majesty 'hath of late found, and tried, by a large number of witnesses, being your faithful subjects, and personages of great honour, worship and discretion', that Cromwell was the most false and corrupt traitor in the king's entire reign.[11]

In fact, no 'trial' had taken place. And one of these 'faithful' witnesses was Richard Rich, the man who had testified – by universal consent falsely – against Thomas More. Marillac, no special friend of Cromwell, called Rich the 'most wretched person in England'.[12]

Cromwell, the attainder continued, had released men convicted or suspected of treason: but no names were mentioned. He had misused and expropriated funds, and enriched himself with bribes – but no amounts or details were produced. He had also made appointments without royal approval. Again, names and offices are missing, and neither is there any evidence that someone improperly appointed was removed from office.

Now for the main charges. Minor charges like retainers and granting passports without authority can be passed over. No creditable historical writer has ever taken these seriously, and in any case they did not amount to treason.

First, Cromwell was a 'detestable heretic' who had spread heretical books (no titles or authors) especially against the Sacrament, all over the kingdom contrary to articles (unspecified) enacted by parliament. Cromwell had even said that it was 'lawful for every Christian man to be a minister of the said sacrament as well as a priest'. This sounds like an attempt to make Cromwell guilty by association with radical heretics like sacramentaries and Lollards. Cromwell was also a 'maintainer and supporter' of heretics. Again names, facts and evidence are all missing, though admittedly it was hardly a secret that Cromwell was a reformer. However, the attainder had now introduced a radically new crime of Cromwell's. He was not just a heretic, but the worst kind of heretic in Henry's view. Though the word 'sacramentary' is missing, the meaning is plain enough, and this was how the prisoner understood it.

The second main charge concerned treasonable talk. When in the parish of St Peter le Poer in London, certain preachers, including Robert Barnes, were reported to Cromwell, he had supported them traitorously, saying: 'If the king would turn from it, yet I would not turn; and if the king did turn, and all his people, I would fight in the field in mine own person, with my sword in my hand against him and all other'. Then he had boasted that 'if I live one year or two, it shall not lie in the king's power to resist or let it if he would'. The attainder's conclusion: Cromwell should be 'adjudged an abominable and detestable heretic and traitor', and suffer due punishment at the king's pleasure.

The offending words were allegedly spoken in the thirtieth year of Henry's reign, which would be 1539. However, no reason was offered to explain why such treason was concealed for up to a year and by whom; or why, with witnesses available, it was necessary to proceed by attainder instead of the normal court of law. It is also rather unlikely that Cromwell would have announced any such aggressive intent to hostile witnesses. Though it is almost certainly true that in the spring of 1540 Cromwell had been planning to oust the bishops opposed to him, there is nothing to suggest that he intended using armed force. He had no need to if convincing evidence could be found. He was not a military man, at least not since his youthful adventures. He had no standing army or militia under his own personal control that he could muster for rebellion. Further, the king *had* turned from the Lutheran way, but Cromwell was not fighting in the field, or preparing to. So the charge is disproved by events. Technically, in law, the fact that he had not carried out his threat might not absolve him entirely from his treasonable words – *if* the words had actually been spoken. Historians and readers, however, are free to consider not just the legal technicalities, but the true probability of guilt.

Also relevant is the fact that although the accusation is an expanded version of the claims made in Henry's message to Marillac, and in the official announcement after Cromwell's arrest, it has become progressively more sensationalized since then. Originally, to Marillac, the context made it clear that the faith for which Cromwell allegedly vowed to fight was the Lutheran one. By the time of the attainder, on the other hand, Cromwell had been turned into a sacramentary. The implications of this should not be overlooked. The German Lutherans strongly opposed armed rebellion against the civil power, and also offensive wars for the sake of religion. Luther believed in spreading the Gospel through the power of the Word, not the sword. However, it was not quite the same everywhere in Europe. The German radical Thomas Müntzer, a bitter enemy of Luther, had formented rebellion during the so-called Peasants' War, while Zwingli died fighting on the battlefield at Kappel. Using the same insurrectionist talk in this different context, therefore, had the effect of transforming Cromwell from a hitherto acceptable evangelical councillor into a seditious radical, a man more akin to Zwingli or even Müntzer than to Luther or Melanchthon.[13]

Nevertheless, though I know of no reputable historian who believes there is any truth in this charge against Cromwell, the possibility that it was not entirely made up must be reckoned with. What if Cromwell, quoting or adapting St Paul, had said: 'I will fight the good fight for the Gospel' – meaning it figuratively, not literally (2 Timothy 4:7)? By altering the wording ever so slightly, a malicious witness could easily have distorted the meaning completely. As for 'bringing things to such a pass that in a year or so it would not lie in the king's power to resist' – we have seen Cromwell strike against Sampson and send his agents after Tunstall and Gardiner. So it is not unthinkable that Cromwell might have said something like this: 'This time next year, by the grace of God, the Reformation will be so far advanced that none can stop it'. This, however, is all getting a little speculative. It is quite possible, maybe quite likely, that the accusation was wholly fabricated. Cromwell never claimed that something he said had been taken out of context or distorted. He simply denied ever using the words at all.

The evidence for the attainder's second main charge – that Cromwell was a closet sacramentary – is just as scant. Even

William Gray, a balladeer and former servant to Cromwell, who reluctantly accepted that his master had been justly condemned as a traitor, still denied he was a sacramentary. Writing after Cromwell's death, Gray insisted that Cromwell had always believed the consecrated bread 'to be the very body of Christ'. Intriguing, too, is the fact that during these few summer days Cromwell's heresy had changed its colours. When he was arrested he was Lutheran; when attainted, a sacramentary. So either the official version at the time of the arrest was false, or the attainder was false. But the official version, so far it went, is *true* – Cromwell *was* Lutheran, and everyone knew it. By simple elimination, therefore, the attainder has to be wrong.[14]

Another curiosity is that a complete silence has descended on Cromwell's alleged treasonous contacts with the Germans, evidenced by those letters found in his house. Marillac was not the only one unable to discover their dreadful secrets. They were never produced in evidence, never quoted against the prisoner, never even referred to afterwards. Not a trace of them remains in the calendared volumes of Cromwell's papers. These letters, if they existed at all, might have had some propaganda value for Anglo-French relations at the time of the arrest, but there was obviously nothing incriminating in them. Most likely they proved only the well-known fact that Cromwell had corresponded amicably with German leaders – quite acceptable and lawful in the 1530s.

So the original Lutheran charge had been dropped, and the sacramentary charge put in its place. One source for this accusation may have been Calais (see pp. 377–9) and especially the welcome Cromwell laid on for the alleged Calais sacramentaries when they arrived in England in May). Adam Damplip and his friends were latent liabilities for Cromwell. On his diplomatic mission to France in February, Norfolk had passed through Calais and spent a day or two there. During this brief visit he had the opportunity to hear Lisle's complaints about sacramentaries, and also Cromwell's apparent lack of zeal in dealing with them. Norfolk could then have reported all of this to Henry anytime after his return in March or April.

It would appear, however, that Norfolk did not in fact do this, because the potentially damaging Calais evidence was *not* part of the original charge against Cromwell. Nothing was said about Cromwell being a sacramentary when he was arrested on 10 June. The sacramentary charge was something dredged up afterwards, in between the arrest and the attainder.

So did someone, shortly after Cromwell's arrest, recall the Calais events and realize what valuable ammunition this was for the prosecution? Plausible though this sounds, it also has to be rejected, and for two reasons. First, Calais is not mentioned on the attainder. Second, most of the Calais sacramentaries, though not Botolf and the conspirators, were later discharged at the king's command under a general pardon issued in July 1540. Chancellor Audley brought the good news to them in prison. Audley warned them sternly to take great care in future because the pardon was not supposed to cover sacramentaries, 'and all of you are called sacramentaries', he admonished. Quite why they were released, when even the Lord Chancellor could not explain it, will have to remain a puzzle. The relevant point is that Barnes, Garrett and Jerome – prominent allies of Cromwell – were specifically exempt from that same general pardon. So Cromwell and the Calais men were *not* closely linked. Had they been among his well-known circle of evangelical protégées, they would never have been set free.[15]

The story of events in Calais, narrated in the *Lisle Letters*, is a hugely absorbing one, but it may be more peripheral than central in the drama of Cromwell's fall. Though it had the potential to do him great harm, it did not actually do so, at least not to any significant degree. Neither the arrest of Cromwell on 10 June, nor the attainder a few days later, relied on evidence from Calais. So something else must account for the sacramentary charge.

It should not be too difficult to guess what it was. The Gardiner party soon realized that the original Lutheran charge was far too feeble. Even they must have recognized that the 'fight in the field' story was a bit stretched. They knew, too, that Cromwell was a powerful man with supporters as well as enemies. They may have recalled Wolsey's attempted comeback after his first fall from power. Hall says that many who rejoiced to hear of Cromwell's arrest still feared 'lest he should escape, although he were imprisoned'. To be sure of Cromwell's speedy destruction, therefore, any potential support for him in the council, parliament or the country would have to be quickly and ruthlessly neutralized. So the sacramentary charge became the essential mortal blow, because under the first of the Six Articles – and this was wholly unique in medieval Christendom – a convicted sacramentary would be condemned to die with no hope of pardon, not even after a recantation. Even to sympathize with such a person would risk death by fire. Just in case this was not enough, a rider was added to the general pardon denying any forgiveness for heresies against the sacrament.[16]

Attention turns now to Anne of Cleves, with whom Cromwell's downfall is customarily connected. This connection may have originated with Gardiner, who, later in Mary's reign, reflected on how dangerous it was to 'take a share in the marriage of princes'. As an example he cited Cromwell for arranging Henry's marriage to Anne 'because he believed that Germany would ever afterwards assist this country for her sake; whereas the marriage only lasted one night and *ruined Cromwell*'.[17]

But if the Cleves marriage was all Cromwell's fault, or if Henry felt misled by Cromwell, why is this subject, and Anne's name, so conspicuously absent from the attainder? With Cromwell locked away and his enemies free to accuse him of anything they liked – and with complete impunity, for the prisoner had no opportunity to reply or defend himself – why not blame him for the whole sorry affair? Amazingly, the idea never crossed the mind of either the king or the Gardiner party. Despite all the subsequent tales about Cromwell pushing and tricking Henry into an ill-matched marriage, nothing he had said or done during the Cleves negotiations could be used against him at his own trial.

In fact, Gardiner was disingenuously covering up his own role in Cromwell's fall. The ruin of Cromwell was not the

Cleves marriage itself. He had easily survived that. Cromwell's ruin began with the Lenten crisis, and it was sealed by Henry's passion for Catherine Howard, stoked up by those feastings and entertainments laid on by wily Winchester at his Episcopal palace. Henry now saw his Lutheran Vicegerent as a threat to the king's headship of the church, and, even more provocatively, the barrier to Anne's removal and Catherine's coronation.

With Cromwell incarcerated, however, the way lay open for yet another royal divorce, and a written statement from the prisoner on the delicate subject of the consummation of the marriage, or lack of it, was now required. On 30 June, Henry sent a delegation to the Tower to demand that Cromwell declare, 'as he would answer before God at the dreadful day of judgement, and also upon the extreme danger and damnation of his soul', all that he knew of the marriage between Henry and Anne. The choice of Norfolk and Audley was doubly ironic. Henry may have intentionally selected one from the old faith and one from the new, but he may not have known that both of these men had, in happier times, pledged Cromwell their lifelong friendship and loyalty. During the Pilgrimage of Grace, Norfolk wrote to Cromwell with effusive thanks for various kindnesses, promising friendship for ever, begging him to keep his letter as proof 'if ever fault of promise shall be found in me'. Audley, after Cromwell helped him acquire Walden Abbey during the suppression, promised that 'ye shall have my heart and good will during my life'. This meeting in the Tower must have been one of the most painfully embarrassing that Audley had ever endured. Here was Cromwell, his former ally, attainted for the Zwinglian heresy when only a few months earlier, in February 1540, Audley had sent cordial greetings to Henry Bullinger, Zwingli's successor in Zürich.[18]

Anyway, Cromwell began to write as commanded. In unsparingly intimate detail, he related all that Henry had told him in private about his lack of feeling for Anne, and how the marriage had not been consummated. At the end Cromwell wished God's blessing on Henry and Prince Edward. Then, with 'heavy heart and trembling hand', he closed with an appeal to the king: 'Most gracious prince, I cry for mercy, mercy, mercy'. Alongside is Cromwell's signature, in the hand Henry knew so well. Firm, clear and muscular as ever, it betrays little sign of a 'trembling hand'.[19]

Some persons seize on these dramatic words in isolation as if Cromwell did nothing else but abjectly cry out for mercy when confined in the Tower. Nothing will ever stop people rejoicing in the misfortunes of good men, but by so doing they give their readers a wholly false picture. Cromwell had not finished his writing yet. A second letter was soon composed, and Cromwell asked that it too might be delivered to the king along with the first. The delegation was taken aback, initially unwillingly. Eventually Ralph Sadler, a Cromwell loyalist now compelled to go along with events, went to Henry to seek the king's permission to bring the letter to him. Henry agreed, though when he read it he might have wished he had not.

The letter began respectfully enough. Besides the questions about Anne, Cromwell had been asked to name anyone he knew who was untrue to the king. Cromwell coolly replied that had he known anyone thus minded, he would have detected them already. Then – and he had *not* been asked to do this – he took the time to answer the attainder charges. A touch of sarcasm mingled with deference as he acknowledged his conviction by parliament on the testimony of 'honest and probable' witnesses. As a loyal subject he was bound to obey laws, and he submitted meekly to their sentence. Then, suddenly, a few simple words wing their way like arrows straight at Henry's conscience: 'though laws be laws ... yet God is God' – and God knows that he had never been a traitor or sacramentary.

The exact wording here is difficult because the document is mutilated. What remains goes as follows:

Albeit laws be laws and in them have ... yet God is God and knoweth both ... towards your Majesty, and your Realm ... how dear your person was, is and ever hath ... much

grieved me, that I should be noted … e I hadde your laws
in my breast, and … mentary God he knowth the … he ton
and the other guiltless.

The last words – 'the one and the other guiltless' – are the crucial ones. Almost certainly they refer to the two main charges
on the attainder – that he was a sacramentary, and that he
threatened to 'fight in the field' against the king.

Cromwell had now aimed a penetrating double thrust at
Henry, a dutiful appeal to the king's goodness and mercy, but
also a fearless denial of the charges against him. If we may be
allowed to cut through the profligate Tudor prose and suggest
a paraphrase of these letters, the substance might read thus:
'Whatever man's laws or attainders may say, you King Henry
know that these charges are false, and God Almighty knows
they are false. I appeal to you to be righteous and merciful'.
Then, aware that he ought not to overdo this, a good deal of
typical Tudor bowing and scraping follows. Again he makes
confessions of human failings, though they are very general
and contain nothing specific. He also appealed to Henry to be
good to his son and the rest of his family. For reasons not stated,
much of the stuff about Anne is then repeated. The letter left
Henry much moved, says Foxe; he asked for it be read to him
three times over.[20]

The trial of Cromwell had now taken an unexpected twist.
To secure his divorce, Henry had demanded a written statement from his minister on the failed marriage, trusting that
a prisoner condemned to death would tell the truth lest he
perjure his soul. This statement Henry duly received. But the
accused, condemned unheard by attainder, though with wits
intact and quick as ever, had grasped this golden opportunity to appeal directly to the conscience of the king. Now if
Henry accepted the statement on the marriage, he was bound
to accept the denial of the charges of heresy and treason as
well, because it was composed under the same solemn oath.
So Henry was confronted with a piercing crisis of conscience.
He had hoped to wash his hands of Cromwell's death by shel-

tering behind that 'petition attainder', because if Cromwell could be condemned by an act of parliament rather than by royal fiat, then accountability would lie with parliament and not the king. Cromwell's unsolicited letter skewered that idea and forced Henry into the unwanted role of a supreme appeal judge. On him, no longer on parliament, lay responsibility for exercising justice, or committing judicial murder.

No man is entirely free from fear when the hour of death is at hand, but Cromwell's humility and appeals in his letters should not be crudely torn from their context. His bearing towards Henry was meek and humble, like any true and obedient servant's should be; but in the presence of Henry's delegates, and in a personal letter to the king, he also called the charges against him a pack of lies, invoking God Almighty and the Day of Judgement as his witness. This is not the spirit that Henry expected from his prisoners. Neither is it the air of a man possessed by fear. Had Cromwell been in state of terror, he would have confessed everything. An instinct for survival may have led him to hope that, even at this late stage, he might somehow be able to drive a wedge between Henry and the Gardiner faction and regain the king's trust.

But it was too late for that, and other men were more ready to gratify Henry's lust for Catherine Howard than Cromwell had been. Gardiner was already drawing up 'an order to be observed in the process for this matter', and divorce arrangements were soon underway. Audley delivered a speech in Convocation on 5 July on the danger to the realm if, though he prayed God would avert it, some accident were to befall Henry's only heir, Prince Edward. A second heir would then be needed, born 'in true and lawful wedlock'. Alas, it was 'doubtful' that such a blessing would be granted from this present marriage due to 'some impediments, which upon inquiry may arise to make the validity of that marriage dubious'. Audley proposed that a delegation from both Houses should go to the king and beg leave to speak with him on this most sensitive matter. The delegation was despatched straight away. Henry replied that he could neither deny nor grant the request, but thought it best to refer the matter to the clergy. As with the 'petition' attainder, everything was carefully stage-managed to make it look as though the initiative came from parliament, not the king.[21]

Another speech by Gardiner on 7 July stated the reasons why the marriage was invalid. Next day Convocation declared Henry free to marry another. Gardiner's prominent role suggests that he had already, before Cromwell's arrest, assured the king how quickly everything could be arranged. The reasons for divorce were these: Anne's pre-contract to Lorraine's son, Henry's unhappiness on meeting her and his reluctance to complete the marriage ceremony, the fact that the marriage was not consummated, and England's need of a male heir in the event of Prince Edward's untimely death. Not a word is to be found about Cromwell misleading the king about Anne. Nor did the woman forsaken raise even a murmur. No lady has ever consented to a divorce settlement more readily than Anne of Cleves. She was, she assured her anxious brother, entirely satisfied with the outcome. Anne is portrayed as pliant and biddable in popular accounts of her, with few historians willing to allow for the possibility that she saw Catherine Howard not as a rival she should be jealous of, but as an escape route to be thankful for. Whatever her true feelings, her adopted country was saddened to see her go. Marillac told Francis about the divorce and the 'great regret of the English people, who loved her and esteemed her much', and how it was 'commonly said' that Henry would soon marry 'a lady of great beauty'. If reports were to be believed, the ambassador added, 'he would say this marriage has already taken place and is consummated, but as this is kept secret he dare not yet certify it as true'. Edward Hall, who covered Anne's reception and marriage in abundant detail, notes her divorce in one terse, solitary paragraph.[22]

The reasons cited for the divorce, and the remarkable speed with which the arrangements were concluded, prove that ending this marriage was never a particularly 'great matter' for Cromwell. It would have been easy – very easy – for him to have survived the summer of 1540. A ruthless, scheming, unprincipled politician could have sacrificed Barnes, Garrett and Jerome, arranged Henry's divorce for him – Anne was willing enough – and remained comfortably in office as Lord Privy Seal and Vicegerent. Instead, Cromwell chose to make a stand for what really was his 'great matter', namely the Reformation in England. Thus the story of Cromwell's fall now closes.

A brief word is now needed on a few sub-plots going on around this time. A rumour was circulating that Cromwell planned to make himself king and marry Mary. The source was Castillon, Marillac's predecessor, and Henry ordered Ambassador Wallop in France to search out the facts. On 5 July Wallop promised he would send a letter from Castillon confirming the claims, but ten days later he had to tell Henry that no news had arrived. Letters continued between Henry and Wallop, but Henry must have lost interest in the tittle-tattle about the danger to his throne from King Thomas and the House of Cromwell. The rumour was never confirmed, and there is nothing about it on the attainder.[23]

On 17 July Barnes, Garrett and Jerome were attainted for heresies 'too long to be rehearsed'. All three, and particularly Barnes, had enjoyed the king's favour until Henry's blunder over faith and good works was expertly brought home to him by Gardiner at Lent. Their fate was sealed by their refusal to recant devoutly and their closeness to Cromwell, while others of the same faith like Cranmer, Latimer and Barlow lived on, for now, unharmed.[24]

Speculation abounded about what manner of death awaited Cromwell, condemned as both a heretic and a traitor. Convicted heretics died at the stake, while traitors were hanged, drawn and quartered unless they were fortunate enough to be of noble stock, in which case they were customarily beheaded. Some were saying Cromwell would be burned, others predicted hanging and quartering because he was not a nobleman by birth. Merriman writes that not until the morning of the execution did Henry commute the sentence to beheading, and he quotes Marillac as his source; but in fact Marillac merely says that 'grace was given him' to die by the axe – he does not say that grace was given only on the day of execution. Despite all the gossip, there was probably never any real danger of either disembowellment at Tyburn or the fires of Smithfield for the former Vicegerent. From Buckingham to More, Fisher and Exeter, Henry's prominent victims were allowed to die with dignity. Besides, though Cromwell's attainder pompously notes his humble origins – 'a man of very base and low degree' before the king exalted him – it thereafter consistently refers to him as 'Thomas Cromwell, earl of Essex', not plain, low born Mr Cromwell.[25]

Little is known of how Cromwell wiled away the time when he was not receiving delegations from the king. Foxe records that official visitors were a touch disquieted by the prisoner's unexpectedly calm and composed demeanour. Foxe gives no details, but his source may have been Ralph Sadler, Cromwell's former secretary who lived on till Elizabeth's reign. Cromwell's last surviving letter, to the Council on 24 July, concerned the so-called Rochepot affair. This had been discussed already (p. 330), but for reasons not stated he was now required to make a statement about it, and he denied taking money unlawfully. This apart, the letter has little interest value except that the style, the grasp of detailed facts and the carefully constructed arguments all point to a man who had lost none of his faculties during his two-month confinement.[26]

'My prayer', Cromwell once said, 'is that God give me no longer life than I shall be glad to use my office in edification and not in destruction'. In a way unforeseeable, yet strangely merciful, that prayer was now answered. Cromwell could only have survived the summer of 1540 by an act of destruction, either the cynical sacrifice of his allies, or the brutal culling of his enemies on rather flimsy evidence. Instead, he was able to mount the scaffold on 28 July with a quiet conscience, and to deliver his valedictory address.[27]

'I am come hither to die', he told the crowd, 'and not to purge myself, as some think peradventure that I will'. So anyone expecting a phoney, wretched confession would be disappointed. He acknowledged he had offended God and the king, and he sought the forgiveness of both; but this was another purely general admission of human failure, with nothing precise. 'I die', he went on, 'in the Catholic faith, not doubting in any article of my faith … nor in any sacrament of the church'. An ironic gallows humour was now at play. He used the word 'Catholic' in the sense that Melanchthon did in the Augsburg Confession, and as Cranmer subsequently did, meaning the 'Holy Catholic and Apostolic Church' of the New Testament and the Nicene Creed, not the medieval Roman church. Then once again came a bold denial of the charges against him, followed by a piece of classic Cromwellian inscrutability:

> Many have slandered me, and reported that I have been a bearer of such as have maintained evil opinions; which is untrue: but I confess, that like as God, by His Holy Spirit, doth instruct us in the truth, so the devil is ready to seduce us; and *I have been seduced*.

If Cromwell was not guilty as charged, as he claimed, then the words in my italics must have puzzled his hearers. They could have been the sort of sweeping, general confession that all believers make from time to time, like 'forgive us our trespasses', or 'all we like sheep have gone astray' (Matthew 5:12; Isaiah 53:6). Or maybe Cromwell, a little out of touch after nearly two months in the Tower, was under the impression that affairs in Calais had contributed more to his downfall than was actually the case. If so, the 'evil opinions' could be the sacramentaries' opinions, and Cromwell had been seduced, not into believing them himself, but by sacramentaries like Damplip pretending to be Lutherans.

A calculated ambiguity, so typical of Cromwell throughout his life, marks these words. He was leaving his hearers waiting and guessing, right up to the last prayer. When that moment arrived, however, all vagueness vanished. He committed his soul to Christ in the sure hope of the blessed resurrection, calling on Him for mercy. For 'I see and acknowledge that there is in myself no hope of salvation, but all my confidence, hope and trust is in thy most merciful goodness. I have no merits or good works which I may allege before thee'. Here was a withering attack on the work righteousness of medieval religion. This is what *he* meant by 'Catholic faith'. Justification by faith alone – the faith that Robert Barnes had preached in Lent, the very faith that Henry had rejected – was now being proclaimed from the scaffold. Merriman has misinterpreted the speech if he thinks that Cromwell parroted a prepared statement, authorised by Henry, in return for commuting the sentence from quartering to beheading. It is highly unlikely that Henry would tell Cromwell to preach justification by faith to a large crowd in public.[28]

The prayer continued, its evangelical flame burning brighter than ever:

> Of sins and evil works, alas, I see a great heap … but through thy mercy, I trust to be in the number of them to whom *thou wilt not impute their sins; but will take and accept me for righteous and just*, and to be the inheritor of everlasting life … Most merciful Saviour … let thy blood cleanse and wash away the spots and foulness of my sins. *Let thy righteousness hide and cover my unrighteousness.* Let the merits of thy Passion and blood-shedding be satisfaction for my sins …'

The entire prayer, but especially the words in my italics, is pure Lutheran. Derived from St Paul, the teaching is not just that God, for Christ's sake, forgives the sinner. It goes further than that. God entirely exonerates, He freely justifies. The righteousness that is found only in Christ is thereby *imputed* to the believer, so 'there is no condemnation to those in Christ Jesus' (Romans 3:21–6; 8:1). And with this classic Lutheran confession, Thomas Cromwell bid the world farewell.[29]

That same day, Henry married Catherine Howard. Three days later a gruesome double execution was staged, almost certainly on Henry's orders. Barnes, Garrett and Jerome suffered the common fate of heretics. According to witnesses, death came mercifully quickly. Less than a stone's throw away, three priests of the old faith – Thomas Abel, Richard Featherstone and Edward Powell – were hanged, drawn and quartered as traitors for resisting the Royal Supremacy. 'Good Lord!' a foreign witness exclaimed. 'How do these people live? Here are the Papists hanged, there are the anti-Papists burned'. Two more of Cromwell's loyal men – the Bible translators Rogers and Coverdale – sought refuge on the continent, where they stayed until Edward's reign. Rogers went to Wittenberg, and after a recommendation from Melanchthon he accepted a pastorate in Germany. When he heard the news from England, Melanchthon called down the wrath of God on Henry for the slaying of Cromwell. In Rome, by contrast, it was noted approvingly that Henry had, at last, taken a turn in the right direction by punishing his recalcitrant chief minister.[30]

Other players in the Cromwellian drama enjoyed mixed fortunes. Though the Calais sacramentaries had been fortuitously pardoned, most of the Calais conspirators were hanged and quartered. An exception was Botolf, the ringleader, who became one of the luckiest men of Henry's reign. He was picked up in Louvain and then set free again thanks to a legal technicality. How he ended his days is not known. Adam Damplip was detained in London for two more years before being sent back to Calais to face more heresy charges, and there this incorrigible troublemaker eventually died a traitor's death for receiving a French crown of Cardinal Pole. The main witnesses against Cromwell – Rich and Throgmorton – were rewarded for their services with lands and allowances. Bishop Sampson was not released until 1541. Lord Lisle, though never convicted, died in the Tower in March 1542, shortly after learning he had been pardoned. The fact that Henry did not release these men immediately after Cromwell's fall suggests that the king was not entirely sure that the suspicions of collaboration with Pole and Rome were false.[31]

Hugely contrasting fates awaited the two leading ladies in the story. Catherine Howard was barely on the throne before she began cuckolding her doting, but increasingly bulky and unappealing husband. Her affection for younger, more handsome men was soon uncovered, and like Anne Boleyn before her she was sent to the block – this time there is no room for any doubt about the queen's guilt. Meanwhile Anne of Cleves, the rejected wife whose arrival in England provided the overture to the drama, was settling contentedly into her new life as the king's 'good sister', with two fine houses, parks and servants, and an allowance of 500 shillings a year.[32]

If, as Hall says, those who rejoiced at Cromwell's demise really did outnumber those who lamented, then the mourners far outclassed their gloating rivals in eloquence. Shortly after seeing Cromwell die, Thomas Wyatt, the poet, penned his own epitaph of his patron, mentor and friend:[33]

> The pillar perished is whereto I leaned,
> The strongest stay of my unquiet mind;
> The like of it no man again can find –
> From east to west, still seeking though he went –
> To mine unhap, for hap away hath rent
> Of all my joy, the very bark and rind,
> And I, alas, by chance am thus assigned
> Dearly to mourn till death do it relent.
> But since that thus it is by destiny,
> What can I more but have a woeful heart,
> My pen in plaint, my voice in woeful cry,
> My mind in woe, my body full of smart,
> And I myself, myself always to hate
> Till dreadful death do ease my doleful state?

Epilogue

In January 1541 John Wallop, Henry's ambassador in France, reported a meeting he had just had with King Francis. Among other matters, Francis made some reference to Cromwell's 'naughty pretended intentions … as well concerning your highness as my lady Mary'. The rumour of Cromwell's designs on Mary had stubbornly persisted, even though no evidence was ever produced.[1]

Wallop presumably expected Henry to find this story diverting, but his flippancy was woefully mistimed. By now Henry had lost interest in tales of Cromwell's alleged misdeeds, whether regarding Mary or not. One day in March, says Marillac, Henry was bitterly berating his ministers, because 'upon light pretexts and by false accusations, they made him put to death the most faithful servant he ever had'. Thus out of all Henry's prominent casualties, Thomas Cromwell became the only one to receive what amounted to a posthumous royal pardon.[2]

Tudor justice had finally prevailed. For of Catherine Howard's guilt there is no doubt. Anne Boleyn and the Exeters were definitely making mischief of some sort, though exactly what sort may remain disputed. And to say that More and Fisher really were Papalists is neither to applaud nor justify the manner of their deaths, but at least they were granted the honour of dying for deeply held convictions. They were not falsely accused of being, say, closet Pelagians, or of seeking the king's injury. But the attainder of Cromwell is lies from first to last, as the king's own words confirm.

What moved Henry to anger with his surviving councillors is not clear – maybe the machinery of government was not running quite as smoothly as before – but this was no isolated royal outburst. Two years later the Gardiner party staged a coup against Cranmer, but this time they failed to win Henry's support. Knowing what was afoot the king turned double agent and disclosed the entire plot to Cranmer. 'Do you not think', Henry demanded, with memories of Cromwell seemingly fixed in his mind, 'that if they have you once in prison, three or four false knaves will soon be procured to witness against you and condemn you, which else now being at your liberty dare not once open their lips or appear before your face?'[3]

It was convenient for Henry to put all the blame on Cromwell's foes, though not especially convincing. As Shakespeare's Brutus said of Mark Antony – 'he can do no more than Caesar's arm when Caesar's head is off' – so even wily Winchester, for all his craft and artifices, could never have touched a hair of Cromwell's head without Henry's sanction. It was the king himself who, uncontrollably infatuated by Catherine Howard, had used Gardiner and his faction to strike his 'most faithful servant' down. If proof is needed, let the king himself provide it. When Henry, in the last days of his life, named a Council of Regency for Prince Edward, Gardiner's name was not on it. Sir Anthony Browne asked whether this was an oversight, but Henry told him to hold his peace; he had left Gardiner out deliberately because of his 'troublesome' nature. 'Marry', went on Henry, 'I myself could use him, and rule him to all manner of purposes, as seemed good unto me; but so shall you never do'.[4]

Why it 'seemed good' to Henry to reject his foremost minister for a giddy nineteen year-old girl, hopelessly ill fitted to be queen of England, only Henry will ever know. It did not 'seem good' to everybody except perhaps, though all too briefly, the victorious Gardiner party. Norfolk and other councillors assured Marillac that Anglo-French relations would be more productive now that the main 'obstacle' to them, that is, Cromwell, was removed. Yet not long after the demolition of this 'obstacle', Henry was at war not only with France but Scotland as well. Cromwell's non-interventionist foreign policy was discarded, and his management of the national economy badly missed as inflation rose sharply in the 1540s. With the costs of Henry's modest military successes quickly spiralling out of control, the king was forced to borrow huge sums from foreign money markets, debase the English currency more severely than ever, re-mint coins and levy yet more taxes from his long-suffering subjects. By the end of his reign, and for little substantial gain, the financial soundness bequeathed by his father and sustained by Cromwell was squandered, and Henry handed on to his heirs a crippling burden of debt that remained outstanding well into Elizabeth's reign. 'Would God England had a Cromwell', exclaimed a harassed Dr Wilson, Principal Secretary to Elizabeth, one day – and he lived in an age overflowing with political and cultural talent.[5]

To turn from the immediate effects of Cromwell's downfall to his place in English history, I have argued that he was a reformer but not a destroyer of the old church. I also believe that he would have continued in this vein even if Henry, like the Scandinavian kings, had accepted the *Augsburg Confession* and granted Cromwell the authority to oversee the Reformation in England. His was a spirit that sought to reform for the better rather than uproot and begin again. His policy regarding shrines and monasteries may appear to run counter to this argument, but these were not exclusively Protestant or Cromwellian measures. The value of much medieval piety had been critiqued by Renaissance humanists like Erasmus as well as by reformers like Luther, and the English dissolution might even have gone ahead without Cromwell, though less efficiently. At the core of the Reformation lay the theology of salvation, not religious houses or traditions. Cromwell mastered the new learning from Germany with an accomplishment that many bishops failed to match, and by means of printed material, persuasion, evangelical appointments, articles and injunctions he used all his skill and ingenuity to restore England to the true faith of the Gospel – or, as Robert Aske accused him during the Pilgrimage of Grace, to fill the realm with heresy. This is a highly charged subjective issue, a matter of conscience even, so Cromwell is destined to remain for ever a controversial figure.[6]

Even for those who would take Aske's side, however, this is the head and front of Cromwell's offending. Elsewhere the same Aske, in a more generous moment, conceded that Cromwell had done him no personal harm. Aske's candid admission sets in context the hostility that Cromwell faced from certain quarters, chiefly the established clergy and also, though perhaps to a lesser extent, the nobility. He was hated not for his ruthlessness or cruelty – those who machinated his ruin were far more ruthless than he – but because, to quote Marillac again, he was the 'principal author' of the Reformation in England. What his opponents feared and loathed was not the bloody, corrupt henchman of Merriman's description, but the formidable intellect, energy and learning of this low born layman who had gained the king's confidence and trust to the extent that he was appointed Vicegerent in the church. So long as Cromwell lived, the existing order felt threatened. He never persuaded Henry to be reconciled to Luther, but loyalists of the old religion were always afraid that he might.[7]

It is one of history's many ironies that the visions, hopes and prayers of this layman were eventually fulfilled in the spiritual realm but not the political. As a Reformer of the church he laid the foundation for the future Protestant England, but he neither visualized nor desired the future constitutional monarchy. Mindful of the previous troubled century, he saw a powerful Tudor monarchy as the guarantor of liberty, stability, civil peace and prosperity. He believed in a righteous kingly absolutism, a prince accountable to God alone. This prince, however, would govern through parliament, not by royal decree. Though the Royal Supremacy was believed to be the divine will, the means of implementing it on earth became parliamentary statute. Consequently Henry's reign, and particularly Cromwell's time, witnessed a strengthening of both crown and parliament, and it takes its distinctive place in English parliamentary and constitutional history, as well as church history.

Knowing the course of the seventeenth as well as sixteenth century, it is easy for us to see an innate tension between the concept of a strong monarchy and an increasingly prestigious parliament. How long could such a parliament be expected to remain unquestioningly loyal to the royal will? The Tudor system needed a minister to manage parliament in the king's interest, and in Cromwell it had one; but no generation can provide an absolutely fail-safe insurance against the mistakes of those who are to follow. No one in Henry's reign could have foreseen the future conflict, still a century ahead, between a Stuart monarch implacably convinced of his divine right, and a parliament so assertive of its own rights that it could take up arms against the king and plunge the nation into the misery of civil war. With men like Cromwell administering it, the Tudor state proved to be an impressively stable one.

His tenure of office as the king's chief minister, if dated from the Act of Appeals to his fall, was a comparatively short seven years, less than half the period enjoyed by Wolsey. Much was achieved, but much remained unfinished when he died. The Royal Supremacy was settled, but reform of the church had a long way to go, and many bills on economic and social affairs were stifled during debates and on committees. Despite the incompleteness, however, the achievement was an enviable one, and only his most churlish opponents could gainsay his rightful place alongside Wolsey and the Cecils as the ablest ministers of state in the Tudor and early Stuart age. He might even stand above them. There is also something especially estimable about distinguished men of state who also treasure the arts and humanities and who willingly befriend and win the good opinion of talented writers, musicians and artists.

S. R. Gardiner, the great historian of seventeenth-century England, said of Robert Cecil that he was 'the first and greatest of that unhappy race of statesmen who were trained for their work as for a profession'. Thomas Cromwell was untrained for statesmanship, but not unprepared. His adventures as a fugitive, traveller and soldier of fortune taught him how to survive, to escape poverty, to learn languages, to hate war and cherish peace; as an accountant, merchant and lawyer he acquired the skills needful to administer the kingdom as the king's Principal Secretary; while his love of the humanities and theology, and his skill in them, ensured that his pre-eminence in the church might be resented but never disputed on grounds of inability or unfitness. In a way he could never have foreseen as a young man his life's experiences dovetailed from many diverse directions to equip him for high office more effectively than any formal training could have done. It was this that gave him a compelling sense of calling, a subject he touched on in his letter to Nicholas Shaxton (see p. 291): 'It hath pleased His Goodness to use me as an instrument, and to work somewhat by me, so I trust I am as ready to serve Him in my calling to my little power'. This is semi-religious language not often used by men of state. Cromwell was one of the few to do so.[8]

Of Cromwell's personal character, enough has been said in Chapter 13. There and elsewhere I argued that allegations of ruthlessness and brutality are mainly exaggerated and frequently distorted, but it will do little good to go over all this again. To arouse wildly contrasting emotions – intense aversion as well as deep admiration – is a mark of distinction that elevates men like Cromwell above the general mass of mankind.

Because history is more than just a study of dry facts and past events, it is not being sentimental to feel drawn to the story of the poor man's son exalted to the king's right hand; or to reflect on the tragedy of a great minister destroyed not by greed for power, or the vaulting ambition of a Macbeth, but by the capriciousness of the prince he had served so well. If, however, the souls of the departed really are able to observe the course of events in the life they have left behind,

Cromwell would not approve of sombre and ultimately inconclusive ruminations. Nor would Cromwell, that great survivor and eternal optimist, have shared the sorrow and gloom that overwhelmed his friends after his passing. He would frown sternly on anything disparaging of his erstwhile earthly king. Cromwell's devotion to Henry, for him a sacred as well as secular duty, was absolute and unconditional, willingly and gladly given. He was content to leave the world at the king's pleasure. After the loss of his wife and children, and the fall of his master, it was Henry who had raised Cromwell above the lords, nobility and dignitaries of the realm, entrusting to him unparalleled authority in church and state. The same Henry had allowed him to bring the Gospel into England and bestow the English Bible, arguably Cromwell's proudest single achievement, on every parish in the land. And whatever his own motives, it was Henry who spared Cromwell the miseries of old age, sickness and failing health, granting him instead a mercifully quick end on Tower Hill; where, no longer constrained by the demands of his office, he could proclaim more freely than ever the message of Christ's redeeming grace to the assembled throng that summer morning.

If this 'most faithful servant' were allowed to write his own epitaph, he might describe himself rather modestly. He might prefer to say, as the disciples were enjoined to say: 'We are unworthy servants; we did only our duty' (Luke 17:10).

Notes

Abbreviations Used in the Notes

AC	*Augsburg Confession*
Apology	Philip Melanchthon's *Apology of the Augsburg Confession*
Bandello	*Tutte le opere di Matteo Bandello,* 2 vols
BIHR	*Bulletin of the Institute of Historical Research*
BSLK	*Die Bekenntnisschriften der Evangelisch-Lutherischen Kirche*
Brecht	Martin Brecht's biography of Luther (3 vols)
BL	British Library
Burnet	G. Burnet, *History of the Reformation of the Church of England* (7 vols)
Cavendish	Cavendish, G., *The Life and Death of Cardinal Wolsey,* ed. R. Sylvester
CR	*Corpus Reformatorum* (28 vols)
Cranmer, *Misc. Writings*	*Miscellaneous Writings and Letters of Thomas Cranmer*
CSP For.,	*Calendar of State Papers, Foreign*
CSP Milan	*Calendar of State Papers, Milan*
CSP, Span	*Calendar of State Papers, Spanish* (15 vols in 20)
CSP, Ven	*Calendar of State Papers, Venetian* (9 vols)
Ellis	*Original Letters Illustrative of English History,* ed. H. Ellis (12 vols)
Elton, *Policy*	G.R. Elton, *Policy and Police: The Enforcement of Reformation in the Age of Thomas Cromwell*
Elton, *Studies*	G.R. Elton, *Studies in Tudor and Stuart Politics and Government* (3 vols)

Elton, *Tudor Cons*	G.R. Elton, *Tudor Constitution: Documents and Commentary* (2nd edn)
Elton, *Tudor Rev*	G.R. Elton, *The Tudor Revolution in Government*
ET	*Epistolae Tigurinae*
HJ	*Historical Journal*
JEH	*Journal of Ecclesiastical History*
Foxe	*Acts and Monuments of John Foxe* (8 vols)
Hall	E. Hall, *A Chronicle containing the History of England … to the end of the reign of Henry VIII*
Holinshed	R. Holinshed, *Chronicles of England …* (6 vols)
Kaulek	*Correspondence Politique de Mm. de Castillon et de Marillac … ed. J. Kaulek*
Lambeth	Lambeth Palace Library
Lisle Letters	*Lisle Letters*, ed M. St C. Byrne (6 vols)
LJ	Journals of the House of Lords
LP	*Letters & Papers, Foreign & Domestic, of the Reign of Henry VIII, 1509-47* (21 vols)
LW	*Luther's Works: American edn* (55 vols)
MBW	*Melanchthons Briefwechsel* (15 vols)
Merriman	R.B. Merriman, *The Life and Letters of Thomas Cromwell* (2 vols)
OL	*Original Letters,* ed. H. Robinson (2 vols)
Pocock	*Records of the Reformation,* ed. N. Pocock (2 vols)
Ribier	Ribier's *Lettres et memoires d'estat*
PRO	Public Records Office
PS	Parker Society
SCJ	*Sixteenth Century Journal*
SP	*State Papers* (11 vols)
SR	*Statutes of the Realm*
Tappert	*The Book of Concord: The Confessions of the Evangelical Lutheran Church,* ed. Tappert
TRHS	*Transactions of the Royal Historical Society*
TRP	*Tudor Royal Proclamations*
UP	University Press
VA, England	Vienna Archives Haus-, Hof-und Staatsarchiv: Staatenabteilungen England, Diplomatische Korrespondenz
WA	*Dr. Martin Luthers Werke* (Weimar edn, 61 vols)
WA, Br	*Dr. Martin Luthers Werke: Briefwechsel* (18 vols)
Wright	*Letters relating to the Suppression of Monasteries* (ed.) Wright
Wriothesley	Wriothesley's *Chronicle of England* (2 vols)

1. In my Lord the Cardinal's Service

1   *Othello* Act 2, Scene 3.
2   *CSP Span., 1534–5*, no. 228. A report by the Venetian ambassador in England to the Venetian senate dated 3 June 1535 also included a short biography of Cromwell, but for reasons best known to themselves, the transcribers left out all the details. See *CSP Ven.* 5, no. 54, p. 26, footnote.
3   From Pole's *Apologia ad Carolum Quintum*, printed in Merriman 1, p. 18.
4   Bandello 1, pp. 1010–11.
5   Foxe 5, pp. 362, 365, 392–3.
6   Merriman, 1 pp. 1–8; *Calendar of Close Rolls ... Henry VII* (London, HMSO, 1963), vol. 2, 1500–1509, no. 57.
7   Ellis 10, pp. 237–9; PRO SP 1/89, fol. 6 = *LP* 8, no. 11; *CSP Span., 1534–5*, no. 165, p. 468. The admission of the mother's age is discussed in context in chap. 7.
8   PRO SP 1/87, fols 97–9 = *LP* 7, no. 1515.
9   Foxe 5, pp. 363–5.
10 *LP* 1, no. 1473 (3556); Elton, *Studies* 3, p. 374; *CSP Span., 1534–5*, no. 228; Merriman 1, p. 12.
11 Foxe 5, p. 365; *LP* 1, no. 3195 (5355); Elton, *Studies* 3, p. 374; G.R. Elton, *Reform & Renewal: Thomas Cromwell and the Common Weal* (Cambridge, 1973), p. 34. Cromwell may have made further visits to Rome on the subject of Boston pardons, because in April 1529 the Guild of our Lady in Boston thanked him for all that he had done for them: *LP* 4 (3), no. 5460.
12 *LP* 3 (1), nos 1026, 1289, 1963; *LP* 3 (2), nos 2437, 2441, 2557.
13 *LP* 3 (2), nos 2447, 2461, 2624, 2754, 3015. For miscellaneous legal affairs see also *LP* 3 (2), nos 2753, 3081, 3502 (from his cousin, Henry Wykys), 3530, 3681 (2).
14 The speech is printed in Merriman 1, pp. 30–44. See also the note in Elton, *Tudor Const.*, p. 309, fn. 170.
15 Merriman 1. p. 313.
16 Elton, *Studies* 1, pp. 277–80.
17 Merriman 1, p. 47; Elton, *Studies*, p. 375; *LP* 3 (2), no. 3657; *LP* 4 (1), nos 106 (7), 294, 304, 327, 368, 388 (2, 7, 2), 393 (2), 643, 681, 969, 979.
18 Merriman 1, pp. 314–15; *LP* 4 (1), nos 1348 (2), 1386, 1794.
19 *LP* 4 (1), nos 1989 (2), 2106, 2229, 2347–8; *LP* 4 (2), nos 2375, 2387, 2400, 2755.
20 *LP* 4 (1), no. 1732; Ellis 9, pp. 338–9.
21 Merriman 1, p. 314; *LP* 4 (1), nos 99, 989–90, 1137, 1138 (2), 1499 (3).
22 J. Youings, *The Dissolution of the Monasteries* (London, 1971), p. 27; Merriman 1, pp. 319–21; *LP* 4 (1), nos 1881, 1964, 2193, 2217; *LP* 4 (2), nos 2538 (8), 2738; *SP* 1, pp. 155–6, 261; *LP* 4 (2), no. 3461.
23 *Remains of Coverdale*, ed. G. Pearson (Cambridge, 1846), pp. 490–92; J.F. Mozley, *Coverdale and his Bibles* (London, 1953), pp. 2–3.
24 *LP* 4 (2), nos 2844, 2989–91, 3014, 3032, 3053 (1), 3079; Merriman 1, pp. 316–18.

25 Foxe 5, p. 365; Cavendish, pp. 37–41, 209.
26 *LP* 14 (2), nos 3197, 4613, 4884, 5034; *LP* 4 (3), nos 6429, 6744.

2. To Make or Mar

1   From the vast amount of material on Henry's first divorce, the follow-
    ing are some of the best accounts (apologies are offered to anyone who
    feels unjustly excluded): G. R. Elton, *England under the Tudors*, chaps 5–6;
    J. Guy, *Tudor England* (Oxford, 1988), pp. 116–53; V. Murphy, 'Literature
    and Propaganda of Henry VIII's First Divorce', in *The Reign of Henry
    VIII, Politics, Policy and Piety*, ed. D. MacCulloch (Basingstoke, 1995),
    pp. 135–58; R. Rex, *Henry VIII and the English Reformation* (Basingstoke,
    1993), pp. 6–11; R. Rex: *The Theology of John Fisher* (Cambridge,
    1991), pp. 162–83; J. Ridley, *Henry VIII* (London, 1984), pp. 157–69; J.
    Scarisbrick, *Henry VIII* (London, 1968), pp. 163–239; D. Starkey, *Six
    Wives: The Queens of Henry VIII* (London, 2003), part 2.

2   Rex, *Henry VIII*, p. 7; Scarisbrick, *Henry VIII*, pp. 139–52.

3   See discussions in Rex, *Theology of John Fisher*, p. 164; Scarisbrick, *Henry
    VIII*, pp. 168–9.

4   Hall, p. 728.

5   Cavendish, pp. 29–35.

6   *CSP Span., 1527–9*, no. 69, pp. 193–4; no. 113, pp. 273, 277; no. 224, pp.
    432–3; Cavendish, pp. 43–4; *LP* 4 (2), no. 3318.

7   *LP* 4 (2), nos 4314, 4433, 4560–61, 4837–8.

8   Merriman 1, pp. 318–25; *LP* 4 (2), nos 4755, 4778, 4872; D. MacCulloch,
    Thomas Cranmer: A Life (New Haven and London, 1996), p. 44.

9   Hall, pp. 755–6.

10 *CSP Span., 1527–9*, no. 550, pp. 789–90; no. 586, p. 846. For a some-
    what more sympathetic interpretation of Wolsey's dealings in the Great
    Matter, see P. Gwyn, *The King's Cardinal: The rise and fall of Thomas Wolsey*
    (London, 1990), chapter 12.

11 Cavendish, pp. 94–5; *CSP Span., 1527–9*, no. 614, p. 877; no. 586, p. 841;
    no. 621, pp. 885–6.

12 Foxe 4, pp. 599–601.

13 *LP* 4 (2), nos 4388, 4542; Hall, p. 750; Merriman 1, pp. 56–63.

14 Merriman 1, p. 325; *LP* 4 (3), nos 5757, 5787, 5792, 5809–11, 6219, 6722.

15 *CSP Span., 1529–30*, no. 135; Ellis 1, p. 310; Cavendish, pp. 96 (15–19),
    232.

16 *LP* 4 (3), nos 5983, 6011, 6018–19.

17 Cavendish, pp. 104–5.

18 Cavendish, pp. 105–110. NB: On two occasions, once to Cavendish and
    once in the presence of Wolsey and others at his last dinner, Cromwell
    claimed that he never received any increase in salary from the cardi-
    nal. On neither occasion was he contradicted. See Cavendish, pp. 105
    (12–14), 109 (23–5).

19 Ellis 10, pp. 171–2.

20 Cavendish, p. 112 (21–5); Merriman 1, pp. 67–9.

21 Elton, *Tudor Rev.*, pp. 77–8; S. Lehmberg, *The Reformation Parliament: 1529–1536* (Cambridge, 1977), p. 27.

22 Hall, p. 765; Lehmberg, *Reformation Parliament*, pp. 69, 76–83.

23 See discussions in Elton, *Studies* 2, pp. 107–35; Lehmberg, *Reformation Parliament,* pp. 83–6; Cavendish pp. 112–13; *LP* 4 (3), no. 6112.

24 *SP* 1, pp. 351–5; *LP* 4 (3), no. 6115; *CSP Span., 1529–30*, no. 232, pp. 366, 368.

25 Merriman 1, pp. 71–2.

26 Elton, *Tudor Rev.*, pp. 81–4; PRO SP 1/56 fol. 252 = *LP* 4 (3), no. 6196.

27 *CSP Span., 1529–30*, no. 257, pp. 449–50; *SP* 1, pp. 360–62; *LP* 4 (3), nos 6151, 6213–14; Merriman 1, p. 75.

28 *SP* 1, pp. 355–6; Cavendish, p. 126; Merriman 1, pp. 73–4.

29 *LP* 4 (3), no. 6213–14; Cavendish, pp. 123–32; Hall, p. 769.

30 Merriman 1, pp. 327–30; *LP* 4 (3), nos 6420, 6467.

31 Hall, p. 773; *CSP Span., 1529–30*, no. 354, pp. 600–601; no. 366, p. 619; E. Hammond, 'Dr. Augustine, Physician to Cardinal Wolsey and King Henry VIII', in *Medical History* 19 (1975): 215–19; *LP* 4 (3), no. 6374.

32 Merriman 1, pp. 326–7.

33 Merriman 1, pp. 327–8; Hall, p. 773.

34 Merriman 1, pp. 328, 334. There is nothing cryptic or sinister in these words; Cromwell simply meant that he would keep Wolsey up to date with news. On these *praemunire* proceedings, see J. Guy, 'Henry VIII and the *Praemunire* Manoeuvres of 1530–31', *EHR* 97 (1982): 481–503. By these manoeuvres, which lasted from July 1530 till November 1531, Henry asserted his control over the clergy. Cromwell carried out some business for the king, but at this stage of his career it is unlikely that he greatly influenced Henry's policy.

35 *CSP Span., 1529–30*, no. 509, pp. 819–20; *CSP Ven.* 4, nos 637, 642.

36 Cavendish, pp. 151–2, 155, 157, 249; Hammond, 'Dr Augustine', pp. 219–25; *CSP Ven.* 4, no. 694, p. 301. Compare De Mendoza in *CSP Span., 1527–29*, no. 69, p. 193; no. 550, p. 790 – see notes 6 and 10 above. Again, a slightly more sympathetic view of Wolsey can be found in his more recent biography – see Gwyn, *Wolsey*, pp. 599–639.

37 *CSP Span., 1534–5*, no. 228, p. 569.

38 Elton, *Tudor Rev.*, pp. 89–90; T. Mayer, *Reginald Pole, Prince and Prophet* (Cambridge, 2000), pp. 78–100; Foxe 5, p. 366; *CSP Span., 1534–5*, no. 228, p. 569.

39 Cavendish, *Wolsey*, p. 126 (18–19).

40 Cavendish, p. 29 (16–19); *CSP Span., 1529–30*, no. 249, p. 116; no. 250, p. 428; *CSP Ven.* 4, nos 601, 694, pp. 294–5; *CSP Span., 1531–3*, index under 'Cromwell', p. 1042.

41 Kaulek, p. 189 = *LP* 15, no. 766.

3. *The Lutheran*

1 The League's letter is *MBW* 2, nos 1127–9 = *CR* 2, cols 472–82. For Henry's reply and discussion see N. Tjernagel, *Henry VIII and the*

Lutherans (St. Louis, 1963), p. 136.

2   *WA* 30 (2), p. 68 (12) – p. 69 (1).

3   Brecht's biography of Luther (see Bibliography) is one of the truly great works on the Reformation published in the last decade. Brecht deals with Luther's most controversial writings in a way that is balanced, mature and fully informative; there is no cheap sensationalising or irrelevant psychoanalysing.

4   Merriman 1, p. 327; *TRP* 1, no. 122, pp. 181–5; no. 129, pp. 193–7.

5   Foxe 8, pp. 712–15; *Complete Works of Thomas More*, vol. 8, ed. L.A. Schuster *et al.* (New Haven and London:Yale UP, 1973), pp.16–17.

6   *LP* 4 (2), nos 4407, 5094; *Sermons and Remains of Latimer*, ed. G.E. Corrie (Cambridge: PS, 1845), p. 468. See also Foxe 5, pp. 688–94.

7   S. Brigden, 'Thomas Cromwell and the Brethren', in C. Cross, D. Loades and J. Scarisbrick (eds), *Law and Government under the Tudors* (Cambridge, 1988), pp. 34– 5.

8   S. Lehmberg, *The Reformation Parliament: 1529–1536* (Cambridge, 1977), pp.112-15.

9   On Vaughan's mission to Tyndale see J.F. Mozley, *William Tyndale* (Westport, Connecticut: Greenwood Press, reprint 1971), chapter 9; D. Daniell, *William Tyndale: A Biography* (New Haven and London, 1994), chap. 8. Both works, especially Mozley, have lengthy extracts of letters from Vaughan to Cromwell and Henry. On the questions re Vaughan, see Daniell, *Tyndale*, p. 201; *LP* 4 (3), no. 5823.

10   Letter printed in Mozley, *Tyndale*, pp. 187–8.

11   Mozley, *Tyndale*, pp. 191–2; Lehmberg, *Reformation Parliament*, pp. 117– 18.

12   Merriman 1, pp. 336–9; Mozley, *Tyndale*, pp. 193–9; Daniell, *Tyndale*, pp. 212–15.

13   Mozley, *Tyndale*, p. 200; Daniell, *Tyndale*, pp. 206–7.

14   *SP* 1, p. 380; Elton, *Tudor Rev.*, p. 90; Lehmberg, *Reformation Parliament*, pp. 59–60, 62, 132; *CSP Ven.* 4, no. 694, p. 297.

15   C. D'Alton, 'William Warham and English heresy policy after the fall of Wolsey', *HR* 77/197 (2004), pp. 337–57; Foxe 4, pp. 652–6, 680–88; Hall, p. 763.

16   Mozley, *Tyndale*, p. 206. See also *LP* 5, nos 532–3.

17   *LP* 5 App. 18, p. 768; Mozley, *Tyndale*, pp. 207–9. Cromwell's letters to Vaughan, dated 6 December, are missing, but certain points in them can be deduced from Vaughan's reply.

18   *LP* 5, no. 585; Tjernagel, *Henry VIII and the Lutherans*, pp. 59–64; *CSP Span., 1531–3*, no. 864, p. 337.

19   *WA*, Br 6, pp. 175–88 = *LW* 50, pp. 27–40; Pocock 1, p. 428; 2, pp. 5–11.

20   Mozley, *Tyndale*, p. 210; Foxe 4, pp. 580–82, 702–6; Lehmberg, *Reformation Parliament*, pp. 142–3.

21   BL Cottonian MS Vitellius B. XX, fol. 259 = *LP* 5, no. 911. A curiosity of this document is that while some of it is quite easy to read, the most interesting part – the sending of the Lutheran confession and the *Apology* – is damaged and very faint.

22   E. Hammond, 'Dr. Augustine, Physician to Cardinal Wolsey and King Henry VIII', in *Medical History* 19 (1975): 215–49, 229–32; Pocock 2, pp. 299–300; *LP* 4 (3), no. 6374.

23   *LP* 5, nos 739, 753, 804, 808, 813, 843, 870; Daniell, *Tyndale*, pp. 186–91; D. MacCulloch, *Reformation: Europe's House Divided* (London, 2003), p. 203.

24   W. Underwood, 'Thomas Cromwell and William Marshall's Protestant Books', *HJ* 47/3 (2004): 519.

25   G.R. Elton, *Reform and Renewal: Thomas Cromwell and the Common Weal* (Cambridge, 1973), pp. 26–8.

26   Brigden, 'Cromwell and the brethren': 36.

27   For the *Apology* on James, see *BSLK*, pp. 207–10 = Tappert, pp. 141–3. For Luther and Melanchthon on James, see J. Schofield, *Philip Melanchthon and the English Reformation*, pp. 46, 62, 65, 85.

28   *CSP Span.*, *1531–3* (cont), no. 1055, p. 618;

29   Merriman 1, pp. 369–70; R. McEntegart, *Henry VIII and the League of Schmalkalden* (Woodbridge, 2002), pp. 15–17 ; *CSP Span.*, *1531–3*, no. 1157, p. 873; *CSP Span.*, *1534–5*, no. 9.

30   *LP* 7, no. 583. Quotes from Strassbourg archives, quoted and discussed in McEntegart, *Henry VIII*, pp. 20–21, 46.

31   On Cranmer, see the discussion in D. MacCulloch, *Thomas Cranmer: A Life* (New Haven and London, 1996), pp. 60–71.

32   Hammond, 'Dr Augustine': 233–49.

4. The King's Councillor

1   Elton, *Studies* 1, p. 182; G.R. Elton, *England under the Tudors* (London, 2001), p. 107; A. Fox, and J. Guy, *Reassessing the Henrician Age: Humanism, politics and reform, 1500–1550* (Oxford, 1986), pp. 165–6; J. Guy, *Tudor England* (Oxford, 1988), pp. 104–5.

2   Hall, p. 728.

3   On Henry and ending his marriage, see Hall, p. 728, and discussions below and also in: V. Murphy, 'The Literature and Propaganda of Henry VIII's First Divorce', in D. MacCulloch (ed.), *The Reign of Henry VIII: Politics, policy and piety* (Basingstoke, 1995), pp. 135; R. Rex, *Theology of John Fisher* (Cambridge, 1991), p. 165); J. Scarisbrick, *Henry VIII* (London, 1968), pp. 181–97. On the princes of Almain: *LP* 4 (3), no. 5476. The 'true vicar of Christ': *SP* 7, p. 185. This *may* be an allusion to a far-fetched scheme in 1527 designed to make Wolsey 'caretaker' Head of the Church while Pope Clement was Charles's prisoner, so that Wolsey would be peacemaker in Europe and secure Henry's divorce. It came to nothing. See S. J. Gunn, 'Wolsey's Foreign Policy and Domestic Crisis' in S. Gunn and P. Lindley (eds), *Cardinal Wolsey: Church, State and Art* (Cambridge, 1991), p. 152. For Chapuys and the French ambassador: *CSP Span.*, *1529–30*, no. 224, pp. 349–50; no. 232, pp. 366–7; *LP* 4 (3), no. 6307.

4 *CSP Span., 1529–30*, no. 445; *CSP Span., 1531–3* (cont.), no. 598, p. 23; *LP* 5, no. 148, p. 69.

5 Fox and Guy, *Reassessing*, pp. 157–61; D. MacCulloch, *Thomas Cranmer: A Life* (New Haven and London, 1996), pp. 54, 59.

6 Elton, *Tudor Cons.*, pp. 350–53; Merriman 1, p. 343; S. Lehmberg, *The Reformation Parliament, 1529–1536* (Cambridge, 1970), pp. 136–8.

7 *LP* 5, no. 738, p. 352; *CSP Ven.* 4, no. 754.

8 For the passage of the Supplication through parliament, see Lehmberg, *Reformation Parliament*, pp. 139–54. For Elton's analysis and discussion see Elton, *Studies* 2, pp. 107–35; Elton, *Tudor Cons.*, pp. 333–5; G.R. Elton, *Reform and Reformation* (London, 1977), pp. 151–6. Elton suggests that the first draft of the Supplication might have been drawn up before the 1532 session began. He admits that definite proof is missing, but suggests that the 1529 session included some of the later complaints against the clergy: as early as 1529 Cromwell's drafts and corrections show him turning general complaints against the clergy into a new form – complaints that the clergy and courts were acting without the king's consent. However, Lehmberg has an extract from an anti-clerical petition in 1529 *before* Cromwell made any alterations to it, and one of its complaints is that the clergy make laws 'without your royal assent' (Lehmberg, *Reformation Parliament*, pp. 85–6). Lehmberg is generally a bit more cautious than Elton on Cromwell's role. He agrees that the Supplication might have been prepared in advance by the government, but there is no definitive evidence and other explanations are possible: the Supplication could have been drafted by Cromwell during the current session, or maybe it was framed by a committee, with Cromwell's support, based on some 1529 drafts (Lehmberg, *Reformation Parliament*, p. 139). This may have to remain an open question.

9 Lehmberg, *Reformation Parliament*, p. 153.

10 Elton, *Tudor Rev.*, p. 99; Lehmberg, *Reformation Parliament*, pp. 159, 161–2; MacCulloch, *Cranmer*, pp. 75–6.

11 *CSP Span., 1527–9*, no. 550, p. 789; *CSP Span., 1529–30*, no. 224, pp. 351–2; *CSP Ven.* 4, no. 437.

12 *CSP Span., 1529–30*, no. 245, p. 405; no. 290, p. 511; no. 347, p. 590.

13 *CSP Span., 1531–3* (cont), nos 608, 612; no. 739, p. 177; no. 765, p. 212.

14 *CSP Span., 1531–3*, no. 980, p. 489; no. 1077, p. 699.

15 *CSP Span., 1531–3* (cont), no. 1003, p. 527; no. 1008, p. 535; *CSP Ven.* 4, nos 802–3; J.A. Froude, (ed.), *The Pilgrim: A Dialogue of the Life and Actions of King Henry VIII*, by W. Thomas, Clerk of the Council to Edward VI (London, 1861), pp. 89–90; *LP* 5, no. 1538; Wright, p. 17 (18).

16 Hall, pp. 790–94; *LP* 5, nos 1430, 1484–5, 1509; *CSP Ven.* 4, nos 820, 824, pp. 365, 368.

17 Hall, p. 794; MacCulloch, *Cranmer*, pp. 637–8. It may be noteworthy that the Elizabethan historian, Ralph Holinshed, presumably after giving the matter some thought, accepts Hall's version of the November marriage: see Holinshed 3, p. 777.

18 MacCulloch, *Cranmer*, p. 83; Lehmberg, *Reformation Parliament*, p. 162; Cranmer, *Misc. Writings*, p. 246.

Notes

19 *CSP Span., 1531–3* (cont), no. 1048, p. 602; no. 1053, p. 609.

20 *CSP Span., 1536–8*, no. 43, p. 82.

21 Elton, *England under the Tudors*, pp. 132–3; Elton, *Tudor Const.*, pp. 353–8; Elton, *Studies* 2, pp. 82–106; Lehmberg, *Reformation Parliament,* pp. 164–9, 174–5.

22 Lehmberg, *Reformation Parliament,* pp. 176–8.

23 Hall, pp. 794–5. Chapuys's despatch (*CSP Span., 1531–3*, no. 1061, pp. 638, 643) is dated 15 April, describing a conversation with Henry on Thursday of Holy Week, which would be 10 April. The Venetian ambassador's letter – *CSP Ven.* 4, no. 870, p. 393 – is interesting. The calendar translates thus: 'I am assured that some months ago', Henry married Anne, and that 'she bore him a son who is several months old' (*Mi vien afirmato za più mezi questa Mts averla sposata, e aver uno fiol di qualche meze con lei*). The editor's translation seems rather free. Literally it reads: 'he has a son of some months with (or by) her'. There is no other record of a son actually born yet, and the Venetian ambassador could hardly have been so badly informed as to think that there was. He probably meant that Anne was now some months pregnant – 'with child' as we would say – and he assumed the child would be a son. Note also the marriage 'some months ago' (*za più mezi*) – from 12 April – may point more to a marriage in mid November than at the end of January.

24 *SP* 7, pp. 428–30, 434.

25 *SP* 7, p. 495.

26 *CSP Ven.* 4, nos 649, 705, 723; 5, no. 1035, p. 633; *LP* 13 (2) no. 804, p. 318; *CSP Span., 1531–3* (cont), no. 1044, p. 588; *LP* 6, no. 208. For more contacts between Francis and Rome around this time, see *LP* 6, nos 91–2. Francis seemed to be trying to induce Rome to look more favourably on Henry's Great Matter, though this was before the news of the second marriage was made public.

27 *CSP Span., 1531–3*, no. 1143, p. 837.

28 *CSP Span., 1529–30*, no. 245, p. 406; *CSP Span., 1531–3*, no. 1061, p. 645. Further evidence that Francis supported Henry, perhaps more than he admitted in public, is as follows: A report of a personal letter to Anne from Francis in March, though addressing her as 'Madame la Marquise', not queen (*LP* 6, no. 242). After Rochford's visit in March, Francis told his cardinals that he still supported Henry's cause (*LP* 6, nos 254–5). Though noting the pope's displeasure with Henry, Francis still wished that Rome would be patient and understand why he was sympathetic to Henry. He trusted that the pope would not drive Henry to further disobedience (*LP* 6, no. 424). The pope, however, was getting impatient with Henry and a little suspicious by now about Francis (*LP* 6, no. 643). There is also an intriguing report claiming that the pope told Francis that the dispensation of Pope Julius allowing Henry and Catherine to marry was not valid, therefore tacitly admitting that the marriage might be unlawful (*LP* 7, nos 1348, 1604).

29 *LP* 6, no. 282.

30 *CSP Span., 1531–3*, no. 1058, pp. 630–31.

31 *SP* 7, pp. 417–18; *LP* 6, nos 525–6; *CSP Span., 1531–3*, no. 1077, p. 700; Lehmberg, *Reformation Parliament*, p. 178–9.

32 *LP* 6, nos 423 (2), 631, 641, 846; MacCulloch, *Cranmer*, pp. 94–5; *CSP Span., 1531–3*, no. 1091, p. 721; *CSP Ven.* 4, no. 923.

33 *LP* 6, nos 1070, 1111. As MacCulloch has already noted (MacCulloch, *Cranmer*, p. 638), the date of Elizabeth's birth, 7 September, means that Anne's pregnancy began in early December the previous year, which provides further evidence for the marriage in mid November, as Hall says.

34 *LP* 6, nos 1386, 1399, 1404, 1426, 1479.

35 *CSP Milan*, nos 927, 932–3; *CSP Span., 1531–3*, no. 1144, pp. 841–2.

36 *CSP Span., 1531–3*, no. 1148, pp. 852–3; *LP* 6, nos 996, 1427. For more on the intrigues of kings and the pope in Du Bellay's miscellaneous memoirs, see the summary in *LP* 6, no. 1572.

37. The Milan ambassador: *CSP Ven.* 4, no. 601.

38 MacCulloch, *Cranmer*, p. 106; Ellis 10, pp. 287–8.

5. Principal Secretary

1 Bandello 1, pp. 1012–16 = Foxe 5, pp. 392–3.

2 *LP* 5, nos 1197, 1413–14, 1657; *LP* 6, nos 156, 1215–16; *LP* 7, no. 923 (26).

3 The standard story of her life is A. Neame, *The Holy Maid of Kent: The Life of Elizabeth Barton 1506–1534* (Hodder and Stroughton, 1971).

4 Merriman 1, p. 361; PRO SP 1/78, fol. 119 = *LP* 6, no. 967; *LP* 6, nos 1149, 1468; Cranmer, *Misc. Writings*, p. 274.

5 Morrison quoted in Neame, *Holy Maid*, pp. 239–41.

6 *LP* 7, nos 48, 52; G.R. Elton, *Reform and Reformation* (London, 1977), p. 180; Elton, *Policy*, pp. 274–5, 390; S. Lehmberg, *The Reformation Parliament: 1529–1536* (Cambridge, 1977), pp. 194–6.

7 PRO SP 1/82, fol. 81 = *LP* 7, no. 70. See also discussion in Lehmberg, *Reformation Parliament*, p. 194.

8 Lehmberg, *Reformation Parliament*, pp. 196–9.

9 Elton, *Tudor Rev.*, pp. 124–5; Merriman 1, p. 380.

10 *LP* 7, nos 1261–3; *CSP Span., 1534–5*, no. 97.

11 Lehmberg, *Reformation Parliament*, p. 202.

12 Elton, *Tudor Const.*, pp. 42, 53–6; Elton, *Reform and Reformation,* pp. 189–90; Lehmberg, *Reformation Parliament*, pp. 206–7.

13 Lehmberg, *Reformation Parliament*, pp. 207–9; *CSP Span., 1534–5*, no. 118, p. 346.

14 Elton, *Policy*, pp. 263–92; Elton, *Tudor Const.*, pp. 62–4; Lehmberg, *Reformation Parliament*, pp. 202–5.

15 Milan ambassador: *CSP Ven.* 4, no. 601.

16 *SR* 1, p. 320; Elton, *Policy*, pp. 288–9.

17 Elton, *Policy* pp. 217, 230–34.

18 Elton, *Policy*, p. 175; A. Fox and J. Guy, *Reassessing the Henrician Age: Humanism, politics and reform, 1500–1550* (Oxford, 1986), p. 101.

19 Pocock 2, pp. 385–421; Elton, *Policy*, p. 176; *LP* 5, no. 1338.

20 Elton *Policy*, p. 177.

21 R. Rex, 'Jasper Fyloll and the Enormities of the Clergy: Two Tracts Written during the Reformation Parliament', *SCJ* 31/4 (2000): 1043–62.

22 Pocock 2, pp. 523–31, 539–52; Elton, *Policy*, pp. 180–84.

23 E. Duffy, *Saints and Sinners: A History of the Popes* (London, 1997), p. 146.

24 Elton, *Policy*, p. 186.

25 D. MacCulloch, *Reformation: Europe's House Divided* (London, 2003), p. 81.

26 Marsiglio of Padua: *The Defender of Peace*, trans. A. Gewirth, (New York, 1956), *passim*.

27 Marsiglio, p. xvii, footnote 1; Elton, *Studies* 2, pp. 228–30; *LP* 11, no. 1355.

28 J. Strype, *Memorial of ... Thomas Cranmer, Archbishop of Canterbury* (Oxford, 1812), vol. 2, pp. 691–3; Cranmer, *Misc Writings*, p. 286; Merriman 1, p. 381.

29 W. Roper, *Life of Thomas More* (London, 1907), p. 70; E.F. Rogers (ed.), *Correspondence of Thomas More* (Princeton, 1947), p. 506 (line 129), p. 517 (128), p. 541 (59), p. 552 (50–54), pp. 554–5.

30 Merriman 1, p. 119; Rogers, *More* pp. 555–9. On More and Cromwell, and More's trial, see also Elton, *Policy*, pp. 402–25.

31 *CSP Span., 1531–3*, no. 1130, p. 813; no. 1133, p. 821.

32 Merriman 1, pp. 373–9.

33 C.A. Hatt (ed.), *The English Works of John Fisher. Bishop of Rochester, 1469–1535* (Oxford, 2002), pp. 12, 350; *LP* 8, no. 856 (39); Rogers, *More*, pp. 559–63.

34 *CSP Span., 1534–5*, no. 178, p. 505; *LP* 8, nos 742, 1117; Merriman 1, pp. 416–19; 427–30.

35 Wright, pp. 40–41.

36 *LP* 8, nos 475, 565, 600.

37 Cranmer, *Misc Writings*, p. 303.

38 *LP* 8, no. 661.

39 *CSP Span., 1534–5*, no. 156, p. 453.

40 *LP* 8, no. 895; *LP* 9, nos 523–4, 1150; D. Knowles, *The Religious Orders in England, vol. 3: The Tudor Age* (Cambridge, 1971), pp. 219–20.

41 *SP* 1, p. 459; Knowles, *Religious Orders* 3, p. 235; Elton, *Policy*, p. 423.

42 Wright, p. 162; Elton, *Policy*, p. 371, fn. 1.

6. Vicegerent

1. *LP* 7, no. 420.

2 For background and details of the vicegerency, see F. Logan, 'Thomas Cromwell and the Vicegerency in Spirituals: a revisitation', *EHR* 103 (1988): 658–67.

3 Foxe 5, p. 368–9, 378; Wright, p. 112. On the government's monastic policy, and the notable lack of evidence for a master plan during the early and middle 1530s, see J. Youings, *The Dissolution of the Monasteries* (London, 1971), pp. 13–14, 21; R. W. Hoyle, 'The Origins

of the Dissolution of the Monasteries', *HJ* 38 (1995): 275 – 305; F. Heal, *Reformation in Britain and Ireland* (Oxford, 2003), pp. 143, 148. The classic Catholic account of the monasteries remains D. Knowles, *The Religious Orders in England, vol. 3: The Tudor Age* (Cambridge, 1971), especially chapters 20–24.

4   Ellis 5, p. 18; *LP* 4 (3), no. 6011; *CSP Span., 1529–30*, no. 211, p. 325; no. 232, pp. 366–7; J. Guy, 'Communications – The Tudor Commonwealth: Revising Thomas Cromwell', *HJ* 23/3 (1980): 683; S. Lehmberg, *The Reformation Parliament: 1529–1536* (Cambridge, 1977), p. 101.

5   *CSP Span., 1529–30*, no. 492, p. 800; *CSP Span., 1531–3*, no. 1056, p. 623.

6   *CSP Span., 1536–8*, no. 43, pp. 83–4.

7   D. M. Loades (ed.), *The Papers of George Wyatt*, Camden Soc., series 4, 5 (1968), p. 159; G.R. Elton, *Reform and Reformation* (London, 1977), pp. 236–7.

8   PRO SP 1/102, fols 5–6 = *LP* 10, no. 254. On this see also the comment in Lehmberg, *Reformation Parliament*, p. 220, footnote 4.

9   Youings, *Dissolution*, pp. 35–6; Elton, *Tudor Const.*, p. 379; Wright, pp. 75–6; *LP* 9, nos 621–2, 630, 651.

10   *LP* 10, no. 364; *LP* 9, nos 457, 533; Wright, pp. 136–7. For some conflicting evidence from the visitors, see Knowles, *Religious Orders* 3, pp. 480–82.

11   The injunctions are printed in Youings, *Dissolution*, pp. 149–52.

12   Merriman 1, p. 347; *LP* 5 no. 1428; *LP* 10, no. 916; Cranmer, *Misc. Writings*, p. 240–41. In the latter, the editor's footnote suggests that the abbot – William Boston or Benson – was a man of shallow convictions, while Ellis calls him a man who 'bent with the times' (Ellis 11, p. 273). Maybe, but the point is still valid. Pliant abbot or genuinely evangelical abbot, Cromwell and Cranmer could still infiltrate the religious orders. See also Cranmer, *Misc. Writings*, pp. 251, 270, 275.

13   *LP* 8, nos 852, 802 (27), 962 (14).

14   Ellis 10, p. 362; *LP* 9, no. 808.

15   PRO SP 1/102, fols 214–15 = *LP* 10, no. 480.

16   PRO SP 1/103, fol. 53 = *LP* 10, no. 588.

17   BL Cottonian MS Cleopatra E.VI, fol. 257 = *LP* 10, no. 723.

18   *LP* 9, no. 1164; Wright, pp. 100–102; *LP* 10, no. 424.

19   Cranmer, *Misc. Writings*, p. 310; D. MacCulloch, *Thomas Cranmer: A Life* (New Haven and London, 1996), p. 135; *CSP Span., 1534–5*, no. 205, p. 542.

20   PRO SP 1/86, fols 161–4 = *LP* 7, no. 1367.

21   *LP* 8, no. 1111; *LP* 9, no. 4.

22   PRO SP 1/89, fol. 145 = *LP* 8, no. 171; BL Cottonian MS, Cleopatra E. IV, fol. 47 = *LP* 9, no. 747.

23   *LP* 9, no. 934.

24   PRO SP 1/95, fols 135–6 = *LP* 9, nos 134–5.

25   PRO SP 1/96, fols 127–8 = LP 9, nos 321–2.

26   BL Cottonian MS Cleopatra E.VI, fol. 261 = *LP* 9, no. 1134.

27   PRO SP 1/100, fol. 103 = *LP* 9, no. 1145.

28 PRO SP 1/89, fol. 57 = *LP* 8, no. 79.

29 Elton, *Policy*, pp. 40–41; *LP* 8, nos 625–6.

30 *LP* 8, no. 959; *LP* 9, nos 314–15.

31 Ellis 10, pp. 295–308; Wright, p. 82.

32 *CSP Span., 1534–5*, no. 112, p. 332.

33 Foxe 5, p. 135; 7, p. 461; *Sermons and Remains of Latimer*, ed. G.E. Corrie (Cambridge, 1845), pp. xv, xviii.

34 Latimer, *Remains*, pp. 368–9, 410–11.

35 *LP* 10, nos 835, 1257 (9); *LP* 11, no. 117.

36 *LP* 6, nos 1226, 1067; 8, no. 839; MacCulloch, *Cranmer*, p. 125.

37 *SP* 2, p. 539.

38 Wright, pp. 77–8, 183; G. Williams, *Wales and the Reformation* (Cardiff, 1997), p. 61; *LP* 10, no. 227.

39 Cranmer, *Misc. Writings*, pp. 239, 262–3, 269.

40 Cranmer, *Misc. Writings*, pp. 276, 295–6; A. Ryrie, *The Gospel and Henry VIII: Evangelicals in the Early English Reformation* (Cambridge, 2003), p. 219.

41 *Correspondence of Matthew Parker*, ed. J. Bruce and T. Perowne (Cambridge, 1853), pp. 5–6; Ellis 2, pp. 46–7.

42 BL Additional MS 19398, fol. 49 = *LP* 8, no. 1056.

43 Anne's religion has been a subject of much discussion. By a majority she was evangelical: see M. Dowling, 'Anne Boleyn and Reform', *JEH* 35 (1984): 30–45; E. Ives, 'Anne Boleyn and the early Reformation in England: The contemporary evidence', *HJ* 37 (1994), pp. 389–400. But not everyone is persuaded by Anne as the evangelical princess. For a touch of scepticism see G.W. Bernard, 'Anne Boleyn's religion', *HJ* 36 (1993), pp. 1–20. For a defence of Foxe's account of Anne, see T.S. Freeman, 'Research, Rumour and Propaganda: Anne Boleyn in Foxe's Book of Martyrs', *HJ* 38/4 (1995):797–819

44 The standard work on the Anglo-Lutheran diplomacy of the 1530s is R. McEntegart, *Henry VIII, The League of Schmalkalden and the English Reformation* (Woodbridge, 2002). For full details of the Anglo-Lutheran discussions during 1535–36, see his chapter 2.

45 McEntegart, *Henry VIII*, pp. 26–7; *LP* 8, nos 174, 270, 272 (p. 110), 273; D. Crouzet, *La Genèse de la Réforme Française, 1520–1562* (Paris, 1996), p. 332; C.L. Manschreck, *Melanchthon, The Quiet Reformer* (Westport, Connecticut, 1975), pp. 222–5.

46 McEntegart, *Henry VIII*, pp. 27–38; Merriman 1, p. 416; *CSP Span., 1534–5*, no. 201, p. 538; no. 213, p. 550.

47 W. Underwood, 'Thomas Cromwell and William Marshall's Protestant Books', *HJ* 47/3 (2004): 517–39.

48 For fuller discussion of the theology of the *Loci*, see J. Schofield, *Philip Melanchthon and the English Reformation* (Ashgate, 2006), pp. 61–7. What follows above is largely a summary.

49 For an analysis of Henry's *Assertion* and Luther's reply, see J. Schofield, 'The Lost Reformation: Why Lutheranism failed in England during the Reigns of Henry VIII and Edward VI' (Newcastle Ph.D., 2003), chap. 1.

50 Wright, pp. 70–72.

51　C. H. and J. W. Cooper, *Annals of Cambridge* (Cambridge, 1842–1908), vol. I, p. 375; Merriman I, p. 421, no. 116; *LP* 9, no. 964. For the significance of Cambridge University in the Reformation, see Ryrie, *Gospel and Henry VIII*, pp. 170–83.

52　Cooper, *Annals of Cambridge* I, p. 376.

53　*LP* 9, nos 312, 708.

7. Her Special Friend

1　*SP* 7, p. 509.

2　*CSP Ven.* 4, no. 846; BL Additional MS 19398, fol. 49 = *LP* 8, no. 1057.

3　*CSP Span., 1531–3*, no. 1058, p. 629; no. 1164, p. 893; no. 1165, pp. 897–8; *LP* 6, nos 1541–3. Catherine seems to have stayed where she was, at least for some time; she sent a letter to Charles from Buckden on 8 February 1534: *CSP Span., 1534–5*, no. 252, p. 605.

4　*CSP Span., 1531–3*, no. 1073, p. 679.

5　*CSP Span., 1531–3*, no. 1100, p. 739.

6　*CSP Span., 1531–3*, nos 1123–4, pp. 788–9.

7　*CSP Span., 1531–3*, no. 1130, p. 811; no. 1154, p. 865; *LP* 6, no. 1572, pp. 637–8.

8　*CSP Span., 1531–3*, no. 1144, pp. 839–41.

9　*CSP Span., 1531–3*, no. 1153, pp. 859, 864.

10　*CSP Span., 1531–3*, no. 1149, p. 854; no. 1157, pp. 870–71; *CSP Span., 1534–5*, no. 75, p. 219.

11　*LP* 7, App. 8, nos 11–13, pp. 630–34; *CSP Span., 1534–5*, no. 26, p. 83; no. 31, p. 95; no. 211.

12　*CSP Span., 1534–5*, no. 45, pp. 125, 129–31.

13　*CSP Span., 1534–5*, no. 10, p. 33; no. 60, pp. 169–72.

14　Catherine's refusal: *LP* 7, no. 786. Catherine's letter: PRO SP 1/85, fol. 157 = *LP* 7, no. 1126. An English translation is printed in T. Hearne, *Sylloge epistolarum, a variis Angliae scriptarum* ... (Oxford, 1716), pp. 107–8.

15　Hall tells us that Catherine could speak French – Hall, p. 756. For Butts, see *LP* 7, no. 1129.

16　*CSP Span., 1534–5*, no. 90, p. 264; J. A. Froude, (ed.), *The Pilgrim: A Dialogue of the Life and Actions of King Henry VIII*, by W. Thomas, Clerk of the Council to Edward VI (London, 1861), pp. 100–103.

17　*CSP Span., 1534–5*, no. 102.

18　*CSP Span., 1534–5*, nos 139, 142–6; no. 150 p. 437; no. 156, p. 454; no. 178, p. 500.

19　*CSP Span., 1534–5*, no. 165, pp. 468–9.

20　*CSP Span., 1534–5*, no. 122, p. 355; no. 170, p. 484.

21　*CSP Span., 1534–5*, no. 239.

22　*CSP Ven.* 5, no. 54, p. 27; *CSP Span., 1534–5*, no. 174, p. 493.

23　*LP* 8, nos 554, 557, 561, 591, 712, 726, 793, 823, 837, 846, 891, 909, 985 (pp. 389–90).

24.　*LP* 9, nos 378, 571; *CSP Span., 1534–5*, no. 229, pp. 569–71. For Henry's forebodings, see note 27 below.

25   *CSP Span., 1536–8*, no. 9, pp. 11–12, 19.
26   Hall, p. 818; *CSP Span., 1536–8*, no. 21, p. 39; Wriothesley 1, p. 33.
27   *CSP Span., 1536–8*, no. 13, p. 28.
28   R. Warnicke, *The Rise and Fall of Anne Boleyn* (Cambridge, 1989); G.R. Elton, *England under the Tudors* (London, 2001), p. 494 (36).
29   *LP* 10, no. 283; *CSP Span., 1536–8*, no. 21, pp. 39–40.
30   See especially, but not only, E. Ives, *The Life and Death of Anne Boleyn* (Oxford, 2004), part 4.

8. In the Line of Duty

1   *CSP For., 1558–9*, no. 1303, pp. 524–34.
2   J. Collier, *An Ecclesiastical History of Great Britain* (London, 1708–1714), 1.2, p. 117.
3   *LP* 14 (2) no. 782, pp. 328–30, 332, 334, 338; *LP* 14 (1), no. 1353.
4   R. McEntegart, *Henry VIII, The League of Schmalkalden and the English Reformation*, pp. 61–76. See also chap. 10.
5   For Barnes, see Foxe 5, p. 436; Starkey: *LP* 11, no. 73; T. Mayer, *Thomas Starkey and the Commonweal: Humanist politics and religion in the reign of Henry VIII* (Cambridge, 1989), p. 241. See also chapter 14 on the later dissolution.
6   *CSP Span., 1534–5*, no. 170, p. 480.
7   Elton, *Studies* 2, pp. 137–54.
8   Burnet 1, p. 331–2.
9   *Chronicle of King Henry VIII of England* … written in Spanish by an unknown hand, trans. and ed. M.A. Hume (London, 1889). Hereafter referred to as *Spanish Chronicle*.
10   *Spanish Chronicle*, pp. 55–61.
11   *Spanish Chronicle*, p. 64; Cranmer, *Misc. Writings*, pp. 323–4.
12   *Spanish Chronicle*, pp. 65–7, 71; *LP* 14 (1), no. 511.
13   *Spanish Chronicle*, pp. 75, 84–5, 96–7.
14   VA, England K.7, Konv. 1536/2, fol. 1 = *CSP Span., 1536–8*, no. 61, p. 137.
15   Collins/Robert, *Concise French Dictionary* (4th edn, Glasgow, 2000), pp. 109, 678.
16   Collins/Robert, p. 510 under '*sur*', points c, d. Similar examples in *Grand Larousse de la langue française* (6 vols, 1972), vol. 6, pp. 5826–7.

9. Around the Throne the Thunder Rolls

1   *Circa Regna tonat* – from Thomas Wyatt's poem on the fall of Anne Boleyn, printed in *Complete Poems of Thomas Wyatt*, ed. R. A. Rebholz (Middlesex, 1978), p. 155.
2   *LP* 9, nos 148, 205, 443, 984, 994, 1001, 1013; *CSP Ven.* 5, no. 80.
3   *LP* 9 App. 7, pp. 404–5; *LP* 9, no. 1038; Merriman 1, pp. 434–6; Merriman 2, p. 1.

4   Merriman 2, pp. 1–2.

5   *CSP, Span., 1536–8*, no. 29, pp. 54–9.

6   *CSP Span., 1531–3*, no. 1043, p. 583; *CSP Span., 1534–5*, no. 71, p. 206; no. 221, p. 563, no. 222; *CSP, Span., 1536–8*, no. 43A, pp. 86–8.

7   Merriman 2, pp. 5–6; *LP* 10, no. 410.

8   *CSP, Span., 1536–8*, no. 29, p. 59; no. 43, pp. 79–85.

9   *LP* 10, no. 615. Solomon (1 Kings 11); Rehoboam (1 King 12:1–11); Haman (Esther 3–5).

10 E. Ives, *The Life and Death of Anne Boleyn* (Oxford, 2004), pp. 307–9.

11 On the Pilgrimage of Grace, see chap.10. Wolsey had also carried the Haman tag – see G. Walker, 'Wolsey and the satirists: the case of Godly Queen Hester re-opened', in S. Gunn and P. Lindley (eds), *Cardinal Wolsey: Church, State and Art* (Cambridge UP, 1991), pp. 243–5. It may have become a catch-all insult for any minister unpopular for some reason or another.

12 E. Ives, 'Anne Boleyn and the early Reformation in England: The contemporary evidence', *HJ* 37 (1994): 398, fn. 76; *LP* 10, nos 797, 910. .

13 *CSP Span., 1536–8*, no. 40.

14 *WA*, Br 7, p. 396 = *LW* 50, pp. 136–8; *LP* 10, no. 665.

15 This and the following discussion, including the events of 18 April, is taken from *CSP Span., 1536–8*, no. 43A, pp. 85–98.

16 Merriman, 1, p. 231.

17 *LP* 10, nos 688, 759. Chapuys knew the French had seen Henry on 19 April. An example of the unpredictability and fluidity of European diplomacy is that shortly after this Cromwell was astonished to hear a report that Charles and Francis were making an alliance, and he asked Chapuys if this was true, and whether their negotiations should be halted: see *CSP Span., 1536–8*, no. 43A, pp. 99–101.

18 *LP* 10, no. 670, p. 269.

19 *CSP Span., 1536–8*, no. 48, pp. 107–8.

20 Cranmer, *Misc Writings*, p. 322.

21 Wriothesley, pp. 189–91, 205; *LP* 10, nos 848, 876.

22 *SP* 7, pp. 683–6 (on the dating, see the note in *LP* 10, no. 726); Merriman 2, p. 10.

23 *LP* 10, no. 736; S. Lehmberg, *The Reformation Parliament: 1529–1536* (Cambridge, 1977), p. 221; *CSP Span., 1536–8*, no. 47, p. 106.

24 Cromwell and Sampson: VA, England K.7, Konv. 1536/1, fol. 98 = *LP* 10, no. 753. (For reasons not clear, this document is not calendared in the *CSP Span.* volumes.) On Sampson see S. Lehmberg, *The Later Parliaments of Henry VIII: 1536–1547* (Cambridge, 1977), p. 2.

25 *CSP Span., 1536–8*, no. 48, pp. 107–8.

26 *LP* 10, nos 669, 673, 675, 738, 742, 747–8, 756, 779, 789, 865, 875.

27 *LP* 10, no. 1036; *William Latymer's Chronicle of Anne Boleyn*, ed. M. Dowling, *Camden Miscellany* 30 (CS 4th series 39, 1990), p. 37.

28 *CSP Span., 1536–8*, no. 48, pp. 107–8.

29 George Constantine, *Memorial to Thomas Cromwell*, ed. T. Amyot in *Arch.* 23 (1831), p. 64.

30   Cromwell was at his home in Stepney on 30 April, from where he wrote a fairly routine letter to Gardiner: Merriman 2, p. 11.

31   *LP* 10, no. 1036, p. 429; Constantine, *Arch. 23*, p. 64.

32   *CSP Span., 1536–8*, no. 58; *LP* 10, nos 798 (p. 338), 956.

33   *LP* 10, nos 793, 869, p. 358.

34   Burnet 1, pp. 316, 330, 332; G. Walker, 'Rethinking the Fall of Anne Boleyn', *HJ* 45 (1) (2000): 1–29; G.W. Bernard, 'The Fall of Anne Boleyn', *EHR* 106 (1991): 584–610. See also the Ives/Bernard debate in *EHR* 107 (1992): 651–74.

35   Bernard, 'Anne Boleyn', *EHR* 107: 667.

36   *CSP Span., 1536–8*, nos 54–5; *LP* 10, no. 901. There is an interesting reference to Cromwell in one of these letters (no. 55, p. 123). Back on the subject of good relations between Henry and Charles, Cromwell reminded Chapuys of his words on St Mathias, and that he 'was right in his predictions with regard to her' (*et que si bien me souvenoye de ce que mavoit tacitement assez declaire et pronosticque ce quen adviendroit*). This seems another free translation, but it may mean only that Cromwell had always been hopeful of favourable outcome generally. St Mathais is 24 February. There is a letter from Chapuys on that date (no. 29) but it contains no specific dire predictions regarding Anne, only a general optimism on Cromwell's part that Anglo-Imperial relations would, despite the difficulties, turn out for the best. Chapuys had also heard from the bishop of Carlisle that Henry claimed that he knew his second marriage would end the way it did (no. 55, p. 127). But if Henry had entertained some suspicions about Anne, the record is quite clear that nothing was done until those three lords went to the king at the end of April. It is always easy to be wise after the event.

37   Burnet 1, pp. 325–7.

38   *LP* 10, no. 965.

39   Merriman 2, pp. 11–12.

40   *LP* 10, nos 953, 964; *Reports of Sir John Spelman*, ed. J. H. Baker, vol. 1 (London, 1977), p. 71.

41   *LP* 10, nos 797, 799, 843, 1036 (p. 429); *CSP Span., 1536–8* no. 48, pp. 107–8.

42   Merriman 2, pp. 46 = *LP* 10, nos 376–7; *LP* 10, nos 254, 341, 827; *William Latymer's Chronicle*, ed. M. Dowling, *Camden Miscellany* 30 (CS 4th series 39, 1990), pp. 23–66 – on p. 28.

43   For Anne's indictment, see Wriothesley 1, p. 191 = *LP* 10.876 (7). Norfolk: *LP* 10, nos 848 (3); 876 (1, 5); 1036, p. 430.

44   Cromwell and Wolsey compared: *CSP Span., 1534–5*, no. 228, p. 569. Anne and her father: *CSP Span., 1531–3*, no. 664, p. 96. Peasants' War: *CSP Span., 1531–3*, no. 1133, pp. 822–3. The parliamentary committee: *CSP Span., 1536–8*, no. 43A, p. 102; Lehmberg, *Reformation Parliament*, p. 223, fn. 4.

45   Merriman 2, p. 21.

10. *A New Queen of the Old Faith*

1   Foxe 5, pp. 376–8, 384; *ET*, p. 10 = *OL* 1, p. 15.

2   *LP* 10, no. 942.

3   Elton: *Policy* pp. 244–5; Merriman 2, pp. 111–13; Burnet 4, pp. 394–5. For the dating, see Elton.

4   R. McEntegart, *Henry VIII, The League of Schmalkalden and the English Reformation*, pp. 61–76.

5   *Letters of Stephen Gardiner*, ed. J.A. Muller (Cambridge 1933), p. 72.

6   S. Lehmberg, *The Later Parliaments of Henry VIII: 1536–1547* (Cambridge, 1977), pp. 1–16.

7   Mary's submission: *LP* 10, no. 1137. Cromwell to Mary: Merriman 2, pp. 17–18 = *LP* 10, no. 1110 (a 'mutilated draft', and this time the *LP* abstract contains more than Merriman; it is also printed in T. Hearne, *Sylloge epistolarum, a variis Angliae scriptarum …* (Oxford: 1716), p. 137.) Mary to Cromwell: *LP* 10, nos 991, 1079, 1108, 1129, 1186; *LP* 11, nos 6, 334, 1269. Originals printed in Hearne, *Sylloge*, pp. 125–33, 144–8.

8   *CSP Span., 1536–8*, no. 70.

9   *CSP Span., 1536–8*, no. 72. There were even rumours that under new Succession Act, Cromwell would become Henry's heir: *LP* 12 (1), nos 201 (3–4), 533.

10   Lehmberg, *Later Parliaments*, p. 37; *LP* 11, no. 202 (3); Merriman 2, p. 134; *LP* 13 (2), no. 508; *CSP Span., 1538–42*, no. 7, p. 19.

11   Lehmberg, *Later Parliaments*, pp. 20–24.

12   *LP* 10, no. 1077; D. MacCulloch, *Thomas Cranmer: A Life* (New haven and London, 1996), p. 150; Lehmberg, *Later Parliaments*, pp. 25–8; Elton, *Policy*, p. 291; Elton, *Tudor Const.*, p. 341. For further parliamentary business, see Lehmberg, *Later Parliaments*, pp. 28–35.

13   McEntegart, *Henry VIII*, p. 73; Lehmberg, *Later Parliaments*, pp. 32, 36, 38; A.G. Dickens, *The English Reformation* (2nd edn, London, 1989), pp. 130, 142–3; Wriothesley 1, pp. 51–2.

14   The Ten Articles are printed in C.H. Williams (ed.), *English Historical Documents, vol. 5, 1485–1588* (London, 1967), pp. 795–805. For a more detailed discussion, including the influence of Melanchthon and the case for Cromwell's authorship, see J. Schofield, *Philip Melanchthon and the English Reformation* (Ashgate, 2006), chapter 5.

15   *English Historical Documents 5*, pp. 805–8.

16   For examples of resistance, or grudging acceptance, of the Injunctions, see Elton, *Policy*, p. 250.

17   G.R. Elton, *England under the Tudors* (London, 2001), p. 133.

18   D. Daniell, *William Tyndale: A Biography* (New Haven and London, 1994), pp. 361–84; *LP* 9, nos 275, 498; *LP* 10, no. 663; Foxe 5, p. 127–8; Hall, p. 818.

19   Daniell, *Tyndale*, pp. 381–3; Foxe 5, p. 127; *LP* 11, no. 1296.

20   *LP* 11, no. 331; *CSP Span., 1536–8*, nos 103, 130.

21   *LP* 8, no. 955; *CSP Span., 1534–5*, no. 257.

22   On the Pilgrimage of Grace, see Elton, *Studies* 3, pp. 183–215; M.L. Bush, *The Pilgrimage of Grace: A study of the rebel armies of October 1536*

(Manchester UP, 1996); R.W. Holye, *The Pilgrimage of Grace and the Politics of the 1530s* (Oxford, 2001).

On Cromwell as the rebels' hate figure, see Elton, *Policy*, pp. 6–8; *LP* 11, no. 841; *LP* 12 (1) nos 163, 853, 976, 1021 (5), and also Bush, *Pilgrimage of Grace*, Index under Cromwell, pp. 438–9.

23 *LP* 11, no. 860, p. 346; *LP* 11, no. 1250; *CSP Span.*, *1536–8*, no. 116, p. 284.

24 Merriman 2, p. 36; *LP* 12 (1) nos 247, 259; Elton: *Policy* p. 253.

25 Chapuys: *LP* 12 (2), no. 292 (3, p. 121). Norfolk: *LP* 12 (1), nos 426, 488, 479.

26 *LP* 12 (1), no. 698.

27 McEntegart, *Henry VIII*, pp. 78–88.

28 *LP* 12 (1), nos 457, 708, 789, p. 346.

29 Foxe 5, pp. 378–84.

30 *LP* 12 (2), nos. 289, 445, 466, 581; Cranmer, *Misc. Writings*, pp. 337–8; *Sermons and Remains of Latimer*, ed. G.E. Corrie (PS, 1845), p. 379.

31 J.F. Mozley, *Coverdale and his Bibles* (London, 1953), pp. 65–71; 111, 115–16, 119–21; S.L. Greenslade (ed.), *The Cambridge History of the Bible* (3 vols, Cambridge, 1987), vol. 3, p. 148.

32 Mozley, *Coverdale*, pp. 110, 123, 136–41; Foxe 4, pp. 121–3. Daniell, *Tyndale*, p. 334–5. For an absorbing comparison of the 'Matthew' with the Tyndale and Coverdale editions, and an analysis of the historical books in the 'Matthew', see Mozley, *Coverdale*, pp. 148–66; Daniell, *Tyndale*, pp. 335–57.

33 Cranmer, *Misc. Writings*, pp. 344–7; Mozley, *Coverdale*, pp. 126–9.

34 Merriman 2, pp. 94–5; *LP* 12 (2), nos 889, 911, 1060.

35 Cranmer, *Misc. Writings*, pp. 83–115, 359–9. For more a detailed discussion, see Schofield, *Melanchthon*, pp. 75–9.

11. *The Administrator*

1   Elton, *Tudor Rev.*, pp. 99–100, 119–20

2   Elton, *Tudor Rev.*, p. 126–7; G.R. Elton, *England under the Tudors* (London, 2001), pp. 182–3.

3   Elton, *Tudor Rev.*, pp. 122, 127–8, 130, 132–3.

4   Elton, *Tudor Rev.*, pp. 129, 133.

5   *CSP Span.*, *1534-5*, no. 228, p. 569; *LP* 12 (2), no. 445; G.R. Elton, *Reform and Renewal: Thomas Cromwell and the Common Weal* (Cambridge, 1973), pp. 10–12.

6   *Life of Thomas More*, by William Roper (London, 1907), p. 55.

7   For a discussion of Luther's 'two kingdoms', see Brecht 2, pp. 116–19.

8   PRO SP 1/125, fol. 253 = *LP* 12 (2), no. 952; LP 10, no. 901.

9   *CSP Ven.* 4, no. 601; *LP* 6, no. 1479, p. 595.

10 *CSP Span.*, *1536–8*, no. 61, p. 161; no. 71, p. 189; no. 98, p. 257.

11 See Chaps 6 (Lutherans), 8 (Poor Law), 9 (Anglo-Imperial relations), 10 (justification and the Bible), 15 (priestly marriage).

12 Henry & Cromwell: *SP* 2, pp. 551–3; *LP* 13 (1), nos 999–1000, 1021, 1303; *LP* 13 (2) no. 433. Cromwell & Cranmer: Foxe 8, p. 27.

13   For discussions on this see Elton, *Tudor Rev.*, pp. 318, 320, 329–32, 342–51; Elton, *England under the Tudors*, pp. 180–84, 479–80; A. Fox and J. Guy, *Reassessing the Henrician Age: Humanism, politics and reform, 1500–1550* (Oxford, 1986), pp. 142–3; J. Guy, *Tudor England* (Oxford, 1988), p. 157, 160–64. However, there is no evidence that the fall of Anne Boleyn or the Pilgrimage of Grace had much to do with Cromwell's governmental reforms.

14   Elton, *Studies* 3, p. 8–9, 11, p. 216; Elton, *Tudor Const.*, pp. 20–21.

15   Elton, *Reform and Renewal*, pp. 70–80; 92–7; 161; 164–5; Elton, *Tudor Const.*, pp. 22, 27–30; S. Lehmberg, *The Later Parliaments of Henry VIII: 1536–1547* (Cambridge, 1977), pp. 75–9; M. Graves, *Tudor Parliaments* (London, 1985), p. 75.

16   Gardiner, S., *Letters of*, ed. J.A. Muller (Cambridge, 1933), p. 399; Merriman 2, pp. 13, 199, 209–10; Lehmberg, *Later Parliaments*, pp. 41–50.

17   S. Lehmberg, *The Reformation Parliament: 1529–1536* (Cambridge, 1977), pp. 255–6; Elton, *Studies* 2, p. 233.

18   Merriman 1, pp. 388–92; Lehmberg, *Reformation Parliament*, pp. 239–41.

19   Lehmberg, *Reformation Parliament*, pp. 209–10.

20   Lehmberg, *Reformation Parliament*, pp. 241–2; P.R. Roberts, 'The Union with England and the Identity of "Anglican Wales"', *TRHS* 22 (1972), pp. 49–70; G. Williams, *Renewal and Reformation: Wales c. 1415–1642* (Oxford, reprint 2002), pp. 259–60; J. Davies, *A History of Wales* (London, 1993), 230–33.

21   Ellis 10, pp. 369–72; 11, pp. 13–14; *LP* 8, no. 947; *LP* 13 (1), no. 152.

22   Ellis 11, pp. 47–9; *LP* 13 (1), no. 371. The Morgan case was followed up by Lee and Cromwell, but the outcome is not certain: see *LP* 13 (1), nos 519, 624, 675, 824.

23   PRO SP 1/98, fol. 7 = *LP* 9, no. 608; *LP* 9, no 607.

24   Wright, pp. 189, p. 207; *LP* 11, no. 1418; *LP* 13 (2), nos 1072–3; G. Williams, *Wales and the Reformation* (Cardiff, 1997), pp. 123–4.

25   F.W. Brooks, *The Council of the North* (London, 1953).

26   S. Ellis, *Ireland in the age of the Tudors, 1447–1603* (London, 1998), pp. 11; 121–3, 125, 132–3.

27   B. Bradshaw, 'Cromwellian reforms and the origin of the Kildare rebellion', *TRHS* 5th series (1977): 69–94; S.G. Ellis, 'The Kildare rebellion and the early Henrician Reformation', *HJ* 19 (1976): 807–30.

28   *CSP Span.*, *1534–5*, no. 70, pp. 204–5; *LP* 7, nos 1457, 1575, 1567, 1573.

29   *LP* 8, no. 1004; *LP* 9, nos 308, 331, 575; *LP* 10, nos 822, 1030 (2.5); Ellis, *Ireland*, pp. 144, 205–7.

30   *LP* 9, nos 234 (p. 78), 1051, 1054; *LP* 10, nos 1032; 1210; 1223–4; *LP* 11, no. 266; *LP* 12 (2), no. 628.

31   *LP* 11, no. 1434; Merriman 2, pp. 80–81; *LP* 12 (1), no. 503; *LP* 14 (1), nos 993–7; Ellis 5, pp. 93–104.

32   See discussion in Ellis, *Ireland*, 195–205.

33   Browne to Cromwell: PRO SP 60/3, fol. 112 = *LP* 11, no. 120. Pelles: Lambeth MS 602, p. 136 = *LP* 11, no. 1248.

34   *SP* 2, pp. 465, 512.

35   *SP* 2, p. 569; *SP* 3, pp. 1, 6, 8, 35; *LP* 13 (1), nos 1037, 1161; *LP* 13 (2), no. 64.

36   *LP* 10, nos 1102–4, 1113, 1196; *LP* 11, nos 1149–50.

37   *LP* 12 (1), no. 1077; *LP* 13 (1), nos 50, 1224, 1303; *LP* 13 (2), nos 181, 195–6, 216, 504, 769, 1027, 1032; *LP* 14 (1), no. 302–3.

38   *LP* 12 (2), nos 76, 86, 146–7.

39   BL Cottonian MS Titus B. IX, fol. 111 = *LP* 10, no. 1030, Cap. 16.

40   *SP* 3, p. 123; *LP* 13 (1), nos 114, 1420; Merriman 2, p. 194. A qualifier may be prudent here. Another piece of legislation passed by the Irish parliament in 1536 was an 'Act against marrying or fostering with Irishmen' – hardly a measure designed to encourage harmony between Gaelic and English Irish (*LP* 10, no. 1030, Cap. 13). But Cromwell was not directing the Dublin parliament in everything because the same session (June 1536) confirmed the succession in favour of Henry and Anne – just when Henry and Cromwell were changing the succession laws in favour of Jane! Obviously some failure in communications between London and Dublin had occurred. The point about Cromwell and the Gaelic Irish remains valid, as the cases of Nangle and the Irish speaking agents show.

41   *LP* 14 (2), nos 355, 363, 617–18, 709–10; *LP* 15, nos 327–8, 341, 441, 649, 654, 683, 830; *SP* 3, p. 208

42   See also the discussion in Ellis, *Ireland*, pp. 352–8.

43.   Foxe 5, p. 395; *CSP Span., 1534–5*, no. 142, p. 427.

44.   *CSP Span., 1534–5*, no. 7, p. 23; *LP* 8, no. 647; *LP* 9, no. 730.

45.   Foxe 8, p. 27; Merriman 1, pp. 370–71.

46.   *LP* 9, nos 746, 765; *LP* 12 (2), no. 26. On Henry, Cromwell and Pole, see chapter 13.

47.   Elton, *Tudor Const.*, pp. 129–3; See also the detailed discussion on Cromwell's supervision of finances in Elton, *Tudor Rev.*, pp. 139–57.

48.   *TRP* 1, nos 180–82, pp. 264–6; no. 189, p. 281–3; Elton, *Reform and Renewal*, pp. 113–21.

49.   See the discussion in R.B. Outhwaite, *Inflation in Tudor and Early Stuart England* (London, 1982), p. 12.

50.   Cromwell's period seems, from these statistics, to be so different from the rest that it would be worthwhile to investigate this subject further. This, however, is a task for a specialist in economic and social history.

51.   Elton *Reform and Renewal*, pp. 101–6; Merriman 1, p.373; Lehmberg, *Reformation Parliament*, p. 188.

52.   Elton, *Reform and Renewal*, pp. 143–7. Cromwell's role in the Statute of Wills, 1540, is less clear: see Lehmberg, *Later Parliaments*, pp. 98–9.

53.   Elton, *Reform and Renewal*, pp. 107–8.

12. The Widows' Helper

1.   Merriman 1, pp. 175–6; Elton, *Policy*, pp. 305, 307.

2.   *LP* 14 (2), no. 49; Wright, pp. 255–61; Kaulek, pp. 140, 145 = *LP* 14 (2), nos 389, 613.

3. Elton, *Policy*, 293–326.
4. Taken from the analysis in Elton, *Policy*, pp. 387–93.
5. Elton, *Policy*, pp. 331–43, 380–82.
6. Elton, *Policy*, pp. 340–51. On Smeaton, see chap. 8
7. Elton, Policy, pp. 353–4, 375–80; *Sermons and Remains of Latimer*, ed. G.E. Corrie (Cambridge, 1845), p. 383.
8. Elton, *Policy*, pp. 18, 31–4, 58–65.
9. Merriman 1, pp. 360–61; Elton *Policy*, p. 19.
10. Ellis 11, pp. 63–7. For a summary of the *History of Florence*, see Q. Skinner, *Machiavelli*, (Oxford, 1981), pp. 78–88.
11. Merriman 1, pp. 85–7, 203; T. Mayer, *Reginald Pole, Prince and Prophet* (Cambridge, 2000), pp. 99–100; For more scepticism about Pole's story, see Elton, *Tudor Rev.*, pp. 73–4; A.G. Dickens, *Thomas Cromwell and the English Reformation* (London, 1959), pp. 76–7. On Morison, see F. Raab, *The English Face of Machiavelli: A changing interpretation, 1500–1700* (London, 1964), pp. 34–40.
12. From N. Machiavelli, *The Prince*, trans. G. Bull (Penguin, 1999).
13. *The Prince*, pp. 38–9.
14. *The Prince*, pp. 51–6.
15. *The Prince*, pp. 56–8.
16. *The Prince*, pp. 65, 71–7.
17. *The Prince*, pp. 79–83.
18. Skinner, *Machiavelli*, pp. 61–4.
19. Skinner, *Machiavelli*, pp. 8–14.
20. G.R. Elton, 'How Corrupt was Thomas Cromwell?', *HJ* 36/4 (1993): 905–8; Merriman 2, pp. 31–2, 49.
21. M.L. Robertson, 'The Art of the Possible: Thomas Cromwell's Management of West Country Government', *HJ* 32/4 (1989): 793–816.
22. Merriman 1, pp. 385–96; 2, pp. 37–9.
23. *LP* 6, no. 1663; 8, no. 32; *LP* 9, no. 317; *LP* 10, no. 1180.
24. *LP* 10, nos 1267, 1276; *LP* 11, no. 1466; *LP* 14 (1), no. 334; *LP* 14 (2), App. 7, p. 360.
25. *LP* 15, no. 318.
26. *LP* 15, no. 1029 (43).
27. *LP* 15, no. 1029 (62).
28. *LP* 6, no. 1414.
29. *LP* 10, no. 1185; *LP* 11, nos 1441, 1449, 1452, 1461.
30. *LP* 11, nos 1470–72.
31. *LP* 11, no. 1488.
32. *LP* 12 (1), no. 928.
33. *LP* 7, nos 1043, 1383. On the likelihood of Cromwell being the receiver, see discussion in S. Lehmberg, *The Reformation Parliament: 1529–1536* (Cambridge, 1977), p. 215.
34. *LP* 7, nos 1071, 1073; *LP* 15, no. 1029 (47).
35. *LP* 9, no. 611.
36. *LP* 11, no. 1467.
37. *LP* 13 (2), no. 1038; *LP* 15, no. 1029 (13).

38. *LP* 12 (2), nos 1073–4, 1153, 1159; *LP* 13 (1), no. 311.
39. *LP* 11, nos 1445, 1474, 1497.
40. *LP* 12 (2), no, 1327; *LP* 15, no. 1029 (44, 55).
41. *LP* 9, no. 1161; *LP* 12 (1), no. 985; *LP* 12 (2), nos 1037–8; *LP* 13 (2), no. 1237.
42. *LP* 13 (1), no. 662; *LP* 14 (1), nos 223, 387–8, 1051; *LP* 14 (2), App. 53, p. 371; *LP* 15, no. 1029 (22).
43. PRO SP 1/155, fol. 10 = *LP* 14 (2), no. 556.

13. Patron and Persona

1. Harvey is quoted and discussed in G.R. Elton, *Reform and Renewal: Thomas Cromwell and the Common Weal* (Cambridge, 1973), pp. 10–12. For Cromwell as Maecenas, see *LP* 10, no. 356; *LP* 12 (1), no. 746.
2. *CSP Span., 1534–5*, no. 228, p. 569; *LP* 10, no. 1130 (an example of a letter in Italian to Cromwell from one Antony Vivali – many more could be given); Ellis 10, pp. 177–8; Elton, *Reform and Renewal*, p. 13.
3. *LP* 13 (2), nos 335, 383, 616, 938.
4. *Letters of Gardiner*, ed. J.A. Muller (Cambridge, 1933), p. 399.
5. Gardiner, *Letters*, pp. xvi, xxiii, 44, 64, 66, 92, 100–22, 136–8, 262, 351, 358.
6. *LP* 4 (3), no. 5860.
7. R. Strong, *Holbein and Henry VIII* (London, 1967), p. 14; S. Foister, *Holbein and England* (London, 2004), pp. 103–6; *LP* 7, no. 1668; *LP* 15, no. 1029 (6), p. 512. Note there is nothing unLutheran about devotional works on Mary.
8. Elton, *Reform and Renewal*, pp. 13–16; *LP* 6, nos 717, 1448.
9. Elton, *Reform and Renewal*, p. 14; *LP* 10, nos 819, 840, 855; Foxe 5, p. 401; *LP* 14 (2), no. 782, p. 333.
10. Elton, *Reform and Renewal*, pp. 48–51; T. Mayer, *Thomas Starkey and the Commonweal: Humanist politics and religion in the reign of Henry VIII* (Cambridge, 1989), pp. 2–3, 216–20, 238–43. On Starkey's *Dialogue*, one of the major political writings of the age, see pp. 139–68 and also T. Mayer, 'Faction and Ideology: Thomas Starkey's *Dialogue*', *HJ* 28/1 (1985): 1–25.
11. Quoted and discussed in B. Thompson, 'Monasteries and their Patrons at Foundation and Dissolution', *TRHS* 6th ser., 4, p. 103.
12. S. Lehmberg, *Sir Thomas Elyot: Tudor Humanist* (Texas, 1960), pp. 30, 115–24, 150–51, 157–8, 167.
13. Elton, *Reform and Renewal*, pp. 18–23.
14. Chapuys: *CSP Span, 1531–3*, no. 1107, p. 752; no. 1132, p. 819; Castillon: Ribier 1, p. 351 = *LP* 13 (2), no. 1162, p. 482; Marillac: Kaulek, p. 108 = *LP* 14 (1), no. 1208; Ribier 1, p. 513 = *LP* 15, no. 486.
15. J. Stow, *A Survey of London*, (Oxford, 1908), vol. 1, p. 179.
16. Stow, *Survey of London*, 1, pp. 89, 91.
17. *LP* 10, no. 1231.
18. PRO SP 1/72, fols 11–12 = *LP* 5, no. 1509; Foxe 5, pp. 391, 394–6.

19. *LP* 8, no. 938; Elton, *Policy*, p. 423.
20. Merriman 2, pp. 133, 135, 161.
21. *LP* 5, nos 1435, 1464, 1467, 1472, 1483, 1509; *LP* 6, nos 1183, 1594; *LP* 7, nos 257, 882, 1151, 1525 (5), 1644; *LP* 14 (2), no. 782.
22. Ellis 9, pp. 341–5; *LP* 5, no. 359; *LP* 6, nos 1011, 1014; *LP* 7, nos 940, 967–8, 1473.
23. *LP* 12 (1), no. 678; *LP* 12 (2), nos 97, 269, 423–4, 629, 881; *LP* 13 (2), no. 967 (54).
24. Ellis 10, pp. 281, 285–6; *LP* 6, no. 1226, Cranmer, *Misc. Writings*, p. 274.
25. *LP* 7, no. 988.
26. Elton, *Policy*, pp. 101–6.
27. J. Strype, *Ecclesiastical Memorials under Henry VIII* (Oxford, 1822), vol. 1 (2), pp. 222–8.
28. Merriman 2, pp. 128–31.
29. *LP* 13 (1), no. 674.
30. *LP* 7, no. 905; *LP* 8, no. 542; Gardiner, *Letters*, pp. 60–61; Cranmer, *Misc. Writings*, p. 304.
31. Merriman 2, p. 136.
32. *Correspondence of Reginald Pole: vol. 1: A Calendar, 1518–1546*, ed. T. Mayer (Aldershot, 2002), pp. 77–86, 98–101, 135–6; *LP* 12 (1), nos 429–30.
33. Mayer, *Correspondence of Pole*, pp. 155–6, 162–7, 177–8.
34. Merriman 2, pp. 84–6.
35. Merriman 2, pp. 86–90.
36. *LP* 12 (1), no. 1032; *LP* 13 (2), nos. 797, pp. 309–10; 830, p. 342 (5); Mayer, *Pole*, p. 67. More cloak and dagger stories can be found in S. Brigden, '"The Shadow that you know": Sir Thomas Wyatt and Sir Francis Bryan at Court and in Embassy', *HJ* 39/1 (1996):1–31.
37. *LP* 8, no. 673; *LP* 11, nos 233, 236; *LP* 12 (1), nos 1157, 1173, *LP* 12 (2), nos. 206, 332.
38. *LP* 12 (2), no. 101.
39. *LP* 6, no. 475; *LP* 12 (2), no. 976, p. 342.
40. *LP* 7, no. 1083; *LP* 8, no. 319; *LP* 12 (1), no. 252.
41. *LP* 12 (2), nos 143, 1049.
42. *LP* 14 (1), nos 160, 425, p. 171.
43. *LP* 12 (2), nos 35, 100–101.
44. *LP* 11, no. 41; *LP* 12 (1), nos 532–3; *LP* 13 (1), no. 1082; *LP* 14 (2), no. 782, pp. 333, 339, 344, entries under 'December'.
45. Merriman 1, p. 61; Wright, p. 243.
46. PRO SP 1/75, fol. 193 = *LP* 6, no. 381; Merriman 1, p. 425; BL Cottonian MS Titus B. I, fol. 340 = *LP* 9, no. 330.
47. *LP* 15, nos 498 (59), 1029 (34).
48. *CSP Span., 1534–5*, no. 118, p. 344; *LP* 7, no. 1655.
49. Ellis 5, pp. 78–82; *LP* 11, no. 312.

14. The Vicegerency in Eclipse

1. R. McEntegart, *Henry VIII, The League of Schmalkalden and the English Reformation* (Woodbridge, 2002), pp. 89–94; Merriman 2, pp. 144–6; J.F. Mozley, *Coverdale and his Bibles* (London, 1953), pp. 168–71; Burnet 6, pp. 206, 210; *LP* 13 (1), nos 1197, 1231; *Sermons and Remains of Latimer*, ed. G.E. Corrie (PS, 1845), pp. 240–44.

2. Ellis 10, pp. 249–67; Hall, pp. 825–6; Wright, pp. 190–91; LP 13 (1), no. 1043; Cranmer, *Misc. Writings*, pp. 365–6; Latimer, *Remains*, pp. 391–2.

3. P. Marshall, 'Papist as Heretic: The Burning of John Forest, 1538', *HJ* 41 (1998): 351–74.

4. Kaulek, pp. 23–4 = *LP* 13 (1) 273–4; Kaulek, p. 73 = *LP* 13 (1), no. 1451, p. 535; Merriman 2, pp. 92–4, 102–5, 122–5, 140–41; *LP* 13 (1), nos 69, 1396; *CSP Span., 1538–42*, no. 7, p. 18. On the summer delegation to England, see McEntegart, *Henry VIII*, pp. 94–107. For the Thirteen Articles, see Cranmer, *Misc Writings*, p. 473 (4). On the Wittenberg Articles, see chap. 8; Melanchthon's *Loci*, chap. 6; Ten Articles and the Bishops' Book, chap. 10.

5. *LP* 13 (1), nos. 1267–9; C. Sturge, *Cuthbert Tunstall: Churchman, Scholar, Statesman, Administrator* (London, 1938), pp. 129–43, 170–87, 360.

6. Latimer, *Remains*, p. 395; *LP* 13 (1), nos. 1054 (p. 388), 1376, 1407.

7. Cranmer, *Misc. Writings*, pp. 377–9. For full details and analysis of the letters between Henry and the Germans, see J. Schofield, *Philip Melanchthon and the English Reformation* (Aldershot, 2006), chapter 7. What follows here is a summary.

8. *English Historical Documents, vol. 5, 1485–1558*, ed. C.H. Williams (London, 1967), pp. 811–14. For Cromwell's previous Injunctions, see chap. 10.

9. *MBW* 2, no. 2111 = *CR* 3, col. 601; *LP* 13 (2), nos 328, 367, 401, 674, 860, 1049. For some government backed historical revisionism on Becket, see Elton, *Policy*, p. 257, fn. 1.

10. *TRP* 1, no. 186, pp. 270–76; no. 188, pp. 278–80; J. Strype, *Memorial of … Thomas Cranmer, Archbishop of Canterbury* (Oxford, 1812), vol. 2, p. 691; *LP* 13 (2), nos 427, 498; Elton, *Policy*, pp. 256–60; McEntegart, *Henry VIII*, pp. 138–9.

11. Foxe 5, pp. 3–15; *LP* 5, nos 1432, 1458; Cranmer, *Misc. Writings*, p. 246; Brecht 3, pp. 56–7.

12. Foxe 5, pp. 230–36.

13. Merriman 2, p. 162; Foxe 5, p. 236.

14. Foxe 5, p. 236.

15. *LP* 13 (2), p. xlvi.

16. M.H and R. Dodds, *The Pilgrimage of Grace and the Exeter Conspiracy* (2 vols, Cambridge, 1915), 2, pp. 277–334.

17. Merriman 2, p. 161; *LP* 14 (1), nos 233, 280; Ribier 1, p. 350 = *LP* 13 (2) no. 1163, p. 483; *LP* 14 (1) no. 37, pp. 15, 18–19; Dodds, *Exeter Conspiracy* 2, pp. 319–20.

18. *CSP Span., 1534–5*, no. 109, p. 325; no. 201, p. 538; no. 213, p. 550.

19. *LP* 13 (2), no. 804, p. 317.
20. *LP* 13 (2), no. 800, p. 313.
21. *LP* 13 (2) nos 955 (8), 979, pp. 418 (7.3), 419 (11).
22. Dodds, *Exeter Conspiracy* 2, pp. 289–90; *LP* 13 (2), nos 765, 957.
23. *LP* 13 (2), nos 827, p. 334; 829 (2), pp. 337–8; 830, p. 341 (2.1); 856, p. 397, 875, p. 363; 954, 961.
24. Ribier 1, p. 247 = *LP* 13 (2), no. 753.
25. On the Court of Augmentations and its work, see J. Youings, *The Dissolution of the Monasteries* (London, 1971), chapter 4. The fish: Wright, pp. 152–4.
26. E. Hallam, 'Henry VIII's refoundations of 1536–37 and the course of the dissolution', *BIHR* 51 (1978): 124–31; Wright, pp. 156–7.
27. Ellis 11, pp. 158–61; Youings, *Dissolution*, pp. 67, 69; Merriman 2, pp. 131–2.
28. Hallam, 'Henry's refoundations', p. 131; D. Knowles, *The Religious Orders in England, vol. 3: The Tudor Age* (Cambridge, 1971), pp. 350–51, 360–66; Wright, p. 254; Youings, *Dissolution*, p. 78.
29. Wright, pp. 203–4; 244–5; *LP* 13 (2) 650.
30. Wright, p. 197.
31. Cranmer, *Misc Writings*, pp. 375–6.
32. Wright, pp. 248–9.
33. Merriman 2, p. 159; Wright, p. 250; *LP* 13 (2), nos 887, 1092; *LP* 14 (1), nos 145, 269.
34. *LP* 14 (1), nos 1006, 1025; *LP* 14 (2) App. 5, p. 359, App. 18, p. 363, App. 25, p. 365.
35. *LP* 12 (1), nos 508 (3), 1147 (2.1); Latimer, *Remains*, pp. 386–7, 406–9.
36. *LP* 13 (1), no. 347; Ellis 12, pp. 223–4; Wright, pp. 236–8; Latimer, *Remains*, pp. 407–8, 410–11.
37. *LP* 11, no. 570; *LP* 13 (1), nos 441, 492, 1262; Wright, pp. 227–31.
38. Ellis 11, pp. 233–4.
39. Ellis 11, pp. 236–8.
40. S. Lehmberg, *The Later Parliaments of Henry VIII: 1536–1547* (Cambridge, 1977), pp. 62–3; G.R. Elton, *England under the Tudors* (Routledge, 2001), pp. 148–9; Youings, *Dissolution*, p. 23.
41. Wright, p. 227.
42. Wright, pp. 238–9; *LP* 13 (2), nos 677, 866; *LP* 14 (1), no. 1191; *LP* 14 (2), no. 787.
43. Kaulek, p. 99 = *LP* 14 (1), no. 988; 31 Henry VIII, c. 9; *LJ* 1, p. 112; Lehmberg, *Later Parliaments*, pp. 66–7.
44. *ET*, p. 209 = *OL* 1, p. 316; *ET*, p. 398 = *OL* 2, p. 614; *LP* 15, no. 379.
45. See discussions in Youings, *Dissolution*, pp. 86–7; G.R. Elton *Reform and Reformation* (London, 1977), pp. 242–4; A. Ryrie, *The Gospel and Henry VIII: Evangelicals in the Early English Reformation* (Cambridge, 2003), pp. 161–4.
46. S. Greenslade (ed.), *The Cambridge History of the Bible* (3 vols, Cambridge, 1987), vol. 3, pp. 148–51; Mozley, *Coverdale*, pp. 7, 171–2, 201–3; Foxe 5, p. 411; *LP* 13 (2), no. 973.

47. *SP* 1, pp. 575–6, 578–9, 589; *SP* 8, p. 62; Coverdale, *Remains* ed. G. Pearson (Cambridge, 1846), pp. 492–7.
48. Mozley, *Coverdale*, p. 206; *LP* 13 (2) 1085; Foxe 5, pp. 411–12.
49. *LP* 13 (2), no. 1136 (2); Mozley, *Coverdale*, 210–11.
50. *LP* 13 (2), nos 148, 1110, 1087–8; 1136 (1).
51. *LP* 13 (2), no. 1163, p. 483; Mozley, *Coverdale*, pp. 207–9, 320–21.
52. Kaulek, pp. 97, 100, 108 = *LP* 14 (1), nos 934, 989, 1208; A. Slavin, 'The Rochepot Affair', *SCJ* 10 (1979): 3–19; Foxe 5, pp. 411–12.
53. *LP* 14 (1), no. 37, p. 19.
54. *TRP* 1, no. 192, pp. 286–7; Elton: *Policy*, pp. 247–8; Elton, *Tudor Const.*, pp. 223, 368; Merriman 2, pp. 111–12.
55. Cranmer, *Misc Writings*, p. 336.
56. Ibid., pp. 371–2
57. Ibid., p. 380.
58. Ibid., p. 380.
59. Ibid., pp. 381–5.
60. Ibid., pp. 386–7.
61. *LP* 14 (2), no. 75.
62. D. MacCulloch, *Thomas Cranmer: A Life* (London, 1996), pp. 221–6.
63. Williams (ed.), *English Historical Documents 5,* p. 609.
64. Elton, *Policy*, pp. 258–9.
65. *LP* 14 (1), nos 295, 839.
66. Coverdale, *Remains*, pp. 498–9; *LP* 13 (2), no. 571; *LP* 14 (1), nos 1052–3.
67. *LP* 13 (2), no. 953; *LP* 14 (1), no. 334.

15. *The Affairs of Kings*

1. Merriman 2, pp. 96–8; *LP* 12 (2), p. 602; *SP* 8, pp. 5–8.
2. Merriman 2, pp. 119–22; J. Scarisbrick, *Henry VIII* (London, 1968), pp. 355–61; *CSP Span.*, *1538–42*, no. 25, pp. 65, 69.
3. Kaulek, p. 50 = *LP* 13 (1), no. 995.
4. Merriman 2, pp. 117–20; Kaulek, p. 11 = *LP* 12 (2), no. 1285, p. 449; Kaulek, pp. 52–3 = *LP* 13 (1), no. 1101; Kaulek, p. 80 = *LP* 13 (2), no. 77; Scarisbrick, *Henry VIII*, pp. 355–61.
5. *CSP Span.*, *1536–8*, no. 225, pp. 530–31; Kaulek, pp. 65–6 = *LP* 13 (1), nos 145, 1320; *LP* 13 (2), p. 770; R. McEntegart, *Henry VIII, The League of Schmalkalden and the English Reformation* (Woodbridge, 2002), p. 142; Merriman 2, p. 174.
6. *CSP Span.*, *1536–8*, no. 21, p. 52; Ribier 1, p. 341 = *LP* 13 (2), no 1162; *LP* 13 (2), nos 923, 1127; *LP* 14 (1), no. 37, p. 18; McEntegart, *Henry VIII*, p. 142.
7. Merriman 2, pp. 174–5; Mont's letters are not calendared, but referred to in Merriman 2, p. 186.
8. Merriman 2, pp. 187, 207; *CSP Span.*, *1538–42*, no. 40, p. 115; *LP* 14 (1), nos 433, 478, p. 190.
9. *LP* 14 (1), no. 489; Merriman 2, pp. 188–90.
10. Merriman 2, pp. 199–201.

11. *LP* 14 (1), nos 36, 62, 372, 446–7, 461; *Correspondence of Reginald Pole: vol. 1: A Calendar, 1518–1546*, ed. T. Mayer (Aldershot, 2002), pp. 209–13; *CSP Span.*, *1538–42*, no. 54, p. 141, no. 76, p. 174.

12. Merriman 1, p. 441; 2, pp. 167–73; *CSP Ven.* 5, no. 35.

13. *LP* 14 (1), no. 200. For fuller discussion, see Pole's biographer: T. Mayer, *Reginald Pole, Prince and Prophet* (Cambridge, 2000), pp. 78–100.

14. On the divorce and supremacy, see chaps 2, 4; on the monasteries, chap. 6; on Pole and historians' reactions, chap. 12.

15. *LP* 14 (1), nos 144, 227; Merriman 2, pp. 180–83; *CSP Span.*, *1538–42*, *Introduction*, p. ii.

16. S. Lehmberg, *The Later Parliaments of Henry VIII: 1536–1547* (Cambridge, 1977); pp. 40–41; Merriman 2, pp. 183–6, 207; *LP* 14 (1), no. 462.

17. *LP* 13 (2), nos 288, 349; Merriman 2, p. 183 = *LP* 14 (1), nos 307, 398–400, 529, 564, 615, 644, 652–5, 662, 682, 940–41.

18. *LP* 14 (1), no. 37, p. 18; Ribier 1, p. 437 = *LP* 14 (1), no. 770; Kaulek, pp. 87–90 = *LP* 14 (1), nos 669–70; Kaulek, pp. 122–3 = *LP* 14 (2), no. 35.

19. *LP* 14 (1), nos 455, 481; Merriman 2, pp. 195, 197.

20. *LP* 14 (1), nos 691, 714, 728, 734–5, 767; Merriman 2, p. 211.

21. *LP* 14 (1), nos 625, 687.

22. *LP* 14 (1), nos 599, 627; Merriman 2, pp. 211–13; Mayer, *Correspondence of Pole*, pp. 213–14, 217–19; Kaulek, p. 111 = *LP* 14 (1), no. 1230; *CSP Span.*, *1538–42*, no. 80.

23. Merriman 2, pp. 202–7; McEntegart, *Henry VIII*, p. 149–52.

24. Merriman 2, pp. 216, 219–22. Some nuns who made their vows while very young, probably not entirely freely, were allowed to marry: *LP* 14 (1), no. 1321.

25. Merriman 1, pp. 272–3; Lehmberg, *Later Parliaments*, pp. 55–7; McEntegart, *Henry VIII*, p. 155–6.

26. *LP* 14 (1), nos 920, 1193.

27. Quoted and discussed in Lehmberg, *Later Parliaments*, pp. 60–61.

28. *LP* 14 (1), nos 955–8, 981; Lehmberg, *Later Parliaments*, pp. 65, 68–74; McEntegart, *Henry VIII*, pp. 157–62.

29. For a fuller analysis of the Six Articles, and Henry's policy behind the act, see J. Schofield, *Philip Melanchthon and the English Reformation* (Ashgate, 2006), chapter 8.

30. Foxe 5, p. 502.

31. *SP* 1, p. 849; A. Chester, *Hugh Latimer: Apostle to the English* (New York, 1978), pp. 149–50.

32. Elton, *Policy*, pp. 105–7.

33. D. MacCulloch, *Thomas Cranmer: A Life* (New haven and London, 1996), p. 251; Cranmer, *Misc Writings*, pp. 393–4.

34. Foxe 5, p. 398; 8, p. 14; Burnet 1, p. 425; Elton, *Studies* 1, p. 213; *LP* 14 (1), nos 693, 764; Merriman 2, p. 215.

35. R. McEntegart, 'England and the League of Schmalkalden, 1531–1547: Faction, Foreign Policy and the English Reformation' (London School of Economics Ph.D., 1992), pp. 372–3, 377–8, 399–400; Elton, *Policy*, pp. 98–9; *LP* 14 (2), no. 301.

36. Ellis 2, pp. 121–2.
37. I was gratified to read that Prof. Scarisbrick also rejects the idea that Cromwell tried to trick or push Henry into an unwanted marriage: Scarisbrick, *Henry VIII*, pp. 373–5.
38. Kaulek, p. 125 = *LP* 14 (2), no. 117.
39. McEntegart, *Henry VIII*, pp. 180–83; *LP* 14 (2), nos 220–21, 285–6.
40. Kaulek, pp. 137–8 = *LP* 14 (2), no. 388.
41. *TRP* 1, no. 192, pp. 286–7; J.F. Mozley, *Coverdale and his Bibles* (London, 1953), pp. 217–18; *Misc Writings*, pp. 118–27, 395–6; Merriman 2, pp. 144–7; Elton, *Policy* pp. 260–61.
42. Hall, pp. 832–3; McEntegart, *Henry VIII*, pp. 179–81, 187–8; *LP* 14 (2), nos 638, 718; *LP* 15, nos 14, 850 (5); *SP* 8, pp. 208–13; J. Strype, *Ecclesiastical Memorials under Henry VIII* (Oxford, 1822) 1 (2), pp. 454–5.
43. Hall, pp. 833–7; Merriman 2, pp. 268–71. A generation later, Hall's account was accepted and followed by the Elizabethan historian, Holinshed – see Holinshed 3, pp. 810–14.
44. Strype, *Ecclesiastical Memorials*, pp. 459, 462–3.
45. Merriman 1, p. 262; *LP* 14 (2), nos 258 (p. 97), 500, 754, 881–2 (pp. 509, 587); Hall, p. 837; Kaulek, p. 151 = *LP* 15, no. 22–3. We can discount the description of Cardinal Farnese to Pope Paul III that Anne was 'old and ugly' (*LP* 15, no. 179). He had not seen her, and like many historians, he assumed she was unattractive simply because Henry did not like her. Besides, Anne was not old – she was only 25.

16. A Treacherous Place

1. *LP* 14 (2), no. 750, pp. 278, 281; Merriman 1, p. 279.
2. R. McEntegart, *Henry VIII, The League of Schmalkalden and the English Reformation* (Woodbridge, 2002), pp. 192–3.
3. *LP* 15, nos 136, 248–9; Ellis 11, pp. 279–83.
4. Kaulek, p. 153 = *LP* 15, no. 121; *LP* 15, nos 145, 189.
5. *LP* 15, nos 222–4.
6. *LP* 15, nos 233, 240, 253; Merriman 2, pp. 250–55.
7. J. Strype, *Ecclesiastical Memorials under Henry VIII* (Oxford, 1822) 1 (2), p. 437; *SP* 8, p. 234; *LP* 15, no. 243.
8. J.F. Mozley, *Coverdale and his Bibles* (London, 1953), pp. 261–88 (quote from p. 269); Foxe 5, pp. 411–12.
9. Henry on justification quoted and discussed in McEntegart, *Henry VIII*, pp. 192–3. I am most indebted to Dr McEntegart's researches in Germany for this vital piece of evidence.
10. See chap 6 (*Loci*), chap. 10 (Ten Articles and the Bishops' Book), chap. 14 (Thirteen Articles). On Taverner, see W. Underwood, 'Thomas Cromwell and William Marshall's Protestant Books', *HJ* 47/3 (2004): 533–5.
11. *LP* 14 (1), nos 206, 412, 775, 890; *ET*, p. 406 = *OL* 2, p .627; *ET*, p. 398 = *OL* 2, p. 614. For a fuller account of this Lenten controversy, see J.

Schofield, *Philip Melanchthon and the English Reformation* (Ashgate, 2006), pp. 137–41. What follows here is a summary.

12. *ET*, p. 209 = *OL* 1, p. 317.

13. Ribier 1, p. 513 = *LP* 15, no. 486.

14. *LP* 15, no. 429. Wallop's letter is dated 31 March, but the date of this dinner is not certain. It was either before the recantations, or at least before anyone in power heard that they were all made as a bit of a joke. See M. St C. Byrne (ed.), *Lisle Letters*, 6 vols (Chicago, 1981) vol. 6, p. 59. There is no evidence for Merriman's suggestion that Cromwell made an apology to Gardiner, as Merriman himself admits. Why he made the suggestion at all is a mystery: Merriman 1, pp. 288–9.

15. Burnet 1, pp. 437–9; S. Lehmberg, *The Later Parliaments of Henery VIII, 1536–1547* (Cambridge, 1977), pp. 85, 90–91.

16. Cromwell resigns as PS: Elton, *Tudor Rev.*, pp. 313–14; *LP* 15, no. 437. Cromwell's ennoblement: Hall, p. 838; *LP* 15, no. 541; Kaulek, p. 179 = *LP* 15, no. 567; Lehmberg, *Later Parliaments*, p. 86; G.R. Elton, 'Thomas Cromwell's Decline and Fall', *Cambridge Historical Journal*, 10 (1951): 174; D. Head, *Ebbs and Flows of Fortune: Life of Thomas Howard, Third Duke of Norfolk* (Georgia, 1995), p. 170. Whether Cromwell's advancement was an intended snub to Norfolk is uncertain. It could be taken that way.

17. Ellis 5, pp. 156–8.

18. Lehmberg, *Later Parliaments*, pp. 91–5; *LP* 15, no. 502.

19. Lehmberg, *Later Parliaments*, pp. 94–5, 103; Kaulek, pp. 181, 184 = *LP* 15, nos 651, 697.

20. Merriman 2, pp. 65–6, 139–40. For a full account of religious troubles at Calais, see *Lisle Letters*, especially vol. 6, *passim*.

21. Foxe 5, pp. 497–501; Cranmer, *Misc. Writings*, pp. 375–6.

22. Merriman 2, pp. 222–8; *LP* 14 (1), nos 1009, 1042, 1058, 1088; *LP* 14 (2), no. 496.

23. *Lisle Letters* 6, pp. 63–6, 72–4, 117; Foxe 5, pp. 515–19. Cromwell's reception of the prisoners comes from Foxe, and it is just possible that Foxe is exaggerating slightly. Foxe does have a tendency to assume that Lutherans like Cromwell, had they lived longer, would have turned into good Calvinists like himself. But it does seem fairly certain that Cromwell did not take the allegations against the men too seriously.

24. *Lisle Letters* 6, pp. 53–121, especially pp. 56, 74, 87, 96–8, 102.

25. *LP* 15, nos 727–8, 1005; Kaulek, pp. 184–5, 195 = *LP* 15, nos 697, 804, p. 378; *Lisle Letters* 5, pp. 352–3; 6, p. 116.

26. *LP* 15, nos 310, 509; Kaulek, p. 184 = *LP* 15, no. 697; Lehmberg, *Later Parliaments*, pp. 102–3.

27. J. Stow, *A Survey of London* (Oxford, 1908), vol. 2, p. 99; Merriman 2, pp. 271–2; Strype, *Ecclesiastical Memorials* 1 (2) 461–2.

28. *ET*, p. 134 = *OL* 1, pp. 201–2.

29. Head, *Norfolk*, pp. 179–80; J. Scarisbrick, *Henry VIII* (London, 1968), p. 429; *LP* 14 (2), no. 572; *LP* 15, nos 21, 613 (12), 686; *LP* 16, no. 1409.

30. *LP* 15, no. 329.

31. Foxe 5, p.401; Kaulek, p. 185 = *LP* 15, nos 697, 721.

32. Kaulek pp. 186–8 = *LP* 15, nos 736–7.
33. *LP* 15, nos 747, 749–50 (see also Index, p. 671).
34. Strype, *Ecclesiastical Memorials* 1 (2), pp. 381–2; *SP* 1, p. 627.
35. Strype, *Ecclesiastical Memorials* 1 (2), pp. 328–9; Burnet 6, pp. 287–8; *LP* 12 (1), nos 987, 939, 1032.
36. BL Cottonian MS Titus B. I, fol. 100 (no matching *LP*); Burnet 6, p. 275; Foxe 6, p. 66.
37. Kaulek, p. 187 = *LP* 15, no. 737.
38. Strype, *Ecclesiastical Memorials* 1 (2), pp. 459–60.
39. *ET*, p. 134 = *OL* 1, p. 202; Foxe 5, p. 402.
40. Elton, *Studies* 3, p. 91; Lehmberg, *Later Parliaments*, pp. 105–6.
41. Kaulek, p. 193 = *LP* 15, no. 804. This is Marillac's account, dated 23 June, nearly two weeks after the event. Marillac received his information from Norfolk and others, so some allowance may have to be made for a bit of embellishing. Nevertheless, Marillac was a politically astute man, well able to sift fact from spin, so there is no real reason to doubt him this time.

17. The Pillar is Perished

1. Hall, p. 838.
2. Kaulek, pp. 190–91 = *LP* 15, no. 767.
3. Kaulek, pp. 189–90 = *LP* 15, no. 766.
4. Kaulek, p. 191 = *LP* 15, no. 785; *SP* 8, p. 264.
5. Kaulek, p. 193 = *LP* 15, no. 804; *SP* 8, pp. 349–50.
6. *SP* 8, pp. 364–5.
7. S. Lehmberg, *The Later Parliaments of Henry VIII: 1536-1547* (Cambridge, 1977), p. 107; Kaulek, p. 194 = *LP* 15, no. 804.
8. Cranmer, *Misc. Writings*, p. 401. Diarmaid MacCulloch dates this letter to 12 June, unlike Cox and *LP*. See D. MacCulloch, *Thomas Cranmer: A Life* (New Haven and London, 1996), p. 270.
9. Merriman 2, pp. 264–7.
10. *LJ* 32 Hen. VIII, pp. 145–6, 149; G.R. Elton, *Reform and Reformation* (London, 1977), pp. 292–3; Lehmberg, *Later Parliaments*, pp. 107, 109, 313, fn. 108.
11. The attainder is printed in Burnet 4, pp. 416–21.
12. Kaulek, p. 195 = *LP* 15, no. 804, p. 378.
13. For Luther and Müntzer, see Brecht 2, pp. 146–57, 172–94. For Zwingli, see G.R. Potter, *Zwingli* (Cambridge, 1976), pp. 413–14. The Lutherans agreed that Christian princes had duty to defend true religion, so a defensive war was acceptable. In 1538 Luther approved resistance to the Emperor, though with misgivings, should he attack the Lutheran states. In that case, Charles would be effectively waging war on behalf of the pope, not his own interests. Normally the Christian would be bound to render obedience even to an unjust government, but this did not apply to the pope because he was not a legitimate ruler. If he or princes

on his behalf waged war, then resistance was justified. See Brecht 3, pp. 199–203; E. Cameron, *The European Reformation* (Oxford, 1991), pp. 353–4. However, this hardly fits Cromwell's case. Maybe he was planning something against the bishops, but not directly against Henry.

14. Gray quoted and discussed in A. Ryrie, *The Gospel and Henry VIII: Evangelicals in the Early English Reformation* (Cambridge, 2003), p. 139.

15. Foxe 5, p. 519; *LP* 15, no. 498, p. 217, II. cap. 49.

16. Hall, p. 838; A.G. Dickens, *The English Reformation* (London, 1989), p. 201; Lehmberg, *Later Parliaments*, pp. 118–19.

17. *CSP Span., 1553*, p. 339.

18. *LP* 12 (2), no. 101; Wright 2, pp. 241–2; *ET*, p. 209 = *OL* 1, p. 317: Nicholas Partridge to Bullinger – Audely 'has conceived a great regard for you'.

19. Merriman 2, pp. 268–73. The original is in Hatfield House, Cecil Papers 1/24–7. I am grateful to Lord Salisbury and the Librarian for allowing me to see a copy.

20. Merriman 2, pp. 273–6 (See also the discussion on these letters in *LP* 15, nos 822–3, editor's note); Foxe 5, pp. 401–2. Actually Foxe does not say for sure which of Cromwell's letters moved Henry this way, but it is most likely this one.

21. *LP* 15, nos 821–2; Lehmberg, *Later Parliaments*, pp. 112–13.

22. Lehmberg, *Later Parliaments*, pp. 114–15; Kaulek, p. 202 = *LP* 15, no. 901; *LP* 15, nos 844–5, 860–61, 908–9, 925; Burnet 4, pp. 446–9; Hall, p. 839. The elusive pre-contract documents had eventually arrived in February, though unfortunately there is no record of Henry's reaction when he saw them, and surviving copies are damaged (*LP* 15, nos 267, 909). Later in July, when Anne's divorce was arranged, the English claimed that the documents did not put the matter beyond doubt after all: J. Strype, *Ecclesiastical Memorials under Henry VIII* (Oxford, 1822), 1 (2), pp. 452–3.

23. *LP* 15, nos 792, 890; *SP* 8, pp. 362, 376.

24. *LJ* 32 Hen. VIII, pp. 157–9; *LP* 15, no. 498, p. 215, I. 58; Lehmberg, *Later Parliaments*, p. 111.

25. Kaulek, p. 194 = *LP* 15, no. 804; Kaulek, p. 198 = *LP* 15, no. 847, p. 418; *CSP Ven.*, 5, no. 220; Merriman 1, p. 296; Kaulek, p. 207 = *LP* 15, no. 926.

26. Foxe 5, p. 401; Merriman 2, pp. 277–8.

27. Merriman 2, p. 129 (In a letter from Cromwell to Shaxton; for the context, see chap. 13).

28. Merriman 1, p. 301.

29. AC: see summary at the end of Article 21, and conclusion, in *BSLK*, pp. 83 (1), 134 (19–20, 24). For the last words and prayer, see Foxe 5, pp. 402–3; Hall, p. 839. Hall says that Cromwell 'made his prayer', but it is Foxe who supplies the words of the prayer. Its strong Lutheran tone may be the reason that Hall, perhaps writing while Henry was still alive, left them out. Richard Hilles reports a rumour that Cromwell, in return for a quick death, confessed that he had 'offended the king' (*OL* 1, p. 203). Hilles admits, however, that it was only a rumour, and he did not know whether it was true. Cromwell did indeed make purely general confes-

sions like this, and not just on the scaffold; he made them in his letters to Henry from the Tower. But he consistently denied the *specific* charges of treason and sacramentary heresy. On the evangelical use of the word 'Catholic', compare also the title of Thomas Cranmer's best known later work, *Defence of the True and Catholic Doctrine of the Sacrament*: Cranmer was contending for the *Reformed* doctrine, arguing that this was the one held by the ancient church.

30. Foxe 5, pp. 438–9; *Works of Coverdale*, ed. G. Pearson (Cambridge, 1846), pp.xi-xii; J. Schofield, *Philip Melanchthon and the English Reformation*, pp. 144–5, 181; *LP* 15, no. 911.

31. *Lisle Letters* 6, pp. 113–15, 180–82, 238; *LP* 15, no. 812; *LP* 16, nos 305 (2), 878 (80), p. 427; Foxe 5, pp. 520–22.

32. Kaulek, p. 274 = *LP* 15, no. 930.

33. Printed in *Complete Poems of Thomas Wyatt*, ed. R.A. Rebholz (Middlesex, 1978), p. 86.

Epilogue

1. *SP* 8, p. 517.

2. Kaulek, p. 274 = *LP* 16, no. 590, p. 285.

3. *Narratives of the Reformation*, ed. J.G. Nichols (Camden Society 1st series 77, 1859), pp. 254–8. For a full discussion of the 'Prebendaries Plot' against Cranmer, see D. MacCulloch, *Thomas Cranmer: A Life* (New Haven and London, 1996), pp. 295–323.

4. *Julius Caesar*, Act 2, scene 1; Foxe 5, pp. 691–2 (italics mine).

5. Kaulek, p. 196 = *LP* 15, no. 804. On Henry's last years see G.R. Elton, *England under the Tudors*, pp.197–9; J. Scarisbrick, *Henry VIII* (London, 1967), pp. 433–57; J. Ridley, *Henry VIII* (London, 1984), pp. 364–400. For Wilson's quote, see G.R. Elton, *Reform and Renewal: Thomas Cromwell and the Common Weal* (Cambridge, 1973), p. 166.

6. *LP* 12 (1), no. 853.

7. Aske's admission: *LP* 12 (1), no. 6, p. 9.

8. Cecil: Gardiner, *History of England* ... 1, p. 91. Cromwell on his calling: Merriman 2, p. 129.

List of Illustrations

Bibliography

Manuscript Sources

British Library   Additional MS, Cottonian MS, Harleian MS
Hatfield House, Herts   Cecil Papers
Lambeth Palace Library   Carew MS
Public Records Office   SP 1, SP 60
Vienna Archives   Haus-,Hof-und Staatsarchiv:
                                   Staatenabteilungen England, Diplomatische
                                   Korrespondenz

Primary Sources

Bandello, M., *Tutte le Opere*, A cura di Francesco Flora (2 vols, Arnoldo
    Mondadori Editiore, 1966)
*Die Bekenntnisschriften der Evangelisch-Lutherischen Kirche, herausgegeben
    im Gedenkjahr der Ausburgischen Konfession 1930* (7 Auflage, reprint
    Göttingen, 1976)
Calendar of Close Rolls … Henry VII (London, HMSO, 1963), vol. 2,
    1500–1509
Calendar of State Papers, Domestic, Edward VI, Philip and Mary, Elizabeth (9
    vols, H.M.S.O., 1856–72)
Calendar of State Papers, Foreign (23 vols, H.M.S.O., 1863–1950)
Calendar of State Papers, Milan, vol. 1, 1385–1618, ed. A. Hinds (London:
    H.M.S.O., 1912).

Calendar of State Papers, Spanish, ed. P. de Gayangos *et al.* (15 vols in 20 H.M.S.O., 1862–1954)

Calendar of State Papers, Venetian, ed. R. Brown *et al.* (9 vols, H.M.S.O., 1864–98)

Cavendish, G., *The Life and Death of Cardinal Wolsey*, ed. R. Sylvester for The Early English Text Society (London: Oxford UP, 1959)

Cromwell, Thomas, *Life and Letters of Thomas Cromwell*, ed. R.B. Merriman (2 vols, Oxford, Clarendon, 1902)

Chronicle of King Henry VIII of England ... written in Spanish by an unknown hand, trans. and ed. M.A. Hume (London: George Bell and Sons, 1889)

Constantine, G., *Memorial to Thomas Cromwell*, ed. T. Amyot in Arch. 23 (1831)

Coverdale, M., *Remains*, ed. G. Pearson (Cambridge: PS, 1846)

——, *Works*, ed. G. Pearson (Cambridge: PS, 1846)

Cranmer, Thomas, *Works of Archbishop Cranmer*, ed. J.E. Cox (Cambridge: PS, 1844)

——, *Miscellaneous Writings and Letters of Thomas Cranmer*, ed. J.E. Cox (Cambridge: PS, 1846)

English Historical Documents, vol. 5, 1485–1558, ed. C.H. Williams (London: Eyre and Spottiswoode, 1967)

Epistolae Tigurinae de rebus potissimum ad ecclesiae Anglicanae Reformationem .... (Cambridge: PS, 1848)

Fisher, J., *The English Works of John Fisher. Bishop of Rochester (1469–1535)*, ed. C. A. Hatt (Oxford: Oxford UP, 2002)

Foxe, J., *Acts and Monuments of John Foxe*, ed. Josiah Pratt (8 vols, 4th edn, London: Religious Tract Society, 1877)

Frith, J., *The Work of*, ed. N.T. Wright, Courtenay Library of Reformation Classics (Appleford: Sutton Courtenay Press, 1978)

Froude, J. A. (ed.), *The Pilgrim: A Dialogue of the Life and Actions of King Henry VIII*, by W. Thomas, Clerk of the Council to Edward VI (London: Parker, Son and Bourn, 1861)

Gardiner, S., *Letters of*, ed. J.A. Muller (Cambridge: Cambridge UP, 1933)

Hall, E., *A Chronicle containing the history of England ... to the end of the reign of Henry VIII* (London: J. Johnson, 1809)

Holinshed, R, *Chronicles of England ...* (6 vols, London: J. Johnson, 1807–8)

Hearne, T., *Sylloge epistolarum, a variis Angliae scriptarum ...* (Oxford, 1716)

Hooper, J., *Early Writings*, ed. S. Carr (Cambridge: PS, 1843)

——, *Later Writings*, ed. C. Nevinson (Cambridge: PS, 1852)

Journals of the House of Lords, 1509ff (10 vols)

Latimer, H., *Sermons*, ed. G.E. Corrie (Cambridge: PS, 1844)

——, *Sermons and Remains*, ed. G.E. Corrie (Cambridge: PS, 1845)

William Latymer's *Chronicle of Anne Boleyn*, ed. M. Dowling, *Camden Miscellany* 30 (CS 4th series 39, 1990), pp.23–66

Bibliography

Letters and Papers, Foreign and Domestic, of the Reign of Henry VIII, 1509–47,
    ed. J.S. Brewer *et al.* (21 vols and 2 vols addenda, H.M.S.O., 1862–1932)

Lisle Letters, ed M. St C. Byrne (6 vols, Chicago: Chicago UP, 1981)

Luther, M. *Dr Martin Luthers Werke: Kritische Gesamtausgabe* (61 vols,
    Weimar: Hermann Böhlaus, 1883–1983)

Luthers Werke, Briefwechsel (18 vols, Weimar: Hermann Böhlaus, 1930–85)

Luther's Works: American edn, ed. J. Pelikan (55 vols, Philadelphia and St.
    Louis: Fortress Press and Concordia, 1955–86)

Machiavelli, N., *The Prince,* trans. G. Bull (Penguin, 1999)

Marsiglio of Padua: The Defender of Peace, trans. A. Gewirth, (New York:
    Harper and Row, 1956)

Melanchthon, P., *Philippi Melanchthonis Opera Quae Supersunt Omnia,* ed.
    C.G. Bretschneider (28 vols, Halle, 1834–60)

—— , *Melancnthons Werke in Auswahl,* ed. R. Stupperich (7 vols to date,
    Gütersloh: Gerd Mohn, 1951–)

—— , *Melanchthons Briefwechsel: Kritische und Kommentierte Gesamtausgabe,*
    ed. H. Scheible (15 vols to date, Stuttgart-Bad Cannstatt: Frommann-
    Holzboog, 1977–)

More, Thomas, *Complete Works of,* vol. 8, ed. L.A. Schuster *et al.* (New
    Haven and London: Yale UP, 1973).

—— , *Correspondence of,* ed. E.F. Rogers (Princeton: Princeton UP, 1947)

—— , *Life of,* by William Roper (London: Chatto and Windus, reprint 1907)

Narratives of the Reformation, ed. J.G. Nichols (Camden Society 1st series,
    vol. 77, 1859)

Original Letters Illustrative of English History, ed. H. Ellis (12 vols, London:
    Bentley, 1846)

Original Letters Relative to the English Reformation, ed. H. Robinson (2 vols,
    Cambridge: PS, 1846–7)

Parker, M., *Correspondence of,* ed. J. Bruce and T. Perowne (Cambridge: PS,
    1853)

Correspondence of Reginald Pole: vol. 1: A Calendar, 1518–1546, ed. T. Mayer
    (Aldershot: Ashgate, 2002)

Records of the Reformation: The Divorce, 1527–1533 ed. N. Pocock (2 vols,
    Oxford: Clarendon, 1870)

Reports of Sir John Spelman, ed. J. H. Baker, vol. 1 (London: Seldon Society, 1977)

Ribier, G., *Lettres et memoires d'estat* … (Paris, 1666).

*State Papers Published under the Authority of His Majesty's Commission, King
    Henry VIII* (11 vols, 1830–52)

Statutes of the Realm (11 vols, London: Dawsons, reprint 1963)

Tappert, T. (ed.), *The Book of Concord: The Confessions of the Evangelical
    Lutheran Church* (Philadelphia: Fortress Press, 1959)

Stow, J., *A Survey of London,* 2 vols, reprinted from the 1603 text by C.L.
    Kingsford (Oxford: Clarendon, 1908)

Tudor Royal Proclamations, vol. 1, ed. P.L. Hughes and J.F Larkin (New Haven and London: Yale UP, 1964)

Tyndale, W., *Expositions and Notes on Sundry Portions of Holy Scriptures, together with the Practice of Prelates*, ed. H. Walter (Cambridge: PS, 1849)

Wriothesley, C., *A Chronicle of England … by*, ed. W.D. Hamilton (2 vols, Camden Society, second series, 1875).

Wright, T. (ed.), *Three Chapters of Letters relating to the Suppression of Monasteries*, Camden Society, vol. 26 (London: John Bowyer Nichols, 1843)

Wyatt, George: *The Papers of George Wyatt*, ed. D. M. Loades, Camden Society, series. 4, 5 (1968).

Wyatt, Thomas, *Complete Poems*, ed. R. A. Rebholz (Middlesex: Penguin, 1978)

Zürich Letters, ed. H. Robinson (2 vols, Cambridge: PS, 1842, 1845)

Secondary Sources

Beckingsale, B.W., *Thomas Cromwell: Tudor Minister* (London: Macmillan, 1978)

Bernard, G. 'The Fall of Anne Boleyn', *EHR* 106 (1991): 584–610

—— , Rejoinder [to Ives, see below], *EHR* 107 (1992): 665–74

—— , 'Anne Boleyn's religion', *HJ* 36 (1993): 1–20

—— , *The King's Reformation: Henry VIII and the Remaking of the English Church* (New Haven and London: Yale UP, 2005)

Bowker, M., 'The Supremacy and the Episcopate: the struggle for control, 1534–40', *HJ* 18 (1975): 227–43

Bradshaw, B., 'Cromwellian Reform and the Origins of the Kildare Rebellion, 1533–34', *TRHS* 5th series 27 (1977), pp. 69–94

—— , and Bottigheimer, K., 'Revisionism and the Irish reformation', *JEH* 51/3 (2000): 581–91

Brecht, M., *Martin Luther*, trans. J.L. Schaff (3 vols, Philadelphia and Minneapolis: Fortress Press, 1985, 1990, 1993) …

—— , 1: *His Road to Reformation, 1485–1521*

—— , 2: *Shaping and Defining the Reformation, 1521–1532*

—— , 3: *The Preservation of the Church, 1532–1545*

Brigden, S., 'Thomas Cromwell and the Brethren', in C. Cross, D. Loades and J. Scarisbrick (eds), *Law and Government under the Tudors* (Cambridge: Cambridge UP, 1988), pp. 31–49

—— , *London and the Reformation* (Oxford: Clarendon, 1989)

—— , '"The Shadow that you know": Sir Thomas Wyatt and Sir Francis Bryan at Court and in Embassy', *HJ* 39/1 (1996):1–31.

Brooks, F.W., *The Council of the North* (London, G. Philip, 1953)

Burnet, G., *History of the Reformation of the Church of England*, ed. N. Pocock (7 vols, Oxford: Clarendon, 1865)

Bush, M., *The Pilgrimage of Grace: A study of the rebel armies of October 1536* (Manchester: Manchester UP, 1996)

Cameron, E., *The European Reformation* (Oxford: Clarendon, 1991)

Carelton, K., *Bishops and Reform in the English Church, 1520–1559* (Woodbridge: Boydell Press, 2001)

Chester, A., *Hugh Latimer: Apostle to the English* (New York: Octagon, 1978)

Cooper, C. H. and J.W., *Annals of Cambridge* (6 vols, Cambridge: Warwick and co., 1842–1908)

Collier, J., *An Ecclesiastical History of Great Britain* (2 vols, London: Samuel Keble and Benjamin Tooke, 1708–1714.)

Collins/Robert, *Concise French Dictionary* (4th edn, Glasgow: Harper Collins, 2000)

Cross, C., Loades, D. and Scarisbrick, J. (eds.), *Law and Government under the Tudors* (Cambridge: Cambridge UP, 1988)

Crouzet, D., *La Genèse de la Réforme Française, 1520–1562* (Paris: Sedes, 1996)

D'Alton, C., 'William Warham and English Heresy Policy after the fall of Wolsey', *HR* 77/197 (2004): 337–57

Daniell, D., *William Tyndale: A Biography* (New Haven and London: Yale UP, 1994)

Davies, J., *A History of Wales* (London: Allen Lane, 1993)

Dickens, A.G., *Thomas Cromwell and the English Reformation* (London: English UP, 1959)

—— , and D. Carr (eds.), *The Reformation in England To The Accession of Elizabeth I* (London: Edward Arnold, 1967)

—— , *The English Reformation* (2nd edn, London: Batsford, 1989)

Dodds, M. H. and R., *The Pilgrimage of Grace and the Exeter Conspiracy* (2 vols, Cambridge: Cambridge UP, 1915)

Dowling, M., 'Anne Boleyn and Reform', *JEH* 35 (1984): 30–45

Duffy, E., The *Stripping of the Altars: Traditional religion in England 1400–1580* (New Haven and London: Yale UP, 1992)

—— , *Saints and Sinners: A history of the popes* (New Haven and London: Yale UP, 1997)

Elliot, J. H., *Imperial Spain, 1469–1716* (London: Edward Arnold, 1963)

Ellis, S. G., 'The Kildare Rebellion and the early Henrician Reformation', *HJ* 19 1976): 807–30

——, 'Thomas Cromwell and Ireland', *HJ* 23 (1980): 479–519

——, *Ireland in the age of the Tudors, 1447–1603* (London: Longman, 1998).

Elton, G.R., 'Thomas Cromwell's Decline and Fall', *Cambridge Historical Journal*, 10 (1951): 150–85

——, *The Tudor Revolution in Government* (Cambridge: Cambridge UP, 1953)

——, *Policy and Police: The Enforcement of Reformation in the age of Thomas Cromwell* (Cambridge: Cambridge UP, 1972)

——, *Reform and Renewal: Thomas Cromwell and the Common Weal* (Cambridge: Cambridge UP, 1973)

——, *Reform and Reformation* (London: Edward Arnold, 1977)

——, *Tudor Constitution: Documents and Commentary* (2nd edn, Cambridge: Cambridge UP, 1982)

——, *Studies in Tudor and Stuart Politics and Government* (3 vols, Cambridge: Cambridge UP, 1974, 1983)

——, 'How corrupt was Thomas Cromwell?', *HJ* 36/4 (1993): 905–8

——, *England under the Tudors* (3rd edn, London: Routledge, 2001)

Foister, S., *Holbein and England* (London: Yale UP, 2004)

Fox, A. and Guy, J., *Reassessing the Henrician Age: Humanism, Politics and Reform, 1500–1550* (Oxford: Blackwell, 1986)

Freeman, T.S., 'Research, Rumour and Propaganda: Anne Boleyn in Foxe's Book of Martyrs', *HJ* 38/4 (1995):797–819

Gardiner, S.R., *History of England … 1603–42* (vol. 10, London: Longman, 1905)

Graves, M., *The Tudor Parliaments: Crown, Lords and Commons, 1585–1603* (London: Longman, 1985)

Grand Larousse de la langue française (6 vols, Paris, Libraire Larousse, 1972)

Greenslade, S.L. (ed.), *The Cambridge History of the Bible* (3 vols, Cambridge: Cambridge UP, 1987)

Gunn, S and Lindley, P. (eds), *Cardinal Wolsey: Church, State and Art* (Cambridge: Cambridge UP, 1991)

Guy, J., 'Communications – The Tudor Commonwealth: Revising Thomas Cromwell', *HJ* 23/3 (1980): 681–7

——, 'Henry VIII and the *Praemunire* Manoeuvres of 1530–31', *EHR* 97 (1982): 481–503

—— , *Tudor England* (Oxford: Oxford UP, 1988)

Gwyn, P., *The King's Cardinal: The Rise and Fall of Thomas Wolsey* (London: Barrie and Jenkins, 1990)

Haigh, C., *English Reformations: Religion, Politics and Society under the Tudors* (Oxford: Oxford UP, 1993)

Hallam, E., 'Henry VIII's Monastic Refoundations of 1536–37 and the course of the Dissolution', *BIHR* 51 (1978): 124–31

Hammond, E., 'Dr. Augustine, Physician to Cardinal Wolsey and King Henry VIII', in *Medical History* 19 (1975): 215–49

Head, D., *Ebbs and Flows of Fortune: Life of Thomas Howard, Third Duke of Norfolk* (Athens: Georgia UP, 1995)

Heal, F., *Reformation in Britain and Ireland* (Oxford: Oxford UP, 2003)

Hildebrandt, E., 'Christopher Mont, Anglo-German diplomat', *SCJ* 15/3 (1984): 281–92

Hoyle, R.W., 'The Origins of the Dissolution of the Monasteries', *HJ* 38 (1995): 275–305

—— , *The Pilgrimage of Grace and the Politics of the 1530s* (Oxford: Oxford UP, 2001)

Ives, E., 'Anne Boleyn and the Early Reformation in England: The contemporary evidence', *HJ* 37 (1994): 389–400

—— , 'The Fall of Anne Boleyn Re-considered', *EHR* 107 (1992): 651–64 [See also Bernard, Rejoinder, above]

—— , *The Life and Death of Anne Boleyn* (Oxford: Blackwell, 2004)

Jeffries, H., 'The Early Tudor Reformation in the Irish Pale', *JEH* 52/1 (2001): 34–62

Knecht, R.J., *Renaissance Warrior and Patron: The Reign of Francis I* (Cambridge: Cambridge UP, 1994)

Knowles, D., *The Religious Orders in England, vol. 3: The Tudor Age* (Cambridge: Cambridge UP, 1971)

Lehmberg, S.E., *Sir Thomas Elyot: Tudor Humanist* (Austin, Texas: Texas UP, 1960)

—— , 'Supremacy and Vicegerency: a Re-examination', *EHR* 81 (1966): 225–35

—— , 'Parliamentary Attainder in the Reign of Henry VIII', *HJ* 18/4 (1975): 675–702

—— , *The Reformation Parliament: 1529–1536* (Cambridge: Cambridge UP, 1977)

—— , *The Later Parliaments of Henry VIII: 1536–1547* (Cambridge: Cambridge UP, 1977)

Loades, D., *Tudor Government: Structures of Authority in the Sixteenth Century* (Oxford: Blackwell, 1997)

Logan, F., 'Thomas Cromwell and the Vicegerency in Spirituals: A Revisitation', *EHR* 103 (1988): 658–67

MacCulloch, D, *Suffolk and the Tudors: Politics and Religion in an English County* (Oxford: Clarendon, 1986)

—— , (ed.), *The Reign of Henry VIII: Politics, Policy and Piety* (Basingstoke, Macmillan, 1995)

—— , *Thomas Cranmer: A Life* (New Haven and London, Yale UP, 1996)

—— , *Reformation: Europe's House Divided* (London, Allen lane, 2003)

Manschreck, C.L., *Melanchthon, The Quiet Reformer* (reprint Westport, Connecticut: Greenwood, 1975)

Marshall, P., 74 'The Rood of Boxley, the Blood of Hailes, and the Defence of the Henrician Church', *JEH* 46 (1995): 689–96

—— , 'Papist as Heretic: The Burning of John Forest, 1538', *HJ* 41 (1998): 351–74

Mattingly, G., *Catherine of Aragon* (London: Jonathan Cape, 1942)

Mayer, T., 'Faction and Ideology: Thomas Starkey's *Dialogue*', *HJ* 28/1 (1985): 1–25

—— , *Thomas Starkey and the Commonweal: Humanist Politics and Religion in the Reign of Henry VIII* (Cambridge: Cambridge UP, 1989)

—— , *Reginald Pole, Prince and Prophet* (Cambridge: Cambridge UP, 2000)

McConica, J., *English Humanists and Reformation Politics under Henry VIII and Edward VI* (Oxford: Clarendon, 1968)

McEntegart, R., 'England and the League of Schmalkalden, 1531–1547: Faction, foreign policy and the English Reformation' (London School of Economics Ph.D., 1992)

—— , *Henry VIII, The League of Schmalkalden and the English Reformation* (Woodbridge: Boydell Press, 2002)

Mozley, J.F., *Coverdale and his Bibles* (London: Lutterworth Press, 1953)

—— , *William Tyndale* (Westport, Connecticut: Greenwood Press, reprint 1971)

Muir, K., *Life and Letters of Sir Thomas Wyatt* (Liverpool: Liverpool UP, 1963)

Murphy, V., 'The Literature and Propaganda of Henry VIII's First Divorce', in D. MacCulloch (ed.), *The Reign of Henry VIII: Politics, policy and piety* (Basingstoke: Macmillan, 1995), pp.135–58

Neame, A., *The Holy Maid of Kent: The Life of Elizabeth Barton 1506–1534* (London: Hodder and Stroughton, 1971)

Outhwaite, R.B., *Inflation in Tudor and Early Stuart England* (2nd edn, London: Macmillan, 1982)

Pettegree, A., (ed.), *The Reformation World* (London: Routledge, 2000)

Potter, G.R., *Zwingli* (Cambridge UP, 1976)

Raab, F., *The English Face of Machiavelli: A changing interpretation, 1500–1700* (London: Routledge, 1964)

Redworth, G., *In Defence of the Church Catholic: Life of Stephen Gardiner* (Oxford: Blackwell, 1990)

Rex, R., 'The English Campaign against Luther in the 1520s', in *TRHS*, 5th series 39 (1989), pp. 85–106.

—— , *The Theology of John Fisher* (Cambridge: Cambridge UP, 1991)

—— , 'The New Learning', *JEH* 44 (1993): 26-44

—— , *Henry VIII and the English Reformation* (Basingstoke: Macmillan, 1993)

—— , 'Jasper Fyloll and the Enormities of the Clergy: Two tracts written during the Reformation Parliament', *SCJ* 31/4 (2000): 1043–62

Richardson, W.C., *Stephen Vaughan: Financial Agent of Henry VIII* (Baton Rouge: Louisiana State University Press, 1953)

Ridley, J.G., *Henry VIII* (London, Constable, 1984)

Roberts, P.R., 'The Union with England and the identity of "Anglican Wales", *TRHS* 22 (1972), pp. 49–70

Robertson, M.L., 'The Art of the Possible: Thomas Cromwell's management of West Country government', *HJ* 32/4 (1989): 793-816

Ryrie, A., *The Gospel and Henry VIII: Evangelicals in the Early English Reformation* (Cambridge: Cambridge UP, 2003)

Scarisbrick, J., *Henry VIII* (London: Eyre and Spottiswoode, 1968)

—— , *The Reformation and the English People* (Oxford: Blackwell, 1984)

Schofield, J., 'The Lost Reformation: Why Lutheranism failed in England during the Reigns of Henry VIII and Edward VI' (Newcastle Ph.D., 2003)

—— , *Philip Melanchthon and the English Reformation* (Aldershot: Ashgate, 2006)

Shagan, E., *Popular Politics and the English Reformation* (Cambridge: Cambridge UP, 2003)

Skinner, Q., *Machiavelli*, (Oxford: Oxford UP, 1981)

Slavin, A. J., 'The Rochepot Affair', *SCJ* 10 (1979): 3–19

Starkey, D., *The Reign of Henry VIII: Personalities and Politics* (London: George Philip, 1985)

—— , *Six Wives: Queens of Henry VIII* (London: Chatto and Windus, 2003)

Strong, R., *Holbein and Henry VIII* (London: Routledge and Keegan Paul, 1967

Strype, J., *Ecclesiastical Memorials under Henry VIII* (3 vols in 6, Oxford: Clarendon, 1822)

—— , *Memorial of … Thomas Cranmer, Archbishop of Canterbury* (2 vols, Oxford: Clarendon, 1812)

Sturge, C., *Cuthbert Tunstall: Churchman, Scholar, Statesman, Administrator* (London: Longmans Green, 1938)

Thompson, B., 'Monasteries and their Patrons at Foundation and Dissolution', *TRHS* 6th series 4, pp. 103–23

Thomson, John A.F., *Popes and Princes, 1417–1517: Politics and polity in the Late Medieval Church* (London: George Allen and Unwin, 1980)

Tjernagel, N.S., *The Reformation Essays of Dr Robert Barnes, Chaplain to Henry VIII* (St. Louis: Concordia, 1963)

—— , *Henry VIII and the Lutherans* (St. Louis: Concordia, 1965)

Trueman, C.R., *Luther's Legacy: Salvation and the English Reformers 1525–1556* (Oxford: Clarendon, 1994)

Underwood, W., 'Thomas Cromwell and William Marshall's Protestant Books', *HJ* 47/3 (2004): 517–39

Walker, G., 'Rethinking the fall of Anne Boleyn', *HJ* 45/1 (2000): 1–29

Warnicke, R.M., *The Rise and Fall of Anne Boleyn* (Cambridge: Cambridge UP, 1989)

—— , *The Marrying of Anne of Cleves: Royal protocol in early modern England* (Cambridge: Cambridge UP, 2000)

Wernham, R.B., *Before the Armada: The Growth of English Foreign Policy, 1485–1588* (London: J. Cape, 1966)

Wilkins, D., *Concilia Magnae Britanniae et Hiberniae* (4 vols, London: R. Gosling, 1737)

Williams, G., *Wales and the Reformation* (Cardiff: University of Wales Press, 1997)

—— , *Renewal and Reformation: Wales c. 1415–1642* (Oxford: Oxford UP, reprint 2002)

Youings, J., *The Dissolution of the Monasteries* (London: George Allen and Unwin, 1971)

Index

Acknowledgements

Any work on Thomas Cromwell must pay tribute to the late Professor G.R. Elton, one of the greatest Tudor historians. His definitive studies and analyses of the Tudor age provide an indispensable foundation for an understanding of Cromwell and his times. Without them, this book could never have been started, let alone written.

The works of a number of other scholars, notably Stanford E. Lehmberg and Rory MacEntegart, have also been invaluable: to them, many thanks. The research for much of the material in Chapters 6, 10 and 16–17 was undertaken as part of my doctoral thesis at Newcastle University, 2000–2003, so I would like to thank once again my supervisor Professor Euan Cameron – then of Newcastle, now at New York – and my examiners, Professor Diarmaid MacCulloch and Emeritus Professor John Derry for all their knowledge, kindness and assistance.

Thanks of a rather different sort are due to R.B. Merriman for his labours nearly a century ago in collating and publishing Cromwell's letters. He has saved me a great deal of time and trouble, so it is not without some regret that I must say that I find much of Merriman's character analysis of Cromwell to be bewilderingly wide of the mark. If my work at times reads like an *Apologia*, then I feel that this is unavoidable given the fact that Merriman's has been for a long time the standard biography of Cromwell. On this point, readers will make their own judgements.

I also thank Newcastle University and particularly Professor Jeremy Boulton, Head of the School of Historical Studies, for accepting me as a guest member and visiting scholar, thereby allowing me to complete this book; the staff of Newcastle and Durham University libraries, the British Library, Public Records Office, Lambeth Palace Library, Hatfield House and the Vienna Archives; Tony Morris for his welcome advice and interest; and Jonathan Reeve and Miranda Embleton-Smith at The History Press for bringing this work to completion.